ASBESTOS – THE LAST MODERNIST OBJECT

Edinburgh Critical Studies in Modernist Culture
Series Editors: Tim Armstrong and Rebecca Beasley

Available

Modernism and Magic: Experiments with Spiritualism, Theosophy and the Occult
Leigh Wilson

Sonic Modernity: Representing Sound in Literature, Culture and the Arts
Sam Halliday

Modernism and the Frankfurt School
Tyrus Miller

Lesbian Modernism: Censorship, Sexuality and Genre Fiction
Elizabeth English

Modern Print Artefacts: Textual Materiality and Literary Value in British Print Culture, 1890–1930s
Patrick Collier

Cheap Modernism: Expanding Markets, Publishers' Series and the Avant-Garde
Lise Jaillant

Portable Modernisms: The Art of Travelling Light
Emily Ridge

Hieroglyphic Modernisms: Writing and New Media in the Twentieth Century
Jesse Schotter

Modernism, Fiction and Mathematics
Nina Engelhardt

Modernist Life Histories: Biological Theory and the Experimental Bildungsroman
Daniel Aureliano Newman

Modernism, Space and the City: Outsiders and Affect in Paris, Vienna, Berlin, and London
Andrew Thacker

Modernism Edited: Marianne Moore and the Dial *Magazine*
Victoria Bazin

Modernism and Time Machines
Charles Tung

Primordial Modernism: Animals, Ideas, Transition (1927–1938)
Cathryn Setz

Modernism and Still Life: Artists, Writers, Dancers
Claudia Tobin

The Modernist Exoskeleton: Insects, War, Literary Form
Rachel Murray

Novel Sensations: Modernist Fiction and the Problem of Qualia
Jon Day

Hotel Modernity: Corporate Space in Literature and Film
Robbie Moore

The Modernist Anthropocene: Nonhuman Life and Planetary Change in James Joyce, Virginia Woolf and Djuna Barnes
Peter Adkins

Asbestos – The Last Modernist Object
Arthur Rose

Forthcoming

Modernism and the Idea of Everyday Life
Leena Kore-Schröder

Modernism and Religion: Poetry and the Rise of Mysticism
Jamie Callison

Abstraction in Modernism and Modernity: Human and Inhuman
Jeff Wallace

Visionary Company: Hart Crane and Modernist Periodicals
Francesca Bratton

Sexological Modernism: Queer Feminism and Sexual Science
Jana Funke

The Modernist Long Poem: Gnosticism, the First World War and the Sympathetic Imagination
Jamie Wood

www.edinburghuniversitypress.com/series/ecsmc

ASBESTOS – THE LAST MODERNIST OBJECT

Arthur Rose

EDINBURGH
University Press

For John and Dorothy Rose
And Arthur, Alan, Peter, Jimmy. . .

Edinburgh University Press is one of the leading university presses in the UK. We publish academic books and journals in our selected subject areas across the humanities and social sciences, combining cutting-edge scholarship with high editorial and production values to produce academic works of lasting importance. For more information visit our website: edinburghuniversitypress.com

We are committed to making research available to a wide audience and are pleased to be publishing an Open Access ebook edition of this title.

© Arthur Rose 2022, 2024 under a Creative Commons Attribution-Non-commercial licence

First published in hardback by Edinburgh University Press 2022

Edinburgh University Press Ltd
The Tun – Holyrood Road
12(2f) Jackson's Entry
Edinburgh EH8 8PJ

Typeset in 10/12.5 Adobe Sabon by
IDSUK (DataConnection) Ltd, and
printed and bound by CPI Group (UK) Ltd, Croydon, CR0 4YY

A CIP record for this book is available from the British Library

ISBN 978 1 4744 8242 4 (hardback)
ISBN 978 1 4744 8243 1 (paperback)
ISBN 978 1 4744 8244 8 (webready PDF)
ISBN 978 1 4744 8245 5 (epub)

The right of Arthur Rose to be identified as the author of this work has been asserted in accordance with the Copyright, Designs and Patents Act 1988, and the Copyright and Related Rights Regulations 2003 (SI No. 2498).

CONTENTS

List of Figures — vi
Acknowledgements — vii
Series Editors' Preface — xi
Preface: What's the Use of Writing about Asbestos? — xii

Introduction: Asbestos and Modernism — 1

Part I: Prefiguring Asbestos
1 A Utopian Impulse — 41
2 Clues and Mysteries — 59

Part II: Configuring Asbestos
3 Salamander Cotton — 87
4 Illness Narratives — 107
5 Compensating for Franz Kafka — 127

Part III: Transforming Asbestos
6 The Mine — 155
7 The Factory — 175
8 The Home — 202
Conclusion: The Dump — 222

Bibliography — 230
Index — 250

LIST OF FIGURES

0.1	Arriving in the Cabin	20
0.2	The Asbestos Roll	20
0.3	Donning the Asbestos Suit	20
0.4	Explanatory Intertitle	22
7.1	The Mining and Transport of Raw Asbestos (© the Heath Robinson Museum)	182
7.2	Patent double action grinder (© the Heath Robinson Museum)	182
7.3	Mixing treated asbestos fibre with cement (© the Heath Robinson Museum)	183
7.4	Powerful machinery (© the Heath Robinson Museum)	183
7.5	In the finishing departments (© the Heath Robinson Museum)	184
8.1	Lady Asbestos	213

ACKNOWLEDGEMENTS

The longer a book takes to write, the longer the list of people whose kind and patient contributions make it possible to bring that writing to a close. But all books begin somewhere, and this one undoubtedly began as a conversation with my father, Peter Rose, that extended over two site visits to Koegas in the Northern Cape and Pomfret in the North West in 2015 and 2019. Without his enthusiastic support of this project, I would never have persevered with it. He also introduced me to Sonja and Ruan Immelman, Jim te Water Naudé, Gill Nelson and François Loots, who gave generously of their time to talk to me about asbestos exposure in South Africa. Equally generous were Kate Hill at the June Hancock Mesothelioma Research Fund, Helen Clayson (formerly at the University of Sheffield), Bev Wears (formerly of the British Lung Foundation), Chris Knighton at the Mick Knighton Mesothelioma Research Fund, Nick Mansell and Rahul Bhatnagar at the University of Bristol, and Jo Barnes-Mannings and Lorna Johns at Asbestos Awareness and Support Cymru, who each contributed to my understanding of mesothelioma in the United Kingdom. Through them, I met the people whose ongoing engagement with the consequences of asbestos exposure gives this book its moral purpose.

Still, a book like this does not emerge from moral purpose alone. I was lucky to receive support from the Wellcome Trust and the University of Bristol for the research and writing up phases of the project. As a postdoctoral research fellow on the Wellcome Trust Senior Investigator Award Life of Breath at Durham University, I had the privilege of working with Jane Macnaughton, without whose mentoring hand I doubt I would have had the courage to write this book, and Mary Robson, who knew the right questions to ask and when to ask them. I was also supported by an amazing team of interdisciplinary researchers on the project, including Havi Carel, Krzysztof Bierski, Kate Binnie, Jordan Collver, James Dodd, Gene Feder, David Fuller, Alice Malpass, Coreen McGuire, Sarah McLusky, Fredrik Nyman, Rebecca Oxley, Corinne Saunders, Andrew Russell, Megan Wainwright, Oriana Walker, Tina Williams and Ronit Yoeli-Tlalim. In the wider Durham community, I owe more than passing debts to Ben Alderson-Day and Helen Sanger, Marco Bernini, Sam Bootle, Marc Botha, Dan Grausam, Francisco-J. Hernández Adrián, Kerstin Oloff, Alastair Renfrew, Zoë Roth, Marc Schachter, Hugh and Lotte Shankland, Rick de Villiers and Michelle Joubert, and Angela Woods. A special word must be given to Will Viney, who provided a model for this book that I completely failed to follow. As a Vice-Chancellor's Fellow at Bristol, I was fortunate to have Maria Vaccarella as an engaging mentor and a committed interlocutor. Ulrika Maude generously stepped up to the role as well. Andrew Bennett, Andrew Blades, Lesel Dawson, Helen Fulton, Cleo Hanaway-Oakley, John Lee, Laurence Publicover and Kirk Sides were considerate colleagues in English. Members of the Centre for Health, Humanities and Science, Victoria Bates, Havi Carel and Giovanni Biglino, gave me an interdisciplinary community, while Colin Nolden and Eleni Michalopoulou were a constant source of transdisciplinary insights. Claire Wrixon, Rachel Dill and the Fellows from the 2017, 2018 and 2019 cohorts offered help at every turn, personal as well as professional. I am particularly indebted to Ryan Davey, Daniel Finch-Race, Tigist Grieve and Liz Haines for their regular check-ins. In Exeter, Gemma Anderson, Lara Choksey, Michael Flexer, Robin Jakob, Ina Linge, Laura Salisbury, Niccolò Tempini and Dóra Vargha all contributed greatly.

I am grateful to many people for their help in accessing various materials. Ken Yates and the University of Leeds Special Collections helped me source a copy of his play, *Dust*. Alice Nutter sent me a copy of her play, *Snow in August*. The Amazwi South African Museum of Literature helped me trawl through South Africa's literary archive. Texas Tech University's Southwest Collection/Special Collections Library sourced work by Rick Bass for me in the middle of a pandemic. Yolanda Wisher allowed me to make use of her work in progress. Jo Barnes-Mannings from the AASC let me use one of her poems. Muireann Maguire put me in contact with Yekaterina Severts, who introduced me to the work of Pavel Bazhov and Semen Schepachev. Geoffrey Beare provided high resolution copies of William Heath Robinson's Asbestos Cement illustrations (photos © the Heath Robinson Museum).

Will Viney, Maria Vaccarella and Maebh Long provided endless fonts of asbestos references.

I was fortunate to try out some of the ideas at some conferences and seminars. Thanks go to the following for inviting me: Simon van Schalkwyk, Merle Williams and Michael Titlestad for inviting me to present at the University of the Witwatersrand, first at the staff seminar and then at the conference, Cultures of Populism. Thando Njovane and Mike Marais, who offered space at the staff seminar in the institution currently known as Rhodes University. Rick de Villiers, who brought me to the staff seminar at the University of the Free State. Madhu Krishnan and Andrew Blades, for having me at the staff seminar at the University of Bristol. Stefanie Heine, for letting me give a class on her mineral aesthetics course at the University of Zurich. Kasia Mika, for involving me in the ASCA Cities Project at the University of Amsterdam. Jean Michel Rabaté and Aaron Levy, for giving me time at the Slought Foundation in Philadelphia. David Watson, for including me in the Crisis and Beyond Conference at the University of Uppsala. Michael Flexer, for involving me in an Engaged Research Workshop at the University of Exeter.

Special thanks to the people who helped me to turn my scattered ideas into something approaching a cogent written form. At Edinburgh University Press, Ersev Ersoy and Susannah Butler provided constant support for the project, Fiona Conn ably managed its production and Caitlin Murphy was responsible for the fitting cover design. Aidan Cross provided excellent copy-editing. Peter Rose, Rick de Villiers and Stefanie Heine read through the draft manuscript in its entirety, as did my editors, Rebecca Beasley and Tim Armstrong. Maria Vaccarella, Ryan Topper, Michelle Rada and Kasia Mika each read key chapters at key moments. When asked, Doug Battersby dropped everything to help me restructure ungainly paragraphs. I also benefitted greatly from comments from Sam Durrant, Philip Dickinson and two anonymous reviewers on a version of Chapter Three, and from comments on a version of Chapter Five by Bruce Holsinger and an anonymous reviewer. Through all this, my errors remained my own. I am grateful to the editors of *New Formations* and Lawrence Wishart for permission to reprint 'Asbestos's Animacy; or, Salamander Cotton', copyright © 2021 New Formations, Lawrence Wishart. This article first appeared in *New Formations* Number 104-5, Autumn/Winter 2021, pages 105–27. I am grateful to the editors of *New Literary History* and Johns Hopkins University Press for permission to reprint "Recovering Franz Kafka's Asbestos Factory", copyright © 2022 New Literary History, The University of Virginia. This article first appeared in *New Literary History* Volume 52, Issue 4, 2022.

As anyone in the habit of reading acknowledgements knows, books such as these owe an unspeakable debt to the writer's family. This is no exception. Sarah, Sean, Seb and Sam provided light and laughter, as did other members of my extended family. But a special debt is owed for continued love and support, despite my absences (and many, many references to asbestos), to Luna and Theo, and for so much more than I can possibly say. They accepted, with much forbearance, my need to make sense of my family's asbestos past. If what results is not quite a reckoning of my family's history, I hope this book goes some way to thinking about the cultural context that gave it sense. It is only fitting, then, that it be dedicated to my father, grandfather, grandmother and uncles, whose stories inspired it.

SERIES EDITORS' PREFACE

Edinburgh Critical Studies in Modernist Culture
Series Editors: Tim Armstrong and Rebecca Beasley

PREFACE

This series of monographs on selected topics in modernism is designed to reflect and extend the range of new work in modernist studies. The studies in the series aim for a breadth of scope and for an expanded sense of the canon of modernism, rather than focusing on individual authors. Literary texts will be considered in terms of contexts including recent cultural histories (modernism and magic; sonic modernity; media studies) and topics of theoretical interest (the everyday; postmodernism; the Frankfurt School); but the series will also re-consider more familiar routes into modernism (modernism and gender; sexuality; politics). The works published will be attentive to the various cultural, intellectual and historical contexts of British, American and European modernisms, and to inter-disciplinary possibilities within modernism, including performance and the visual and plastic arts.

PREFACE: WHAT'S THE USE OF WRITING ABOUT ASBESTOS?

To write about asbestos is, first and foremost, to write about its use. Some 3,000 products, asbestos information websites will tell you, 'used' asbestos, ranging from cement sheets and insulation boards to cigarette filters and tampons.[1] Asbestos 'was widely used' in construction, factories, home improvement and shipbuilding.[2] This use-value stemmed from the mineral's properties: its composition of soft and flexible fibres resistant to heat, electricity and corrosion.[3] It is, moreover, a substance that refuses the perfective 'used up': objects made from asbestos – fire suits and funeral attire, napkins and purses – would be thrown upon open flames only to emerge as they were, unscathed.[4] This refusal accounts for the uses our bodies make of asbestos fibres, as they enter our lungs or guts. Unable to dislodge the shards of fibre piercing and lacerating internal tissue, the body struggles to enfold these fibres, to digest them, to 'use' them up.[5] This effort causes inflammation and apoptosis. The body turns against itself, generating fearsome asbestos-related diseases: asbestosis, mesothelioma, lung cancer and pleural plaques. Asbestos use culminates in a body's abuse.

As collective awareness of these diseases grew, so asbestos changed. We learned of the companies that dissimulated and disavowed the consequences of asbestos use, the governments that backed these companies; the lobbyists, the lawmakers and the lawyers.[6] With knowledge of asbestos's misuse, there emerged new forms of 'creative use': the 'creative use' of data by lobbyists to diminish concerns about asbestos-related diseases, for instance, or the 'creative use' of procedural devices by the judiciary and lawyers to enact court-based tort reform.⁷ This creativity depended on strategies often associated with textual interpretation. Data was mediated through cherry-picked quotes and the 'infowhelm' of competing and contradictory studies.⁸ Manufacturers labelled contaminated products 'no detectable asbestos' rather than certifying they were 'asbestos-free'.⁹ Industry researchers established the 'chrysotile defense', exploiting differences between asbestos types to exonerate chrysotile ('white asbestos') at the expense of other commercial forms (amosite, or 'brown asbestos' and crocidolite, or 'blue asbestos').¹⁰ Lobbyists developed 'the controlled use' fiction, as an alternative to total bans, to palliate fears about illnesses with promises about regulation.¹¹ Even the 'one fibre rule', which holds that a single fibre can cause mesothelioma, is a legal fiction, albeit a necessary one, that allows survivors some recourse to compensation.¹² When language use is so fraught and carries such obvious material effects, it is unsurprising that the litany of asbestos's uses seems neither welcoming nor in need of the ambiguities that attend the mediation and representation of cultural objects. What's the use, in this actual and continuing crisis, of cultural responses to asbestos?

Sara Ahmed suggests that the question 'what's the use?' seems to assert 'the pointlessness of doing something', while also, more productively, raising the possibility of doing this something differently.¹³ Asking about 'use', after all, 'brings things to mind'. To illustrate this possibility, she turns to a moment in Virginia Woolf's 1937 novel, *The Years*, when Peggy interrupts her family's discussion of her brother, North, by asking: 'What's the use? [. . .] You'll marry. You'll have children. What'll you do then? Make money. Write little books to make money . . . "¹⁴ Peggy worries about North's plans, certainly, but what was meant as an impersonal statement has become a personal attack. '"You'll write one little book, then another little book" she said viciously, "instead of living . . . living differently, differently"' (342). If Peggy, at this point, stops, unable to say 'the thing she had seen', even though 'she had tried to say it', Ahmed completes Peggy's thought: by asking 'about the point of *anything*', we can address how 'some things we do, things we are used to, things we are asked to get used to, are in the way of a feminist project of living differently.'¹⁵

This book aims to think 'differently' about the narratives used to tell the asbestos story. It does so in three parts. First, it considers how closely linked these historical, legal and medical narratives are to literary genres like the utopia, the detective novel and the horror story. Then, it draws on these literary connections to make a bolder claim: that literary thinking brings to light aspects of asbestos experiences generally ignored in history, law and medicine. And finally, it shows how these literary connections can help us to find new ways of understanding the places where we find asbestos: mines, factories, homes and businesses, and waste sites. In repositioning the literary as a necessary, if overlooked voice in existing debates around asbestos, I attempt to formalise a family discussion about asbestos use with my father and my grandfather. Mostly absent from the text proper, they are nonetheless my ideal readers. Informed by five years of intermittent conversations with my father, I try to imagine what my grandfather, long dead, might have thought of his decades working as a mine manager in the Northern Cape of South Africa for the multinational company, Cape Asbestos. Rather than adopt a direct biographical approach, I have tried to resurrect cultural narratives to represent my family's changing attachments to asbestos and its consequences. Much like Peggy, I forego 'easy' arguments for or against my grandfather's involvement – 'money', with its companions, 'marriage' and 'family' – to think instead about social legacy, a concept that lurks behind her notions of 'little books' and 'living differently'.

First as the deputy mine manager at Koegas, in the Northern Cape, then as manager at Pomfret, and finally back as manager of Koegas, much of my grandfather's working life was spent on the extraction of asbestos from the earth for commercial use. But he, like many of his generation, believed that the value of his work obtained as much in its contribution to improving 'society' as by the profit it accrued. Accordingly, I would imagine that his answer to the 'what's the use' question would link asbestos to larger ideals: development, progress, technological advancement. In a word: modernity.

At the same time, I can't help but wonder if this 'nobler' ideal wasn't supplemented by a professional satisfaction in his technical work for an extractive industry that was, in the words of Walter Arnold Rukeyser, 'more of an art than a science'.[16] In his 1932 account of his consultancy work for the Soviet asbestos industry, Rukeyser calls the mining of asbestos 'an art' because it relied upon technology that needed to be adapted to the specific conditions of particular mines by able and open-minded engineers. By 1932, modern mining and milling techniques were only a couple of decades old. Moreover, 'the industry, since the post-war depression, has never been financially strong enough to dig its way out of certain unavoidable ruts' (56). Although Rukeyser never clarifies what these ruts might be, his insistence on 'operating experience in the Canadian field' suggests that modern techniques developed through onsite trial and error, rather than as an outcome of technical research (56). As Rukeyser observes,

> asbestos [. . .] is not always asbestos. It is unique in that its quality plays the leading role in determining its value. Quality depends upon such factors as length of fibre, tensile strength, harshness or softness, silkiness, color, divisibility into microscopically fine strands, resistance to heat, iron content – in other words, upon both *physical* and *chemical* properties. (56)

These variations mean that even asbestos from the same mine may have 'vastly different characteristics' (56). The technical process that works for one source of fibre may not work for another. The engineer must therefore 'become entirely familiar with the geological and other peculiarities of that district', 'have a suitable background of actual operating experience', and 'keep a completely open mind [to] build up a technique for the particular problem at hand' (57). The palpable intellectual curiosity with which Rukeyser describes his craft can be found, more or less consistently, across other 'scientific' responses to asbestos that sought to popularise its use, in works by Robert H. Jones, A. Leonard Summers and Oliver Bowles.[17]

Still, I can only imagine my grandfather's response. We never talked about the uses of asbestos or his work in the industry. So, instead, I try to reconstruct the cultural understanding of asbestos that he, born in 1913, would have grown up with. To take my grandfather's commitment to asbestos seriously, I engage with the history that has discredited this magic mineral, while trying to hold it at arm's length. As a whole, the industry dissembled about asbestos-related diseases and, in its South African iteration, disavowed its reliance on the political economy of Apartheid. But, if we imagine that simply knowing this serves to correct it, then we have not really called into question the conditions of belief that made my grandfather's commitment possible. To understand his ideals, his professionalism and his curiosity, I have turned not to historical record, but to a reflective form of literary criticism. In literature, we perhaps find ways of doing things differently. If so, literary criticism offers a means, necessarily imperfect, to explain how such ways might themselves be found.

NOTES

1. Mesothelioma + Asbestos Awareness Centre, https://www.maacenter.org/asbestos/products/
2. Epps, *International Trade and Health Protection*, p. 206.
3. Asbestos.com, https://www.asbestos.com/asbestos/
4. Oliver Bowles, *Asbestos: The Silk of the Mineral Kingdom* (np: Ruberoid Co., 1946), p. 13.
5. Martha L. Warnock and Andrew M. Churg, 'Asbestos Bodies', 77 *Chest* (1980), pp. 129–30.
6. The evolving nature of these relations may be tracked across the archive of the International Ban Asbestos Secretariat, http://ibasecretariat.org. Accessed 15 November 2021.
7. For 'creative use' in developing court-based tout reform, see Jeb Barnes, *Dust-Up: Asbestos Litigation and the Failure of Commonsense Policy Reform* (Georgetown University Press, 2011).
8. On the notion of 'infowhelm', see Heather Houser, *Infowhelm: Environmental Art and Literature in an Age of Data* (New York: Columbia UP, 2020).
9. David Rosner, Gerald Markowitz and Merlin Chowkwanyun, '"Nondetected": The Politics of Measurement of Asbestos in Talc, 1971–1976. 109 *American Journal of Public Health* (2019), pp. 969–74.

10. Jock McCulloch and Geoffrey Tweedale, *Defending the Indefensible: The Global Asbestos Industry and its Fight for Survival* (Oxford: Oxford University Press, 2008), pp. 127–37.
11. McCulloch and Tweedale, *Defending*, pp. 137–45.
12. As there is no minimum threshold of safe exposure to asbestos, courts have used any exposure to asbestos to show a material increase in risk of injury. In the case of Fairchild v Glenhaven Funeral Services Ltd [2002] UKHL 22, Lord Hoffmann found that a material increase in risk satisfied the causal requirements for liability.
13. Sara Ahmed, *What's the Use? On the Uses of Use* (Durham: Duke University Press, 2019), p. 2.
14. Virginia Woolf, *The Years*, intro. Susan Hill and Steven Connor (London: Vintage, 2004), p. 341.
15. Ahmed, *Use*, p. 2.
16. Walter Arnold Rukeyser, *Working for the Soviets: An American Engineer in Russia* (New York: Covici Friede Publishers, 1932), p. 55.
17. Robert H. Jones, *Asbestos, Its Production and Use: With Some Account of the Asbestos Mines of Canada* (London: Crosby Lockwood & Son, 1888); A. Leonard Summers, *Asbestos and the Asbestos Industry: The World's Most Wonderful Mineral and Other Fireproof Materials* (London: Pitman, 1919); Bowles, *Asbestos*.

INTRODUCTION: ASBESTOS AND MODERNISM

On 14 March 1924, shortly before the writer, Franz Kafka, left Berlin for the last time, a factory worker named Nellie Kershaw passed away in the English town of Rochdale. Kafka would outlive Kershaw by less than three months: after a few days in Prague, he would go on to Vienna and then to Dr Hoffmann's sanatorium in Kierling, where he died on 2 June. The lives of the two 'K's bear little resemblance to each other. Kershaw, a textile worker, began work in a cotton mill in 1903 aged 12. Kafka, a law student in 1903, would go on to take his Doctor of Laws and, later, become an insurance officer, responsible for processing and investigating claims made to the Worker's Accident Insurance Institute for the Kingdom of Bohemia. It is at this point, however, that I might begin to sketch an imagined intersection between the worker and the insurance officer. For, some months after she began to work in the cotton mill, Kershaw changed her employment to Garside's asbestos mill. In 1917, she took up another job at Turner Brothers Asbestos, where she was tasked with spinning raw asbestos fibre into yarn. Around the same time, her attendance began to be 'intermittent'. In 1920, she started treatment for a lung condition that would, in July 1922, see her certified as unfit to work because of 'asbestos poisoning' and, upon her death in March 1924, find her the first person to have 'pulmonary asbestosis' listed as the cause of death.[1] With this final twist, Kershaw's relation to Kafka takes on a different aspect because, of course, Kafka co-owned an asbestos factory, Prager Asbestwerke Hermann & Co.

Three sets of social relations connect Kershaw and Kafka. First, there is a sympathetic congruity between two patients with respiratory illnesses. William Cooke, Kershaw's pathologist, found traces of tuberculosis in her lungs, the original cause given for Kershaw's death and, undeniably, the pathogen behind Kafka's.[2] Second, professional complementarity ties the worker exposed to an occupational hazard to the insurance officer responsible for assessing such hazards. But Kershaw's cause of death complicates this speculative relation, turning an alignment based on shared illness and professional ethics into an antagonism between labour and capital. For, third, Kafka's capital relied upon the exploitation of women like Kershaw. This scarcely seems a matter for literature or literary criticism. Of the identities listed – Kafka the invalid, Kafka the insurance officer, Kafka the capitalist – Kafka the writer is conspicuously absent.

And yet, it is Kafka's prose that makes this intersection with Kershaw meaningful; indeed, this will anticipate the larger argument of this book, that literature about asbestos can help us to make meaning of our encounters with this strangely wonderous, terrible material. Following her diagnosis of 'asbestos poisoning', Kershaw found herself in the singularly uncomfortable position of being unable to claim health benefits from either her National Health Insurance fund or her employer (via the Workmen's Compensation Act). The fund deemed her ineligible for benefits because her condition was related to her occupation. But she was also denied compensation because, as the board of Turner Brothers Asbestos decided in their minutes: 'We repudiate the term "Asbestos Poisoning". Asbestos is not poisonous and no definition or knowledge of such a disease exists.'[3] In recognising Kafka's 'voice or his habits' in the outrageous dilemma Kershaw's case produced, an 'idiosyncrasy' emerges I might not have perceived 'if Kafka had not written'.[4] '"It is characteristic of this legal system," conjectures K. in *Der Prozess* [*The Trial*], "that one is sentenced not only in innocence but also in ignorance."'[5] If it is K who is ignorant of the court protocols, Kershaw faced the ignorance of the entire medical-legal-commercial establishment. Falling into the cracks between nonoccupational and occupational disease, Kershaw's circumstances bear all the hallmarks of a differend: 'a case,' observes Jean-François Lyotard, 'where the plaintiff is divested of the means to argue and becomes for that reason a victim.'[6] For Lyotard, a double bind occurs when attempting to testify to both damages (a compensable complaint) and a wrong (a miscarriage of justice): 'either the damages you complain about never took place and your testimony is false; or else they took place, and since you are able to testify to them, it is not a wrong that has been done to you, but merely damages, and your testimony is still false' (5). Kershaw's case offers a third possibility: the wrong occurs because the damages are not recognised by either occupational or public health. Unable to 'establish what is not without criticizing what is',

Kershaw was left adrift in a situation that 'Kafka warned us about [.] It is impossible to establish one's innocence, in and of itself. It is a nothingness' (9).

Kershaw's case points to 'a lack of a common measure' or incommensurability, when it comes to linking illness, recognition and compensation in the asbestos story.[7] I can recognise this incommensurability because, today, the causal link between asbestos and these conditions has been recognised. They have become commensurable, and in no small way because of Kershaw. By linking the deaths of Kershaw and others to asbestos exposure, medical cases notes, occupational health surveys and epidemiological research paved the way for the legal recognition of liability.[8] As thinking in asbestos medical cases was increasingly accepted in legal case thinking, liability was attributed to the companies, who paid compensation accordingly.[9] The heterogenous concerns of medical findings, principles of legal liability and awards of damages became equivalent as they began to be grasped together as a narrative, a causal sequence.

Of course, Kafka's own fictions played no part in the process. And yet, the parallels are such that they might have done. This 'might have done' opens up the possibility, pursued through this book, that other literary narratives have grasped together the medical, legal, occupational and environmental histories of asbestos. These testify to asbestos's commensurability with a literary and cultural history extending from modernism to the present. But, Kafka's work makes literary, medical, legal and economic values seem commensurable, paradoxically, by showing how odd this equivalence is: registering their incompatibility as an occasion for the properly absurd within the narrative, while expecting the reader to reconcile these absurdities as they grapple with the text. In real life, the values of medicine, law and money seldom correlate without a protracted struggle for recognition, as Kershaw's case teaches us. And yet, when recognition is achieved, many forget the struggle. This may be why asbestos, though still widely mined and used, appears to be yesterday's problem. It is commensurable with a previous phase in capitalist development, already safely dealt with in the past. This quick resolution misses the point: as much as the equivalence of medicine, law and money seems commensurable to those unaffected by asbestos, the lack of a common measure is all too real for those whose lives it explodes.

When literary plots challenge their audiences, spectators or readers to choose between the values of medicine, law and money, they recall the torsions involved in imagining new relations of commensurability. At the same time, reading in this way impacts our understanding of literature. Textual interpretation is not catalytic conversion. K's maxim about ignorance and the legal system is striking, but, when one looks closer, one finds it is based on an assumption. Prevented from looking at some books lying on a table in the empty courtroom by the wife of one of the court ushers, K. says 'they're probably law books', before decrying the legal system's characteristics.[10] When K. does see the books, a page or two later, one contains 'an indecent picture' and the other is a novel. Nevertheless, he follows his earlier assumption, concluding, 'these are the law books they study [. . .] I'm to be judged by such men' (64). From the opening line, where the narrator assumes that 'someone must have slandered Josef K', such assumptions echo through the novel (24). If ignorance is often understood as the absence of knowledge, it may also be understood as an assumption about what is known, 'to deny either its importance or its very existence [or] to overlook it.'[11] Ignorance in *The Trial* plays on both senses: K. might not know very much, but he hardly helps himself with what he assumes to know.

As I trace the history of asbestos use through the twentieth century, I need to address the ignorance that coalesced around it not merely as an absence of knowledge, but as a series of assumptions whose rate of change was slower than circumstance demanded. By the advent of modernism, asbestos was already established as a widely used commodity. This explains why modernist texts can use asbestos objects, without dwelling on them. Its traces everywhere, asbestos itself remains unthought. From theatre curtains in Djuna Barnes, H. D. and Lawrence Durrell to gas fittings in John Rodker, Samuel Beckett and Patrick Hamilton, asbestos emerges in the infrastructure of modernism only to disappear once again, its reference a confident reminder that, for all the anxieties produced in the period by war, illness and social change, 'new' uses for materials like asbestos emerged to offer alternative forms of security and social reliance. After all, it is not simply unthought in modernism because it is taken for granted; as a fire retardant and insulator, it provided protection from fire and from anxieties about fire. In other words, it was meant to be taken for granted.

Paradoxically, these assumptions recall many of the positive, or at least ambivalent, connotations absent in contemporary accounts of asbestos: the sense of wonder it evoked, the security it provided, the social responsibility it implied and the possibility of a better world it anticipated. The image on this book's cover realises these connotations in concrete form. Depicting a man in an asbestos fire suit against a backdrop of flames, the metal relief by the Art Deco muralist, Hildreth Meière, appeared above the main entrance to the Johns Manville building at the 1939 New York World's Fair. *Asbestos – the Magic Mineral* personified the humble function of fire resistance through a noble figure that appeared to manage and defy the elements. But to think of the mural only in terms of its content fails, I think, to appreciate how Meière's bold combination of flowing lines and modern materials encourages the viewer to imagine the mineral's role in building the 'World of Tomorrow'. Transient as it was, Meière's work exemplifies a cultural response excited by asbestos's utopian, world-building possibilities.[12]

Still, overt declarations about asbestos's transformative potential are generally outnumbered by those that demurely mention it in passing, to assure without undue emphasis. Calling attention to the manner in which modernism takes asbestos for granted helps us to appreciate the manner in which asbestos, for all its regulations, scares and 'public awareness', continues to be taken for granted in the present. Objects that pose possible or actual future risk, from carbon nanotubes and glyphosate to opioids and AI in healthcare, are often described as 'the next asbestos'. But, apart from a short précis about asbestos's dangers, little information is given as to why such an association is necessary or useful. Always the source of the metaphor, never its target, asbestos remains, even when in plain sight, a matter of received wisdom.

As a preliminary step, I need to establish how such wisdom comes to be received. To do this, I identify a corpus of literary works – some traditionally 'modernist', others 'proletarian', still others in the catch-all category of 'genre fiction' – stretching across the twentieth century, that, through use or mention, can help us understand asbestos's 'meaning'. These works show how, for all our changing awareness about what it does, the methods used to represent asbestos's problems remain deeply indebted to early twentieth-century efforts to advertise it. Such formal concerns are not simply a matter of rarefied literary discourse; they determine how activists agitate for action, how doctors inform their patients, how lawyers advocate for their clients, and how policy makers determine when a site is 'rehabilitated'. This continued reliance on techniques used by the industry to sell its products may constitute an impediment to thinking about asbestos in the future, beyond bans, remediation and medical interventions. But it also helps us track asbestos as a commodity on the world market, extracted to resolve particular problems in machinofactured capitalism, and subject to the laws of exchange.

Transnational traffic inaugurated and sustained the supply-demand, production-consumption cycles that made asbestos endemic in the built environment, as the material passed from mines in Canada, Russia and South Africa, through production centres in Australia, mainland Europe, the United Kingdom and the United States, to its general, if uneven, distribution across the Global North and Global South.[13] In this light, the asbestos mine expands from being 'a discrete sociotechnical object' to become what Martín Arboleda calls 'a dense network of territorial infrastructures and spatial technologies vastly dispersed across space.'[14] For Arboleda, the result is the planetary mine. In finessing this concept, first advanced by Mazen Labban, Martín Arboleda argues that the planetary mine produces relative surplus value at the world scale, with national economies taken as its alliquot parts (6). For Arboleda, the planetary mine emerges not simply through the *long durée* of resource imperialism explained in the work of Immanuel Wallerstein, Giovanni Arrighi and Stephen Bunker and Paul Ciccantell, but the accompanying revolutions in technology (Lewis Mumford) and logistics (Deborah Cowen).[15] Nineteenth-century technological developments in machinofacturing made fire-retardants, like asbestos, absolutely essential for insulating large machinery, the factories that housed them, and the surrounding housing estates. The global asbestos industry was built on the planetary mine. Profits depended upon disaggregated labour, vertical integration across national borders, and cartelism. Even the process by which asbestos companies divested themselves of responsibility for asbestos torts, through the creation of shell relief funds and the transfer of assets offshore, resonates with a much bigger story about the division of industrial and financial capital in Europe and North America in the latter half of the twentieth century, as the former was redirected to Asia and the Global South and the latter was increasingly deregulated in the Global North.

There is a rich tradition in thinking about how literature can bear witness to these effects. The Warwick Research Collective, for instance, imagines the intersection between 'a single but radically uneven world-system; a singular modernity, combined and uneven; and a literature that variously registers this combined unevenness in both its form and its content to reveal itself as, properly speaking, world-literature.'[16] Here literature 'registers' the impacts of a capitalist modernity, scaled up to account for interactions between geographically distinct polities. By concentrating, in particular, on asbestos, I show how a planetary literature, when responding to the planetary mine, may help to render 'visible how human bodies become possessed (and often obliterated by uncanny forces and nonhuman objects become animated with powers over life and death.'[17] 'Crucially,' writes Arboleda, 'the shift from the global to the planetary is also understood as a stepping stone towards novel formations of collective consciousness and of collective agency' (16). In this regard, asbestos is not simply one example amongst others; it already offers a clear model for novel formations of collectivity. Of all the substances that have proliferated through this combination of system, modernity and literature, asbestos has generated perhaps the richest, most detailed scholarship on generalised harm, the most comprehensive judicial remedies for these harms, and, perhaps most importantly, the strongest combination of grassroots and legislative activism. International asbestos activism has produced an exemplary site of community development that could provide a model for transnational praxis, from climate change to forced mass migration, pandemics to plastic pollution. As yet, however, there is no comprehensive, critical account of cultural texts responding to asbestos. This book aims to offer such an account.

But even when framed by asbestos's extra-literary concerns, literature helps us do some important, if undervalued, concept work. The book begins by showing how these assumptions are encoded in the very genres that seem most appropriate to telling the asbestos story: the utopia and the dystopia; or the mystery, crime novel and horror story.[18] These genres establish a socially accepted understanding of asbestos, which shapes more experimental writing about asbestos, during and after modernism. Experimentalism helps to reframe my assumptions about asbestos, but I must be wary of the epistemic virtue it claims.[19] To offset the claim such writing is 'valuable' simply because it is epistemically interesting, I consider how it might transform our understanding of asbestos's movement across the world market, from the mine to the factory, into the built environment, and then to the dump. Although all texts partake in codes and traditions that help us to identify them, reflexively, with genres, many, if not all, develop some minimal difference that marks them as singular and devised for some particular purpose. By dividing these texts according to generic structure, experimental poetics and proletarian outlook, I make distinctions meant to be usefully heuristic, rather than necessary, exclusive and essential. In many cases, the texts transcend these categories, but the categories themselves afford opportunities for learning. Genre teaches me about the assumptions that shape my understanding, experimentalism helps me to challenge these assumptions, and more politically motivated literature can direct my attention to new forms of resolution.

Before I begin these framing analyses, however, I want to bring together modernism and asbestos to show they can be of mutual interest. In this introduction, I follow some asbestos objects in modernist texts, to evidence the presence of asbestos to the modernists and to explain their textual interpretation to asbestos scholars. Following these objects, or, more precisely, their function as metaphors, establishes a much larger semantic set of assumptions about asbestos than their isolated appearance might suggest. Metaphors are not simply substitutes for other words, they are referents that can change our entire understanding of a sentence or paragraph: a metaphor can establish a 'new semantic pertinence' that helps to 'redescribe reality'.[20] When asbestos is used as a metaphor for new forms of reliance in modernist literature or for new threats today, it redescribes the reality in which it is embedded. Unearthing the narrative context for these metaphors might help to make sense of asbestos's strange temporalities: its slow development over geological epochs, its long latency in the body, the illnesses it causes. Accordingly, I draw on Paul Ricoeur's work on metaphor, time and narrative not simply to address the new semantic pertinences of asbestos metaphors, but to explain how narrative may order asbestos's temporalities. His related notions of prefiguration, configuration and refiguration have the added benefit of explaining, in the loosest sense, the processes that define the book's three sections: genres prefigure our understanding of what asbestos is and does; experimental literature configures these understandings in new ways; politicised literature refigures these understandings to particular extra-literary ends.[21] This work finds its relevance in the ongoing contamination of our environment by asbestos products, and the ongoing burden of disease faced by many, many people. I relate these discussions of asbestos in modernism to its legacy in the present. At the same time, I want to frame these formal concerns by addressing the racial, gendered and classed assumptions that obtain in the small, but not unimportant role asbestos plays in the history and philosophy of western science and modernity. So, through a reading of Buster Keaton's *The Paleface* (1922), I consider how knowledge and ignorance play against each other when thinking of asbestos as, in the words of Bruno Latour, 'the last modernist object'. In following the presence of asbestos in modernism through to these consequences, I prefigure the book to come.

Modernism's Infrastructures

When asbestos appears in modernist literature, it is primarily there to be relied upon. In other words, it fits within a material and metaphoric infrastructure. To understand asbestos as a material of infrastructure, I follow the lead of David Trotter, in his work on Bakelite and vulcanised rubber, and Mimi Sheller, in her examination of aluminium, in considering how asbestos, like the other new materials of modernism, fits into a physical network of exchange across lines of combined and uneven development, in an emotional network, that translates their appearance into affective states like anxiety, hope and insecurity, and in a temporal network, that observes how these spatial and emotional networks shift and change over time, in relation to political, social, and economic pressures.[22] Like most infrastructures, these networks are easiest to identify as and when they fall apart or begin to break down.[23] But certain objects can be shown to exemplify the network, even in peak working order. One such object in modernism's cultural life was the asbestos curtain.

The asbestos curtain was a safety curtain, mandatory in theatres, that was raised at the beginning of a performance and lowered at its end. By virtue of its ubiquity, the asbestos curtain infiltrated the metaphoric language of literary modernism, where it served to signal beginnings and endings. Thus, the asbestos curtain presents an exemplary point of intersection between asbestos's material and cultural histories, as mundane reality becomes figurative device. As a metaphor, it is primarily associated with marking a narrative terminus. It therefore also limns this book's concern with meaning, time, and narrative: namely, how narratives about asbestos, explicitly or implicitly, help me come to terms with the strain the material puts on my relations with time. 'With narrative,' Ricoeur writes, 'the semantic innovation lies in the inventing of another work of synthesis – a plot. By means of the plot, goals, causes and chance are brought together within the temporal unity of a whole and complete action.'[24] By a process of 'grasping together', narrative refigures multiple scattered events into a whole and complete story. In what follows, I 'grasp together' the historical and metaphorical use of the asbestos curtain to illustrate and explain both asbestos's place in modernism's infrastructure and, in parallel, time's relation to narrative.

The relation between the asbestos curtain metaphor, time, and narrative can be found in a letter by the Imagist poet H. D. [Hilda Doolittle] to Havelock

Ellis, dated 30 August [1933]: 'I am glad now to feel an "asbestos" curtain drop between certain phases of me and my past.'[25] The metaphor describes the outcome of H. D.'s analysis with Freud. The same image appears in *Advent* (1956), the notebook she kept during her analysis: 'an asbestos curtain had dropped between me and my past, my not-so-far-past bitter severance from love and friendship.'[26] Here, the curtain presents a physical, spatial image of division to describe the more complex, temporal process of psychic compartmentalisation. It translates the 'asbestos curtain' to the realm of psychoanalysis. Far from marking the juxtaposition of asbestos and curtain as strange, H. D.'s scare quotes refer to the tendency to label such curtains 'Asbestos' in the theatres where they were to be found. H. D. relies on the image being itself pedestrian enough not to intrude on her reader's understanding of her insulation from 'psychic death'. Finding the right words to describe asbestos and its effects is difficult, not least because asbestos is being used as a metaphoric source to describe other things.

H. D.'s metaphor demands a fuller history of the asbestos curtain. Introduced as a device to separate the stage, and its lights, from the plush (and flammable) furnishings of the auditorium, the asbestos curtain began to replace existing safety curtains in the 1870s.[27] In 1897, Edwin O. Sachs documented more than 10,000 deaths by theatre fires worldwide in the preceding century, largely as a result of stage fires, caused by lighting requirements, that spread to the auditorium.[28] There was, therefore, a pressing need for a non-flammable barrier that could divide the two: the asbestos curtain, which separated the theatre's audience from the stage. Such was the hubris offered by its protection that Chicago's Iroquois Theatre billed itself as 'Absolutely Fireproof' before suffering the deadliest single-building fire in US history (at least 602 fatalities). It was determined that the fire was, in part, due to poor maintenance of the curtain, which failed to drop fully when the fire broke out, and to the poor quality of the curtain itself, which, made mainly from wood pulp mixed with asbestos, was 'of no value in a fire'. This failure, far from curtailing the fortunes of the asbestos curtain, led to its institution in building and fire codes. By 1909, legislation in most US cities mandated that this curtain be made from asbestos.

When I focus on the structural elements of this story, I can use it to explain how narrative works. The casual introduction of the asbestos curtain leads to its haphazard use, culminating in catastrophe. The aftermath of this catastrophe, the *anagnorisis* or moment of realisation that permits narrative resolution, is the codification of the asbestos curtain as a fixed feature of modernism's built environment. The reader is pushed towards a (inevitable) teleology that sees the curtain reign victorious, even as the tragedy immerses them in the accidental and the contingent. What gives this narrative its force, Ricoeur might argue, is its reliance on plot: not only do events follow on from each other, but they affect each other (through cause-and-effect) and may be divided into a recognisable beginning, middle and end. Haphazard general use is interrupted by the fire (crisis), which causes a tightening of regulations. This progression, which Ricoeur takes from Aristotle's notion of *muthos* (emplotment), emphasises itself as a single dramatic action. But, insofar as this action must be represented, it demands a *mimetic* action ('the imitation or representation of action' and 'the organization of the events'). This action is not just the action represented within the work (its configuration, or what Ricoeur will call 'mimesis$_2$'). It includes the presumption that both storyteller and her audience have the narrative competence to identify the structural, symbolic and temporal features of the work and its represented actions (its prefiguration, or 'mimesis$_1$'). For narrative action to be represented, I must apprehend that actions have goals and ethical implications, and that they are shaped by my experience of time. Further, the work must be received by a spectator or reader, which allows its represented actions to be understood in relation to time, their place in the world and their significance (its refiguration, or 'mimesis$_3$'). The contents of the work, its production and its reception each rely on their own mimetic actions, which must be thought of as interdependent on one another.

The asbestos curtain was an important material and metaphoric object in modernist culture, but it can also illustrate Ricoeur's thoughts on narrative. Since it marked the beginning and the end of every cinematic or theatrical performance, the curtain separates three distinct periods that map onto the standard division of the performance's time into before (prefiguration), during (configuration) and after (refiguration). My anticipation of the performance to come, like my memory of the performance just seen, is as much a part of the overall action as my attention to the performance itself. This, my experience of time, is anchored to the movements of the asbestos curtain, which announces the material breaks or puncta in that experience.

The history of the asbestos curtain serves as preamble to a further narrative that follows it through modernism's literary canon. Its prosaic importance is indicated by the givenness with which these texts use it, without dreaming it might need further explanation. In a human-interest story on a fireman, Djuna Barnes imagines him spending his evenings 'supervising the rising of the asbestos curtain of the last act.'[29] As befits the vox-pop-profile nature of her piece, Barnes marginalises the excitement of the theatrical production to emphasise the necessary, repetitive functionalism of Michael Quinn's work as a fire warden, overseeing the curtain as a feature of fire safety. Barnes's actual curtain serves to remind us of cultural modernism's reliance on emerging forms of materiality, and that the sources of these metaphors were real objects, whose initial phase of marvel were quickly dampened by the expectations of habit.

Most metaphoric asbestos curtains in modernist literature target associations with the end of performances. In Lawrence Durrell's *The Black Book*

(1938), the quasi-autobiographical protagonist, Lawrence Lucifer, reminisces on his sexual exploits with the prostitute, Hilda, by imagining their coupling as a theological-theatrical performance. Durrell extends the metaphor by referring to a non-existent audience ('it was a wonderful house tonight'), whose approval warrants 'seven calls before the curtain' before 'the curtain slips down giddily, bearing one apocalyptic word: Asbestos.'[30] Asbestos, Greek for inextinguishable, perhaps also implies a heat of passion absent from Durrell's description of the sex itself. Qualifying the word as apocalyptic (Greek for 'revelation') suggests it uncovers what the curtain so decorously attempts to disguise: that sex with Hilda, even evocations of Hilda as the Virgin Mary, do not slow the relentless narcissism that characterises Lucifer's narrative voice.

e. e. cummings also uses the asbestos curtain to disclose sexual practices it is meant to censor. In his memoir, *The Enormous Room* (1922), cummings discretely turns his gaze away from the sexual exploits of his fellow prisoners by invoking this physical feature of the theatre: 'Now let the curtain fall, and the reader be satisfied with the significant word "Asbestos" which is part of all first-rate performances.'[31] Ostensibly a factual account of cummings's internment at La Ferté Macé in 1917 for anti-war behaviour, contemporary reviewers qualified their praise for *The Enormous Room* by regretting 'its crudities'.[32] It presented a 'calculated indecency' that might be seen to be a feature of Modernist texts more generally.[33] Drawing down the asbestos curtain, then, signals a metaphoric self-censorship against even more graphic descriptions. In a text, however, that, as Hazel Hutchison has argued, 'presents the struggle for self-expression and freedom of conscience [. . .] as the real war within the war', both curtain and signal become part of a performance: a wink acknowledging that activities have been covered over, which should have been eliminated entirely.[34] For cummings, the asbestos curtain presented the distinction between what one can say, and what one can't, to highlight the latter.

For Durrell and cummings, the asbestos curtain marks a divergence between narration (the act of telling the story or utterance) and narrative (the story being told or statement). In both novels, the curtain punctures a realist narrative with an allegorical turn, since it is substituted for more graphic descriptions of sexual acts. The asbestos curtain acts simultaneously as censoring device and as marker outlining, more or less explicitly, what is being censored. In acting for both, however, the curtain implicitly stands for the time each takes to be completed: therefore, it sutures together the times of narration and narrative. The result is what Ricoeur calls

> a three-tiered scheme: utterance-statement-world of the text, to which correspond a time of narrating, a narrated time, and a fictive experience of time projected by the conjunction/disjunction between the time it takes to narrate and narrated time.[35]

When Durrell's 'apocalyptic' and cummings's 'Now' signal an intrusion of the narrator that splits narration from narrative, they rely on the curtain to stand in for this divergence: a reliance that reinforces the curtain's role as a marker of time.

It still marks time in Elizabeth Bowen's final novel, *Eva Trout; or Changing Scenes* (1968). Here, the asbestos curtain signals the end of Eva's time at the 'experimentary' castle school, after her roommate Elsinore attempts suicide: 'With the coming-into-the-room of Elsinore's mother, all here ended. From that instant, down came oblivion – asbestos curtain. Whether Elsinore died or lived no one told Eva.'[36] Again, the asbestos curtain announces a moment of transition. It censors what the baffled, inarticulate Eva knows, or knows to ask, peremptorily foreclosing both the narrative about the school experience and any questions it might have caused. The difficult questions that might be asked about Elsinore are dismissed; like death itself, the episode concludes pre-emptively, without plot resolution and in 'oblivion'. And yet, Bowen gives us an asbestos curtain to mark that it has ended, however unsatisfying that end might be. Ending doesn't just happen, as a teleology might imply; it is marked, staged or otherwise performed. As in H. D., Durrell and cummings, the asbestos curtain functions as a *cordon sanitaire*, separating the consequences of events in the narrative from their prosaic narration. It functions as a liminal marker that discloses those same occlusions it is meant to obstruct from view.

When modernist writers call on a tradition of theatre-going that accepts the asbestos curtain as the physical end of a performance, they use this tradition to disrupt the reader's expectations about how the scene will unfold. The scene ends, and yet it goes on. The consequence is a radical foreclosing of the future: not, as was usual in the nineteenth-century novel, with a death, a marriage or an inheritance, but as the announcement that a narrative arc has been abandoned to 'oblivion', a death, in other words, to narration. Historically, the asbestos curtain offered modernist writers a metaphoric source that allowed them to draw moral or temporal lines, marking moments of transition in their works. Crucially, it also highlighted the drawing of lines as a narrative gesture, self-reflexively incorporating the physical curtain to relate the plot to 'all first-rate performances'. Since the asbestos curtain marked the beginning and end of performances, it materialises the boundaries of Ricoeur's three mimetic divisions: the configuration of the work itself or what Ricoeur calls $mimesis_2$, as separated from the prefiguration of narrative ($mimesis_1$) and its refiguration ($mimesis_3$) through reception. The different permutations of the asbestos curtain mentioned above serve as fitting examples of a material object absorbed into a cultural imaginary. They demonstrate asbestos's unacknowledged presence as an infrastructure of modernism. Tellingly, these examples all make use of the asbestos curtain as the source, rather than target, of their metaphoric conceit: they rely on their reader knowing what an asbestos curtain is, in order to concretise more complicated arguments about censorship, memory and narrative.

The use of asbestos curtains, even as a metaphoric source, provokes thoughts about their discursive meaning, even if, perhaps especially if, that meaning is assumed to be fixed and stable. It blurs material history into cultural history. It introduces a concern with time and narrative that will prove very useful in the chapters to come. But, thought textually, the asbestos curtain also foregrounds a narrative will-not-to-know. Its intrusion marks a conscious refusal to elaborate on a scene, effectively disqualifying any narrative resolution. The result is a sticking point; even as I continue to read, I return to these moments as unresolved and irresolvable.

Entanglements

By now, I can say that modernism's relationship with asbestos is more significant than its absorption into the infrastructure might suggest. I argued that, in its curtain form, it played a metaphoric role in describing time and narrative. But these casual observations gain their real significance only in retrospect, as knowledge about what asbestos does becomes general. Moreover, where asbestos in modernist texts plays the role of the ordinary object, more recent writing about asbestos, literary and theoretical, draws on modernist techniques to highlight asbestos's resistance to ordinary description. Or, to adapt Dora Zhang's discussion of Henry James, when ordinary description encounters asbestos, it becomes 'about something other than how things look [. . .] but it is quite specific with respect to qualities and effects.'[37] After all, the distortions of time and space now associated with asbestos fibres and their attendant diseases – its microscopic scale; the long latency periods – lend themselves to consciously experimental writing, which seeks, like Zhang's James, 'to imagine what it is like to feel an atmosphere.'

For Montana-based nature writer, Rick Bass, the story of asbestos 'is a big story comprised of millions of tiny parts. It defies structure. It drifts along the breeze, settles and lands where it may.'[38] This accounts for Bass's structural choices in 'With Every Great Breath: Living and Dying in Lincoln Country', his essay about asbestos contamination at the vermiculite mine in Libby, Montana, the alleged cover-up by the mine's owner, W. R. Grace & Co., and its eventual acknowledgement as a public health disaster by the Environmental Protection Agency.[39] Told as a series of vignettes, anecdotes, observations and accounts, ranging in length from a paragraph to a few pages, the essay imagines itself 'identifying safe paths and sealing over old wounds', 'just as the scar tissue in a body seeks to isolate an infection, attempts to seal the pustulous wound'.[40] It exemplifies 'the rhetoric of exposure' that Steve Schwarze identifies in earlier responses to Libby: a rhetoric that juxtaposes evidence credited with different epistemic value – personal experience, scientific studies, official press releases

– to overcome *'uncertainty* about material conditions and relationships and *inertia* on the part of institutions responsible for investigating and addressing those conditions.'[41] Juxtaposition brings together competing temporalities in Bass's essay: the risks to his own life, the illnesses in his neighbours and his dog, the culpability of the corporations, and the fibres' effect. Although Bass claims the story of asbestos defies structure, the vignette offers him a form that simultaneously isolates its 'millions of tiny parts', even as it grasps these together through juxtaposition. But what matters, Bass decides, is not the number of people affected at Libby, but 'the fact that our story is new and use-able by others'.[42] This rhetoric motivates public action about the specific concern, and about comparable concerns in the future.

When describing the forms of uncertainty and inertia that emerge with comparable asbestos contaminations in Northern Italy's Balangero Mine and the Eternit factory at Casale Monferrato, the São Félix mine in Bahia or the Jeffrey Mine next to Asbestos, Quebec, cultural critics and anthropologists like Serenella Iovino, Agata Mazzeo, Sasha Litvintseva and Enrico Cesaretti turn to Rob Nixon's work on 'slow violence': 'a violence', Nixon explains, 'that occurs gradually and out of sight, a violence of delayed destruction that is dispersed across time and space, an attritional violence that is typically not viewed as violence at all.'[43] The slow violence of asbestos is measured, first and foremost, in the long latencies of diseases like mesothelioma. Iovino, Litvintseva and Cesaretti agree that asbestos diseases open up pathways for understanding asbestos's other forms of slow violence, which they characterise as a series of 'intra-actions' (Iovino), 'haptics' (Litvintseva) or 'entanglements' (Cesaretti) that connect fibre to flesh on a cellular level, exposure to illness on a personal level, and contamination to communities on a historical level.[44] Asbestos's rate of change, measured in geological epochs, jibes against the moment needed by a breath to bring the fibre into the body, while, between them, the decades it takes a fibre to generate mutations in a human cell spar with the months or years these cells then take to kill you.

The three critics find inspiration in Feminist New Materialism: in particular, Karen Barad's 'entanglement', which suggests 'individuals emerge through and as part of their entangled intra-relating', and Stacy Alaimo's 'trans-corporeality', in which 'the human is always intermeshed with the more-than-human world'.[45] The human and the more-than-human, too often thought of as distinct entities, are intimately related and ethically intertwined. Still, this relationality risks leaving something out. '[R]ather than focus on an ethics based on relationality and entanglement,' Eva Haifa Giraud wonders whether 'it is important to more fully flesh out an ethics of exclusion, which pays attention to the entities, practices, and ways of being that are foreclosed when other entangled realities are materialized?'[46] Or, as Giraud and others have argued elsewhere, as interesting as Barad is on entanglement, too little attention is paid to her work on 'agential cuts': the determinate boundaries that apparatuses produce, and which are necessary for turning phenomena (the ontologically inseparable intra-agents of entanglement) into meaningful objects of knowledge.[47] Asbestos, after all, was once thought of as a substance that could produce boundaries, freeing us from touch or attachment. This irony needs to be remembered, to appreciate fully why it was that people came to invest time and life in its production.

At the same time that asbestos performs agential cuts, it is clear that attempts to trace 'the alliances through which stone's long temporality enmeshes with human story' become more fraught when those alliances kill.[48] The lithic alliance may register human ephemerality in the vertiginous terms of the geologic, but it renders some humans more ephemeral than others. Here, Mazzeo offers a more complex account of how people come to terms with time. Mazzeo, an anthropologist working with Brazilian anti-asbestos activists, uses 'time' to elaborate on 'the lack of synchronicity between asbestos mining, human and environmental temporalities, and the Brazilian anti-asbestos activists' practices and narratives.'[49] Her attention remains on the human. This reminds us of the tension in the relation between the more-than-human focus of New Materialism and Nixon's slow violence, which, after all, Nixon developed to articulate an 'environmentalism of the poor'. Not parsing this tension risks recapitulating precisely the problem Nixon and, before him, Johan Galtung sought to diagnose with 'slow' and 'structural violence' respectively: when multi-species being is invoked, at the expense of the human, it is usually the poor who are excluded first. In structural violence, Galtung 'sought to foreground the vast structures that can give rise to acts of personal violence and constitute forms of violence in and of themselves'.[50] For Nixon, slow violence elaborates on the stasis of structural violence 'to foreground questions of time, movement, and change, however gradual' (11). Expanding on the static determinism of structural violence, slow violence projects itself from the past through the present into the future, but it is measured, mainly, through its effects on communities, and in the writings of people trying to make those effects more visible.

If witnessing slow violence offers a nuanced understanding of asbestos's effects on human communities, it is not, in and of itself, sufficient. Slow violence could be, and was, used by the asbestos industry to justify inaction. In a memo, the Johns-Manville medical officer at Asbestos, Kenneth Smith, would note of the 708 workers he surveyed in 1948:

> It must be remembered that although these men have the X-ray evidence of asbestosis, they are working today and definitely are not disabled from asbestosis. They have not been told of this diagnosis for it is felt that as long as the man feels well, is happy at home and work, and his physical condition remains good, nothing should be said. When he becomes disabled and sick, then the diagnosis should be made and the

claim submitted by the Company. The fibrosis of the disease is irreversible and permanent so that eventually compensation will be paid to each of these men. But as long as the man is not disabled it is felt that he should not be told of his condition so that he can live and work in peace and that the Company can benefit from his many years of experience. Should the man be told of his condition today there is a very definite possibility that he would become mentally and physically ill, simply through the knowledge that he has asbestosis.[51]

Smith is aware that asbestosis is a slowly violent, disabling disease; he is also concerned, sincerely I must imagine, that anxieties may provoke their own illnesses. In contrasting asbestosis to the 'possibility' of becoming 'physically ill', his document is certainly cynical. But it also shows how slow violence can, and has, been used against its own activist ambitions, for the 'peace' of the worker and the 'benefit' of the Company. Its concern with feeling well, happy and good trades on something like Lauren Berlant's 'cruel optimism', a desire that obstructs people's flourishing. In its visceral ordinariness, cruel optimism represents a zone 'where life building and the attrition of human life are indistinguishable'.[52] Paralleling Rob Nixon's 'slow violence', Berlant identifies these zones with 'slow death' 'the physical wearing out of a population in a way that points to its deterioration as a defining condition of its experience and historical existence' (95). Indeed, awareness of asbestos's role in the creation of conditions of 'slow death' is almost exactly coincident with Nixon and Berlant's tendency to focus on 'the present' of late capitalism, from the 1960s and 1970s onward.

Both Berlant and Nixon insist that they describe conditions of violence and attrition that rely upon 'ordinariness' to become invisible. The processes of slow violence and slow death depend upon tenacious fantasies: misrecognitions involved in 'seeing selves and worlds as continuous', whether motivated by profit or other attachments (122). These fantasies cover up the effects of slow violence and slow death, while motivating people to keep these effects covered up. We only see this violence, they suggest, when we look at it twice: the first time, for how it appears, and the second, for how it really is. This double look invests my first impressions of the ordinary with a catalogue of horrific effects. The asbestos curtain presents just such an ordinary image. Suddenly, its glib associations with apocalypse and closure take on frightening and oppressive connotations. My sense of it is destabilised as I anticipate future consequences for those unsuspecting theatre workers who might have been exposed, on the basis of my memories of other victims of exposure.

On the basis of my discussion of 'slow violence' and 'slow death' I can return to Ricoeur's preoccupation with time and narrative with a better sense of its consequences for history. In other words, the cultural history of asbestos combines with the formal dimensions of Ricoeur's argument to create a materialist poetics.⁵³ Ricoeur, remember, brings together the 'completeness' and 'wholeness' of plot to its discordant counterpart, temporality:

> the world unfolded by every narrative work is always a temporal world [. . .] time becomes human time to the extent that it is organized after the manner of a narrative; narrative, in turn, is meaningful to the extent that it portrays the features of temporal experience.⁵⁴

Ricoeur's gambit is that Aristotle, in order to preserve the concordance of plot, forgets time in his *Poetics*, while Augustine, Ricoeur's other point of departure, provides a reciprocal aporia when he insists on the discordance of time, at the expense of plot, in his *Confessions*. In keeping with his hermeneutic method, Ricoeur uses this circularity as the starting point for establishing how time and narrative become mutually constitutive: my desire for the concordance offered by narrative remains in tense relation with the discordance provoked by my experience of time passing. This insight suggests that narrative might recuperate the alien time scales of asbestos itself for narrative, but, more importantly, it does so for the experience of asbestos-related disease. Indeed, narrative medicine might be said to rest upon this basic assumption: narratives provide solace ('concordance') after an illness upsets my normal experience of time passing ('discordance').⁵⁵

Whether apprehending the effects of slow violence and slow death or simply addressing the metaphor of the asbestos curtain, I need to bring my appreciation of phenomenological temporality (past, present, future) together with a more standard progression of linear or cosmological time (before, during, after) to form a third, 'historical' or 'narrative' time. Like the clock that determines the play's duration or the calendar its assignation, the asbestos curtain does not simply define different periods in the production; it sutures my experience of the production to physical markers of time passing: my expectation before the curtain is raised, my attention when it is raised, and my memory after it falls. To address this in greater detail, I turn, with Ricoeur, to Augustine.

When Augustine describes the human experience of time, he suggests it is best understood as a threefold present: the present of past things, or memory, the present of present things, or attention, and the present of future things, or expectation.⁵⁶ Whereas cosmological time measures itself against the movement of material things, like the sun, temporality is time as experienced by human subjects, who, locked as they are in an unfolding present, must experience both the past and the future as mediated through this present. By recasting temporality into a threefold present, Augustine raises the possibility of thinking about time experience as a set of actions, wherein I attend to a present in negotiation with an expectation of that which is coming and a remembering of that which is past. Time's extension relies on this distention of the soul (*disentio animi*) into the past or the future, a distention that will provoke time's discordances. Whether I am impatient for the curtain to be raised, or distressed when it falls, my concern with the past and future disturb my sense of equanimity in the present.

Speculations about the movements of cosmological time and the actions of temporality demand some stable point against which these dynamics might be measured. For Augustine, this limiting idea is eternity, not simply registered as God, but as that which is not, or outside, time. But this also provides a hinge that Ricoeur will use to introduce what is absent from Augustine's speculation about time: narrative emplotment. If the temporality of illness causes discordances through a distension of the soul, narrative provides a concordance through its engagement of a plot. Behind the internal discordances of the plot that impel me towards its telos, resolution or conclusion, lies narrative's concordant security: like Augustine's eternity, the narrative presupposes the story is already finished, the page is written, the world is complete. My experience of temporality as the plot unfolds relies upon an expectation that this plot will resolve itself by the final page. Thus, as I read forwards, experiencing the within-time of the characters as they try to make choices constrained by circumstance, I also understand the plot as an achronic structure that stabilises my sense of within-time with a completeness provided by its 'sense of an ending'. Here Ricoeur finds, in narrative temporality's complement, the concordance necessary to make sense of its discordance.

Ricoeur's argument clarifies the narrative purpose of apprehension in contexts of slow violence and slow death. When I become 'aware' of the underlying violence of ordinary life, I am forced to distend my attention on the present into my memories of contiguous catastrophes, while extending these consequences, through anticipation, to future, as yet undiagnosed events. Meditating on the limits of his attempt to reconcile time and narrative, Ricoeur wonders whether narrative can ever truly come to terms with the forms of 'deep temporality' with which Nixon is concerned. Narrative can originate in the deep temporality of within-time, proceeding in due course to the historical understanding offered by tradition, but can it reverse this direction, he wonders, moving from historical repetition back to phenomenological experience of time? Berlant would say it can't; that our means of coping must simply navigate the affective disposition we adopt to history. Nixon finds more hope in the potential for communities who, in enacting political change, refigure our responses to the time of events. As I detail in my conclusion, I favour Nixon's optimism to Berlant's, since asbestos activism provides a compelling case study in the power of communities to enact change. But the substance itself has shifted our sense of the world in strange ways we may not see at first. After all, it is a measure of asbestos's psychosocial success that we no longer associate cinemas or theatres with the possibility of a fiery death. In this, asbestos proved itself a vanishing mediator, the means by which society transitioned from a pervasive fear about fire to a confidence about the built environment.[57] Like most vanishing mediators, it imperfectly erased itself when, task done, time came for it to disappear. Today, we bear the material costs for that imperfect vanishing act.

Staging Ignorance

By now, I have established the stakes of this vanishing mediator for modernism and the present. What has been assumed, thus far, is the reflexive approach I have taken to cultural interpretation: a reflexivity that allows me to recuperate a past knowledge that, without being entirely aware of its consequences, cannot simply be dismissed as ignorant. This approach situates my study in a recent turn in modernist studies that encompasses notions as distinct as Aaron Jaffe's 'second modernism', Paul K. Saint-Amour's 'subjunctive historicism' and Elizabeth Outka's 'absent present'.[58] Each finds a latent concern within modernism whose subsequent manifestations are explained and enriched by their juxtaposition with these hidden origins. Are these not simply cases of presentism, where the historical circumstances of today dictate searches of yesterday for a fictive cause? Not if we can identify in yesterday a prevailing cultural logic that signals this cause, argue Jaffe, Saint-Amour and Outka. For Jaffe, this is the logic of second modernity, when social concerns shifted from monitoring the distribution of wealth to the distribution of risk.[59] Saint-Amour finds it in the sense of anticipatory catastrophe that accompanied the interwar's 'real-time experience of remembering a past war while awaiting and theorizing a future one'.[60] Outka traces its effects in the miasmic atmospheres that surround silences about the 1918 influenza pandemic, nowhere spoken about but everywhere present.[61] A comparable cultural logic emerges when the racialised narratives of technological advancement that characterise capitalist modernity intersect with a substance that, at first, exemplifies modernist advancement, before becoming a signature of humanity's hubris. To illustrate this intersection, I turn to Buster Keaton's *The Paleface*, a film that, despite, or perhaps because of, its racist use of redface and stereotype, and its occlusion of Indigenous subjectivities, exemplifies the assumptions bound up in asbestos use.

In the film, an oil company tries to take over the land of a peaceful Native American 'tribe'. Keaton, a naïve lepidopterist, is caught in the midst of the escalating hostilities. Two scenes, in particular, turn on asbestos's properties as a fire-resistant fibre that can be woven into a fabric. Keaton, pursued by men in the tribe, finds his way to a log cabin. In the cabin, there is a roll of asbestos cloth, which Keaton, intuiting his eventual capture, sews into a set of underclothes.

Figure 0.1 Arriving in the Cabin

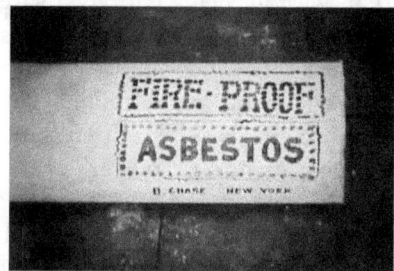

Figure 0.2 The Asbestos Roll

Figure 0.3 Donning the Asbestos Suit

After the men capture him, they try to burn him at the stake. As the ropes fall away, an unharmed Keaton steps out of the fire and nonchalantly lights a cigarette. The awestruck men immediately bow down before him.

The film repeats what Daniel Heath Justice calls the 'corrosive' story of 'Indigenous deficiency' by relying on the old, racist trope that peoples, coexisting in the same time and space, may be differentiated by their 'stages of development' or the degree to which they have realised a (Western) modernity.[62]

Without discounting the film's overt racism, an increased attentiveness to its use of asbestos helps to puncture the hubris of this trope. To understand why, I must reckon with the film's use of asbestos as a gimmick, 'an *ambivalent* judgment', writes Sianne Ngai, 'tied to a *compromised* form'.[63] For Ngai, gimmicks, from the word's first appearance in 1926, are 'overrated devices that strike us as working too little (labor-saving tricks) but also as working too hard (strained efforts to get our attention)' (1). Keaton's asbestos clothes are gimmicky because they short-circuit other, more reasonable methods of resolving his lepidopterist's dilemma, while depending on a developed sense of what asbestos does. In this regard, they join a rich tradition of gimmickry that brought the substance to the attention of potential consumers: the comic book supervillains, Asbestos Lady and Asbestos Man, whose asbestos suits made them uniquely impervious antagonists for Fantastic Four member the Human Torch; asbestos cigarette filters, designed to protect against lung cancer; a limited edition of Ray Bradbury's *Farenheit 451* bound in asbestos, to protect it against the book-burning censors described within. The degree to which I understand these examples as gimmicky or not reflects the position of judgment I occupy: gimmick 'is what we say when we want to demonstrate that we, unlike others implicitly invoked or imagined in the same moment, are not buying into what a capitalist device is promising' (5). If it 'does not strike us as suspiciously over- or underperforming, we will not perceive it as a gimmick but as a neutral device'. Like the asbestos conceit, or, indeed, 'every made thing in capitalism', devices can turn into gimmicks at any moment, or vice versa. The judgment process that Ngai observes in the gimmick might well describe my retrospective understanding of mass-produced asbestos, not simply in villains, filters, book covers or underwear, but the entire history of its use.

Obviously, asbestos was not, in the vast majority of cases, used as a gimmick. Still, Ngai's argument can help me to address asbestos through aesthetic modes of judgment, and this is valuable for three reasons. First, gimmickry is an aesthetically coded manner of seeing and judging objects that is produced by, rather than alongside, capitalism. Second, when people make use of the gimmick, they acknowledge its ambivalence but pursue it anyway because it helps them cope with capitalism's depredations, especially those that capitalism renders vulnerable through racial, gendered or classist differentiations. Finally, physical objects may drift in and out of its frame of reference, depending on individual or historical circumstance. Gimmicks aren't gimmicks all the time and forever. Even if I don't see or judge asbestos to be a gimmick in all cases, it encodes forms of seeing and judging that are shaped by capitalism, forms that linger even as public understanding changes. *The Paleface* captures something of these lingering forms as they relate to asbestos, ignorance and capitalist modernity.

In the film, asbestos indexes a standard, if exaggerated, correspondence between twinned dialectics: knowledge-ignorance and civilisation-barbarity. Replicating the discursive soft power of Empire, the white male subject finds some asbestos, turns it into underwear, and thereby ensures that he is immune to fire. The foolish barbarians, ignorant of the fire-retardant qualities of asbestos, elevate the white subject to the position of minor godhead. As the film ages, however, so do responses to the material object, asbestos, that sits at its heart. Today's viewers know something that Buster Keaton and his audience did not: asbestos has toxic qualities. I can map my own knowledge on to their ignorance, as a demonstration of scientific progress.

How, then, does this change my relationship with those who came before? Does this make the people of the past my 'barbarians'? One might well think so. Then I must sit with an uneasy speculation about the future, when my judgment about the audience is, in turn, judged, when I, laughing, am in turn laughed at. Such ironies are anticipated in the film itself. Between the scenes of Keaton sewing the asbestos and finally putting it on, the audience is presented with a short text: 'Strictly fireproof – Asbestos BVDs'.

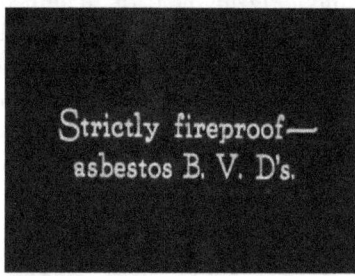

Figure 0.4 Explanatory Intertitle

For the film to make sense, it needs to make certain that the audience knows what, only two minutes later, they will be laughing at Native Americans for not knowing. The audience may laugh at the apparent ignorance of the Native Americans, but, whether they realise it or not, they are also laughing at themselves, at their own implied need for a cue.

The film imagines an epistemic break between the modern understanding of material cause and effect and a pre-modern reliance on magical thinking. The break is contingent on the knowledge it assumes of its audience. As a result, in each successive stage of its reception, the modern is recast as now, the pre-modern as the stage immediately preceding it. From the Native Americans watching Keaton within the film, to the 1922 audience, to the audience of 2022, each audience treats its predecessor as ignorant. I laugh at the audience of 1922 as they laughed at Keaton's Native Americans. At the same time, the laughter that erupts from the modern in judgment over the pre-modern presumes a knowledge of the present moment whose ignorance becomes apparent in the future. Here, the Native American response, grossly stereotyped as it is, proves the most sophisticated. Rather than taking asbestos to be an inert natural phenomenon, whose social implications are measured only in its capacity to shock and awe, they attend to it as magical object, or, in other words, a concern coproduced by nature and society.

Almost 100 years later, American comedies are still using the asbestos gimmick. In a 2018 episode of *Schitt's Creek*, for instance, the long-suffering Jocelyn Schitt stages an asbestos festival to raise funds for her dilapidated town.[64] When the ignorant owner of the town, Moira Rose, offers to perform at the festival, the play she proposes is, in her words, 'a tale of perseverance, much like your quest to bring asbestos back to the town.' 'We're trying to get rid of the asbestos, Moira,' replies an exasperated Jocelyn. Asbestos's significance has, by now, undergone a full inversion, from miraculous object to well-known contaminant. Behind this change in content, however, I detect formal continuities: the reliance on a knowledgeable audience that understands this significance, the assumption that the position of ignorance is risible, even the subtle inclusion of the knowledge the audience is assumed to know (at the end of the episode, Moira will say, 'nothing is colder than the chill I get when I think of the dangers of asbestos poisoning.'). The form of the asbestos joke still distinguishes between the ignorant and the knowledgeable.

The subdued genealogy that runs from *The Paleface* to *Schitt's Creek* depends upon a persistent formalism that maps across the knowledge divide, from the prior understanding that asbestos secured its users from enmeshment, entanglement and attachment to the subsequent understanding that it enmeshes, entangles and attaches. But if, like all art objects, *The Paleface* and *Schitt's Creek* are both implicated in capitalism as commodities, *The Paleface* does at least entertain a reading wherein asbestos creates an epistemic crisis that mere knowledge won't fix. Alternative readings are more difficult to spin from *Schitt's Creek*, where the schema of knowledge and ignorance is fixed. When the former, however unintentionally, pushes the limits of its own epistemic position, it acquires an artistic autonomy that complicates its inexcusable racism.

In arguing about the possibility of autonomous art objects after modernism, Nicholas Brown avoids differentiating art objects (*The Paleface*, in my example) from mere cultural products (*Schitt's Creek*) by their implication in, or resistance to, capitalism.[65] Both are implicated. Rather, the object differentiates itself when it manages to push the formal limits previously set for it by genre or social expectation. Brown tries to resuscitate the possibility of an artistic autonomy as a matter of philosophical aesthetics. Earlier efforts by modernists and their critics had asserted the art object's autonomy by claiming it was external to commodification. The materialist turn of the New Modernist studies has confirmed what earlier work on the institutions of modernism already knew: modernism's intimate relation with commodification. Brown rescues the art object by separating its formal concerns from its position within a social commodity chain. Although art objects are commodities, they are not commodities like any other: their engagement with each other as part of a developing aesthetic tradition demands interpretation, which grants a meaning separable from mere market desire, and therefore implies an intentionality (i.e. autonomy) distinct from the conditions of their production.

This replicates for aesthetics a similar claim made by Bruno Latour about modernism in its sociological sense, where the 'fabulous dissonance' in modernist culture lies 'between what modernists say (emancipation from all attachments!) and what they do (create ever-more attachments!).'[66] 'Modernism', in Latour's reading, claims to attenuate the conditions of risk, while embroiling its subjects the more squarely within them. Based on Brown's argument, *The Paleface* might acquire an aesthetic autonomy, while still illustrating Latour's sociological concerns. The arguments open up parallel, semi-autonomous reflections on art and social life. Even so, I want to bear in mind that my response to asbestos is primarily a matter of making aesthetic judgments about a commodity in aesthetic and scientific texts. Indeed, it is insofar as asbestos serves as a hinge between the aesthetic, the scientific and the social that it concretises the concerns raised by Ngai apropos the gimmick, a nonaesthetic object determined through aesthetic modes of seeing and judging. The gimmick ultimately undercuts Brown's argument about artistic autonomy, since it shows that aesthetic judgment, upon which he bases his distinction between formal innovation and mere marketing, may itself be compromised by its intimate relation to value, time and labour. But it complements his general sense that interpretation matters when making meaning. At the same time as these theoretical positions lend credence to the idea that asbestos can be understood aesthetically, this judgment must be reconciled with its distinctly nonaesthetic status as an object of science.

To this end, I want to return to Latour and his seminal 'anthropology of science', *We Have Never Been Modern* (1993). Principally an account of seventeenth-century science, which consolidated divisions between the human and the nonhuman, *We Have Never Been Modern* also invites us to think of the connections, up until now only hinted at, between modernism as a literary period and Western Modernity as reflexive sociological condition. We have, Latour argues, been blinded to the co-production of society with nature. When Robert Boyle and the Royal Society set down the first principles for the study of nature, they freed it from human influence by suggesting that observation might be made independent of any consideration of the observer. At the same time, Thomas Hobbes developed a method for studying society as characterised by human conflicts and agreements that could be distinguished from nature. The studies of nature and society purified themselves of each other, reciprocally expunged the other from their purview. Thus, for Latour, modernity insists on an artificial distinction between the two in the discourses of the natural and human sciences, which 'we' do not recognise in actual life because 'we' have never been modern. For the audience of 1922, Keaton's asbestos underwear follows rules of nature, which don't, in themselves, change their understanding of Keaton as a bumbling extra on the pathway of progress. For both Keaton's Native Americans and the audience of today, the unknown qualities of the asbestos (whether its fire-resistance or its negative health effects) reflect back on to Keaton, granting him the powers of either all-knowing god or unknowing fool. In either case, this reflection breaks the barrier between the natural and the social by implicating the natural qualities of asbestos in social concerns, either of magic or public health.

The historical break Latour marks between sociological modernism and postmodernism may be compared to the epistemic break he observes between matters of fact and matters of concern. In *Politics of Nature*, Latour describes asbestos as 'probably the last objects that can be called modernist'.[67] For Latour, modernist describes a particular epistemic orientation towards scientific facts that insists on their objective, apolitical truth value. Likewise, an object, here, means something closer to the 'object' in 'an object of inquiry' than a regular thing. Latour, in his discussion of the modernist orientation towards asbestos as an object of inquiry, understands both its qualities and its effects as 'matters of fact'. Matters of fact insist on scientific objectivity in four ways: they have clear boundaries defined by 'strict laws of causality, efficacity, profitability, and truth'; the researchers and technicians who produce them remain invisible and therefore excluded from the social understanding of the objects themselves; whatever expected or unexpected consequences the object may bring, 'these [are] always conceived in the form of an impact on a *different* universe' (23); and, because of this apparent translation, the objects' 'cataclysmic consequences [have] no retroactive effects on the objects' responsibilities or their definitions' (24). Indeed, if, like asbestos, they have cataclysmic consequences, such matters of fact often shore up a collective belief in scientific progress by insisting that these effects have been discovered through further scientific inquiry.

He then contrasts such matters of fact with the emergence of 'matters of concern', which, by inverting these four characteristics, lead the natural sciences into crises of objectivity. To find a pertinent matter of concern, we need only think of the early stages of the Coronavirus pandemic in the United Kingdom. Ongoing assurances that political decision-making 'followed the science' meant that 'the science' was reciprocally politicised. As the pandemic progressed, politicians would present daily press briefings flanked by scientists whose ostensible role as informants seemed far less important than their implicit role as supportive authorities. Since these presentations were often performing the unfolding of scientific information about the virus as it was happening for scientists themselves, scientific understanding of the virus became politically entangled. The proliferation of stories about the possible origin of the virus, at the wet markets in Wuhan or the military complexes outside, suggested that the public were not 'surprised' by the virus, even if they were taken aback by its virulence and scale. It was, after all, continuous with the coronavirus pandemics with earlier respiratory syndromes (SARS, MIRS), not to mention 'predicted' by cultural products ranging from Albert Camus to Dean Koontz. Matters of concern trouble the society/nature division, which is why they become the sites of an emergent political ecology, or the relationship between political, social and economic factors in environmental issues.

For Latour, asbestos never transgressed the society/nature divide and never coopted its scientists as a social force. When it became known as a public health risk, this didn't retrospectively affect scientific understandings of its definition or substance; rather, it was taken as a precautionary lesson in how natural objects might have unintended consequences for society without transgressing the divide between the two. In a sense, this is true. Both the companies defending asbestos use and the activists seeking bans rely on scientific authority to underwrite their concerns. Even the scientific studies designed to deflect or dissimulate the links between asbestos and its diseases are often patiently picked apart, rather than simply dismissed as junk science.

At the same time, this fails to acknowledge how asbestos also operates as perhaps the prototypical matter of concern. Scientists raising the health concerns about asbestos were immediately politicised and either vilified (Irving Selikoff) or coopted (Richard Doll; J. C. Wagner).[68] Strict laws of causality appear to be suspended in the etiology of asbestos diseases itself: no one knows who will get it, or why.[69] The increase of risk for people with greater exposure, in this respect, should not obscure that less exposure still produces surprising illnesses, and it was the illnesses of the least exposed that did most to raise public concern. In this sense, the last modernist object becomes the first postmodernist object; a matter of fact that is also a matter of concern; its 'lastness', the hinge upon which an ambiguous change may already be charted. Or, paradoxically, we might say that asbestos itself becomes proof that we have never been modern.

On Formalism and Thinking Differently

For Walter Rukeyser, mining asbestos meant contributing something useful. Treated historically, I might consign this understanding to the dustbin of failed ideals. But to do so fails, I think, to appreciate how the form of such ideals continues to hold us, even when their content becomes manifestly different, even contradictory, to that original sentiment. Adrienne Rich's observation about formalism, that 'like asbestos gloves, it allowed me to handle materials I couldn't pick up bare-handed', serves both to illustrate this irony and explain it.[70] Rich sources asbestos gloves for her simile because they offer a material protection (insulation) that she parallels with the psychological security of depersonalised formalism in her poem's 'objective, observant tone' (22). Rich remains ambivalent about this protection, however, since the tone creates distance that threatens to disconnect her from her 'materials': the split 'between the girl [. . .] who defined herself in writing poems and the girl who was to define herself by her relationships with men' (21). The gloves' associations with female domesticity capture Rich's anxieties about formalism, not simply because they remind us of her alienated self, defined 'by her relationships with men', but because both gloves and formalism rely upon a disconnection that reinscribes the split itself.

Rich regarded her use of formalism to be transitional, allowing her to weather psychological disconnection to establish more clearly the terms of this disconnection. For us, Rich's asbestos gloves recall the paradox that, in protecting ourselves from touching dangerous materials, we ended up touching asbestos. But, if I am to take Rich's lesson seriously, then I must reflect on the material effects of such formalism, both in the writing before, where the disconnection remains unacknowledged except at the level of form, and the writing after, where a new honesty about disconnection means that the form can be surpassed but only at the cost of everything that form offered. This explains why I have framed this as a book about modernist culture, while ranging across texts from more than two millenia. To understand what asbestos means for modernism, culturally, materially and socially, I have considered not only narratives that emerge within modernism, but those whose trajectories pass it by the way, beyond its traditional boundaries.

As a consequence of following asbestos from modernist literature to the contemporary moment, I find a formal continuity in literary uses of asbestos. Asbestos's meaning changes, but, as a mediator, its function is consistent. This is clearest when tracked in genre fiction, whose 'strategic value', I recall from Frederic Jameson, 'lies in [their] mediatory function [. . .] which allows the coordination of immanent formal analysis of the individual text with the twinned diachronic perspective of the history of forms and the evolution of social life.'[71] To make sense of this, I turn, in Part 1, to the two genres that parallel the two social narratives that accompany asbestos's use: the utopia and the mystery.

In Chapter 1, I consider how asbestos facilitates the future-oriented sociology implied by the utopian genre, by tracking those moments when it appears in the infrastructure of utopian texts. This, I argue, allows us to appreciate the way that asbestos use was, and remains, characterised by an orientation towards the future, even if, on the one hand, that orientation historically signified open and reliable possibility and, on the other, now signifies the foreclosure of such possibility. In Chapter 2, I contrast the appearance of asbestos as given, in the infrastructure, with asbestos as a clue or sign of some mystery. Following asbestos as it appears in mystery novels that move towards either the detective genre or the horror story, I consider how asbestos also came to be used as a marker of a past that troubles the present.

Part 1 makes 'strategic' use of genre to correlate the use of asbestos in literature ('the history of forms') with its historical use in the built environment ('the evolution of social life'). But, as the horror genre demonstrates, some kernel of significance remains in asbestos that this socially-oriented understanding fails to grasp. Moreover, recognising that asbestos has a functional continuity in genre cannot, in itself, make sense of asbestos as a mediator: it simply testifies to a residual impact. In Part 2, then, I consider how asbestos takes on a life of its own, assuming a vitalism that might explain both its excess of meaning and its mediating role. Accordingly, I track asbestos through the resurrection of early modern science writings about asbestos and salamanders in late modernist lyrics by Marianne Moore, Yves Bonnefoy and Octavio Paz (Chapter 3), the genesis and establishment of asbestos illness writing (Chapter 4), and the consideration of traditions of justice and compensation in late modernist work by Alan Bennett and James Kelman (Chapter 5). The ways in which writers mediate discussions of asbestos, through salamanders, their individual responses to their illnesses, or even Kafka's factory, become the means of articulating concerns about asbestos that more direct responses can't quite seem to catch.

Finally, in Part 3, I attempt to synthesise the social uses of asbestos with its excess vitality by considering how asbestos's inhuman, 'lithic' temporality impacts on certain semi-porous sites of sociality: the mine (Chapter 6), the factory (Chapter 7), the built environment (Chapter 8) and the dump (Conclusion). In places where asbestos use prevails, as it did for my grandfather, in the whole purpose of the enterprise, such use is, necessarily, underwritten. To insist overly on its function is to open up the possibility of questioning 'use' when such a question is, for practical reasons, foreclosed: when my job, my livelihood and my purpose are wrapped up in producing asbestos, when, but in the dark moments of the early morning, will I question its usefulness? By tracking these sites through texts that share a proletarian impulse, I implicitly rely upon recent efforts by Kristin Bluemel, Michael McCluskey and Nick Hubble to expand my understanding of modernism, not simply by including pulp or genre fiction (as in Part 1), but to consider it against the contemporaneous literary emergence of a 'rural modernity', in new forms of 'proletarian literature'.[72]

Whether or not tracking the use of asbestos in literature is, ultimately, useful, I hope this book offers some useful reflections on asbestos's imbrication within modernism, an imbrication for which, no doubt, modernism is guilty, but whose presence also enjoins us to find, in modernist literature, the possibility of thinking, and living, differently.

NOTES

1. W. E. Cooke, 'Fibrosis of the Lungs due to the Inhalation of Asbestos', 2 (3317) *BMJ* (1924), pp. 140–2; 147, 147; Irving J. Selikoff and Morris Greenberg, 'A Landmark Case in Asbestosis', 265 (7) *JAMA* (1991), pp. 898–901, 898.
2. Cooke, 'Fibrosis', p. 147.
3. David J. Jeremy, 'Corporate Responses to the Emergent Recognition of a Health Hazard in the UK Asbestos Industry: The Case of Turner & Newall, 1920–1960', 24 (1) *Business and Economic History* (1995), pp. 254–65, 254.
4. Jorge Luis Borges, 'Kafka and his Precursors', *The Total Library: Non-Fiction 1922–1986*, trans. Eliot Weinberger (London: Penguin, 2001), pp. 363–5, 363.
5. Walter Benjamin, 'Franz Kafka: On the Tenth Anniversary of His Death', *Selected Writings 2, 1927–1934*, eds M. W. Jennings, H. Eiland, and G. Smith, trans. R. Livingstone et al. (Cambridge, MA: Belknap Press, 1999), pp. 794–818, 796–7.
6. Jean-François Lyotard, *The Differend: Phrases in Dispute*, trans. Georges Van Den Abeele (Minneapolis: University of Minnesota Press, 1988), p. 9.
7. Ruth Chang, 'Incommensurability (and Incomparability)', in *The International Encyclopedia of Ethics*, ed. Hugh LaFollette (Oxford: Blackwells, 2013), pp. 2591–604, 2591.
8. This trajectory is well-known: it runs from Kershaw's case (Cooke), through the 1930 Merewether and Price survey of the asbestos industry, to Richard Doll's 1955 study of lung cancer, and papers on mesothelioma by Wagner et al. (1960) and Newhouse and Thompson (1965). Merewether, E. R. A. and C. W. Price, *Report on Effects of Asbestos Dust on the Lungs and Dust Suppression in the Asbestos Industry* (London: HMSO 1930); Richard Doll, 'Mortality from Lung Cancer in Asbestos Workers', 12 *British Journal of Industrial Medicine* (1955), pp. 81–6; J. C. Wagner, C. A. Sleggs and P. Marchand, 'Diffuse Pleural Mesothelioma and Asbestos Exposure in the North Western Cape Province', 17 (4) *British Journal of Industrial Medicine* (1960), pp. 260–71; Muriel L. Newhouse and Hilda Thompson, 'Mesothelioma of Pleura and Peritoneum following Exposure to Asbestos in the London Area', 22 (4) *British Journal of Industrial Medicine* (1965), pp. 261–9.
9. See John Forrester, *Thinking in Cases* (Cambridge: Polity Press, 2017). On transnational convergence of asbestos compensation mechanisms, see Andrea Boggio, *Compensating Asbestos Victims: Law and the Dark Side of Industrialization* (Abingdon: Routledge, 2013), and for a US-focused case study of the inefficiency this produces, see Barnes, *Dust-up*.
10. Franz Kafka, *The Trial* [1925], trans. Breon Mitchell (New York: Schocken Books, 1998), p. 62.
11. Renata Salecl, *A Passion for Ignorance: What We Choose Not to Know and Why* (Princeton: Princeton University Press, 2020), p. 15.
12. See José Esteban Muños, *Cruising Utopia: The Then and There of Queer Futurity* (New York: New York University Press, 2009); Pheng Cheah, *What is a World?*

(Durham, NC: Duke University Press, 2016); Eric Hayot, *On Literary Worlds* (Oxford: Oxford University Press, 2012).
13. For a less Eurocentric story, we might consider the mining/production processes in India, Korea or Japan. Mahasweta Devi, 'Sabbath' and 'Countryside', in *Dust on the Road* (Kolkata: Seagull Books, 2000); *Breathless*, dir. Daniel Lambo (np: Storyhouse Film, 2018); Y. R. Yoon, K. M. Kwak, Y. Choi, K. Youn, J. Bahk, D. M. Kang, D. Paek, 'The Asbestos Ban in Korea from a Grassroots Perspective: Why Did It Occur?, 15 (2) *International Journal of Environmental Research and Public Health* (2018), pp. 198–209. *Sennan Asbestos Disaster*, dir. Kazuo Hara (Shisso Productions, 2016).
14. Martín Arboleda, *Planetary Mine: Territories of Extraction under Late Capitalism* (London: Verso, 2020), p. 5.
15. Ibid., Chapter 2.
16. WReC, *Combined and Uneven Development: Towards a New Theory of World-Literature* (Liverpool: Liverpool University Press, 2015), p. 49.
17. Arboleda, *Planetary*, p. 18.
18. As this book was being copy-edited, I read Elizabeth Carolyn Miller's *Extraction Ecologies and the Literature of the Long Exhaustion* (Princeton: Princeton University Press, 2021). Although no dialogue was possible, her use of genre to track trends in extractivist logics resonates with my own efforts to think about genre in Part 1 and realist and mythopoetic modes in Chapter 6.
19. Natalia Cesire, *Experimental: American Literature and the Aesthetics of Knowledge* (Baltimore, MD: Johns Hopkins University Press, 2019), pp. ix–xi; 3–5.
20. Paul Ricoeur, *The Rule of Metaphor*, trans. Robert Czerny, with Kathleen McLaughlin and John Costello [1977] (London: Routledge, 1997), p. 7.
21. Daniel Hartley adapts Ricoeur's mimesis into a structuring sequence in *The Politics of Style: Towards a Marxist Poetics* [2016] (Chicago: Haymarket Books, 2017).
22. David Trotter, *Literature in the First Media Age: Britain between the Wars* (Cambridge, MA: Harvard University Press, 2013); Mimi Sheller, *Aluminum Dreams: The Making of Light Modernity* (Cambridge, MA: MIT Press, 2014). See also Marsha Bryant, 'Polymers: Fantastic Plastics in Postwar America', *Impact of Materials on Society*, eds Sophia Krzys Acord, Kevin S. Jones, Marsha Bryant, Debra Dauphin-Jones and Pamela Hupp (Gainesville: Library Press @ UF, 2021).
23. Michael Rubenstein, *Public Works: Infrastructure, Irish Modernism, and the Postcolonial* (Notre Dame, IN: University of Notre Dame Press, 2010), pp. 5–7. See also Susan Leigh Star, 'The Ethnography of Infrastructure', 43 (3) *American Behavioral Scientist* (1999), pp. 377–91.
24. Paul Ricoeur, *Time and Narrative: Volume 1*, trans. Kathleen McLaughlin and David Pellauer (Chicago: Chicago University Press, 1984), p. ix.
25. Hilda Doolittle (H. D.) and others, *Analyzing Freud: Letters of H. D., Bryher and their Circle*, ed. Susan Stanford Friedman (New York: New Directions, 2002), p. 377. H. D. notes that this was lifted from her friend, Stephen Guest.
26. Hilda Doolittle (H. D.), *Tribute to Freud*, introduction by Adam Philips, Afterword by Norman Holmes Pearson (New York: New Directions, 2012), p. 159.
27. Rachel Maines, *Asbestos and Fire: Technological Trade-offs and the Body at Risk* (New Brunswick: Rutgers University Press, 2005), Ch. 3.

28. Edwin O. Sachs, *Fires and Public Entertainments: A Study of Some 1100 Notable Fires at Theatres, Music Halls, Circus Buildings and Temporary Structures During the Last 100 Years* (London: Charles and Edwin Layton, 1897).
29. Djuna Barnes, 'Fireman Michael Quinn: 40 Years a Flame Fighter', *Brooklyn Daily Eagle*, 2 November 1913, Part 4, p. 22.
30. Lawrence Durrell, *The Black Book* [1938] (New York: Dutton & Co, 1960), p. 104.
31. e. e. cummings, *The Enormous Room* (London: Jonathan Cape, 1928), p. 107.
32. Thomas L. Masson, 'A Pilgrim's Progress in France', *New York Times Book Review*, 28 May 1922, p. 10.
33. Michael North, *Reading 1922: A Return to the Scene of the Modern* (Oxford: Oxford University Press, 1999), p. 150.
34. Hazel Hutchison, *The War That Used Up Words: American Writers and the First World War* (New Haven: Yale University Press, 2015), p. 199.
35. Paul Ricoeur, *Time and Narrative: Volume 2*, trans. Kathleen McLaughlin and David Pellauer (Chicago: Chicago University Press, 1985), p. 77.
36. Elizabeth Bowen, *Eva Trout; or Changing Scenes*, intro. Tessa Hadley (London: Vintage, 2011), p. 13, 61.
37. Dora Zhang, *Strange Likeness: Description and the Modernist Novel* (Chicago: University of Chicago Press, 2020), p. 63.
38. Rick Bass, 'With Every Great Breath: Living and Dying in Lincoln Country', Box 24, Folder 4, *Rick Bass Papers, 1986–2013 and Undated*, Southwest Collection/Special Collections Library, Texas Tech University, Lubbock, Texas. 89.
39. See also Andrea Peacock, *Libby, Montana: Asbestos and the Deadly Silence of an American Corporation* (Boulder, CO: Johnson Books, 2003) and Andrew Schneider and and David McCumber, *An Air that Kills: How the Asbestos Poisoning of Libby, Montana, Uncovered a National Scandal* (New York: G. P. Putnam's Sons, 2004).
40. Bass, 'Breath', p. 130; 129.
41. Steve Schwarze, 'Juxtaposition in Environmental Health Rhetoric: Exposing Asbestos Contamination in Libby, Montana', 6 (2) *Rhetoric & Public Affairs* (2003), p. 316.
42. Bass, 'Breath', p. 130.
43. Rob Nixon, *Slow Violence and the Environmentalism of the Poor* (Cambridge: Harvard University Press, 2011), p. 2.
44. Serenella Iovino, *Ecocriticism and Italy: Ecology, Resistance, and Liberation* (London: Bloomsbury, 2016), p. 151; Sasha Litvintseva, 'Asbestos: Inside and Outside, Toxic and Haptic', 11 (1) *Environmental Humanities* (2019), p. 158; Enrico Cesaretti, *Elemental Narratives: Reading Environmental Entanglements in Modern Italy* (University Park, PA: Penn State University Press, 2020), p. 144.
45. Karen Barad, *Meeting the Universe Halfway: Quantum Physics and the Entanglement of Matter and Meaning* (Durham, NC: Duke University Press, 2007), p. ix; Stacy Alaimo, *Bodily Natures: Science, Environment, and the Material Self* (Bloomington: Indiana University Press, 2010), p. 2.
46. Eva Haifa Giraud, *What Comes After Entanglement?* (Durham, NC: Duke University Press, 2019), p. 2.

47. See Gregory Hollin, Isla Forsyth, Eva Giraud, and Tracey Potts. '(Dis)Entangling Barad: Materialisms and Ethics', 47 (6) *Social Studies of Science* (2017), pp. 918–41.
48. Jeffrey Jerome Cohen, *Stone: An Ecology of the Inhuman* (Minneapolis: University of Minnesota Press, 2015), p. 198.
49. Agata Mazzeo, 'The Temporalities of Asbestos Mining and Community Activism', 5 (2) *The Extractive Industries and Society* (2018), p. 223. See also Agata Mazzeo, *Dust Inside: Fighting and Living with Asbestos-Related Disasters in Brazil* (New York: Berghahn, 2020).
50. Nixon, *Slow*, p. 10.
51. Smith qtd. in David Kotelchuck, 'Asbestos: The Funeral Dress of Kings', In *Dying for Work: Workers' Safety and Health in Twentieth-Century America*, eds David Rosner and Gerald Markowitz (Bloomington, IN: Indiana University Press, 1987), p. 203.
52. Lauren Berlant, *Cruel Optimism* (Durham: Duke University Press, 2011), p. 96.
53. See Daniel Hartley, *The Politics of Style: Towards a Marxist Poetics* (Chicago: Haymarket Books, 2017), pp. 56–63.
54. Ricoeur, *Time 1*, p. 3.
55. Rita Charon, *Narrative Medicine: Honoring the Stories of Illness* (Oxford: Oxford University Press, 2006), p. 42.
56. Ricoeur, *Time 1*, p. 11.
57. See Fredric Jameson, 'The Vanishing Mediator: Narrative Structure in Max Weber', 1 *New German Critique* (1973), p. 78.
58. Aaron Jaffe, *The Way Things Go: An Essay on the Matter of Second Modernism* (Minneapolis: University of Minnesota Press, 2014), pp. 18–19; Paul K. Saint-Amour, *Tense Future: Total War, Encyclopedic Form* (Oxford: Oxford University Press, 2015), p. 33; Elizabeth Outka, *Viral Modernism: The Influenza Pandemic and Interwar Literature* (New York: Columbia University Press, 2019), p. 5.
59. Jaffe, *Second*, p. 94.
60. Saint-Amour, *Tense*, p. 305.
61. Outka, *Viral*, p. 34.
62. Daniel Heath Justice, *Why Indigenous Literatures Matter* (Waterloo: Wilfrid Laurier University Press, 2018), p. 2.
63. Sianne Ngai, *Theory of the Gimmick* (Cambridge, MA: Harvard University Press, 2020), p. 1.
64. 'Asbestos Fest', *Schitt's Creek* (CBC, 23 January 2018).
65. See Nicholas Brown, *Autonomy: The Social Ontology of Art Under Capitalism* (Durham, NC: Duke University Press, 2019), 'Introduction'.
66. Bruno Latour, 'Love Your Monsters', 2 *Breakthrough Journal* (2011): online. https://thebreakthrough.org/journal/issue-2/love-your-monsters
67. Bruno Latour, *Politics of Nature: How to Bring the Sciences into Democracy* (Cambridge, MA: Harvard University Press, 2004), p. 23.
68. See Jock McCulloch and Geoffrey Tweedale, 'Science Is Not Sufficient: Irving J. Selikoff and the Asbestos Tragedy', 17 (4) *New Solutions: A Journal of Environmental and Occupational Health Policy* (2008), pp. 293–310; Tweedale, 'Hero or Villain? Sir Richard Doll and Occupational Cancer', 13 (2) *International Journal of Occupational*

Environmental Health (2007), pp. 233–5; and McCulloch, 'Saving the Asbestos Industry, 1960 to 2006', 121 (5) *Public Health Reports* (2006), pp. 609–14.
69. Eduardo Solbes and Richard W. Harper, 'Biological Responses to Asbestos Inhalation and Pathogenesis of Asbestos-Related Benign and Malignant Disease', 66 *Journal of Investigative Medicine* (2018), pp. 721–7.
70. Adrienne Rich, 'When We Dead Awaken: Writing as Re-Vision', 34 (1) *College English* (1972), p. 22.
71. Fredric Jameson, *The Political Unconscious: Narrative as a Socially Symbolic Act* (London: Routledge, 2002), p. 92.
72. See Kristin Bluemel and Michael McCluskey, *Rural Modernity in Britain: A Critical Intervention* (Edinburgh: Edinburgh University Press, 2018) and Nick Hubble, *The Proletarian Answer to the Modernist Question* (Edinburgh: Edinburgh University Press, 2017).

PART I
PREFIGURING ASBESTOS

The twentieth-century history of asbestos appears as a utopian dream turned nightmare imbroglio of mystery, conspiracy and horror. Until recently, historians of asbestos have generally relied upon a combination of medical, legal, industrial and governmental archives to argue for understanding asbestos as either a failed utopia or a vast conspiracy.[1] The first forgives asbestos companies. In this narrative, the material presented utopian solutions to endemic problems of industrial modernity – fire, insulation and a lack of affordable housing – and these technological imperatives combined with medical uncertainties to obscure its dystopian consequences.[2] The second castigates them for perpetuating the industry. Despite the solutions asbestos provided for problems endemic to industrial capitalism, it created health problems, whose public revelation was delayed by asbestos companies who, separately and in concert, conspired to suppress and obfuscate knowledge.[3]

In part, the impasse between these two positions may be explained by scale. Company campaigns that manufactured 'strategic ignorance', as Barry Castleman, Jock McCulloch and Geoffrey Tweedale argue, undoubtedly helped asbestos to remain socially acceptable.[4] But Peter Bartrip and Rachel Maines aren't wrong to relate these machinations to larger social narratives that permitted a general will-not-to-know. If one focuses on company histories, then the conspiracy theory is entirely justified. A general social history, evidenced through government building codes, makes the utopian explanation equally compelling. Rather than reconcile these conflicting traditions in asbestos historiography, I use their resemblance to the utopia and the mystery, broadly conceived, to show how these genres prefigure responses to asbestos. Asbestos historiography implicitly relies on a logic of utopias and dystopias when it conceives of asbestos as an imperfect means to a more perfect world. So, for instance, Maines discusses asbestos as a 'technological tradeoff', facilitated by its instantiation in US Building Code regulations. Bartrip notes that, in the laissez-faire capitalism of the nineteenth century, the UK Factory Acts were designed to limit, rather than extend, overt interventions. Both make much of the fear of fire that heralded the emergence of the asbestos curtain. Conversely, the historiography relies on mystery, crime and conspiracy when Castleman traces asbestos diseases back to Strabo, Tweedale outlines the suppression tactics used by Turner & Newall and McCulloch traces the close relation between Cape Asbestos and the Apartheid government.

I don't need to dive into the history to observe the political stakes of these 'phrases in dispute' or the acrimony they have generated. For Castleman, McCulloch and Tweedale, the conditions of suspicion created by the active dissembling of the companies demands a clear argument that damns their actions. To do otherwise compromises ongoing scientific, legal and historical work that demonstrates the causal connections between asbestos and disease. For Bartrip and Maines, the wasteful excesses of the asbestos tort industry demand a historical curbing of claims to absolute responsibility. In the broadest sense, then, the two positions replicate the approaches of the mystery and the utopia as genres. Facts, for the latter, are the building blocks to a total image of society. For the former, they highlight inconsistencies in the story of reality that society tells itself. For Bartrip and Maines, particular facts evidence narratives that address society as a totality: the key premise of both the utopia and the dystopia. Castleman, McCulloch and Tweedale, by contrast, find evidence in these facts that the social fabric has been torn apart by the conspiracies of the companies: a first principle for a good mystery story.

Genre is not, then, simply the means of categorising texts: it offers an analytic for establishing how responses to asbestos are 'prefigured' by the dominant narratives in its history. 'Genre study,' writes Ralph Cohen, 'is more than another approach to literature or to social institutions or scientific practices, it analyzes our procedures for acquiring and accumulating knowledge, including the changes that knowledge undergoes.'[5] In the two chapters that follow, I link literary understandings of the material to its function in social history, by tracing its use in utopian and mystery genre fiction. As my argument develops, it unsettles expectations that these literary texts simply follow, albeit with some delay, the change in public understanding of asbestos already marked out by the historical scholarship. While this change is certainly there, and nowhere more evident in the movement of asbestos from utopian texts in the early twentieth century to their dystopian counterparts in the late twentieth and early twenty-first, behind this change I discern a formal continuity, in the function asbestos plays for the text itself.

This should be less surprising than it first appears. Where once particular media were used to insist on asbestos's security, now the same forms generate anxiety and fear. Adverts featuring house schematics once suggested places where asbestos products might be added; now they draw attention to the same places to advocate its removal. Propaganda about asbestos once testified to more than 2,000 years of use; now it implies that its abuses stretch across the same length of time. Although this redirection of affect has achieved some good, I want to call into question its continued reliance on the forms of dissemination favoured by the companies. To change the content of what I know about asbestos, I need to change the form that knowledge takes. Before I can, however, I must understand what is at work in these formal continuities. And so, I track asbestos, on the one hand, through the utopia to the dystopia, and, on the other, across genres that rely on mysteries, whether the adventure tale, the police procedural or the ghost story.

NOTES

1. For the relatively recent turn to approaches that nuance this division, without exonerating the companies or sacrificing worker agency, see Lundy Braun, et al. 'Scientific Controversy and Asbestos: Making Disease Invisible', 9 (3) *International Journal of Occupational and Environmental Health* (2003), pp. 194–205; Lundy Braun and Sophia Kisting, 'Asbestos-Related Disease in South Africa: The Social Production of an Invisible Epidemic', 96 (8) *American Journal of Public Health* (2006), pp. 1386–96, and Lundy Braun, 'Structuring Silence: Asbestos and Biomedical Research in Britain and South Africa', 50 (1) *Race & Class* (2008), pp. 59–78; Jessica Van Horssen, *A Town Called Asbestos: Environmental Contamination, Health, and Resilience in a Resource Community* (Vancouver, BC: University of British Columbia Press, 2015); Mazzeo, *Dust*; John Trimbur, *Grassroots Literacy and the Written Record: A Textual History of Asbestos Activism in South Africa* (Bristol: Multilingual Matters, 2020).
2. See Peter Bartrip, *Beyond the Factory Gates: Asbestos and Health in Twentieth Century America* (London: Continuum, 2006); Maines, *Asbestos*.
3. See Barry Castleman, *Asbestos: Medical and Legal Aspects*, 5th ed (New York: Aspen Publishers, 2005); Ronald Johnson and Arthur McIvor, *Lethal Work: A History of the Asbestos Tragedy in Scotland* (East Linton: Tuckwell, 2000); Jock McCulloch, *Asbestos Blues: Labour, Capital, Physicians and the State in South Africa* (Bloomington: Indiana University Press, 2002); Geoffrey Tweedale, *Magic Mineral to Killer Dust: Turner & Newall and the Asbestos Hazard* (Oxford: Oxford University Press, 2001); McCulloch and Tweedale, *Defending*. On the role of public research in achieving similar obfuscations, albeit without malice, see Lundy Braun and Hannah Kopinski, 'Causal Understandings: Controversy, Social Context, and Mesothelioma Research', 13 *Biosocieties* (2018), pp. 557–79.

4. For discussions of 'strategic ignorance', see Linsey McGoey, *The Unknowers: How Strategic Ignorance Rules the World* (London: Zed Books, 2019).
5. Ralph Cohen, 'Introduction: Theorizing Genre', 34 (2) *New Literary History* (2003), p. iv.

I

A UTOPIAN IMPULSE

In 1959, the US Bureau of Mines co-produced a twenty-minute promotional film titled *Asbestos... A Matter of Time*, with Johns Manville, the largest US manufacturer of asbestos-related products.[1] Its ostensible purpose was to usher in a new era for asbestos, a 'miracle mineral' whose versatility would propel its application to all aspects of daily life. It describes how weaving asbestos, a mineral fibre noteworthy for its efficacy as a fire-retardant and an insulator, into fabrics or casting it with cement sheets will translate these qualities to the built environment. The propaganda announced the universal use of asbestos as an inevitability, 'a matter of time'. However misguided, however motivated by profit, this orientation towards the future attaches a utopian impulse to asbestos use, a hopefulness about its capacity to facilitate change that I unpack in this chapter.

Asbestos's Utopian Impulse

In the work of Ernst Bloch and Fredric Jameson, the utopian impulse identifies an alternative, more obscure line of descent for the Utopia. The more recognisable line of descent, understood as 'the realization of the Utopian program', describes 'revolutionary political practice, when it aims at founding a whole new society, alongside written exercises in the literary genre'.[2] The utopian impulse, however, can be found in what Bloch calls the 'discovery and unmistakable notation of the "Not-Yet-Conscious"', or, in Jameson's gloss, as that which 'governs everything future-oriented in life and culture; and encompassing everything from games to patent medicines, from myths to mass entertainment, from iconography to technology, from architecture to eros.'[3] In other words, it is the expression, often concealed or repressed, of utopianism in the present.

For Bloch, the excavation of this latent utopianism, even within the most virulently capitalist objects, presents important lessons for philosophy, if it is to 'have conscience of tomorrow, commitment to the future, knowledge of hope' (7). Attending to these operations of anticipation 'in the field of hope' allows us to understand hope 'as emotion, as the opposite of fear (because fear too can of course anticipate), but more essentially as a directing act of a cognitive kind (and here the opposite is then not fear, but memory)' (12). Insofar as asbestos resolves fears about fires by offering a practical safeguard against them, it presents a vehicle both for carrying hopeful emotions and for realising them through a 'directing act'. If this reading of asbestos appears naïve, it is meant to. Jameson reminds us that the utopian impulse also 'serves as the mere lure and bait for ideology (hope being after all also the principle of the cruellest confidence games and of hucksterism as a fine art)' (3). *Asbestos . . . A Matter of Time* carries and orients a hope riddled with painful contradictions.

These contradictions become particularly apparent when I consider the darker connotations of the film's title. The 'matter of time', which once projected into the future its unlimited potential uses, now implicates the substance with debilitating illness and death. Asbestos is banned in over sixty countries as a result of its toxicity, the health effects of which manifest primarily in Asbestos-Related Diseases (ARDs), which take years, even decades, to develop. Asbestos exposure is, in the popular imagination, terminal, its fatal consequences inevitable, death 'a matter of time'.

The two interpretations of the film's title signal two distinct phases in the public understanding about asbestos: a Before, when the utopian possibilities of asbestos seemed to have almost limitless potential, and an After, when the public realised that this potential came with grave consequences that had been deliberately obscured by interested parties. In this regard, it appears to offer a useful starting point for thinking about asbestos's history as marked by a rupture between two opposing epistemic positions. But, at the same time, and without denying its historical importance, this transition obscures the anticipation that runs from asbestos's utopian impulse, its 'hopes', to its dystopian consequences, 'its realized fears'.

This continued reliance on anticipation hints why asbestos, when tracked in utopian and dystopian texts of the long twentieth century, retains the same basic function as infrastructure. Texts in this trajectory refer to asbestos in background exposition without fully explaining its significance. *Where* it appears changes with its place in the popular imagination: it goes from objects and houses to toxic waste sites. But *how* it is presented does not: its significance is not explained in any great detail, but left largely implicit and self-evident. Whether the text is utopian or dystopian, regardless of the material's changing face, these expositions of the future anticipate that future readers will understand the implicit significance of the asbestos in their background descriptions. This functional continuity, which I will go on to demonstrate in greater depth, suggests that, even in 'the realization of the Utopian program', asbestos remains the exponent of a utopian impulse, a covert form that transmits both Utopian desires and their frustration.[4]

To track the continuity in these phases, I turn now to utopian and dystopian texts, whose 'imaginative framework', in Darko Suvin's terms, provides an 'alternative to the author's empirical environment'.[5] Such texts are 'distinguished by the narrative dominance or hegemony of a fictional "novum" (novelty, innovation) validated by cognitive logic' (63). In other words, the fiction distances, or estranges, itself from reality by introducing a novelty, while implying or explicating a set of logical steps that connect the empirical environment with this estranged reality. Asbestos is not an example of Suvin's novum. Rather, and regardless of whether it is imagined as a saviour or as a villain, it is a small but crucial relic of the empirical environment, grounding the text's estranged reality. Recognisable in the author's own time, asbestos also projects itself forward into the imagined future, anchoring it to the present. In this regard, asbestos use is congruent with the utopianism Nathan Waddell explores in early modernism (i.e. 1900–1920), which 'took the world *as it was* as the basis of the world *as it might be*'.[6] Accordingly, I now turn to moments where asbestos appears as infrastructure in utopian and dystopian texts, to mark it out as an infrastructure of literature.

The Asbestos Utopia

In 1887, Edward Bellamy published *Looking Backward*, a bestselling socialist utopia that imagines a future United States. Told by a somnolescent narrator, Julian West, who goes to bed in 1887 only to wake in 2000, Bellamy's text makes one small but significant reference to asbestos. West is able to sleep for 113 years because he is put into a somnolescent state by a mesmerist. Nobody disturbs him because he sleeps in a vault underneath his house, to escape the noise of the city's traffic. Here, 'in order that the room might serve also as a vault equally proof against violence and flames, for the storage of valuables, I had roofed it with stone slabs hermetically sealed, and the outer door was of iron with a thick coating of asbestos'.[7] These embellishments are 'tinged', in Jean Pfaelzer's gloss, 'with wondrous new technology'.[8] But, the sleeplessness, the hypnotic state and even the vault itself, Pfaelzer notes, resemble the archaisms of Edgar Allan Poe. When one considers the whole scenario as a simple plot mechanism for transferring the narrator into the utopian future, Chris Ferns suggests, it 'goes so far beyond the minimum demands of narrative plausibility as to prompt questions as to its deeper significance'.[9] Buried within the political progressivism of the content, Ferns argues, lies a formal conservatism disguised by prosaically modern elaborations like asbestos.

At the beginning of the nineteenth century, asbestos still played a mythic role in poetic metaphor. 'Fly', commands Robert Southey, 'Salamanders, on Asbestos' wings, to wanton in my Delia's *fiery* glance!'[10] 'The asbestos robe which the chaste style arrays', consoles Anna Seward, will be 'Impassive shield from Envy's lurid blaze'.[11] The metaphoric protection offered by such wings and clothes is realised only in fantasy. When the devil appears before the grog-seller to warn him of his fate, in W. H. Burleigh's version of the temperance poem, 'The Grog-seller's Dream', he wears 'a quaint and silvery gleaming vest' that seems to be made from asbestos.[12] Similarly, Zóphiël, the eponymous heroine of the poem by Maria Gowen Brooks, finds Tahathyam, the ruler of the Gnomes, wearing 'rich attire' composed of 'fibres of asbestos, bleached in fire'.[13] Elizabeth Barrett Browning will offer asbestos as the contrast to a metaphoric burning in her *Casa Guidi Windows* – 'Priestcraft burns out, the twinèd linen blazes;/Not, like asbestos, to grow white and clear,/But all to perish' – while in 'Eric and Amabel', Amabel will spin a 'downy web', 'from the soft asbestos won' to veil Eric's 'scorch'd and throbbing brow [. . .] from fiery spark and burning gale'.[14] In the latter half of the nineteenth century, asbestos still allows for a magical appearance, while providing, in itself, the explanation of a more prosaic scientism. This might be an alternative description for the transformation of the protogimmick into a gimmick. The protogimmick becomes the gimmick when what once appeared rare and miraculous becomes, through common use, cheap and tawdry. R. D. Blackmore's *Alice Lorraine* (1875), for example, relies on asbestos as a scientific explanation for a magical appearance. Blackmore resolves the tricky financial situation of his heroine's family by entrusting to them an inherited box containing valuable opals and pearls, whose magic appearance is explained, in part, because it is 'lined with asbestos'. Blackmore's box recalls a past where such items were rare and valuable, while also appearing at a moment when asbestos lining was becoming common.

By this point, woven asbestos products were nothing new (See Chapter 3). They proliferate through the quasi-mythic history of asbestos, from Roman funereal shrouds through Charlemagne's napkins to Benjamin Franklin's purse. It is a plausible conceit for a box created in the early seventeenth century, or, for that matter, Seward's robe, Burleigh's vest and Browning's linen. But, as lining, asbestos was undergoing something of a mechanical revolution in the 1870s and 1880s. Vast asbestos reserves had just been discovered in Quebec. With abundant supply came abundant use. In 1888, the year after *Looking Backward* was published, Robert H. Jones observes the increased use of 'asbestos millboard as a lining for fireproof cases and deed boxes', 'as a refractory for lining furnaces' and in lining 'cold storage buildings'.¹⁵ Bellamy's passing reference to asbestos plays an important role in orienting the formal anachronisms of West's vault towards the future, by locating it in a rather prosaically possible present.

The brevity of Bellamy's reference is also telling, since its lack of gloss assumes the average reader knows what asbestos lining might mean. In 1888, Jones could already acknowledge that his information was 'not new' but justified his introductory work to the substance by noting that while the use of 'asbestos [. . .] is now rapidly assuming such large proportions that [. . .] it will presently be found more difficult to say to what purposes it cannot be applied', it was still 'a subject on which so little appears to be generally known' (3). Still, Bellamy could assume his readers would know what asbestos could do and what it meant. This assumption takes on the character of a formal trope when linked to other asbestos references in the utopian literature, not least in the lineage of works directly influenced by Bellamy, for good or ill.

Charlotte Perkins Gilman's first novel, *What Diantha Did* (1910) tells the story of the eponymous heroine's elevation from domestic servant to diversified business owner, offering, amongst other domestic services, cooked-food delivery.¹⁶ From the beginning of the novel, the reader is prepared to appreciate Diantha's cooking skills. But, of course, her meals are constrained to the place and time of their preparation. At a key moment, Diantha's investor, Mrs Weatherstone, introduces her to the technological means by which she might transport these meals and keep them hot: a motor wagon and a food container. The food container is made of 'aluminum [. . .] All lined and interlined with asbestos' (148). When its qualities are later appreciated, Mrs Ree, the character introduced to appreciate its novelty, enjoys her soup 'hot', 'ice cream hard' and coffee almost able to 'burn the tongue': '"I don't understand about the heat and cold," she said, and they showed her the asbestos-lined compartments' (154). Again, asbestos linings serve as their own explanation, quietly ushering in new forms of capitalist modernity that facilitate, among a great many other things, the emancipation of women. In this regard, Charlotte J. Rich has observed that Bellamy was a notable influence on the novel, in particular on the model of the cooperative that Diantha and her mother develop: 'with the enterprises that Diantha pursues [. . .] Gilman's debt to Bellamy is clear.'¹⁷ Certainly, *What Diantha Did* anticipates Gilman's more well-known feminist utopia, *Herland* (1915), by offering a legitimation of 'the social and financial benefits of "organized housekeeping"' through 'a liberatory, if not unproblematic, vision of female entrepreneurship' (1; 4). Like Bellamy, Gilman develops a political economy that is utopian, even if, in Gilman's case, it is the repurposing of household expense as it is understood in her present. Both Bellamy and Gilman assume that technological progress may be facilitated by the use of asbestos; moreover, this use remains so unremarkable as to require no comment.

This is perhaps even clearer in Stephen Leacock's parody of Bellamy's novel, 'The Man in Asbestos: An Allegory of the Future' (1913), written shortly after Gilman's novel.[18] Leacock's narrator falls asleep, only to awaken in a world transformed into a socialist nightmare, in a museum of old, discarded artefacts. Beside him sits a man, dressed in clothes 'like the grey ashes of paper that had burned and kept its shape' (209). They are, the man explains, made of 'asbestos [. . .] they last hundreds of years. We have one suit each, and there are billions of them piled up, if anybody wants a new one' (211). The titular Man in Asbestos guides him through the conditions of this new reality, where there is no longer any need for food, fashion, housing or work, and the problems of death, disease and even inclement weather have all been solved. Unlike the more famous dystopias of Huxley and Orwell, Leacock's nightmare is not an agonistic account of an individual at odds with totalitarian conformity, enforced from above through carefully controlled media narratives or drug-induced euphoria. By contrast, it presents a situation wherein the rational elimination of human need and desire leads to a future in which matters of aesthetics, novelty and industry simply no longer matter.

As in Bellamy and Gilman, asbestos plays a small role in Leacock's image of the future. It simply provides materials for clothing. But clothing can hardly be insignificant for a political economist trained, as Leacock was, by Thorstein Veblen. Indeed, the drabness of Leacock's future may be attributed, in part, to its elimination of conspicuous consumption, Veblen's term for economic consumption based on a desire for prestige rather than utility.[19] Leacock's asbestos clothing satirises Bellamy's po-faced approach to fashion, exemplified in West's benign uninterest: 'It did not appear that any very startling revolution in men's attire had been among the great changes my host had spoken of, for, barring a few details, my new habiliments did not puzzle me at all.'[20] But, when mere existence has become an end in itself, Leacock suggests, the insignificance of what one wears is itself significant. The Man, and his culture, value asbestos as apparel because of its longevity. Asbestos, the inextinguishable, indestructible mineral fibre, serves them well because it does not change.

Leacock's sartorial choice signals asbestos's role as an infrastructural agent in utopian fiction over the long twentieth century. After all, asbestos is the only material named in Leacock's future whose qualities would also be recognisable to Leacock's present. Other substances in the story do bear striking resemblance to prototypes in their 'past', like food pills that obviate the need to eat. But it is asbestos that anchors Leacock's vision for the future in a recognisable present for his readers, and for good reasons. If in 1887, asbestos was a sufficiently 'wondrous new technology' that it could still 'tinge' utopias, as Pfaelzer believes, by 1913, it is far more plausible to think of it as a useful background detail that would link infrastructures in the present with those of the future.

Utopias offer, through their engagement with futurity, a glimpse of conditions in the present that may, or may not, lead to the realisation of this future. In order to anchor such futures to the present, as evolutions of the present into that future, they need to describe a future that remains broadly recognisable to contemporary readers. Here, asbestos's very purpose – to insulate and protect the possibility of a future from possible risk – easily intersected with the interests of the utopia.

Such undiagnosed uses of asbestos to describe future infrastructures can be found, even if it becomes less and less a signifier of wonderous futurity than as a grubby indicator of an all-too-cheap modernity. Near the end of Evelyn Waugh's 1953 novella, *Love Among the Ruins*, the reader discovers that the protagonist, Max Plastic, has been living in a hostel divided up into 'asbestos cubicles'.[21] With its 'reek of State sausages' and its clear inability to keep out the surrounding noises of wirelesses playing and sub-officials coughing, the cubicle confirms that Waugh's dystopia is, like the asbestos it contains, cheap and ugly. Waugh's reproduction of an earlier anti-asbestos classism aside, the story does offer more than merely a further example of asbestos as an unquestioned part of the infrastructure. To understand this, however, I want to reflect on why Waugh chooses to mention the asbestos in the cubicles, in which Max has been living for quite some time, only at the novella's end.

The asbestos discovery happens after Max has committed his signature act of arson: he has burnt down the Rehabilitation Centre where he was reeducated, and which he left at the beginning of the novella. His decision to burn down the Centre, Mountjoy, follows a visit to Clara, his onetime lover, who has consented to an abortion and to disfiguring facial surgery. When first encountered, both Mountjoy and Clara explicitly prompt memories of an earlier time: Mountjoy is a repurposed stately home, while Clara, sporting a full and luscious blonde beard and a collection of old masterpieces, appeals to an older aesthetic sensibility that is also decidedly queer. As they merge in his imagination, Max contemplates his decision to burn down Mountjoy as an attempt to make 'a desert in his imagination which he might call peace'.

The story ends with Max's state-sanctioned marriage and the promise that a new Mountjoy, modelled on a 'standard packing-case, set on end', 'will arise from the ashes'. It is not surprising, then, that Ashley Maher has argued that Max's merging of Clara with Mountjoy presents his recognition that 'older aesthetic forms are bankrupt'.[22] The affordances of the packing-case 'fitted':

> It fell into place precisely in the void of his mind, satisfying all the needs for which his education had prepared him. The conditioned personality recognized its proper pre-ordained environment. All else was insubstantial; the gardens of Mountjoy, Clara's cracked Crown Derby and her enveloping beard were trophies of a fading dream.
>
> The Modern Man was home.

Waugh's 'Modern Man', Maher argues, is formed from the standardisation of objects, environments and homes. Asbestos played a critical role in this standardisation. In 1953, asbestos construction materials were in the midst of a boom that extended from the post-war period into the 1960s, as supplies previously reserved for the military became widely available for civilian use. During the Second World War, Michael Frayn recalls in his memoir *My Father's Fortune* (2010), 'great grey corrugated cliffs and hillsides of asbestos cement' housed 'aircraft and munitions, locomotives and troops' in 'lifeless greyness' that strikes the young Frayn as 'profoundly dreary'.[23] This dreariness seems to be what Waugh wants to capture with his asbestos cubicles.

The only sign that Max has not entirely interpolated his identity as 'Modern Man' are found in the final lines of the novel, when Max fidgets through his wedding ceremony with what proves 'to be his cigarette-lighter, a most uncertain apparatus. He pressed the catch and instantly, surprisingly there burst out a tiny flame – gemlike, hymeneal, auspicious.' However, the uncertainty of the lighter and its surprising, auspicious flame augur rather fewer possibilities than the reader might think. Asbestos, after all, is fire-resistant. Whereas the materials of the older Mountjoy were flammable, the reference to asbestos late in the story seems to imply that the new Mountjoy will be similarly constructed. The old world was vulnerable to fire, but the new world is not. Like Bellamy's vault, asbestos presents a prosaic image of the future through a present reality. Unpleasant as it might be, Waugh suggests, the future is now, and that future is asbestos.

Yoking Bellamy together with Waugh confirms that, even as its context shifted from overt utopia to implicit dystopia, asbestos remained a useful infrastructure for imagining the future. As utopias age, discrepancies emerge between the future they predict and the present that future actually becomes. Whether futuristic wonder product or homogenous culture-trash, for Bellamy and Waugh asbestos is not a cancerous pariah. Rather, it promises security, or freedom from harm and care. To be free from care is to live without fear about that which might harm you. Although fear now dominates most people's response to asbestos, it seems to me that this fear occurs even when, perhaps especially when, they do not know how it causes harm. This inversion is not so much the consequence of knowledge, as a redirection of affect, from freedom from fear to feelings of fear.

This redirection of affect parallels, more or less, the development of three distinct phases in the history of security. For much of the nineteenth century, argues François Ewald, the moral obligation towards oneself and others played a greater role than legal obligation in personal security: a world 'in which one must recognize his or her weakness and fragility, subject to incessant reversals of fortune; it is a world of chance events.'[24] Offering 'a paradigm of responsibility', physical harm was understood to be the result of providence and individual action, and therefore demands a clear line of causality; without a person to fault for an injury, the injured party had no claim as a victim (273). Providence, however, provides few systemic solutions to the out-of-pocket creditor. The social response to this problem, Ewald argued, was to absorb the problem of personal responsibility by distributing it socially, in a paradigm of solidarity. This deferred responsibility for security to the whole of society, i.e. through a narrative of risk. In replacing fault with risk, this paradigm ensured the protection of all without attributing fault. Risk replaced cause with distribution by creating a means of reparation 'which, without involving examination of the behaviour of the worker or the boss, attributes them globally to the job and the firm' (277). Or, in the words of Edouard Thoulon, writing in 1898, 'All work has its risks; accidents are the sad but inevitable consequence of work itself.'[25] The technical language of risk came to verbalise systematic anxieties about the future, supported by paradigms of solidarity, compensation and prevention. Prevention, 'the vocabulary of which henceforth replaced that of providence', realised 'the 19th century's dream of security':

> A scientific utopia ever more capable of controlling risks. While one cannot eliminate risks altogether (there is never zero risk), they will have been reduced sufficiently to be able to be dealt with collectively: accidents are the by-product, necessary although always more marginalized, of scientific and technical progress. (282)

The mitigation of risk explains how asbestos came to be embedded in our infrastructure. It is found in our schools, our hospitals, our houses and our shops. It is moulded into the pipes that bring us our water and take away our waste. It lines our cables and our boilers. This proliferation of asbestos remains, for the most part, invisible to us, emerging only exceptionally and with great anxiety, like cracks in a wall previously thought to be sound. But, for the most part, its threat passes over us, its patina of 1950s futurity an anachronism that announces asbestos's obsolescence and, by extension, its disappearance. Because we (wrongly) think it has vanished from our lives, we (wrongly) believe it can no longer hurt us. This is why its irruption into our lives is so upsetting.

Ewald's third phase of security, identified with the rise of the precautionary principle, may well be understood as a direct response to asbestos's evolution into a dystopian problem. The precautionary principle, writes Ewald, is marked by two features: 'a context of scientific uncertainty on the one hand and the possibility of serious and irreversible damage on the other' (284–5). Indeed, it was largely in response to substances like asbestos that the precautionary principle developed, as is evident from the European Environmental Agency's inclusion of asbestos as a late lesson, in its report, *Late Lessons from Early Warnings: The Precautionary Principle, 1896–2000*.[26] Ewald notes that the precautionary principle is based on a latent contradiction, wherein the dilation of time, 'between cause and harmful effect', 'invites one to anticipate what one does not yet know, to take into account doubtful hypotheses and simple suspicions' (289). Thought of in this way, the precautionary principle inverts one's relationship with the future from Bloch's principle of hope into what Hans Jonas calls 'a heuristics of fear.'[27] A similar transformation emerges in the contemporary dystopia.

From Dystopia to Matters of Time

In Neal Stephenson's cyberpunk dystopia, *Snow Crash* (1992), 'Sacrifice Zones' describe 'parcels of land whose clean-up cost exceeds their total future economic value'.[28] One such Sacrifice Zone is 'an abandoned shipyard', contaminated with 'discarded asbestos from the ship-building industry'. At night it glitters, 'an immense carpet of broken glass and shredded asbestos'. Later echoes of Stephenson's asbestos-strewn Sacrifice Zone may be heard in 'the Great Concavity' of David Foster Wallace's *Infinite Jest* (1996) or the Thetford of Cory Doctorow's *Walkaway* (2017), which both draw on Quebec's history of asbestos mining to anticipate similar sites of environmental exception. Doctorow, in particular, recalls Stephenson's language when he calls Thetford a 'zone abandoned a decade before, when asbestos contamination went critical and even the federal government couldn't ignore it.'[29]

On the surface, there is little that recalls the asbestos futurism of Bellamy and Waugh in the desolation it signals for Stephenson and Doctorow. When one burrows into these landscapes, however, one realises that asbestos's toxicity is as taken for granted by Stephenson and Doctorow as its building properties once were by Bellamy and Waugh. It remains an under-explained feature of the landscape, as crucial a feature of immanent toxicity as previously it was of immanent futurity. Rather than projecting asbestos forth into future meanings, these passing references are entirely subsumed by the understanding of asbestos in the writers' own present. If asbestos, in these works, can gesture to the changing historical understanding of the substance, it also signals a continuity in the textual use of the substance, as an undiagnosed textual shorthand for modernity's effects. Asbestos, in the utopia, effectively pulls the world of the future, whether positively or negatively, back into the infrastructure of the present.

If this observation reiterates my point that asbestos metaphors often presume too much, I make it again to situate it within what might be broadly considered to be a sociology of the future, or what Ruth Levitas describes as the desire for a better world. To realise this desire, Levitas suggests an architecture is necessary, which she describes as 'imagining a reconstructed world and describing its social institutions'.[30] Despite their differences, Jameson largely agrees with Levitas's construction metaphor, identifying 'the city itself as a fundamental form of the Utopian image' and 'the individual building as a space of Utopian investment'.[31] This architecture depends upon infrastructure, which, propose Nikhil Anand, Akhil Gupta and Hannah Appel, promises relationships to the future that it may or may not keep, relationships that, again, demarcate an uneven and unequal relationality.[32] And so asbestos's appearance in utopian infrastructure implies an orientation to the future that returns us to *Asbestos. . . A Matter of Time* and its temporal concerns.

Time, in the original sense granted by the film's title, describes an external sequence of events that progress in a linear fashion from the past into the present and so on into the future. This time, which for ease of reference I call cosmological time, is measured in the film by asbestos's obdurate perdurance, as something originating in the deep past that has transformed the present and will continue to transform the future. In the title's subsequent, revised sense, time describes the human experience of such events, as a lived, phenomenological temporality. Instead of progressing as a linear sequence, 'phenomenological time' distends from my present experiences: backward, as my recollection of past events, and forward, as my anticipation of future events. The tension between these two forms of time will help me to describe a fundamental paradox in thinking about asbestos as a matter of time. Even as asbestos persists across linear time, I experience it as something that recedes into the infrastructure only to reappear at some point in the future in a new, and altogether unfamiliar, place. Despite the continuous presence of asbestos across linear time, it is this phenomenological reappearance that causes me concern in present, about the future and the death it may, or may not, foretell, and about the past and the exposure I may, or may not, have had.

It is telling that this tension emerges only when expectations about asbestos begin to break down. Effectively, this reverses a tendency in the Utopia, observed by Jameson, to reunite phenomenological and cosmological time. If 'discussions of temporality always bifurcate into two paths of existential experience [. . .] and of historical time,' Jameson argues, 'in Utopia these two dimensions are seamlessly reunited [when] existential time is taken up into a historical time which is paradoxically also the end of time, the end of history.'[33] As the asbestos infrastructure separates itself from its environment in my reading, so it challenges the seamless reunification of my experience of time with its objective passing. All these assumptions about asbestos, this unquestioned use of it as infrastructure, speaks to a collective ideology wherein asbestos maintains the same imaginary relations for people, despite the terms of these relations changing to accommodate the realities of the situation. This hopefully becomes clearer if I separate the purely historical understanding of asbestos-related diseases from the epistemic battle that has raged over their recognition. Once I know that asbestos is not the miracle substance being touted, I can, in retrospect, find clues that asbestos had been suspicious all along. This is manifestly easier because of a generally recognised shift in a shared public understanding of what asbestos means and does. Whether one calls this an 'epistemic rupture', after Gaston Bachelard, or a 'paradigm shift', after Thomas Kuhn, this change coincides with the year *Asbestos . . . A Matter of Time* was produced: 1959. The real question is how much significance I should accord this date.

Certainly, 1959 anticipates the beginning of the end for asbestos as a freely traded commodity. For, in February of that year, Chris Wagner and Chris Sleggs gave papers at the Witwatersrand Pneumoconiosis Conference that, while not definitively proving an association between diffuse pleural mesothelioma and asbestos, offered 'sufficient evidence to warrant a fuller investigation of the problem'.[34] Indeed, the consequence of this fuller investigation would be a 1960 paper published in *The British Journal of Industrial Medicine* that would emphasise the association between blue asbestos exposure and mesothelioma, and, by extension, the etiology of mesothelioma as an asbestos-related disease.[35] According to Robert Murray, British inspector of factories from 1946 to 1956 and later medical advisor to the Trades Union Congress, this paper would take 'the scientific world by storm'.[36] It became one of the most cited works in the field of industrial medicine.

Mesothelioma, more than lung cancer or asbestosis, would change public feelings about asbestos. Unlike lung cancer, which could always be complicated by tobacco use, there was a clear etiology: mesothelioma could be overwhelmingly associated with asbestos exposure. Unlike asbestosis, which generally developed from protracted exposure and seemed to be mitigated by greater dust control, there was no observable minimum dose: mesothelioma could develop from the barest of environmental, rather than occupational, exposures. Asbestos, already a hazard for workers, turned into a hazard for their families – and, indeed, for everyone else.

Jameson observes that the periodisation offered by such stark dates 'obliterates difference and projects an idea of the historical period as massive homogeneity'.[37] Indeed, the history of asbestos has tended towards such homogeneity, as suggested by my Before and After division. The briefest survey of Geoffrey Tweedale and Jock McCulloch's *Defending the Indefensible*, the most significant work to synthesise the strategies used by the global asbestos industry, helps to challenge the homogeneity of this response.

Tweedale and McCulloch begin with a paradox that coalesces around the auspicious 1960 publication: far from leading to a decline in production, asbestos production actually increased after 1960. Between 1900 and 2004, approximately 182 million tons of asbestos were produced. Of this, 143 million tons were produced between 1960 and 2004. 'Put another way, nearly 80 per cent of world asbestos production in the twentieth century was produced after the world learned that asbestos could cause mesothelioma!'[38] The reasons Tweedale and McCulloch put forward – the political and commercial considerations that allowed the industry to mount a successful defence based on misinformation and conspiracy – are important and convincing. They note, in particular, the industry's general shift from outright denials of asbestos-related diseases (although these still occurred) to amelioration. In this regard, one of the most important developments was the 'chrysotile defence': 'white asbestos is benign and that the amphiboles alone are responsible for ARDs, especially mesothelioma' (127). Before 1960, chrysotile and amphibole asbestoses had generally been differentiated by use. They were otherwise treated similarly, by cultural and medical discourses. For this reason, I use the generic term asbestos in this book, rather than specify its types. With the publication of the Wagner paper, this changed. Chrysotile manufacturers used the paper's focus on crocidolite, an amphibole, as the basis for initiating large research programmes, whose aim, as the minutes of one 1971 meeting put it, 'to tell the chrysotile story and discredit other fibres'.[39] Sacrificing crocidolite and amosite made political sense – the only significant producer of either was Apartheid South Africa – but it was also economically bearable: crocidolite had only ever made up about 2–3% of the total asbestos market. Capital, in other words, accommodated to increased knowledge about asbestos-related diseases by jettisoning a fraction of its market to preserve the majority of it.

Far from marking the moment when ignorance changed to knowledge in a simple linear progression, 1959 might be better understood as marking a site of epistemic contestation, where the stakes were not simply a general understanding of asbestos in the present and future, but in the past as well. The two interpretations of the film's title, time as possibility or time as finality, are incompossible, in the sense that they each put forward an understanding of asbestos that is total, now and always. These rival claims to truth explain why both asbestos promoters and anti-asbestos activists turn to Classical texts for precursors: both need to own the past, as well as the present or future. *Asbestos: A Matter of Time*, like the promotional texts produced by Keasbey & Mattison or Ruberoid, combines utopian descriptions of asbestos's present and future uses with an evocation of its geological and classical pre-history.[40] Asbestos's physical formation finds its human counterpart in a long durée that harks back to Ancient Greece. So, in a historical literature that ranges from the promotional to the propagandistic, the same litany of characters appears: Theophrastus, Pliny and Strabo to Augustine and Charlemagne. Far from disputing the 'long use' narrative, anti-asbestos histories also rely on texts by Pliny and Strabo, albeit to avow incidents of asbestos disease even in Ancient Greece. This formal congruity suggests that the historical understanding of asbestos is contested only as a matter of access: the knowledge was always already there, for those who knew where to look.

The participants of this contest slip from science into ideology when they orient all historical facts to realise their own position as universally correct.

There is, however, an underlying continuity between the two positions, which emerges when we return to the film. *Asbestos... A Matter of Time* appears to reconcile the passing of time with human experience. This is what makes the title's changing significance so ironic. Both positions approach this reconciliation as a shift in risk, either from the individual to society or vice versa. The utopian impulse offered by asbestos offsets anxieties about death by transferring them from the individual to a larger polity as an area of concern. Its failure creates a parallel, darker impulse, whereby the problem of death is passed from the polity to the individual through the very mechanisms once charged with protecting it. In other words, the infrastructure assumes the same mediating function, despite the differing approaches to thinking about asbestos effects as 'a matter of time'.

As a piece of propaganda, *Asbestos... A Matter of Time* exemplifies the rhetorical strategies used by the industry to interpolate asbestos into social reality. The film opens on a scene of cataclysmic formation, a world in genesis. 'About a billion years ago,' the narrator confidently explains, 'when time was young, our earth was a lonely barren world.' Accompanied by tinny music and sporting graphics that recall 1950s Science Fiction films like *Forbidden Planet* and *This Island Earth*, the film ushers its audience into this protoplasmic moment when 'violent forces were at work, contesting, moulding, preparing for time to come.' The play on time continues when the narrator explains: 'In time, millions of years of time,' there was formed 'the most unusual and useful mineral fibre known to man. Largely unseen, seldom recognised, it has played a tremendously important role in improving our standard of living.' The film moves from time's agency to the product of this agency, a conceptual move that is supported visually by a graphic representation of geological formation that morphs into a photo of actual asbestos ore. At the same time, the narrator links this fossil of geological time to the time of human history, reflecting that the Greeks had a name for this fibre: 'they called it the unquenchable, indestructible stone. They called it asbestos.'

Wrought by the geological force of deep time, this matter of time is characterised by its resistances, not least to time itself: 'Unaffected by fire. Unchanged by weather. Untouched by time's dark captains, rust, rot and decay.' And yet, even as the narrator insists on asbestos's inert perdurability across time, a pair of hands take hold of a polished piece of asbestos stone and break it apart, its graphite surfaces cobwebbing into fibres that, themselves, are 'so fine' that they must be observed through a 'powerful electron microscope'. Here, 'they appear delicate, gracefully hiding the fact that they are incredibly strong [and] remarkably flexible.' As the film continues to enumerate the three dominant types of asbestos – chrysotile (white), crocidolite (blue) and amosite (brown) – where they may be found, how they are mined, and their many, many uses, the underlying message is, above all, that asbestos presents an exemplary case of modernity's success that projects itself into the future space race. 'For asbestos,' the film concludes, 'it is still a matter of time.'

The film combines a visual enumeration of asbestos's uses with an authoritative voice-over that clarifies the relationship between asbestos and these images. Establishing shots – cutting between scenes of architecture, household appliances, infrastructure, forms of travel (cars, buses, trains, planes and ships), and industrial processes – extend asbestos use to encompass the domestic, transportation and industrial spheres. Dividing these establishing shots are more focused medium or close-up images to present or represent asbestos products. When the product is visually striking, like the asbestos tile, its image is presented directly; when it is not, as in the asbestos brake pad, the camera dwells on a foot landing on the brake pedal of a car. Because the film overwhelms its viewer with the sheer quantity of images, with a logic that often diverges precisely between immediate presentation and mediated representation, the voice-over's offer of trained judgment calms even as it guides the viewer's eye.

As media is produced and viewed, argues Stuart Hall, it relies on the encoding and decoding of certain messages.[41] Most often, the viewing or decoding is as intended by the hegemon responsible for its encoding. This is why most popular culture serves to underscore the status quo. But Hall challenges the traditional denigration of popular culture as only ideology fodder. Accordingly, viewers may also decode the message from two other positions: the negotiated and the oppositional. The negotiated position typically accepts the global importance of the dominant position, while seeking to contextualise certain immediate conditions to work around their own beliefs, while the oppositional position simply decodes the message against the dominant, in line with an alternative frame of reference.

Hall's concepts of the dominant, negotiated and oppositional positions build on the descriptions of hegemony advanced by Antonio Gramsci and Raymond Williams. Hegemony, according to Williams, describes that 'whole body of practices and expectations; our assignments of energy, our ordinary understanding of the nature of man and of his world.'[42] It is constitutive of 'a sense of reality for most people in the society, a sense of absolute because experienced reality' (43). Such dominant positions breed, of course, their oppositions and their alternatives, which may, in turn, be accommodated within the dominant, even as the dominant ejects those parts no longer useful to it. Shifting responses to the film suggest a parallel shift in the dominant's views on asbestos, which run concurrent to, but are not the same as, its historical developments.

It is easy to see how the two interpretations of the film might then be aligned with Hall's practices of decoding: the first, a dominant-hegemonic decoding that prioritises asbestos's continued usefulness through time, and the second, an oppositional decoding that announces its time is up. Certainly, the second, more recent interpretation opposes the utopian impulse developed through the course of the film. But it fails, I think, to adequately account for the diachronic shift in the dominant response to asbestos. Indeed, when the film was made, or encoded, the first interpretation would have described its dominant-hegemonic decoding. Now, however, the oppositional decoding has become more natural, at least in the reception of the film's title. When considered independently of the film, the second interpretation of the title suggests an overall shift in the dominant-hegemonic position, from a position where the decoding process would entirely align with that imagined by the producer to a negotiated position that takes the film as a product of its time, while being alive to the ironies produced by its anachronisms.

Taking a negotiated position to the film's internal paradoxes provides some intimation of this irony. Even as I am told that asbestos is unchanging, I see hands manipulate it into web and then fibre from varnished rock. Its natural metamorphoses are compounded by the film's images of industry, as asbestos is repurposed into a variety of household objects, even the very substance of the house itself. Its futuristic qualities, underwritten by the evocation of SF aesthetics, are grounded in geological, rather than historical time. The film's ostensible teleology, a future of infinite use, finds justification not in asbestos's miraculous modernism, but its security as something that has always been. And yet, asbestos remains, even in 1959, 'largely unseen' and 'seldom recognized', anticipating its latent lethality. Watching the film today, I find that its concern with time and historicity still make sense, even if its significance has been inverted. The profound historical shift in public understanding of asbestos did not invalidate the film's concerns so much as reconfigure the ground of its reception. Even as the affective response changes, asbestos continues to challenge conventions of both time and narrative. Its morphological freedom (as stone, fibre and particle) jars with its inertia. Unaffected though it might be 'by time's dark captains', the story of asbestos's future must, it seems, be told through the changes exerted upon it within the deep past. With its fusion of arche-myths about creation with utopian visions of the future, the contemporary progress narrative that runs through *Asbestos. . . A Matter of Time* might well be regarded as superficially modernist in its aesthetic, since it follows the now rather hackneyed idea that the redemption of the avant-garde is guaranteed in the traditions offered by the deep past.

I can, by now, identify this guarantee as an infrastructural continuity that will play across the historiography of asbestos supporters and detractors, much like the asbestos infrastructures that persist across the utopia and dystopia. What should also be clearer is the material role that asbestos used to play in reconciling existential anxieties about temporality, or the human experience of time, with the passing of historical, or objective, time. Understood in this light, the collapse of asbestos as a utopian material coincides with the fracturing of its ability to suture together these divergent aspects of time. The vestiges of its infrastructural function provide critical dystopias with the means to highlight this fracture, to use the existential anxiety about an untransformed near future as the impetus to cleave to the realisation of a historical Utopia. Of course, this consternation is far more likely to produce a sociology of mystery, conspiracy and horror, as I discuss in my next chapter. But it also anticipates a logic of thinking differently about asbestos that I hope to track in this book, whereby asbestos provides us with the impetus to think differently about our societies, to imagine them anew.

NOTES

1. *Asbestos . . . A Matter of Time* (U.S. Bureau of Mines with Johns-Manville Corporation, 1959).
2. Fredric Jameson, *Archaeologies of the Future: The Desire Called Utopia and Other Science Fictions* (London: Verso, 2007), p. 3.
3. Ernst Bloch, *The Principle of Hope: Volume 1*, trans. Neville Plaice, Stephen Plaice and Paul Knight (Oxford: Blackwell, 1986), p. 13; Jameson, *Archaeologies*, p. 2.
4. Jameson, *Archaeologies*, p. 3.
5. Darko Suvin, *Metamorphoses of Science Fiction: On the Poetics and History of a Literary Genre* (New Haven: Yale University Press, 1979), p. 63.
6. Nathan Waddell, *Modernist Nowheres: Politics and Utopia in Early Modernist Writing, 1900–1920* (Basingstoke, Palgrave Macmillan, 2012), p. 14.
7. Edward Bellamy, *Looking Backward from 2000–1887*, ed. Matthew Beaumont (Oxford: Oxford University Press, 2009), p. 14. Although he does not mention asbestos's role, Michael Osman notes how Bellamy's text anticipates the rise of cold storage facilities in *Modernism's Visible Hand: Architecture and Regulation in America* (Minneapolis, MN: University of Minnesota Press, 2018), Ch. 2.
8. Jean Pfaelzer, *The Utopian Novel in America, 1886–1896: The Politics of Form* (Pittsburgh: University of Pittsburgh Press, 1985), p. 28.
9. Christopher S. Ferns, *Narrating Utopia: Ideology, Gender, Form in Utopian Literature* (Liverpool: Liverpool University Press, 1999), p. 85.
10. Robert Southey, *The Poetical Works of Robert Southey* (London: Longmans, Green, and Co, 1866), p. 115.
11. Anna Seward, *The Poetical Works*, ed. Walter Scott (Edinburgh: James Ballantyne, 1810), p. 392.
12. J. N. Stearns, *The Temperance Speaker* (New York: National Temperance Society, 1870), p. 67.
13. Maria Gowen Brooks, *Zóphiël, or the Bride of Seven* (London: R. J. Kennett, 1833), p. 135.
14. Elizabeth Barrett Browning, *Poetical Works, Volume 3* (London: Chapman Hall, 1866), p. 300; *The Atheneum*, p. 674.
15. Jones, *Asbestos*, p. 61; 49; 67.
16. Gilman, Charlotte Perkins, *What Diantha Did*, intro. Charlotte J. Rich (Durham, NC: Duke University Press, 2005), p. 149, 148.
17. Charlotte J. Rich, 'Introduction', In *Diantha*, p. 19.
18. Stephen Leacock, *Nonsense Novels* (London: The Bodley Head, 1914).

19. See Veblen, *Leisure Class*. For Leacock's satire of conspicuous consumption, see *Arcadian Adventures* (1914).
20. Bellamy, *Looking*, p. 23.
21. Waugh, Evelyn, 'Love Among the Ruins: A Romance of the Near Future', *Commonweal*, 31 July 1953, *Commonweal Website*, accessed 23 February 2021: https://www.commonwealmagazine.org/love-among-ruins-0
22. Ashley Maher, *Reconstructing Modernism: British Literature, Modern Architecture, and the State* (Oxford: Oxford University Press, 2020), p. 220.
23. Michael Frayn, *My Father's Fortune: A Life* (London: Faber & Faber, 2010), p. 101.
24. François Ewald, 'The Return of Descartes's Malicious Demon: An Outline of a Philosophy of Precaution', trans. Stephen Utz, in *Embracing Risk: The Changing Culture of Insurance and Responsibility*, eds Tom Baker and Jonathan Simon (Chicago, IL: University of Chicago Press, 2002), p. 276.
25. Edouard Thoulon qtd Ewald, 'Return', p. 277.
26. Poul Harremoës et al., *Late Lessons from Early Warnings: the Precautionary Principle, 1896–2000*, Environmental Issue Report 22 (Copenhagen: European Environment Agency, 2001).
27. Hans Jonas, *The Imperative of Responsibility. In Search of an Ethics for the Technological Age* (Chicago, IL: University of Chicago Press, 1984), p. 27.
28. Neal Stephenson, *Snow Crash* (London: Penguin Books, 1994), p. 219–20.
29. Cory Doctorow, *Walkaway* (London: Head of Zeus, 2017), p. 246–7.
30. Ruth Levitas, *Utopia as Method* (Basingstoke: Palgrave Macmillan, 2013), p. 197.
31. Jameson, *Archaeologies*, p. 4.
32. See Nikhil Anand, Akhil Gupta and Hannah Appel, *The Promise of Infrastructure* (Durham, NC: Duke University Press, 2018), Introduction.
33. Jameson, *Archaeologies*, p. 7.
34. Peter Bartrip, *The Way From Dusty Death: Turner and Newall and the Regulation of the British Asbestos Industry 1890s–1970* (London: The Athlone Press, 2001), p. 174.
35. J. C. Wagner, C. A. Sleggs, P. Marchand, 'Diffuse pleural mesothelioma and asbestos exposure in the North Western Cape Province', 17 (4) *British Journal of Industrial Medicine* (1960), p. 260–71.
36. Robert Murray, 'Asbestos: A Chronology of Its Origins and Health Effects', 47 (6) *British Journal of Industrial Medicine* (1990), p. 363.
37. Fredric Jameson, *Postmodernism; or, The Cultural Logic of Late Capitalism* (London: Verso, 1992), p. 3.
38. Tweedale and McCulloch, *Defending*, p. 14.
39. Memo qtd in Tweedale and McCulloch, *Defending*, p. 128.
40. See *Legends of Asbestos* (Ambler, PA: Keasbey & Mattison, 1940); Bowles, *Asbestos*.
41. Stuart Hall, 'Encoding/Decoding', In *Media and Cultural Studies: Keyworks*, eds Meenakshi Gigi Durham and Douglas M. Kellner (Oxford: Blackwell, 2006), pp. 163–173.
42. Raymond Williams, *Culture and Materialism* (London: Verso, 2020), p. 43.

2

CLUES AND MYSTERIES

In this chapter, I engage with asbestos as a mystery that results from 'an irruption of the *world* in the heart of *reality*' where *world* designates all that is and is possible, and *reality* that which 'is stabilized by pre-established formats that are sustained by institutions'.[1] As in Chapter 1, I follow a trajectory of texts across the long twentieth century, to show how a latent continuity disrupts the more obvious historical break in attitudes about asbestos. Whereas *there* I paid particular attention to the way that asbestos infrastructures reconciled or disrupted time with narrative, *here* I want to be a little more attentive to asbestos as a link between different plots in mysteries, or, in other words, when it assumes the role of a clue.

Asbestos as Clue

In his influential essay on the clue, Carlo Ginzburg notes how 'traces that may be infinitesimal make it possible to understand a deeper reality [i.e. the world] than would otherwise be attainable'.[2] Ginzburg notes how, in the late nineteenth century, methods in art history, psychoanalysis and (fictional) detecting drew on parallel forms of semiotic analysis, not least 'the model of medical semiotics that makes it possible to diagnose diseases not recognizable through a direct observation and based on superficial symptoms sometimes irrelevant to the layman' (280). If, on the one hand, semiotics provided a useful diagnostic function, it also allowed for more precise forms of classification and social control, especially in identifying cases of criminal recidivism. In order to identify recidivists, it was necessary to prove both a prior conviction and the identity of past convict with new offender. Therefore, the eventual success of the fingerprint method: 'To catch the elusive uniqueness of individuals, the clue provided by a small detail like papillary ridges proved more useful than the complex description of macroscopic bodily features' (283).

To explain how asbestos comes to be used as a clue, to identify its 'fingerprint', I need to explain the changing nature of the 'solution' it signals. Two narratives serve to illustrate how, even as circumstances changed, asbestos maintains a formal continuity in the form of the clue. The first is a 1917 catalogue from Keasbey & Mattison called *A Spark may cost a Farm*.[3] As its emotive title suggests, *A Spark may cost a Farm* represents a significant departure from asbestos catalogues of the 1880s and 1890s, where a single page served to introduce the asbestos product and its company. As the catalogues became glossier and more enticing, so too did the stories that prefaced their products. In *A Spark may cost a Farm*, fully one third of the publication is dedicated to creating a sense of anxiety that only asbestos could resolve.

As its title suggests, the catalogue begins by imagining how 'one spark on the roof [. . .] may bring your home down in ruins about you while you sleep' (1). This is a story, it insists, too common for the newspapers, 'repeated thousands upon thousands of times on the American farm' (1). 'But to you,' it warns, 'the loss of your home is a crushing blow. It means the work of a lifetime sacrificed to a spark. Loved ones homeless. Things and surroundings [. . .] wiped out in minutes by a spark – a single spark [. . .] It can happen to you anytime' (1). Here, as elsewhere, I can find parallels between the methods used by the asbestos industry, to sell asbestos as the best means to immunise against other, more imminent threats, and those used by anti-asbestos activists to instill the necessary sense of panic. 'A single spark' is, after all, not so different from the 'single fibre' that threatens. Like the fibre, the spark becomes significant precisely through its insignificance, its potential to be overlooked. This means that it cannot be guarded against through conscious vigilance – it can happen 'while you sleep' or 'anytime'. It requires a roof one can 'trust': 'a roof covering that CANNOT BURN or CARRY FIRE to other buildings. Then [. . .] you can rest secure that your roof is an absolutely dependable protection against FIRE. Your loved ones are SAFE' (2). It introduces, as its solution, a principle of reliance: the asbestos roof may be relied upon to disperse any stray sparks. Asbestos, here, preemptively solves a problem that never happened, by anticipating, and guarding against, the spark. In the absence of the spark, asbestos explains why nature's crime was foiled. As a text, *A Spark may cost a Farm* creates a double motion that is familiar to anyone who has read a crime novel: a crime is imagined by the author, only to be solved by the author's proxy, the detective.

My second example, Will Gluck's 2018 adaptation of *Peter Rabbit*, also takes asbestos to be a clue.[4] When Peter's long-time nemesis, Mr McGregor, dies at the beginning of the film, the narrator tells the audience that this is the culmination of '78 years of terrible lifestyle choices'. A montage explains these choices. Although most of its scenes show McGregor eating and drinking, one has him rubbing down a wall, as he stands on a ladder from which dangles a bucket comically labelled 'Asbestos'. It is, in other words, a clue. But to what?

Responses to the film found the narrator's explanation to be misleading, if not offensive. Describing asbestos as 'a bad lifestyle choice' caused some consternation amongst the asbestos activist community, who rightly pointed out that 'making it seem that people chose to get [asbestos-related diseases] is wildly unfair'.[5] 'Asbestos', blogged another, 'is not a joke, it is an extremely dangerous and harmful substance'.[6] These responses replayed earlier, more widespread criticisms about another scene, where Peter forces his new antagonist, McGregor's nephew, to swallow blackberries after finding out that he is allergic to them. Critics accused the film of failing to be more sensitive to food-allergies and the bullying associated with it. Unsurprisingly, the very same arguments used to legitimate the criticism – why include such irrelevant and hurtful details in a film meant for children? – were replayed by the critics' critics: why make such a big deal about a film meant for children?

Side-stepping this debate, Richard Brody, writing for *The New Yorker*, suggested a more nuanced criticism of the film, which, he notes, contrasts an exaggerated, cartoonish violence with a 'mechanistic moralism [. . .] imparting values in the form of equation-like talking points'.[7] Against this 'emotional realism', 'the scene involving a life-threatening allergy is all the more conspicuous: while the rest of the movie marches in lockstep with its edifying narrative, that scene is out of place. It doesn't follow the script.' With its implied condemnation of unhealthy eating, the McGregor montage provides a particularly obvious presentation of the film's mechanistic moralism. For that reason, the inclusion of asbestos is similarly 'out of place', for those with eyes to see.

The McGregor side-plot is a detective story, told in miniature. To explain the 'terrible lifestyle choices' behind McGregor's heart attack, it presents a visually coherent narrative through the juxtaposition of a series of clues. Following Tzvetan Todorov's formulation of the detective story as 'not one but two stories', the heart attack and its ensuing montage present the story of the crime and the story of the investigation.[8] The montage offers an abbreviated history that effectively becomes its own discrete story within the film: a narrative investigation that proves Peter committed no crime.

For Todorov, the two stories in the detective tale 'have no point in common' (44). *Pace* Todorov, Franco Moretti observes the two stories are linked by the clue, which, when it appears in the story of the investigation, gestures to the cycle of events in the story of the crime.[9] Here, the investigation presents the clues as evidence that the 'crime', McGregor's death, was an act of self-harm. The montage relies upon this implicit understanding of the clue when it 'explains' McGregor's heart attack as the result of 'terrible lifestyle choices'. It assumes I understand the link between certain foods and heart disease, and it draws that out to emphasise certain socio-cultural norms or codes. In this regard, it follows the pattern of the classic detective story.

In such stories, the clue frequently reappears in the denouement, to explain how all that seemed out of place before is now contained by a satisfyingly social explanation. When an alternative line of significance displaces this explanatory value, however, these clues subvert, rather than reinforce, narrative coherency. By emphasising the importance of McGregor's asbestos bucket, the viewers concerned with asbestos didn't just recognise an unacceptable tendency to diminish, or dissimulate, asbestos's importance, they also challenged the film's narrative coherence (and by extension its mechanistic moralism). When one suspects that asbestos is not treated as seriously as it should be, references to it are more likely to confirm that suspicion than dispel it.

For the purposes of this chapter, I am going to take for granted that readerly suspicion explored in recent crime fiction studies. 'In response to the deliberate duplicity of the mystery writer', observes Stewart King, 'crime fiction readers learn to interrogate the way information is presented to them'.[10] King notes how readers are trained by crime fiction to read contingently. In this he follows Lisa Zunshine, for whom readers must 'store information under advisement and, then, once the truth-value of this information is decided, to think back to the beginning of the story and to readjust [their] understanding of a whole series of occurrences.'[11] Close encounters with asbestos, allergens or other 'hidden hazards' train people into a parallel readerly suspicion, as the fallout from *Peter Rabbit* illustrates. But, as *A Spark may cost a Farm* demonstrates, asbestos companies too had a stake in developing this suspicious disposition: protective devices are difficult to market, if one is ignorant of, or inured to, the dangers that they protect against. In a more tragic vein, this process of detection echoes the experiences of people who, as they suffer from asbestos-related diseases, must try to recall apparently inconsequential moments of exposure in their life's trajectory to build a case for compensation. For the moment, however, I want to mark the connection between this trained suspicion and the genre's 'strong orientation towards the ending'.[12]

In my utopian texts, asbestos offered the means of anticipating the future as already given in the present. In one sense, its presence as infrastructure reflects the inert nature of the utopian plot, which often consists of a sequential description of the future anterior in which the narrator finds herself. By comparison, the mystery story inverts this process of 'presenting' the future, preferring instead to defer any sense of certainty about future resolution to its very ending. This extends beyond the standard narrative closure, offered or denied at the conclusion of most narrative.[13] 'Rather than simply piecing together the puzzle and tying up loose ends,' argue Gulddal, King and Rolls, 'the crime novel ends with an act of self-interpretation, presented explicitly in the form of the detective protagonist's solution, which replaces mystery with what appears to be complete clarity in regard to actions and motivations.'[14] The mystery explicitly asserts a social coherence that tries to cover over any suggestion of disconnections between time and narrative. But, as my earlier discussion of Ricoeur suggested, mere claims will not serve to relieve tensions between time and narrative: they just make such claims seem all the more fragile.

This fragility shifts my focus from the universality of experience, imagined in utopian time, to the differentiation of experience that occurs across actually existing world-systems. Cultural expressions about asbestos reflect a system that orders itself through combined and uneven development. Asbestos was, and is, primarily encountered as a commodity, produced by human labour and offered as a product for general sale upon the market. Its success as a commodity was assured not simply through the properties of the material itself, but through the machinations of transnational companies, whose cartel, when it divided the global market in 1929, described itself as a 'miniature League of Nations'.[15] This cartel maintained 'a principle of mutual help' across the industry to replace a prior 'atmosphere of distrust and suspicion' (25). But it still relied on vertical integration: incorporating the mining, milling, transportation, manufacture and sales processes to make themselves more resilient to market shocks. By relegating these processes to geographically distant areas of the globe, McCulloch and Tweedale observe, the companies made the development of a transnational solidarity amongst its workers difficult, if not impossible. These connections between the holders of capital, and the concomitant disconnections between their workers, served the companies well when it came to 'dissuading' countries from instituting bans on the material and developing 'corporate science' to dissimulate concerns about asbestos's health effects and, later, to insist on the chrysotile distinction. It is against the backdrop of this transnational political economy that I consider how both the detective novel and the horror story, as exponents of world literature, also speak to asbestos's place within the world-system.

Debates over the meaning of 'world literature', extensive as they are, have tended to revolve around works whose canonical status has ensured their circulation outside of their country of origin. This focus on 'literary' works, formed from aesthetic snobbery and the fear of academic censure, delayed the recognition of genre fiction as an important site of world literature until comparatively recently. Nevertheless, the very reproducibility of such fiction, enabled by established codes and trained readers, makes it a particularly useful site for comparison. In *Crime Fiction as World Literature* (2017), Louise Nilsson, David Damrosch and Theo D'haen observe that crime fiction gives 'local expression to such global phenomena as human trafficking, human rights, upheavals in gender, class or political relations, and globalization itself.'[16] Descriptions of these global phenomena, when framed by the familiar structures of the detective genre, are more easily translated across different localities, into different languages and for different readers. In other words, they enter into a circulatory logic that dictates their dissemination.

These processes of circulation affect, and are affected by, processes of production. As texts circulate, they encourage their readers to refigure their stories to account for different conditions, inspiring these readers, perhaps, to write their own texts, which refine, revise or otherwise rework their conceits in ways that, in turn, shift and develop our understanding of the genre, as an evolving and self-regulating system. These new texts document the material circumstances of the world-system and the singular capitalist modernity that caused it, as both products of, and commentary upon, these processes. This means that, together with the Warwick Research Collective (WReC), I can grasp world literature 'as neither a canon of masterworks nor a mode of reading, but as a *system* [. . .] structured not on *difference* but on *inequality*.'[17] For WReC, capitalist 'modernity is both what world-literature indexes or is "about" and what gives world-literature its distinguishing formal characteristics' (15). Such a modernity is characterised not just by imperial distinctions between core, periphery and semi-periphery, but by the ways that capitalism's flows depend on the creation of these very distinctions. Criticism's work, in this account, should track the cross-over between the ebbs and flow of global capital and the forms that literature develops to track these flows.

To capture the play between the imperial structures of core, periphery and semi-periphery and the mobility of capital, I now turn to two stories from the early twentieth century that depend upon established expectations of genre fiction to convey alternative meanings for asbestos. Casual references to asbestos in Algernon Blackwood's 'The Nemesis of Fire' (1908) and F. Scott Fitzgerald's 'A Diamond as Big as the Ritz' (1922) provide clues to more 'global concerns', with the unexpected consequences of Empire and the tension between speculative and investment capital, respectively.[18] These works effectively model concerns for later mysteries that either make asbestos explainable (i.e. in detective novels) or unexplainable (i.e. in ghost stories).

Asbestos and the Mystery Story

'The Nemesis of Fire', a Dr John Silence story by the occultist Algernon Blackwood, gestures to an unexplainable mystery associated with asbestos, all while orienting it back to an explanation that Blackwood would consider natural. When Colonel Wragge invites Silence, Blackwood's psychic detective, to Manor House, he introduces his 'need for help of a peculiar kind' with some of the 'queer stories' that have emerged from the estate (144; 165). The 'something very serious amiss', it turns out, is an unsettled Egyptian mummy, whose rest has been disturbed by its translocation to England and the theft of its scarabaeus (145). One of the queer stories turns on a dog chasing an invisible creature, who is likely the mummy. After the ensuing scuffle, the dog returns with 'something like white hair stuck to its jaws (166). 'It was curious looking stuff, something like asbestos,' the Colonel muses, but when analysed, it is 'neither animal, vegetable, nor mineral', and soon disappears without a trace (166). The story of the white hair contributes to a larger, composite understanding of the situation as out of joint. The asbestos itself appears to carry little significance. But Blackwood's single casual reference disguises a number of interesting connections with the rest of the story that can, in turn, help to unpack some assumptions about asbestos.

It can hardly be coincidental that asbestos appears to clothe the mummy when so much of the story turns around fears about fire. All the other queer stories from the estate turn around acts of incendiarism: fire attacks in and around the house. These have been caused by a fire-elemental, under the control of the mummy and sent to exact retribution for the theft of its scarabaeus. The asbestos is, in a sense, the means by which the mummy endures the fire, physically, even as it anticipates the need for the more supernatural protections that Strange himself will provide, as the protagonists seek to 'appease the anger of the Fire, and to bring peace again to [the] household' (239). Even in this minor role, asbestos acts as a clue, in Ginzburg's sense, since it still reflects the story's deeper preoccupation with fire and its containment.

However, 'The Nemesis of Fire' does seem to violate Luc Boltanski's basic premise of detective stories: the detective story depends upon a mundane, unexceptional reality, where interruptions are, themselves, explainable by natural means. In late nineteenth-century society, argues Boltanski, social reality came to be presented in a 'robust, organized, and thus predictable fashion'.[19] In contrast to real factual conditions, the establishment of social reality 'presupposes that one can count on a set of regularities that are maintained no matter what situation is envisaged and that frame each event' (10). To reconcile the story with Boltanski's thesis, however, I need only to recall Blackwood's own, well-documented commitment to the supernatural, since, as Emily Alder has noted, it amounted to a belief that the natural should extend to the more-than-visible.[20] After all, as Silence explains, 'I have yet to come across a problem that is not natural, and has not a natural explanation. It's merely a question of how much one knows – and admits' (173).

Certainly, the story illustrates Blackwood's desire to reorient the natural-unnatural binary, rather than discard it completely. Strange, although receptive to the supernatural, is often marked by his 'natural' poise. By contrast, when Wragge attempts to explain the incendiarism, in and around the house, he realises 'at last that the "natural" explanation he had held on to all along was becoming impossible, and he hated it. It made him angry' (171). In both examples, Blackwood reframes the distinction between natural, unnatural and supernatural, by drawing on an opposition between order and disorder. The mummy is not, in and of itself, unnatural, even if it is supernatural; what makes it unnatural is a disruption of order, the theft of its scarabaeus, which wakes it from its slumber and causes the 'unnatural' heat that accompanies it (149). Under these circumstances, the supernatural simply explains that which is natural, but has not yet been absorbed into scientific certainty.[21]

Importantly, it helps me emphasise, with Boltanski, how the mundane mystery aimed not only to assert social reality, but challenge, and thereby reveal, its causal structures. Reciprocally, it serves to show how the inquiry into such causal structures could, potentially, destabilise precisely the reality effect they were designed to support. Alder suggests that 'the gap between an intuitive leap and logical deduction makes space for the weird [. . .] leaving us on the limits of the known.'[22] If so, then the substitution of an intuitive leap for a logical deduction when treating the limits of the known might, conversely, render this weird gap invisible, dangerous and incalculable. Asbestos use, although based upon logical deduction, seems so contingent to our eyes in the present, as to take on the form of an intuitive leap. In like fashion, we might say that the weird space it occupies in mysteries of the early twentieth century augurs not simply its transformation into an explainable phenomenon, for detective stories and conspiracy theories, but also as the inexplicable cause of horror.

For Roger Luckhurst, 'The Nemesis of Fire' introduces Blackwood's longtime interest in the Egyptian Gothic.[23] Although Luckhurst dismisses the story as conventional mummy revenge fiction, he does situate it in the longer trajectory of Blackwood's work, which would come to find in Egypt 'an abstract figuration of ruins that point beyond themselves to the primordial and enduring structure of subjectivity itself' (182). According to Luckhurst, Blackwood's lack of interest in Egypt's specificity speaks to its 'colonial framing', wherein Egypt provokes in Blackwood the same interest that archaeology produced for Freud: as a model for accessing some primal consciousness (182). If, as Luckhurst argues, 'Blackwood *introjects* Egypt into the ego' (182), I suspect, after Ranjana Khanna, that this introjection has failed to absorb its love object properly.[24] After all, Blackwood's rampaging fire elementals, who tear up the English countryside at the behest of their mummy master, are primarily motivated by vengeance, first for the mummy's translocation and then for the theft of its scarabaeus. You don't need be Freud to understand this 'colonial melancholia' as the manifestation of a palpable anxiety about the consequences of colonial expansion.[25] The asbestos hair, which appears in the tale only to disappear, seems to function as a metonym for a much more pervasive haunting of Britain by the discontents of their distant Empire: the mummy's vengeance a literal product of the colonial system that brought him over, and a figurative representation of the imperial anxieties. Blackwood turns Egypt into a periphery, and, in so doing, provides a practical demonstration of what

I, following many others, mean when I claim that empire (and capital) produces, rather than highlights, cores, peripheries and semi-peripheries. Egypt, in Blackwood's tale, is reduced to a mysterious origin point; likewise, London, the point of departure for Silence and his amanuensis, functions as the core, from whence they can travel to the Manor House, the semi-periphery, where core and periphery meet.

F. Scott Fitzgerald's mystery tale, 'The Diamond as Big as the Ritz', occupies a similarly weird space, when it mixes elements from adventure, spy and American Dream genres. At the beginning of the story, the protagonist, John T. Unger, receives 'an asbestos pocket-book stuffed with money' from his father, along with the fatherly admonishment that he will always be welcome at home, where they'll keep 'the home fires burning', and that he is 'an Unger from Hades' (5). Here, Fitzgerald makes playful reference to asbestos's qualities as a fire retardant, a common conceit in Little Magazines like *The Smart Set* where the novella was published in June 1922, and where asbestos products were often advertised. The asbestos pocket-book fits into Fitzgerald's extended metaphor about middle-class, midwestern America as 'hell', where 'the inhabitants have been so long out of the world that, though they make a great show of keeping up to date in dress and manners and literature, they depend to a great extent on hearsay' (5). The pocket-book immediately disappears from sight, suggesting it plays no great role in the story that follows. John is invited to visit the farm of his friend Percy Washington. The farm, as he discovers, holds the secrets to the Washington family's wealth: not only is the house built on the largest diamond in the world, its labour is provided entirely by African American slaves. To keep these secrets, the farm is protected by batteries of anti-aircraft guns. When guests like John visit, they are murdered to protect the family's secrets. The evening of John's murder coincides with an air raid, which culminates in John escaping with the Washington daughters, Kismine and Jasmine, as the rest of the family blow themselves up with the diamond. Kismine has carried out some of the family jewels, but, John discovers, these are worthless rhinestones. The Washingtons' remaining wealth, investments in radium distributed in 'a thousand banks', can only be accessed with bank-books, which are 'consumed' in the explosion (28). The three will have to return to Hades, where John's father 'is just as liable as not to cut me off with a hot coal' (28) This proposed return to Hades invites us to return to John's abandoned asbestos pocket-book, as potentially holding more than mere money.

To understand this significance, we need to think a little bit more about the meaning of the money John's pocket-book ostensibly protects in 'The Diamond'. The pocket-book is 'stuffed with money' when John receives it from his father. This money is the product of an older, 'moral' form of capital, that is capital accumulated through saving. By contrast, the Washingtons rely on a riskier, speculative capital: the radium, the rhinestones, even the diamond itself, are only worth something because of their scarcity. To realise their value would threaten this scarcity and, therefore, the value itself. As the Washington grandfather realises, when he first discovers his diamond, 'If it were offered for sale not only would the bottom fall out of the market, but also, if the value should vary with its size in the usual arithmetic progression, there would not be enough gold in the world to buy a tenth part of it' (21). This speculative capital does translate into means for the Washingtons, but it functions by virtue of trust and secrets. Should the diamond be discovered, it will render the very possibility of scarcity-based value contingent and untrustworthy, thus obviating all other scarcity-based measures of wealth. More than anything, this speculative capital must make use of its magnitude, while covering over its source. It does so by abstracting its value, through the bank-books and the contents of Kismine's pockets. This abstraction carries its own risks: when the books are consumed, and the pockets are shown to contain worthless rhinestones, their value disappears. John's pocket book offers a more straightforward, concrete protection for a more straightforward unit of wealth, commonly accepted as the universal equivalent.

Laura Key and Richard Godden have argued that 'The Diamond' allegorises a mélange of anxieties Fitzgerald had about monetary exchange, the gold standard and the value of fiction.[26] Both Key and Godden link the novella to what Key calls 'the ideological conflict' that developed around the introduction of new credit facilities, 'between the traditional imperative of saving earned money [. . .] and this modern system of instant gratification, in which intangible credit money allowed people to spend beyond their immediate means' (656–7). Though neither Key nor Godden mention it, the pocket-book can be seen to replay this conflict in miniature. Parallels between actual wealth in the pocket-book and the speculative wealth contained in the bank-books or Kismine's pockets serve to highlight the risk of the latter and relative freedom from risk of the former. Whereas not even a bribe to God can save the Washingtons' fortune, the asbestos pocket-book can, at least, represent John and Kismine's remaining option: a return to Hades and a life of hard work.

Rather than rely on existing capital, credit sets its trust in future earnings. As Key explains, 'the introduction of credit forced the American people to think about their lives in the wider sense of present versus future, where borrowing and debt in the present were offset in people's imaginations by the perceived future ability to pay' (659). If the asbestos pocket-book protected an earlier, more moral form of capital, it was able to do so because it was made from a 'modern improvement' designed to reduce risk.[27] For all that the Washingtons rely on 'modern', speculative capital, their antiquated antebellum lifestyle – their reliance on slaves and on personal 'providence' – suggests that they have not acclimatised to modern understandings of risk. When Kismine imagines her previous life to have been 'all a dream' at the end of the novella, we can identify the dream as her inurement to the riskiness, the possible transience, of that life. But for John, whose 'shabby gift of disillusion' at the end parallels his gift of the pocket-book at the beginning, is more able to understand their current circumstances, because, in a way, the pocket-book already presaged them, a logic of risk already coded into its offer of prevention (28)

Fitzgerald's asbestos pocket-book illuminates an intersection between asbestos, moral economy and socialised risk. As asbestos shifted its role from a preventative measure that mitigated social risk to an aggravator of social risk, so its position in the moral economy changed. From a substance that served to insulate people from risks, whether to health or to capital, asbestos became a risky object in itself, whose use implicated companies, doctors and legislators in morally dubious behaviour. But Fitzgerald's mystery also turns on a secret that impinges on the moral fabric of US society: the Washington farm is a secret whose diamond threatens the US economy, whose use of slaves violates the US constitution, and whose geographical excision from survey maps invalidates US political sovereignty. Fitzgerald's preoccupation with the secret that must be uncovered, or not, to preserve social cohesion means that even the story's outlandish plot twists are corralled to support the banality of a social reality built on capital.

Blackwood and Fitzgerald, for all their differences, vacillate over treating asbestos as an explainable or unexplainable mystery. This presages a subsequent, more pronounced divergence in twenty-first-century treatments of asbestos, between detective fiction, on the one hand, and horror, on the other. These works testify to the impact of asbestos across the world-system, while registering this impact in specifically local ways, according to histories dominated by its mining, for example, or its manufacture. Now, to address this history in a more concrete way, I look at three detective novels that take place in three nations that were, historically, amongst the largest producers and consumers of asbestos: two asbestos mining nations, Canada and South Africa, and one of the largest manufacturers of asbestos products, the United Kingdom. Richard Kunzmann's *Salamander Cotton* (2006), Louise Penny's *The Long Way Home* (2014) and Damien Boyd's *Death Sentence* (2016) all give some prominence to asbestos in their plots.[28] Each text uses asbestos as, variously, the motive for murder, the method of murder or the impetus to investigate a disappearance. At the same time, their comparison sheds light on regional understandings of asbestos that develop alongside its more 'universal' toxic effects. I conclude the chapter with two haunted town novels, from Canada and Australia, to consider how the mystery of asbestos might also be understood as unexplained, or unexplainable: Cassie Bérard's *Qu'il est bon de se noyer* [*How good it is to drown*] (2016) and Lois Murphy's *Soon* (2018).[29]

THE ASBESTOS DETECTIVE STORY

Salamander Cotton begins with the murder of Bernard Klamm, a former executive of an asbestos company, at his home in Johannesburg. As the investigation progresses, Klamm's estranged wife, Henrietta Campbell, asks the detective in charge, Jacob Tshabalala, to recommend a private investigator to support a parallel inquiry in the Northern Cape, where the couple owned a farm. Tshabalala enlists the help of his former colleague, Harry Mason. Mason is not charged with finding Klamm's killer; rather, Campbell wants him to resurrect a 'cold case' search for their daughter, Claudette, who disappeared in 1965. Her assumption is that Claudette was killed by Klamm, after he found out that she was in a relationship with Klamm's employee, José Cauto, later found guilty of her rape and murder. When Mason visits the farm, he discovers the remains of an old asbestos mining operation, run by Klamm and managed by Cauto. In a flashback, we learn that one of their employees, the father of Obed Dithlolelo, was gravely injured in a mining accident and died because they didn't bother to send him to the hospital. Obed, it transpires, murdered Claudette; Klamm and Campbell allowed Cauto to take the blame because they objected to the couples' interracial relationship; Cauto, in turn, murdered Klamm, with the assistance of Campbell's boyfriend, Tobias, who wanted to sell the farm to settle his debts. The death of Obed's father prompts a cycle of revenge that works through Claudette and Cauto, and eventually leads to Klamm's murder. When this is revealed at the denouement, Tobias shoots Cauto, thus confirming the truth of the story.

The Long Way Home opens not with a murder but a disappearance. The artist Clara Morrow asks retired Chief Inspector Armand Gamache to find her husband, Peter. Clara and Peter separated when Clara's career started to eclipse Peter's, but they had planned a rendezvous that Peter has not kept. As Gamache tracks Peter's movements across Quebec and Ontario, he learns how both Peter and Clara were educated at the Ontario College of Canadian Arts in Toronto, how one of their teachers, Professor Norman, publicly humiliated Clara for her work, and how another, Professor Massey, was instrumental in Norman being fired because of it. Here, asbestos provides not the motive but the means; in an implausible plot twist, canvases exchanged between the two professors have been lined with asbestos dust, with the ostensible aim of committing a murder as slow as Nixon's slow violence. Norman, dying of mesothelioma, has retreated to an isolated fishing village on the Gulf of St Lawrence, where Peter finds him and, being the reason for his disappearance, has stayed to nurse him through the final stages of his illness. But, if asbestos causes the illness that should have killed Norman, Massey's impatience gets the better of him: he kills Norman with a hunting knife. At the novel's climax, Gamache realises that, contrary to his initial suspicion that the canvases were provided by Norman to Massey as revenge for losing his job, Massey provided Norman with the canvases, his motive a more opaque jealousy about how Norman's talent outshone his own. At this moment, Massey himself reappears with Clara as his hostage. She is saved by Peter, but at the cost of his own life; Massey stabs him in the chest.

At first, the murder that opens *Death Sentence* appears unrelated to the murder that the police detectives are to investigate. This latter murder, it seems, is an act of vengeance for the victim's complicity with asbestos exposure. The victim, a captain in the army during the Falklands/Malvinas war, ordered four soldiers to dismantle mobile radar units that turned out to be lined with asbestos. As the novel progresses, we discover that the soldiers have each developed mesothelioma and are suing for compensation. But, the detective realises, the captain's order was itself an act of retribution: the soldiers had assaulted the captain some weeks before, in battle, when he threatened to report their comrade for deserting. Although this comrade went on to be killed during the fighting, his indictment in the captain's subsequent report cost him a posthumous commendation. The murder, it transpires, is committed by the dead soldier's son, Adrian Kandes. Although the soldiers supported the novel's opening murder, where Kandes kills the defense attorney in retribution for stymying the soldiers' mesothelioma claims, the son's rationale for murdering the captain is not related to the asbestos exposure. Rather, he justifies it as an honour killing, avenging his father for the denied commendation. When he is trapped by the police, Kandes decides to die in a gunfight rather than be captured.

All three novels find their resolution in sacrifice and confession: Cauto is killed by Campbell's boyfriend when he confesses to their conspiracy to kill Klamm; Peter is killed by Massey when he tries to protect Clara, after Massey confesses; Adrian Kandes is killed by the police after he reveals the conspiracy to murder the lawyers. These deaths appear to offer some resolution to the deep disquiet produced by each novel's engagement with historical violence, jealousy or sullied honor, their 'self-interpretations', clarifying all actions and motivations, signed and sealed with the blood of a scapegoat. For us, however, it is remarkable that each novel marginalises the asbestos that, at first, appeared so central to their plots.

Although Klamm's history with asbestos mining seems as likely a motive for his murder as any, Kunzmann's exploration, through Mason, of a parallel plot involving Claudette, proves that this link is more illuminating when addressed as a reflection on Apartheid's historical cycles of racialised violence. Although Obed's father dies as a result of injuries sustained in an asbestos mine, it is the institutionalised lack of care, exhibited by Cauto and Klamm, that motivates Obed to seek revenge. Similarly, the motives of the vengeful son in Boyd's *Death Sentence* are not, as they first appear, explained by the asbestos exposure suffered by his father's friends, but, again, by his regard for his father's posthumous honor. At risk of conflating motive with means, we might find a parallel in Massey's decision to interrupt his own, slow murder of Norman when he preempts the work of the asbestos and slashes Norman's throat. Indeed, each novel dismisses asbestos in the final moment of revelation. Like Blackwood's asbestos hair, it appears only to disappear, once it has served its purpose.

The conclusion of each story swerves away from the problems created by the asbestos itself, preferring to resolve their plots with more intimate, affective motives, like revenge, greed or jealousy. If, as Boltanski argues, the genre's social function is to reconcile divergent challenges to social reality, then these exemplars are united by a failure to perform this recuperative work for asbestos's legacy. This lack of social coherence proves a useful site of horror, as I'll go on to show, but it also prompts us to look for alternative narrative forms to try and secure that indelible remainder constituted by the asbestos fibre itself, when it is stripped of its social function, whether as an insulator or as a pollutant. There is something inhuman about asbestos and its temporalities that shirks any conventional resolution of its ill-effects. The failure of these novels to contain it may be a measure of the writer's limits, or the genre's, certainly, but it also speaks to a manifest difficulty that the substance itself presents to discursive containment.

That said, our interrogation of this inhuman remainder should not blind us to the real effects its commodification has on the world-system. Here, the internal movements of asbestos in the novels still proves useful in demonstrating how cores, peripheries and semi-peripheries come to be created for the production and circulation of capital. In *Salamander Cotton*, the movement between the Johannesburg and Prieska/Leopold Ridge stories dramatises the separation between those sites where executive decisions were made about the mines and those places where the mining took place, and which are often still imperfectly remediated sites of contamination. At the same time, the novel makes it clear that both Johannesburg and Prieska were themselves semi-peripheries for transnational asbestos concerns, which were based in London but often relied on devolved, small scale operations like Klamm's. The social and geographical dislocations in the novel remind us not simply of those inequalities that mark a continuity from South Africa's Apartheid period into the present, but also the asbestos industry's tendency to rely on such dislocations to contain evidence of asbestos's health effects.

Whereas *Salamander Cotton* foregrounds the political economy of asbestos in South Africa, *The Long Way Home*, set in Quebec and with a significant asbestos side-plot, is remarkable for largely ignoring Quebec's long and important history of asbestos mining: the Asbestos Strike of 1949, which Pierre Trudeau called 'a violent announcement that a new era had begun'; the mobilisation of the Strike within the political mythology of the Quebec separatist movement; the continued support of the asbestos industry by the Canadian federal government as a way to mollify Quebec nationalists. Although the novel acknowledges the economic opportunities that asbestos offered Quebec – 'a godsend to a hardscrabble region' (376) – the asbestos it uses to guide its plot has been salvaged from an abatement project at the Toronto art college. Instead of staying with the mine to tracking changing attitudes to asbestos,

Penny breaks the potential parallel to direct criticism at the building trade: 'asbestos turned out to be the thalidomide of building materials' (376). When considering asbestos as a hidden harm, the novel dislocates the substance from its place of extraction on the periphery to focus on its role within the metropolitan infrastructure.

For Kunzmann and Penny, asbestos reflects anxieties about landscapes that bear the historical scars of large-scale, long-term mineral extraction, either by dwelling on the unresolvable conditions of these landscapes or by occluding these scars altogether. But for Boyd, asbestos is less connected to landscape than it is to anxieties about masculinity and empire. Given that the asbestos exposure event in *Death Sentence* happens during the Falklands/Malvinas War, because of the misuse of military authority, and as the point of connection between the murders of the army captain and the defense lawyers, it can be read as marking an anxiety, paralleling Blackwood's, about bringing the consequences of empire home.

Again, we find the novel swerving away from fully engaging with the consequences of the asbestos exposure it relies upon. *Death Sentence* resolves the hanging matter of the soldiers' asbestos trial not by granting them compensation through the European Court, but by suspending it in favour of a national compensation scheme aimed at service personnel. The historical veracity of this solution should not deter us from noting that this preferment of British sovereignty to European justice mimics the nationalist discourses that developed around the British EU membership Referendum in 2016, the same year that the novel was published. But, by emphasising the murderer's concern with honour at the end of the novel, it suggests, obscurely, that anxieties generated by empire are best resolved by precisely those discursive structures – honor, loyalty, patriotism – which empire tended to deploy most cynically.

When asbestos is presented as a clue, to explain how or why a murder is committed, or to mark differences in the security of savings or speculative capital, or to provide a naturalist explanation for a supernatural phenomenon, it curiously disappears from sight, often at the moment when explaining it might prove too demanding on the reader's understanding of its social function. I have already intimated that something about this challenge discloses asbestos's resistance to recuperation within a social functionalism. Something was already, decidedly queer about asbestos, before the health concerns were made public, or even known; before it was heralded as a magic mineral; before any of the social discourses that have already resolved its meaning for miners and factory workers, for boiler engineers, plumbers and electricians, for DIY specialists, school teachers, health professionals or service personnel, or for all their families and carers. Given this queer condition, it is perhaps unsurprising that, of the three genres I have mentioned, it is horror that seems best adapted to deal with asbestos's social meaning.

The Asbestos Ghost Story

In keeping with my transnational comparison, I conclude with two haunted town novels that consider the legacy of asbestos mining in Canada and Australia, in particular Asbestos (now Val-des-Sources) in Cassie Bérard's *Qu'il est bon de se noyer* (2016) and Wittenoom in Lois Murphy's *Soon* (2018).[30] Set in 2012, when the Quebec Government was contemplating a bailout that would reopen Asbestos's Jeffrey Mine, Bérard's *How Good it is to Drown* tells the story of Jacinthe, a young woman who returns to Asbestos years after her brother, Alec, went missing. Jacinthe's story is punctuated by accounts of unexplained drownings, starting with an incident involving three children, in the surrounding area. These remind her not only of Alec's disappearance, but her own childhood experience of nearly drowning. Drowning, Bérard makes clear, is an analogue for the asbestos-related diseases that have struck down so many in the town: when she comes to describe her grandfather's death by mesothelioma in her afterward, she calls it 'a drowning that would last for months' (315). Both rely on suffocation, as Jacinthe observes when, visiting her own grandfather's house, she is enveloped in dust ['la poussière m'ont enveloppée'] and 'I was suffocating, I was suffocating as if I had been struggling underwater, in the ocean, anywhere, drowning' (34). In these moments of exposure, we recall both Jacinthe's memories of playing with fibrous rocks at her grandfather's house or climbing over asbestos tailings with her brother and her tendency to cough, a sign of incipient disease, whenever she exerts herself.

Bérard comes close to diagnosing Jacinthe's cough when, near the end of the novel, an asbestos abatement worker tells her that the chalet she wants to rent has been insulated with asbestos-contaminated vermiculite: 'there's asbestos, my pet, coughs the old man' (295). But Jacinthe turns away from this explanation: remembering a moment when running with her brother, their pockets full of asbestos rocks, she decides that 'the speed and the nervousness took their breath away, not the asbestos, asbestos had nothing to do with all of this' (295). Instead of a full acknowledgment, which, we imagine, might bring asbestos together with Jacinthe's not-so-latent illness and the drownings, we are left with an ominous point-counterpoint at the end of the chapter: having just claimed 'I have always stayed away from the mine', the worker breaks down into a fit of coughing; 'the problem is' the chapter concludes, 'whatever you do, the mine never leaves you alone' (296).

Drowning helps Bérard to overcome some of the representational problems that emerge when trying to describe asbestos-related disease: it shortens the dying process from months, if not years, to a few agonising minutes and it simplifies the cause of death from the seemingly random placement of a single microscopic fibre to a self-explanatory immersion in water. By figuring such deaths as scenes of drowning while keeping their circumstances random and mysterious, Bérard turns our attention away from the vagaries of etiological process to the scenes where such processes take place, without immediately feeling the need to explain such scenes through the macroscale culpability of the asbestos industry. This strategy opens up a space where, without either burrowing into medical details or decrying industrial conspiracy, the reader can apprehend how unsettling asbestos diseases actually are.

Where Bérard imagines Asbestos as plagued by a series of inexplicable drownings, we can find its parallel in *Soon* (2017), where Lois Murphy literalises the ghosts often said to haunt Australia's most infamous asbestos mining town, Wittenoom. The novel takes place in an obscure 'former mining town', Nebula, whose inhabitants are plagued by a mist that descends when the sun sets. The mist attempts to lure the few people still living outside to their deaths, by presenting material apparitions of loved ones, already lost. Like Stephen King's *The Mist, Soon* imagines its spectres to be violent, tormented, treacherous and bloodthirsty.[31] It links their appearance to a group of grey-suited individuals who appear one day in black SUVs and conduct a strange ritual in the local cemetery. In a literal sense, then, the ghosts emerge as part of an opaque plot to remove the residents of Nebula from the land. In this reading, the 'grey men' signify the forces of capital that, through their arcane power, raise the spectre of environmental contamination. By associating the grey men with the ghosts directly, Murphy develops a clear trajectory between the 'nebulous' investors of capital and the harm these investments bring, thereby granting an agency to capital. Since the harm is supernatural, Murphy can strip away all signs of actual industry from the town, which would only complicate this causal chain.

Soon's entire relation to Wittenoom is simply a matter of paratext: it is only in the publisher's material, and in the author's subsequent remarks, that we find out *Soon* is 'partially inspired by the true story of Wittenoom, the ill-fated West Australian asbestos town.' Unlike Bérard's novel, where asbestos diseases appear in counterpoint to the mysterious drownings, the ghosts in *Soon* only remind the reader of Wittenoom's ongoing asbestos contamination when read through the lens of this paratext. In this allegorical reading, the grey men might equally represent the forces of capital or the government. After all, the Australian government has spent considerable time and effort in trying to eliminate the town of Wittenoom: degazetted and stripped of its townsite status in 2007, the Minister for Regional Government at the time, Jon Ford, gave as his 'ultimate goal', 'to remove all signs of the town's existence and wipe it off the map'.[32] The Manichean role played by the bureaucratic grey suits in the novel may equally signal the industry that originally contaminated the site, or the government that seeks to scare people away from it. This, like Nebula's mining history, remains unexplained by the novel's conclusion.

This ambiguity is, perhaps, less surprising when we consider how Murphy herself has responded to the book's reception as a horror story:

> it was intended to be a book about people, and their attempts at resilience [...] Ordinary people who have fallen through the cracks, trying to survive in the face of a force they can't understand or explain.[33]

Instead of horror, Murphy would rather it was classified as an example of *uhtceore*: the Old English term for 'the anxiety experienced before dawn'. King, elsewhere, approaches a similar sense of anxiety or dread as being exactly horror's point: 'the work of horror is really a dance – a moving, rhythmic search. And what it's looking for is the play where you, the viewer or the reader, live at your most primitive level.'[34] Whether or not we subscribe to King's vulgar Freudian notion of 'primitivism', his articulation of such 'phobic pressure points' serves to explain how both *How Good it is to Drown* and *Soon* open up a space where 'the burden of history', made intolerably large by the combination of illness, ignorance and necessity, can be displaced onto a set of mysterious circumstances that act out this randomness in ways that, if still inexplicable, are easier to understand.

Elaine Freedgood hints at the usefulness of ghost stories in achieving this end, when she considers how most ghost stories end with two distinct ontological 'realms': 'the one in which ghosts do exist and the one in which they do not.'[35] If the ghost frequently emerges in response to an unsolved crime that requires resolution, thus providing a relatively simple explanation *why* ghosts are present, this simplicity conceals the ghost story's reluctance to resolve *what* a ghost is. The ghost's double ontology parallels the double personhood of the liberal subject, necessarily split into an embodied, 'consuming, desiring, reproducing, social self' and an 'abstracted, formalized and spiritualized' legal persona (46). By refusing to 'give up the ghost', we might tarry with the material aspects of figurative ghosts or the figurative aspects of material ghosts. But, deferring the decision of belief or disbelief has larger consequences: 'the ghostly reference promises relief from meaning, from guilt, and from the burden of history that it avows and then displaces onto the apparitional, a category that is never resolved' (50). The ghost is a means of avowing a history that need not fully be resolved.

If ghosts are literal presences in *Soon* and conspicuously absent from *How Good it is to Drown*, we can nevertheless follow Freedgood in thinking about both novels as trying to find figures to represent an admission of history, without an acknowledgment of guilt. Héloïse Pillayre implies the importance of such spaces, when she details the range of normative meanings that survivors ascribe to compensation mechanisms in France.[36] Pillayre argues that survivors may or may not blame their employer for their exposure, depending on their career path, their trust in their employer and the legal intermediaries they meet (doctors or victims' associations). This reinforces earlier findings by Linda Waldman, who, in her comparative study of asbestos compensation in England, India and South Africa, established that cultural concerns with masculinity (England), family (India) and economic security (South Africa) often shape survivors' feelings about the industry.[37] Survivor affects, in other words, are complicated, ambiguous and may attach to a wide range of different objects. This complexity, we might add, is largely ironed out of the conspiracy narrative, where the ill are to be understood primarily as victims and the companies as perpetrators. Of course, this doesn't make the conspiracy narrative any less true or important for the larger case against the industry. After all, drownings in Bérard's novel do not simply replace the experiences of asbestos-related illnesses, which, although undiagnosed, remain very much in evidence for its characters. Instead, I think these horror stories cathect a deep uneasiness about the narrative solutions hitherto offered for the crime of asbestos. If asbestos is both utopian infrastructure and mysterious clue, then it demonstrates too much liveliness to function simply as the passive container of human desires: like the ghosts of *Soon*, it shrieks from the outside; like the lakes of *How Good it is to Drown*, it demands its mysterious agency be reckoned with. This may be why, when more mundane detective stories engage with asbestos, they shy away from its uncanny implications. What is clear is that this agency needs to be addressed in greater detail than can be offered by its absorption into sociological texts.

Bérard's novel presents us with a possible way into this configuration, via its complex references to Stéphane Mallarmé's *Un coup de dés jamais n'abolira le hasard* [*A roll of the dice will never abolish chance*] (1897). Mallarmé's poem famously exploits typographical breaks to create large sections of white space on the page ('prismatic subdivisions of the idea'). Not only does this control the speed with which the eye reads, it reproduces in its material structure the philosophical conceit inherent in Mallarmé's title: chance is intimately bound up with death, and no attempt to realise this relation through an action (by, say, throwing dice) will ever resolve all its potentialities (and thereby 'abolish' it). The poem offers no answer, suggests Maurice Blanchot, 'no other certainty than the concentration of chance, its stellar glorification, its elevation to the point where its rupture "rains down absence"'.[38]

One of Bérard's great contributions is to bring the material poetics of *Un coup de dés* into closer alignment with the role of chance in asbestos disease. Two moments, in particular, play on the ontological indeterminacy of rolling the dice. In the process of renovating her grandfather's house, amidst 'the friable matter floating around her', Jacinthe stumbles across a box containing two dice (253). The game calls for the player to throw until the result is not a double, when they lose. She commits to the game: 'You give it a go because otherwise nothing will happen; that nothingness will spread over the world, gestures of all kinds will become futile and suspect' (253). And rolls a double. And another, and another, and another, until she is found, coughing and covered in whitish threads, still throwing. The chapter ends: 'We can never, this is how it works, abolish chance' (254).

At the end of the novel, we return to the dice game. Here, Jacinthe has just arrived at the house where, the reader soon realises, the three children whose drowning opened the book are still alive and well. In a scene that leaves unresolved whether the encounter is imagined or remembered, Jacinthe is left in charge of the children, suggesting, perhaps, it is she who will be responsible for their eventual drowning. As she teaches them the dice game, one child asks 'and when does it end?' 'If you're lucky,' comes the reply, 'it never ends' (309). The ominous ending invites us to imagine asbestos exposure as setting in motion a terrible dice game, where one's only option is to continue to roll, to hope for doubles, to stop the nothingness from spreading, making all gestures futile and suspect. It also invites us to return to the configuration of the asbestos narrative, through the structure of the modernist lyric.

Notes

1. Luc Boltanski, *Mysteries & Conspiracies* (Cambridge: Polity, 2014), p. 3.
2. Carlo Ginzburg, 'Clues: Roots of a Scientific Paradigm' 7 (3) *Theory and Society* (1979), p. 280.
3. *A Spark may cost a Farm* (Ambler, PA: Keasbey & Mattison, 1917).
4. *Peter Rabbit*, dir. Will Gluck (Columbia Pictures, 2018).
5. Mavis Nye, 'Peter Rabbit shows Mr McGregor scrapping #Asbestos from walls while eating? Really?', *A Diary Of A Mesowarrior Living With #Mesothelioma blog*, Accessed 23 February 2021: https://rayandmave.wordpress.com/2018/03/19/a-diary-of-a-mesowarrior-living-with-mesothelioma-peter-rabbit-shows-mr-mcgregor-scrapping-asbestos-from-walls-while-eating-really/
6. Samantha McAleer, 'Is using asbestos a "bad lifestyle choice!?"', *Thompsons Solicitors Scotland Blog*, Accessed 23 February 2021: https://www.thompsons-scotland.co.uk/blog/28-disease-compensation-claims/2847-is-using-asbestos-a-bad-lifestyle-choice
7. Richard Brody, 'The Real Problem with *Peter Rabbit*'s Allergy Scene', *The New Yorker*, 14 February 2018. Accessed 23 February 2021: https://www.newyorker.com/culture/culture-desk/the-real-problem-with-peter-rabbit-s-allergy-scene
8. Tzvetan Todorov, *The Poetics of Prose*, trans. Richard Howard (Ithaca: Cornell University Press, 1977), p. 44.
9. Franco Moretti, 'The Slaughterhouse of Literature', 61 (1) *MLQ* (2000), pp. 207–27.
10. Stewart King, 'The Reader and World Crime Fiction: The (Private) Eye of the Beholder', in *Criminal Moves*, eds Gulddal, King and Rolls, p. 201.
11. Lisa Zunshine, *Why We Read Fiction: Theory of Mind and the Novel* (Columbus, OH: Ohio State University Press, 2006), p. 132.
12. Jesper Gulddal, Stewart King, and Alistair Rolls, eds, *Criminal Moves: Modes of Mobility in Crime Fiction* (Liverpool: Liverpool University Press, 2020), p. 5.

13. See Frank Kermode, *The Sense of an Ending: Studies in the Theory of Fiction* (Oxford: Oxford University Press, 2000); H. Porter Abbott, *Real Mysteries: Narrative and the Unknowable* (Columbus, OH: Ohio State University Press, 2013).
14. Guldall, King and Rolls, *Criminals*, p. 5.
15. T&N memo qtd Tweedale and McCulloch, *Defending*, p. 25.
16. Louise Nilsson, David Damrosch, and Theo D'haen, eds, *Crime Fiction as World Literature* (London: Bloomsbury, 2017), p. 5.
17. WReC, *Combined and Uneven Development: Towards a New Theory of World-Literature* (Liverpool: Liverpool University Press, 2015), p. 7.
18. Algernon Blackwood, *John Silence: Physician Extraordinary* (New York, Brentano's, 1910); F. Scott Fitzgerald, 'The Diamond as Big as the Ritz', 68 (2) *Smart Set* (June 1922), pp. 5–29.
19. Boltanski, *Mysteries*, p. 15.
20. Emily Alder, *Weird Fiction and Science at the Fin de Siècle* (London: Palgrave Macmillan, 2020), p. 132.
21. In this regard, we might consider Blackwood as proto-Fortean.
22. Alder, *Weird*, p. 132.
23. Roger Luckhurst, *The Mummy's Curse: The True History of a Dark Fantasy* (Oxford: Oxford University Press, 2012).
24. See Ranjana Khanna, *Dark Continents: Psychoanalysis and Colonialism* (Durham, NC: Duke University Press, 2003), pp. 257–8.
25. See Megan Vaughn, 'Colonial Melancholia', 37 (1) *Raritan* (2017), p. 118–28.
26. Laura E. B. Key, '"A Love-Hate Relationship": F. Scott Fitzgerald, Money Management and "The Diamond as Big as the Ritz"', 95 (6) *English Studies* (2014), pp. 654–73; Richard Godden, 'A Diamond Bigger than the Ritz: F. Scott Fitzgerald and the Gold Standard', 95 (3) *ELH* (2010), pp. 589–613.
27. Fitzgerald mentions asbestos in his litany of 'modern improvements' in his libretto to the musical *Fie! Fie! Fi-Fi* (1914).
28. Richard Kunzmann, *Salamander Cotton* (London: Pan Macmillan, 2007); Louise Penny, *The Long Way Home* (London: Little, Brown, 2016); Damien Boyd, *Death Sentence* (Seattle: Thomas & Mercer, 2016).
29. Cassie Bérard, *Qu'il est bon de se noyer* (Montréal: Éditions Druide, 2016); Lois Murphy, *Soon* (Yarravile: Transit Lounge, 2017).
30. On horror as a genre also adapted to discussions of world literature, in response to Bérard's novel, see Isabelle Kirouac-Massicotte, 'L'horreur comme littérature-monde, le cas de la littérature québécoise: *Mort-Terrain* de Biz et *Qu'il est bon de se noyer* de Cassie Bérard', 53 (3) *Journal of Canadian Studies* (2019), pp. 555–76.
31. *Soon* is heavily indebted to King, not least in its overt use of a mysterious mist that has descended upon a town and kills anyone caught out in it (*The Mist*; *The Langoliers*).
32. Ford qtd in Britta Kuhlenbeck, *Re-writing Spatiality: The Production of Space in the Pilbara Region in Western Australia* (Münster: Lit Verlag, 2010), p. 176.
33. Lois Murphy 'On writing "Soon"', *Kill Your Darlings*, 9 November 2017. Accessed 7 September 2021. https://www.killyourdarlings.com.au/2017/11/november-first-book-club-lois-murphy-on-writing-soon/
34. Stephen King, *Danse Macabre* (New York: Gallery Books, 2010), p. 10.

35. Elaine Freedgood, 'Ghostly Reference', 125 (1) *Representations* (2014), p. 45.
36. Héloïse Pillayre, 'Compensation Funds, Trials and the Meaning of Claims: The Example of Asbestos-Related Illness Compensation in France', 30 (2) *Social & Legal Studies* (2021), pp. 180–202.
37. Linda Waldman, *The Politics of Asbestos: Understandings of Risk, Disease and Protest* (Abingdon: Earthscan, 2011).
38. Maurice Blanchot, *The Space of Literature*, trans. Ann Smock (Lincoln, NE: University of Nebraska Press, 1982), p. 118.

PART II
CONFIGURING ASBESTOS

Genre fiction takes us a long way in understanding some of the more general assumptions related to asbestos. Since this fiction reflects dominant cultural perspectives, it gives us some insight into asbestos's social life. 'Commodities, like persons,' writes Arjun Appadurai, 'have social lives.'[1] Through asbestos's *social* life, disclosed in utopias and mysteries, we began to appreciate its value for political economy, first to preserve the health of the community and then as an issue to rally the community against. But these texts move their attention away from the material precisely when we might expect literary thinking to offer us some other way of understanding it. Over and above its connotations of utopianism or associations with corporate conspiracy, literature helps us to think differently about asbestos by emphasising its social *life*.

    This is not so far fetched as it might seem. In a casual conversation I once had with a boiler engineer, he called asbestos 'that stuff that comes alive in you'. By tracing a long tradition connecting asbestos to salamanders, I suggest that this throwaway comment opens up a bigger conversation about how asbestos, like the salamander in the late modernist lyric, is often caught between animacy and inanimacy, life and non-life. If asbestos life is indeterminate, this indeterminacy parallels the strange temporalities associated with asbestos-related diseases, where exposure and diagnosis occur decades apart. To offset this temporal disconnect, writers create a compensatory narrative by linking their moments of exposure, diagnosis and death, often with recourse to those ideas, images or logics best known to them. Such compensation is, of course, to be admired;

furthermore, it plays a role in more formal applications for monetary compensation. But such compensation is not justice, in the words of Scottish writer James Kelman. Some material change is needed. If literary thinking addresses an instability in asbestos's social life, as it will in Part 2, such thinking must be brought back into the world. This will be the task of Part 3, which will follow asbestos along its life course.

As I move from Part 1, where asbestos was discussed as the medium for human desires and anxieties, towards Parts 2 and 3, where closer attention is paid to the thing itself, I remember Appadurai's warning about tracking things-in-motion:

> Even if our own approach to things is conditioned necessarily by the view that things have no meanings apart from those that human transactions, attributions, and motivations endow them with, the anthropological problem is that this formal truth does not illuminate the concrete, historical circulation of things. For that we have to follow the things themselves, for their meanings are inscribed in their forms, their uses, their trajectories. It is only through the analysis of these trajectories that we can interpret the human transactions and calculations that enliven things. Thus, even though from a *theoretical* point of view human actors encode things with significance, from a *methodological* point of view it is the things-in-motion that illuminate their human and social context. No social analysis of things (whether the analyst is an economist, an art historian, or an anthropologist) can avoid a minimum level of what might be called methodological fetishism. (5)

Theoretically, it is humans who invest asbestos with value. To observe this value, however, they must follow the substance around. Appadurai's attention to the 'trajectories' of 'things-in-motion' anticipates my decision in Part 3 to follow asbestos as it moves along the commodity pathway, from mine to factory to home to dump. But, before that is possible, I want to consider the fetishism this might entail. As Peter Pels observes in a perceptive close reading of 'methodological fetishism', Appadurai does not sufficiently recognise the 'threat of the fetish to undercut the primacy of human signification by the materiality of the object'.[2]

Here, Pels builds on William Pietz's genealogy of the fetish, which locates its emergence in 'the cross-cultural spaces of the coast of West Africa during the sixteenth and seventeenth centuries'.[3] Far from identifying an essential condition of African animist religious practice, the fetish is specific to 'the problematic of the social value of material object as revealed in situations formed by the encounter of radically heterogenous social systems' (7). These conditions combine to grant the fetish certain important qualities. It has an 'irreducible materiality', in that it materially embodies itself, rather than representing another, immaterial body (as in the idol or icon) (7). It forges 'an identity of articulated relations between certain otherwise heterogeneous things' that also establishes a practice 'fixed by the fetish' (7–8). It explains away the difficulties in assessing the value of material things when that value is determined by different institutional systems (8). From these qualities, Pels determines that Appadurai's concern with the thing's 'systematic social life' downplays the fetish's role as 'an object that has the quality to singularize itself and disrupt the circulation and commensurability of a system of human values' (98).

Responses to asbestos come closest to fetishism when narrating its metamorphoses. Descriptions of asbestos frequently dwell upon its transformations from stone to fibre, or, when exposed to flame, from white to red to pale grey. On his arrival at South Africa's Asbestos Mountains in his *Travels in Southern Africa* (1822), William Burchell remarks upon the interest of Indigenous South Africans in what they called 'doeksteen [cloth-stone]', which has 'the singular property of becoming, on being rubbed between the fingers, a soft cotton-like substance, resembling that which they made from their old handkerchiefs for the purpose of tinder.'[4] The plot of Henry Herbert Knibbs's prospecting narrative, *Lost Farm Camp* (1912), relies on 'a shining, dark-green mineral with little white cracks on its grained surface," which can be 'shredded to a white fibre' that, when held to a flame, 'grows red, then pale to a grayish white ash, but [leaves] the substance unconsumed.'[5] Pavel Bazhov's 1947 folktale about the discovery of asbestos in the Urals has a needlewoman, Marfuša, remember a soft, green stone on Silk Mountain [Šelkovaja gorka], which, when beaten with something heavy, fluffs up like tow (broken flax prepared for spinning) and is called 'rock flax [kudeli kamennoj])'.[6] When Koopman, a character in Jim Williams's *Rock Reject* (2012), closes his hand 'around the shiny green stone and squeezed, grinding it in his fist,' he reveals, upon opening it, 'a handful of long, white fibres. "Metamorphosis," he said. "Fibres from stone."'[7]

When the asbestos is manipulated by hand, or hand tools, it metamorphoses from rock to fibre. Burchell, Knibbs, Bazhov and Williams each describe a social encounter, when a specific stone is invested with the wonder of the observer, through the skill and knowledge of its handler. Since the stone mediates this knowledge in its very materiality, it acts as a fetish object. But this value cannot be exchanged, since it inheres in the moment that knowledge is transferred: once the qualities are known, stones that are otherwise identical cannot generate the same wonder. If these encounters depend upon the fetish value of asbestos, they are unstable examples: the stones gain and lose their status as fetishes almost immediately, their status as exemplars contradicting the fetish's singularity. Most importantly, they, like all the literary examples in this book, are textual descriptions that cannot partake of the fetish's materiality.

Perhaps, however, they can help me to develop a mode of reading that approximates Appadurai's methodological fetishism. If Part 1 adopted the theoretical position of observing how humans encode asbestos with meanings, and Part 3 adopts the methodological position of following things in motion, in Part 2 I want to elaborate a fetishism wherein asbestos is singularised to disrupt the circulation and commensurability of human values across different systems. This will mean that, when I do move to Part 3 and the movement of asbestos across the supply chain, I can be more attentive to the ways that it breaks down across these supply chains, as a function of its fetishism within scientific, medical and legal traditions. To fix asbestos's metamorphoses to these traditions, I identify the salamander, the diagnosis and, perhaps most bizarrely, the figure of Franz Kafka as names for their uncanny relations. The salamander emerges in response to an indeterminacy that plagues efforts to categorise asbestos as an animal, vegetable or mineral product; a diagnosis forces the sufferers of asbestos-related diseases to address the irrational disconnection between temporally distant moments of exposure, symptom, diagnosis and death; and 'Kafka' raises the problem of equating compensation with justice for both that writer's work and the asbestos tort industry. Together, they imagine variant answers to three deceptively simple questions: what is asbestos, what does it do to us, and what response does it demand?

Notes

1. Arjun Appadurai, 'Commodities and the Politics of Value', in *The Social Life of Things: Commodities in Cultural Perspective*, ed. Arjun Appadurai (Cambridge: Cambridge University Press, 1986), p. 3.
2. Peter Pels, 'The Spirit of Matter: On Fetish, Rarity, Fact, and Fancy', in *Border Fetishisms*, ed. Patricia Spyer (New York: Routledge, 1998), p. 93; 98.
3. William Pietz, 'The Problem of the Fetish, I', 9 *RES: Anthropology and Aesthetics* (1985), p. 5. For an Afro-Atlantic perspective on this origin story, see J. Lorand Matory, *The Fetish Revisited: Marx, Freud, and the Gods Black People Make* (Durham: Duke University Press, 2018).
4. William J. Burchell, *Travels in the Interior of Southern Africa, Vol 1* (London: Longman et al., 1822), p. 333.
5. Henry Herbert Knibbs, *Lost Farm Camp* (New York: Grosset & Dunlap, 1912), p. 51.
6. Pavel Bazhov, 'Šëlkovaja gorka', *Uralsky Rabochy*, 7 Nov 1947.
7. Jim Williams, *Rock Reject* (Halifax: Roseway, 2012), p. 29.

3

SALAMANDER COTTON

In this chapter, I consider how asbestos comes to be invested with 'liveliness'. As Ancient Greek, Roman and Chinese sources grappled with identifying asbestos as animal product, vegetable matter or mineral element, their categories invested it with an animated inorganic life. Early modern science writers, from Marco Polo to Thomas Browne, attempted to resolve the paradox of asbestos' inorganic liveliness by refuting a common straw man: the fiction of the salamander, who was cast as a creature that produces asbestos (once known as 'salamander cotton'). Here, I propose to use the salamander straw man to name an incommensurable relation between asbestos's claim to life and scientific acceptance that it is an inert matter. Drawing on three late Modernist lyrics, by Marianne Moore, Yves Bonnefoy, and Octavio Paz, I show how the salamander illustrates the forms of agency asbestos exerts. Reviving the history of the salamander provides a tradition for thinking through asbestos's excess vitality.

Toxic Animacy

To determine the stakes of this vitality, I turn to the lyric, 'Pleased to Meet You', by Joanne Barnes, a mesothelioma support worker for the Asbestos Awareness & Support Cymru who lost her father to the disease in 2012. 'Pleased to Meet You' imagines asbestos itself as the speaker, 'I', who reforms itself as 'blue', 'brown' and 'white' (colours that correspond to the three main commercial types of asbestos: crocidolite, amosite, and chrysotile).[1] 'I' lies 'dormant', 'lurking' in homes and environments, awaiting the opportunity to 'surprise' the listener, 'you'. Underpinning its shifting form, then, we can identify a language that emphasises asbestos's latency: something is present but unacknowledged and unannounced.[2] Beginning and ending with the opening lines of the Rolling Stones's 'Sympathy for the Devil' – 'Pleased to meet you/ Won't you guess my name?' – the poem implicates responses to asbestos in a theology, where the substance is 'evil', causing 'all kinds of chaos'. The poem does not restrict this imaginative evil to an empirically acceptable target, like the industry, although it is mentioned. Rather, asbestos is understood to be doing something itself, on its own: 'I separate my particles', 'travel', 'roam free' and 'come home from work'.

The poem implies a need for a language of animacy when it apostrophises asbestos to channel negative feelings. The substance's effects on its victims feel too personal, proximate or immediate to be routed through a language focused on the uncaring channels of global capital. Asbestos's animus, the mode of its animacy, affords it a Manicheanism obscured by the impersonal language of accident and exposure or condemnations of corporate self-interest and greed.[3] As important as blaming the corporation is for the compensation process, ultimately it risks eliding feelings that the body has betrayed itself by housing the interloping material. By allowing the substance itself to participate as an actant, the poem responds to an unspoken need to have substances themselves evince a hostility its victims already feel.

The animacy implied in this excessive hostility is taken as a constitutive feature of the substance. But a further source of anxiety is, likely as not, the indeterminacy that emerges in asbestos's dialectical play between animation and inanimation. After all, the feelings asbestos evokes are so difficult to grasp because it is neither entirely animate nor entirely inanimate. This may be because the division between animation and inanimation is, as David Wills has shown, more fraught than it might appear. Beginning with John Donne's understanding of inanimation as, paradoxically, that which 'enlivens, animates, quickens, infuses life into', Wills finds in the word a challenge to think '*what is inanimate in animation*, documenting the extent to which *the inanimate animates*'.[4] 'The inanimate', postulates Wills, 'does not simply fall away, vehicled by mechanism, into the category of nonlife but continues to operate as an uncanny force across the divide that supposedly protects and defines life' (6). Wills's argument about inanimation interests me because it advances a conceptual frame for understanding asbestos less as animate than as an inert substance that mobilises animacy, troubling the ground between life and nonlife. Wills, like Mel Y. Chen, offers an alternative approach to animacy to that offered by Indigenous cosmologies.[5] Finding in the mechanistic philosophy of Descartes a starting point for a trenchant deconstruction of the 'physocentrism of the natural as prior to, opposed to, and distinguishable from the artificial' and a rejection of 'the oppositional categories of mechanism and vitalism, and the presumed inertness of matter', Wills elaborates a conceptual contradiction in animacy that mirrors Chen's observations on linguistic contradiction (7). I adopt this alternative approach not because I am resistant to working with Indigenous cosmology; rather, like Wills, I want to use an intellectual history of asbestos's ontological indeterminacy as the means to elucidate the epistemological problem of animacy.

Like lead paint or mercury, asbestos seems to fit into a special group of substances whose interactions with fleshy life yield toxic effects. Their material consequences are inflected by their complex interaction with a grammatical feature called animacy, an expression of the sentience or aliveness of a noun's referent. Chen's *Animacies* considers how the biological implications of lead paint and mercury evoke a feral consideration of linguistic animacy, given the strongly political ways in which both substances have been mobilised in racialised and ableist discourses. Such toxicants, Chen argues, violate implicit hierarchies of animacy. These hierarchies operate grammatically and conceptually, to reinforce the sedimented expectations that manifest through implicit bias, structural inequality, and more explicit racism, sexism, classism, ableism, and phobias about sexuality and gender identity. Such hierarchies can be traced at least as far back as Aristotle's *De Anima*. For Aristotle, life may be differentiated by its capacity to grow and reproduce, to move and feel, and to think and to reflect (characteristics of, respectively, the vegetative soul possessed by all living entities, the sensitive soul possessed by all animals, and the rational soul possessed by human animals). Higher order beings share the animate qualities of lower order beings, while also having additional qualities of animacy that mark them as different. Stones, like asbestos, or metals, like lead or mercury, occupy the lowest order of animacy, being essentially inanimate. But this hierarchy is frequently violated, demonstrates Chen in her consideration of the racialisation of lead and mercury, and for reasons that evidence the ways in which animacy plays across divisions between the linguistic and extra-linguistic.

Asbestos, like lead and mercury, operates as a substance with greater animacy than its place in the hierarchy ostensibly suggests. When lead and mercury function as toxicants, they violate implicit hierarchies where stones and metals are treated as either absolutely or relatively 'dead' or 'inanimate'. Invoking larger racial or ableist contexts, like the Chinese 'lead panic' in the United States or the controversial links between autism and the neurotoxicity of environmental mercury, Chen demonstrates how toxicants, with 'a potency that can directly implicate the vulnerability of a living body', challenge us to rethink relations where 'the animacy criteria of lifelines, subjectivity and humanness (where the human wins) come up short against mobility and sentience (where the toxicant wins)' (203). Chen's examples play across three main categories: words, animals and metals. As words develop animacy, they cause us to challenge the implicit hierarchies that subordinate animals to humans, and metals to animals. Chen's account troubles that standard division that often opens guessing games: is it an animal, vegetable or mineral? What makes asbestos a fascinating interlocutor for Chen's work is that, unlike mercury or lead, whose animacy emerges through juxtaposing their effects on bodies and discourses with their fixed ontological status as metals, asbestos's animacy is 'queered' when one recalls that its history has always been characterised by ontological indeterminacy.

Discussions of asbestos's animacy seem doomed to play out a theoretical tug-of-war between New Materialism, New Animism, Object Oriented Ontology, Thing Theory and Vibrant Matter. In my introduction, I mentioned how Iovino, Litvintseva and Cesaretti had used New Materialist analytics to link asbestos to bodies and their environments. 'The toxic hapticity of asbestos,' writes Litvintseva, 'operates by breaching of the boundary that appears to separate the insides of our bodies from our outward environments.'[6] And yet, as she notes, it is difficult, when considering asbestos workers,

> to distinguish [their toxic embodiment] from what could be thought of as a form of psychological toxic embodiment latent in the capitalist reconfiguration of the relations between human and environment: a psychological suspension that put profit and growth over health and survival. (161)

This difficulty stems as much, I think, from the desubjectifying lens of Litvintseva's New Materialism, a problem shared by many of the other object studies approaches, as from its comparative failure to address asbestos workers' interpolation into capitalism. Louise Green has noted how recent celebrations of vibrant matter and new materialism often risk recapitulating the animacy that capitalism accords to matter in general, in order to facilitate the circulation of commodities.[7] So, if it is easy enough to assert a kind of liveliness to asbestos, we still need to establish how that liveliness might help us to think differently.

Green finds the means to resist a generalisation of animacy in the fetish's materiality: 'its meaning is inaugurated at a moment of contact between different conceptual schemes and different regimes of value [. . .] It invites us to consider which objects have value but cannot be exchanged' (317). We can begin to see the outlines of a fetishism in the need to speak about asbestos's animacy, or liveliness, as something that emerges specifically through our interactions with it. Recall, asbestos is 'the stuff that comes alive inside of you'. Perhaps in response to the psychological suspension Litvintseva identifies, this fetishistic animacy emerges not as denial of subjectivity or personhood but as the means by which it is salvaged. As Peter Pels puts it, 'fetishism is animism with a vengeance. Its matter strikes back.'[8] Crucially, with Pietz, Pels, Green and many others, I want to observe that my use of fetishism is not intended to imply some kind of false consciousness in efforts to animate asbestos. If anything, it recognises a double consciousness in general attitudes to asbestos that is 'false and functional [. . .] a form of misrecognition *as well as* recognition of reality.'[9] Here, I follow Harry Garuba's suggestion that we think about animism less as an object in itself, a rigidly orthodox religious understanding of the world, and more as a means of thinking, a '"fugitive" materialist practice [which he describes as] a socio-cultural phenomenon produced and reproduced by particular institutions, employing specific institutional procedures that carry the imprint of power and authority.'[10] Thinking about animism as a materialist practice may be extended to asbestos historiography, which, as an institution, has always presented asbestos as ontologically indeterminant: from the earlier natural histories to the exposés of industry critics and the defences by corporate apologists. In this respect, it anticipates a further point made by Pels, that the Early Modern history of the fetish coincides with the emergence of the rarity, whose 'wonder' coincides with fetish's 'fancy' (107–111). Indeed, the function of asbestos as a rarity in these discourses, and its 'explanation' through its juxtaposition with salamanders, simply present different terms for asbestos's fetishistic treatment. Asbestos came to be fused together with the salamander in medieval natural history because of a popular misrecognition. But it also paved the way for a useful recognition of asbestos's animacy.

Marianne Moore's Salamanders

The paradox of asbestos is that it is both animate and inanimate at the same time. This incommensurable relation may be fixed through the salamander, which served as its textual fetish for nearly a millennium. Marianne Moore encodes much of this history in the middle three stanzas of 'His Shield' (1944), the first of which I reproduce below:

> Pig-fur won't do, I'll wrap
> > myself in salamander-skin like Presbyter John.
> > A lizard in the midst of flames, a firebrand
> that is life, asbestos-eyed asbestos-eared, with tattooed nap
> > and permanent pig on
> > the instep; he can withstand
> fire and won't drown.[11]

In the first stanza, the speaker had imagined adopting the protective reflex of the hedgehog. Here, however, she dismisses this 'pig-fur' in favour of wrapping 'myself in salamander-skin, like Presbyter John'. The protection this offers, 'asbestos-eyed, asbestos-eared', is not simply against fire and water. For, as the poem develops, the presbyter-turned-salamander also offers 'a formula safer than/an armorer's', a 'humility' (the eponymous 'shield' of the poem) manifested in 'the power of relinquishing/what one would keep'. Protected by armour as the speaker might be, Moore concludes they should also 'be/dull. Don't be envied or/armed with a measuring-rod'.

Moore's references to asbestos, salamanders and Presbyter John introduce a fascinating tradition, to which I turn shortly. But, before I do, I want to establish why it is that Moore's poem proves so productive as a starting point for exploring this tradition. First, it links my discussions of asbestos to a general preoccupation in Moore's poetry with animals, armour, protection and humility. Second, it invites me to imagine what affordances the lyric, as a genre, offers, as I begin to configure a new semantic pertinence for asbestos and salamanders.

'His Shield' has generally been read as an illustration of Moore's armoured poetics, at least as far back as Randall Jarrell's 1952 review, 'Thoughts about Marianne Moore' (later republished as 'Her Shield' in *Poetry and the Age*).[12] But, as Sabine Sielke has argued, 'the common notion that Moore's defensive discourse primarily serves to protect a self supposedly hidden beyond the textual surface misses the mark.'[13] Rather, the image serves to 'construct a subject by protecting its body', the armour being, as Moore herself would write for Mary Austen's *Everyman's Genius* (1925), 'impressively poetic. The moveable plates suggest the wearer; one is reminded of the armadillo and recalls the beauty of the ancient testudo [. . .] an armor in which beauty outweighs the thought of painful self-protectiveness.'[14] Armour, for Moore, merges the subject with their appearance, an insight one 'remembers' via animals that are coextensive with their armour, like the armadillo, the testudo or the iguana. Jarrell may have been ostensibly correct when he noted that 'His Shield' no longer trusts in armour in the same way as Moore's earlier poems. However, he misses the ways in which Moore's creaturely analogues (her 'animiles') were always designed to subvert straightforward interpretations of armour as protective of a hidden subject. Indeed, it seems that Moore's animals serve to reanimate innervated subjects, by suggesting their armour may itself be animated.

Dancy Mason, taking issue with the tendency to read Moore's animiles as 'animal collectibles' (Rieke), 'self-portraits' (Bazin) or 'postcards' (Jarrell), argues that 'Moore's animiles use figurative prosthesis (foreign additions to the body through metaphors and similes) to hyperextend her animal depictions beyond contained definitions of the animal, just as a limb or joint can hyperextend beyond its normal limits.'[15] Moore, herself, suggests as much in *Everyman's Genius*, since she provides the image of animal armour to illustrate the following explanation of a poem's origin:

> An attitude, physical or mental – a thought suggested by reading or in conversation – recurs with insistence. A few words coincident with the initial suggestion, suggests other words. Upon scrutiny, these words

seem to have distorted the concept. The effort to effect a unit – in this case a poem – is perhaps abandoned. If the original, propelling sentiment reasserts itself with sufficient liveliness, a truer progress almost invariably accompanies it. (339)

The 'liveliness' of the sentiment drives the progress of the poem, but only through 'reasserting' itself, as through a feedback loop. In my introduction, I pointed to Adrienne Rich's use of asbestos gloves to imagine how form acts as a kind of shield; here, however, such easy distinctions between hand and glove, protected and protecting object, seem less possible. The salamander-skin gives as much liveliness as it receives.

This is apparent in 'His Shield' when Moore switches the speaker's focus from the hedgehog to the salamander. The salamander becomes more fascinating when it is considered as a natural wonder that extends examples of the creaturely beyond the limits of reason. Moreover, when the 'I' (an unusual pronoun in Moore's later work), wraps themselves in salamander-skin like Presbyter John, they become 'a lizard in the midst of flames', which blurs into a 'he'. This metamorphosis is completed in the lines, 'the inextinguishable/ salamander styled himself but presbyter'. Sheathing the self in salamander skin effectively turns the I, like Presbyter John before, into a salamander, not through a process of actual transformation, but through the pressure the poem places on conventional syntax, a pressure we will see repeated in the salamanders of Bonnefoy and Paz. Using the animal is not, or not simply, an analogy in these cases. It fuses illustration to reality in a way that, like an animal's armouring, or, indeed, like the fetish, makes it impossible to separate image from the connection imagined.

For all the protection that armour offers, Moore's speaker wants to suggest that an even more powerful protection may be found in humility. Parenthetically, asbestos aspires to a similar humility in the modernist period: as it recedes into the infrastructure, it does not simply protect people from fire but from their anxieties about fire. Moore's use of humility also offers a useful point of transition to the legend of Presbyter John, since, in her later essay, 'Humility, Concentration, and Gusto', Moore would link the armoring power of humility to the work of tradition itself: 'Humility ... is armor, for it realizes that it is impossible to be original, in the sense of doing something that has never been thought of before.'[16] In keeping with the impossibility of originality, I turn now to Moore's antecedents: the historiography of asbestos, salamanders and Presbyter (Prester) John.

The Salamander Tradition

Iterations about asbestos from the philosopher Theophrastus onwards display a surprising fluidity as asbestos transitions from a stone to a plant or an animal product. Rachel Maines, for instance, suggests that 'descriptions of it in the middle Ages, and even well into the early modern period have mythical quality that would do justice to Ripley's "Believe It or Not."[17] When the 'origin story' has been replicated by these histories, it has tended to repeat that problem identified by J. Alfred Fisher as early as 1892–1893:

> Much has already been written on the subject of asbestos, but I have been astonished to notice the great similarity in descriptive articles which have appeared from time to time in newspapers – even including scientific and technical papers and magazines. The writers seem, with amusing unanimity, to refer to some old encyclopaedia, and reproduce, with various comments, certain hackneyed statements about the use of asbestos cloth by the ancients of Greece and Rome, who thousands of years ago, wrapped the bodies of their dead in this material, and who made dinner napkins of asbestos, cleansing them after use by throwing them into a fire, and then exhibiting them to their amazed guests.[18]

Both Clare Browne and Maines present histories that are more critically engaged with their sources than those targeted by Fischer's historiography.[19] However, they are still oriented towards the resolution of asbestos's indeterminacy. Maines's engagement with historical antecedents serves principally to refute historicist assumptions about the disease association in the classical texts. While activist scholarship asserts that asbestos diseases may be traced as far back as the Greek geographer Strabo, Maines demonstrates the claim has no basis (26). Browne, whose aim is less political, contextualises late seventeenth-century debates around asbestos's nature in the Royal Society of London. Nevertheless, she displays a lingering Whiggishness when she imagines that earlier anxieties around asbestos's ontological indeterminacy were resolved by determinations that it was a mineral. Instead of simply repeating this pattern of historical revelation, I want to suggest that efforts to resolve asbestos's indeterminacy might be understood as exercises in autoimmunity, whereby assertions about its nature could stand in for the anxious state of wonder that it provoked. This state of wonder is more readily identifiable in an earlier explanation for its nature: that asbestos was the product of the salamander.

As Browne demonstrates, members of the Royal Society were debating asbestos classification in 1684, as a matter of scientific conjecture and refutation. But there was already a strong tradition that sought to establish asbestos's minerality through refutation. In his 1646 *Pseudodoxia Epidemica* [Vulgar Errors], Thomas Browne aimed to disprove the 'common error' that associated asbestos with salamanders:

> That a Salamander is able to live in flames, to endure and put out fire, is an assertion, not only of great antiquity, but confirmed by frequent,

and not contemptible testimony [. . .] It hath been much promoted by Stories of incombustible napkins and textures which endure the fire, whose materials are called by the name of Salamanders wool [. . .] Nor is this Salamanders wool desumed from any Animal, but a Mineral substance Metaphorically so called from this received opinion.[20]

T. Browne aimed to correct erroneous understandings about the salamander, rather than asbestos, which would be the focus of the textile explorations of the Royal Society. In order to reappraise the mythology that had accumulated around the animal, from both 'great antiquity' and 'frequent, and not contemptible testimony', he turns to the asbestos association because it presents the salamander's flame-retardant qualities as correlative to, and therefore potentially, co-extensive with the mineral's. Tellingly, he first iterates sources that speak of salamanders and then of asbestos, but, since the sources are frequently the same, the impression this leaves the reader is that these parallels reflect connections the source materials themselves did, or should have, made, which is by no means the case. If T. Browne's method echoed the style of classical and medieval historiography (i.e. presenting a taxonomy of sources), Marco Polo had already disputed the conjunction on the basis of claims to direct experience in his *Livre des Merveilles du Monde* (c. 1300), also known as *The Travels of Marco Polo*:

And you must know that in the same mountain there is a vein of the substance from which Salamander is made. For the real truth is that the Salamander is no beast, as they allege in our part of the world, but is a substance found in the earth; and I will tell you about it.[21]

Both T. Browne and Marco Polo reference the common, and faulty, understanding that salamanders and asbestos are, somehow, folded together, whether the salamander produces asbestos ('desumed from any Animal'), or may be identified as asbestos itself, 'as they allege'. Both suggest that the asbestos/salamander relation does function 'metaphorically', but that the metaphor has been misapprehended as identifying the substance's true nature. So, while they avow the ontological indeterminacy that I will presently trace in earlier natural histories of asbestos, they also seek to dispute this indeterminacy by presenting the 'real truth'. Behind their claims about the asbestos/salamander relation, however, lies a convoluted history of fake narratives.

In the Natural Histories, asbestos is recognised to be a rather odd duck. Theophrastus's *On Stones* (ca. 300 BCE), asbestos is given as 'a stone which was like rotten wood in appearance. Whenever oil was poured on it, it burnt, but when the oil had been used up, the stone stopped burning, as if it were itself unaffected.'[22] An earlier tradition in Chinese history had already identified asbestos as a linen, including in the *Liezi* (c. 400 BC).[23] When Pliny the Elder similarly describes asbestos as a 'live linen', he suggests that asbestos cloths (*asbestinon*) might be sewn from something constitutively different from the asbestos gemstones (*amiantus*) he mentions elsewhere.[24] In Book 19, on flax, he describes it as a 'plant [that] grows in the deserts and sun-scorched regions of India where no rain falls, the haunts of deadly snakes, and it is habituated to living in burning heat', while in Book 37, on gemstones, asbestos is described as coming from the mountains of Arcadia and being of a red colour. In Book 36, on stones, Pliny associates asbestos with magic: 'Amiantus resembles alumen in appearance, and suffers no diminution from the action of fire. This substance effectually counteracts all noxious spells, those wrought by magicians in particular'. The ontological difference Pliny marks between *amiantus* and *asbestinon*, which simply identifies 'raw' asbestos and its 'woven' state, would prove to be a recurrent confusion that only became more confusing as associations with salamanders developed.

At the same time, the connotations with magic, parsed by Pliny in Book 36, would find its correlative in other traditions. Ko Hung, in 320 CE, named asbestos alongside gold and cinnabar as highly esteemed traditional Chinese medicines for 'an eternal life'.[25] If, for Pliny and Ko Hung, asbestos had intrinsic powers of protection and preservation, when Augustine writes of asbestos, in Chapter 5, Book 21 of *The City of God*, it is more useful for its associative significance: he uses it as an exemplar for his argument that God performs miracles, under the heading 'That there are many things which reason cannot account for, and which are nevertheless true.'[26] For Augustine, 'there is a stone found in Arcadia, and called asbestos, because once lit, it cannot be put out'. Since marvels such as these cannot be explained by reason, it follows that reason's inability to explain God's miracles is not a sufficient basis to argue their inexistence.

Augustine's 'confusion', as Maines calls it, that asbestos will burn forever once lit, continues in the works of Isidore of Seville, Marbode of Rennes and Albertus Magnus, and on through the patristics. Its origins, however, are less interesting to me than its context: Book 21 of *The City of God* aims to examine the fiery punishment that awaits inhabitants of the City of God's counterpart, the City of the Devil. If a stone that burns is conceivable, so, too, might be the punishment by fire that awaits the sinner. It must then also be possible for bodies to survive indefinite immersion in fire. By way of evidence, Augustine refers to salamanders, three chapters earlier: in 'springs of water so hot that no one can put his hand in it with impunity a species of worm is found, which not only lives there, but cannot live elsewhere' (404). These 'salamanders', he continues in Chapter 4, provide sufficiently convincing examples that 'everything which burns is not consumed' (406). Critically, Augustine does not relate salamanders to asbestos, even if their juxtaposition, in Book 21's theological argument about eternal flame, explains subsequent assumptions that he did.

In *Asbest in der Vormoderne* [*Asbestos in the Pre-Modern*], Jan Ulrich Büttner tracks the salamander/asbestos interface over the long Middle Ages.[27] *Contra* T. Browne, he demonstrates that the association is not definitively made until the appearance of the Letter of Prester John (ca. 1165) and the consolidation of the *Roman d'Alixandre* by Alexandre of Paris (ca. 1180). From these two, apparently independent sources, traces of the association proliferate in both courtly poetry and natural history through the later twelfth and early thirteenth centuries. This dual reception may be explained, Büttner notes, by the ambiguities surrounding the Letter, in particular, which would later find its way into Moore's poem. Written in the form of a communique between the Byzantine emperor, Manuel Comnenus, and a Christian priest-king ruling over a hitherto unknown kingdom in Central Asia, the Letter claimed to detail the many wonders of the kingdom. The source of confusion about salamanders and asbestos may be found in this passage:

> In one of our lands, hight Zone, are worms called in our tongue Salamanders. These worms can only live in fire, and they build cocoons like silk-worms, which are unwound by the ladies of our palace, and spun into cloth and dresses, which are worn by our Exaltedness. These dresses, in order to be cleaned and washed, are cast into flames . . .[28]

This description would be combined with the accounts of Pliny and Isidore in the natural histories of Gervasius of Tilbury (ca. 1209–1214), Jacques de Vitrys (1220/21), Thomas von Cantimpré (1226) and Bartholomaeus Anglicus (1235). Marco Polo and T. Browne are writing against this tradition, and it is in the to-and-fro of these arguments that we can mark Moore's humble contribution.

It seems fair criticism to note that animal products, like wool, are not lively, whether they come from sheep or salamanders. Here, the refutations of Marco Polo and T. Browne actually instantiate the liveliness they attempt to dispute, even as Moore's armour reanimates her poetic subjects. By returning asbestos to its mineral classification, they undermine the metaphoric protection that salamanders, in their mythical intransigence, afforded as magical explanations for the properties of the material. Marco Polo, for instance, speaks of the salamander being itself the material, while T. Browne reckons its natural incombustibility is 'the more remarkable'. When associations with the salamander elevated asbestos in an implicit animacy hierarchy, its affective claims became more reasonable, for being explained by magic. By denying this relationship and insisting on asbestos's minerality, the accounts of Marco Polo and T. Browne threaten this order, albeit without registering it as a threat, since they open up the question of asbestos's incombustibility without proffering an affective or empirical explanation for how it works, beyond the marvellous.

The long conceptual history of asbestos and salamanders suggests the animacy tension is neither new nor isolated, even if responses (like those of Marco Polo and T. Browne) have sought to 'deny, disallow, disavow, discredit' such animacy. Such disparagements of animacy, argues Caroline Rooney, lead to 'a double disavowal: an anti-naturalism that seeks to deny that all human beings are a part of nature; and a certain hyper-materialism that seeks to deny the vitality or dynamism of matter.'[29] The salamander, then, emerges as a fetish for fixing this incommensurability to a material, if fictional, object. Since the fetish object is fictional, we must recover it through poems, like Moore's 'His Shield'. But Moore's poem is also part of other traditions: her own, which I have already discussed, and that of late Modernist lyrics about salamanders.

The Salamander Lyric

In *Theory of the Lyric* (2015), Jonathan Culler offers four concerns that mobilise the lyric.[30] In lieu of a general definition or taxonomy of essential features, Culler observes the lyric's preoccupation with enunciative apparatus (to create 'effects of voicing'); its attempt to be, rather than represent, an event ('to create the impression of something happening now, in the present time of discourse'); its attention to 'a ritualistic as opposed to fictional aspect, making them texts composed for *re*performance'; and its hyperbolic attempt at 'animating the world, investing mundane objects or occurrence with meaning' (pp. 35; 37; 38). Returning briefly to 'His Shield', we might note that, alongside the speaking voice that utters a number of commands ('don't be envied'), other 'effects of voicing' include the repetition of the 's' in 'salamander-skin' or 'salamander styled' and the 'p' of 'permanent pig' and 'presbyter'. For our purposes, I want to stress the sense of ritual utterance they effect, a ritual that recalls the salamander tradition to Moore's readers. When the lyric 'animates' the world of salamanders, it does not simply represent a metamorphosis where a speaker turns into a salamander; it actually performs this metamorphosis.

Moore's poem helps to enchant asbestos, to animate it, via the figure of the salamander. But it can also be located within a broader late modernist tradition of salamander poems, notably Yves Bonnefoy's 'Lieu de la salamandre [Place of the Salamander]' (1953), and Octavio Paz's 'Salamandra [Salamander]' (1962).[31] When put in conversation with the natural histories mentioned above, these poems are also deliberately returning to animist modes of mythopoesis, either from within so-called 'Western' traditions (Bonnefoy), or from an interstitial point of communion between Western and Indigenous cosmologies (Paz). Their respective use of the salamander, and its historiographic mutations, can be itself one mode of recognising a material that remains ambiguous in its interanimation.

In 'La Poésie français et la principe d'identité [French Poetry and the Principle of Identity]', Yves Bonnefoy meditates on a moment when he sees a salamander on the wall. He can 'mentally separate this tiny life from the other data of the world and classify it, as the language of prose would, telling myself: "A salamander," then continue my walk, absent-minded as ever.'[32] Rather than a mythopoetic beast, salamander, here, is a classification, a scientific refinement of a more generic lizard. Bonnefoy's response to the salamander illustrates a phenomenological process, whereby what is first apprehended as world is gradually distinguished, separated, through mental classification. But should 'this reality [the world] come together again',

> it is as if I had accepted, *lived*, that salamander, and henceforth, far from having to be explained by other aspects of reality, it is the salamander, present now as the gently beating heart of the earth, which becomes the origin of all that is [. . .] the salamander has revealed itself, becoming or rebecoming *the* salamander [. . .] in a pure act of existing in which its essence is seized and understood. (247–8)

To reassert, as Moore might say, the salamander 'with sufficient liveliness' in this way reorients the world, as it is received, around the salamander, which becomes a point of 'origin'. For the observing poet, this reoriented origin impacts the unity of place as a continuity and a sufficiency (comparable to its *stimmung* or attunement): '[the salamander's] essence has spread into the essence of other beings, like the flow of an analogy by which I perceive everything in the continuity and sufficiency of a *place*, and in the transparency of *unity*' (248). Bonnefoy's salamander is, therefore, the correlative to Moore's iguana, mentioned at the end of her response to Austen, since both function to return the poet to a moment that seemed to be lost, whether through the agglutination of words (for Moore) or through the classifying impulse (for Bonnefoy). Both enliven the perceptive capacity of the observing subject, through 'the flow of an analogy': the lizards spread their essence into other things not least because their association revivifies the meaning of 'armour' or of 'the unity of place' for poetic language. By subverting efforts to objectify the lizards and insisting on their surprising relations, both poets develop a context whereby the salamander's animacy might be translated to speak of asbestos's strange animacy.

John Naughton and Layla Roesler have both linked Bonnefoy's 1965 essay to the Salamander poems in his 1953 collection, *Du mouvement et de l'immobilité de Douve* [*On the Motion and Immobility of Douve*].[33] The poem that most obviously anticipates the later essay is 'Lieu de la salamandre [Place of the salamander]'.[34] Comprising an opening quintet, followed by three quatrains, the poem develops the image of 'the startled salamander [la salamander surprise]' who 'freezes [s'immobilise]/and feigns death', from its physical place, 'halfway up/the wall, in the light of our windows', to the force it exerts on the poet and other bodies: 'How I love that which gives itself to the stars by the inert/Mass of its whole body'.

Bonnefoy's salamander is not, however, wholly subtracted from its mythical origins. For, if the alliterative endings of 'surprise' and 's'immobilise' already anticipated the salamander's response as an astonishment (i.e. to be stunned), the poem goes on to parse this astonishment as a transition from consciousness to stone, as if through a fiery transfer of spirit: 'This is the first step of consciousness into stone,/The purest myth [Le mythe le plus pur],/A great fire passed through, which is spirit.' The Hegelian undertones refer back to the collection's epigraph, taken from Hegel's preface to *Phenomenology of Spirit*: 'But the life of the spirit is not the life that shrinks from death and keeps itself untouched by devastation. It is the life that endures it and maintains itself in it.' Whatever else we might say of the myth 'le plus pur', by invoking stones, purity and fire, the poem implies a connection to 'amiante', French for asbestos and derived from the Greek 'amiantos' meaning 'undefiled'. Such stones are themselves reanimated by the salamander, which is, according to Bonnefoy, 'allegory/of all that is pure', since even if 'Its gaze was merely a stone,/But I could see its heart beating eternal'. The stony gaze is reanimated by an eternally beating heart, maintained by the devastation that surrounds it.

While Bonnefoy's salamander seems to bear but little resemblance to Moore's, or those of the classical, medieval and early modern periods, both the poem and the poetics clearly accord a transgressive animism to the creature as it flits from reptile to stone to spirit. Again, this is facilitated through a syntax that violates implicit hierarchies, which might shy away from 'first steps from conscience into stones'. Oriented, as Bonnefoy and Moore are, to systems of thinking that conflate Western and the Universal, their salamanders remain products of naïve orientalism, albeit an orientalism shared by key Chinese and Sanskrit thinkers.[35] Insofar as the salamander remains rooted in the Prester John tradition, its exotic usefulness as an asbestos analogue still relies on the orientalism problematised by Edward Said. This links back to a concern I already hinted at: my appropriation of animism into a Western episteme threatens to undermine the real and significant work the term performs for cosmologies that do not conform so readily to these assumptions. In this regard, I am as guilty as Chen or Wills, neither of whom reconcile their respective approaches with the Indigenous cosmologies so often understood to be the source of this thinking. If the particularity of the linguistic appears to run beneath the ethnographic while the generality of the philosophical rises above it, both nevertheless risk making covert claims to essentialism and universality. Chen and Wills are vigilant of this risk and endeavour to guard against it theoretically. My own guide has been Garuba, who maintains animism as a fugitive practice. This concern becomes more obvious in my final example, Octavio Paz's 'Salamandra [Salamander]'.

Reading 'Salamandra' is, as with other instances of Paz's appropriation of Indigenous identity, not unproblematic. Writing of Paz's representations of Indigenous persons, Analisa Taylor remarks that it 'exemplifies an indigenista literary sensibility. Because indigenous peoples speak languages that are incomprehensible to the author [. . .] they are bestowed with an eloquent silence.'[36] Nevertheless, 'Salamandra' does offer a response to the salamander that is perhaps less Eurocentric than its antecedents: not, I hasten to add, because it includes Indigenous cosmology (which, Taylor suggests, is part of the problem), but because it effaces structural markers of preference or hierarchy.

John Fein observes that, in the collection as a whole, Paz abandoned the relationship between structure and theme that overdetermined works like *El laberinto de la soledad* [*The Labyrinth of Solitude*] (1950/1961), in favour of themes that developed through the intensification of the poetic subject.[37] Fein suggests that this intensification, and its concomitant 'destructuring', is managed by omitting punctuation and making greater use of columnar typography, both of which are evident in 'Salamandra'. The poem reads like an exercise in paratactic enumeration: each feature of the salamander presented as a discrete conceptual unit that evokes a particular understanding of the salamander. The overall effect of the juxtaposition is a salamander that metamorphoses in different natural, cultural or political milieus. Were the reader to be generous, then, Paz's inclusion of Indigenous cosmology in *Salamandra* might be taken not so much as appropriation, as a recognition of the salamander's place in Mexico's longer history.

All but one of the poem's strophes begin by invoking the 'Salamandra', from which each develops a different abstract, historical, physical or theological association. These assays reflect the diverse ways in which the salamander has been conceived in history, as well as the immense heterogeneity of salamanders that exist in the natural world (there are some 655 living species). By refusing to differentiate the salamanders in empirical research from those that appear in earlier natural histories and religious texts, Paz produces a composite salamander, bound to processes of becoming, transience and decay. Two strophes are, in particular, useful for our argument, since they invoke, respectively, the European myth of the salamander (complete with asbestos) and the religious appearance of the axolotl in Aztec cosmology.

> Salamander
> ancient name of fire
>   and ancient
>   antidote to fire
> flayed sole of the foot
> on hot coals
> amianthus amante amianthus

In Strophe 2, the salamander is recalled as 'ancient name of fire / and ancient antidote to fire'. It both names the fire and immunises the subject from it, represented in the ambiguous next line, 'y desollada planta sobre brasas [flayed sole of the foot over hot coals]'. If we endorse Denise Levertov's translation, the flayed foot might be an obscure allusion to Plutarch's account of Pyrrhus, whose toe survives his funeral pyre (mentioned by both Pliny and Thomas Browne). However, the 'desollada planta' may also be translated as a flayed plant, thereby reprising the confusion between plants and stones in Pliny's *Natural History*. This confusion is authorised by Paz because the next and final line of the strophe is 'amianto amante amianto', which Levertov gives as 'amianthus *amante* amianthus', but which retains both its strangeness and its relation to my argument if translated as 'asbestos lover asbestos'. Levertov clearly aims to maintain the repetition in each word's onset 'am', but Paz's decision to enclose his 'lover' in two 'asbestoses' is perhaps more interesting when we follow the 'ama' of 'amante' to the poem's repetition of 'Sal*ama*ndra', to the various 'll*ama*s [flames]' through which the salamander passes, including those at the end, when the poet suggests that if the salamander carves herself in flames, this will only result in her setting fire to this 'monument'.

The confusion of these contingent transformations find resolution in the thirteenth strophe of the poem, the longest and the only one not to begin with a salamander invocation.

> The sun nailed to the sky's center does not throb
> does not breathe
> life does not commence without blood
> without the embers of sacrifice
> the wheel of days does not revolve
> Xolotl refuses to consume himself
> [. . .]
> the Double-Being
>   'and then they killed him'
> Movement began, the world was set in motion
> [. . .]
> Xolotl the axolotl

The strophe details the story of the Aztec God, Xólotl, 'el dos-seres [the twin-being]', who, like the axolotl he resembles, metamorphosises to escape death.[38] When the sun stops, it is expected that Xólotl will eat himself, but he refuses, transforming instead into maize, then agave and finally an axolotl. In each form he is found, and, finally, he is killed, enabling the sun to move once more. Xólotl, Paz recalls, is a psychopomp, guiding the dead to their final destination. Like most psychopomps, this means he navigates between worlds and between hierarchies of animacy. But he is also tied to natural forms of metamorphosis through the axolotl, which is a neotenic salamander. Although neotenic animals generally reach adulthood without undergoing metamorphosis, axolotls have been known to complete metamorphosis if they ingest enough iodine, sometimes achieved through cannibalism. Thus the injunction that Xólotl should eat himself might also be understood as a charge to complete metamorphosis, or the process of becoming, that Xólotl abjures in favour of a Protean myriad of forms. Xólotl's abjuration prolongs a momentary halt to time in which the God makes free use of his ability to transition across apparently inviolable hierarchies of animacy. But the halt must necessarily be transitory. Like the autopoesis of the salamander's carving, which, being made of flames, consumes itself as monument, the fleeing God must eventually be found and killed to restart time and conclude its metamorphosis.

If this reading of Paz's poem is necessarily partial, it also appears to have taken my discussion off course. For, while asbestos describes a substance that is, like Xólotl, polymorphous, that, like Xólotl, move in temporalities out of synch with those readily apprehended by the human, Paz's subordination of the asbestos myth to merely one of the salamander's many incarnations suggest the marginality of the substance to any but the more superficial discussions of the creature. This conclusion is only compounded by Bonnefoy, who does not mention it all. Even Moore, who gives it more attention than the others, develops her argument as a response to Prester John. In following their explorations of the mythos of the salamander, then, my readings of Moore, Bonnefoy and Paz have carried me quite a distance from asbestos itself. Nevertheless, by what Bonnefoy might call 'the flow of an analogy', I want to suggest these readings open up an alternative approach to asbestos and animacy.

One of the problems I identified at the opening of this chapter was the internal contradiction between identifying asbestos's agency and its agents when considering the victims of asbestos-related diseases. To reassert the substance's animacy, I found a 'solution' in its ontological indeterminacy, realised philosophically, through the play between animation and inanimation (Wills), and linguistically, through the play across implicit hierarchies of animacy (Chen). Applying this solution directly, however, produces a further problem: that such reflection only distances our treatment of the substance from its position as an everyday object, where it sits, latent but inert. Moreover, when responding to asbestos, efforts to grant it agency must be balanced against capital, which, in its exploitation of asbestos, whether through mining, production, commercial use or disposal, or through the legacy of this exploitation, remains wholly responsible for its hazardous disposition. Whether through its inertia in the everyday or its subordination by the coordinators of capital, asbestos must be mobilised into animation, rather than imagined as already animate. Therefore, in place of asserting a quasi-mystical animacy for the substance itself, the salamander emerges as conduit for this animacy, an illustration that also operates as its necessary mediation. Precisely because the salamander is not asbestos, but is, in its natural history, wholly imbricated with it, the salamander can be understood to be the necessary analogue for asbestos's animacy.

Notes

1. Joanne Barnes, 'Pleased to meet you', *Asbestos Awareness and Support Cymru*, Accessed 23 February 2021: http://a-a-s-c.org.uk/wp-content/uploads/2012/01/pleased-to-meet-you.pdf
2. Hans Ulrich Gumbrecht, 'How (if at all) can we Encounter what Remains Latent in Texts?' 7 (1) *Partial Answers* (2009), p. 88.
3. See Eva Horn, *The Future as Catastrophe: Imagining Disaster in the Modern Age*, trans. by Valentine Pakis (New York: Columbia University Press, 2018), Chapter 4.
4. David Wills, *Inanimation* (Minneapolis, University of Minnesota Press, 2016), p. ix; x.
5. Mel Y. Chen, *Animacies: Biopolitics, Racial Mattering, and Queer Affect* (Durham, NC: Duke University Press, 2012).
6. Litvintseva, 'Asbestos', p. 171.
7. Louise Green, 'Thinking Outside the Body: New Materialism and the Challenge of the Fetish', 5 (3) *Cambridge Journal of Postcolonial Literary Inquiry* (2018), p. 317.
8. Pels, 'Spirit', p. 91.
9. Ibid, p. 102.
10. Harry Garuba, 'Explorations in Animist Materialism: Notes on Reading/Writing African Literature, Culture, and Society', 15 (2) *Public Culture* (2003), p. 268.
11. Marianne Moore, *New Collected Poems*, ed. Heather Cass White (New York: Farrar, Straus & Giroux, 2017), p. 179.
12. Randall Jarrell, 'Thoughts about Marianne Moore', 19 (6) *The Partisan Review* (1952), p. 687–700.
13. Sabine Sielke, *Fashioning the Female Subject: The Intertextual Networking of Dickinson, Moore, and Rich* (Ann Arbor: University of Michigan Press, 1997), p. 62.
14. Marianne Moore, 'Marianne Moore: Poet', in Mary Austen, *Everyman's Genius* (Indianapolis, The Bobbs-Merrill Company, 1925), p. 339.
15. Dancy Mason, '"Another armored animal": modernist prosthesis and Marianne Moore's posthumanist animiles', 1 (3) *Feminist Modernist Studies* (2018), p. 320.
16. Marianne Moore, 'Humility Concentration, and Gusto', in *The Norton Anthology of Modern and Contemporary Poetry*, vol 1, eds. Jahan Ramazani, Richard Ellmann, Robert O'Clair (New York: Norton, 2003), p. 995.
17. Maines, *Asbestos*, p. 24.
18. J. Alfred Fischer, 'The Mining, Manufacture and Uses of Asbestos', *Transactions of the Institute of Marine Engineers* (1892–1893), p. 5.
19. Clare Browne, 'Salamander's Wool: The Historical Evidence for Textiles Woven with Asbestos Fibre', 34 (1) *Textile History* (2003), p. 64–73.
20. Thomas Browne, 'That a Salamander lives in the fire', *Pseudodoxia Epidemica* (1646/1672). *Sir Thomas Browne*, Accessed 24 September 2019: https://penelope.uchicago.edu/pseudodoxia/pseudodoxia.shtml

21. Marco Polo, *The Travels of Marco Polo*, trans. by Henry Yule, ed. Henri Cordier (London, John Murray, 1920), p. 595.
22. Theophrastus, *On Stones*, intro., trans. and comm. Earle R. Caley and John F. C. Richards (Columbus, University of Ohio Press, 1957), p. 48; 87. According to N. F. Moore, in *Ancient Minerology*, New York, 1857, this passage alludes to asbestos. However, Caley and Richards dispute this, stating it more likely that Theophrastus refers to brown fibrous lignite (88). Since my own interest is in asbestos's disputed nature, this dispute emphasises the confusions around *subsequent* efforts to identify asbestos in ancient sources.
23. For an in-depth survey of Chinese sources, see Berthold Laufer, 'Asbestos and Salamander, an Essay in Chinese and Hellenistic Folk-Lore', 16 (3) *T'oung Pao* (1915), p. 299–373.
24. Pliny, *Natural History*, translated by H. Rackham, W. H. S. Jones and D. E. Eichholz. Wikisource. Accessed 24 September 2019: https://en.wikisource.org/wiki/Natural_History_(Rackham,_Jones,_%26_Eichholz)
25. Ko Hung, qtd in Maines, *Asbestos*, p. 26.
26. Augustine, *The City of God*, vols I & II, ed. and trans. Marcus Dods (Edinburgh: T&T Clark, 1871), p. 407.
27. Jan Ulrich Büttner, *Asbest in der Vormoderne: Vom Mythos zur Wissenschaft* (Münster, Waxmann Verlag GmbH, 2004), p. 51–61.
28. 'Letter of Prester John', *Selections from the Hengwrt Mss. Preserved in the Peniarth Library*, ed. and trans. Robert Williams, London, Thomas Richards, 1892. Reproduced at Celtic Literature Collective, Accessed 24 September 2019: http://www.maryjones.us/ctexts/presterjohn.html
29. Caroline Rooney, *African Literature, Animism and Politics* (Abingdon: Routledge, 2000), p. 18.
30. Jonathan Culler, *Theory of the Lyric* (Cambridge, MA: Harvard University Press, 2015).
31. Yves Bonnefoy, *On the Motion and Immobility of Douve*, ed. Timothy Mathews, trans. Galway Kinnell (Hexham, Bloodaxe Books, 1992), p. 140/141; Octavio Paz, *The Collected Poems of Octavio Paz: 1957–1987*, ed. and trans. Eliot Weinberger (and others) (New York: New Directions, 1987), p. 138.
32. Yves Bonnefoy, *L'Improbable et autres essais* (Paris: Gallimard, 1980), 246–7. Translations of the passage are taken from John T. Naughton, *The Poetics of Yves Bonnefoy* (Chicago: The University of Chicago Press, 1984), p. 136.
33. Naughton, *Poetics*, p. 136; Layla Roesler, 'Allegory and Event: Two Ways of Saying the Salamander in Yves Bonnefoy', *Trans—*, vol 10 (2010), Accessed 24 September 2019: http://journals.openedition.org/trans/378
34. Although Galway Kinnell's translations of Bonnefoy are, in the words of Herbert Lomas, 'poor' and 'the inaccuracies work against, not for, effect', they remain, unfortunately, the standard English version of *Douve*. Since my argument does not turn overly on their accuracy, I have used them as my source material. Herbert Lomas, 'On the Motion and Immobility of Douve by Yves Bonnefoy, translated by Galway Kinnell', 132 *Ambit* (1993), p. 71.
35. See Laufer, 'Asbestos', and Péter-Dániel Szántó, 'Asbestos and Salamander in India', 63 *Indo-Iranian Journal* (2020), p. 335–70.

36. Analisa Taylor, *Indigeneity in the Mexican Cultural Imagination: Thresholds of Belonging* (Tucson: University of Arizona Press, 2009), p. 12.
37. John M. Fein, *Toward Octavio Paz: A Reading of His Major Poems, 1957–1976* (Lexington: The University Press of Kentucky, 1986), p. 41.
38. Fein notes that these lines 'correspond precisely with a passage from [Bernardino de] Sahagún's *Historia general de las cosas de Nueva España* (ca. 1577)' (56).

4

ILLNESS NARRATIVES

The salamander, in my previous chapter, testified to asbestos's animacy by suspending straightforward scientific understandings of the substance. I justified this gesture by recalling a tendency to treat asbestos as if it was animate by people faced with asbestos-related diseases. Now, I address asbestos's relation with disease more explicitly and, in particular, what is taken for granted when narratives mediate this relation: how they rely on figures like the absolute victim and the resilient subject, how these figures evoke affective responses, like shame, anger and innocence, and how these responses mobilise anxieties about exposure, latency and financial support. In attempting to find a language coeval to these demands, such narratives try to reconcile death's finality with narrative closure. This closure presents itself, however imperfectly, in their recourse to languages of theology, scientific risk, and larger socio-political context.

To understand why these narrative subjectivities and their processes of meaning-making matter, I need to consider their place within a historiography divided, as I explained in Part 1, between accounts of exploitative corporations, on the one hand, and, on the other, explanations of ameliorative, social trade-offs. When asbestos's capacity to cause disease is addressed, however, the case for amelioration holds less sway than the case for exploitation. Legal cases demand clear demarcations of victims and perpetrators. Given how difficult it is to prove an exposure in the distant past, idiosyncratic 'subtlety' must usually be sacrificed for straightforward narrative causality.

In these narratives, asbestos and, behind it, the asbestos industry, provides an overdetermined agent of harm. In part, this may be a matter of overcorrection: although asbestos 'causes' these diseases, the time they take to manifest, the conditions that determine why one person develops an illness while another does not, and the rapid deterioration after they manifest, all present, perhaps, too complex a challenge for narratives offered the option of a much simpler agentive device. Far from resulting in a greater narrative ease, however, this agent proves too dominant: it deprives the disease sufferer of any agency whatsoever, turning them into absolute victims of circumstance.

In what follows, I consider narratives that, despite being framed within the context of corporate malfeasance, challenge a correlative tendency to consign survivors to positions of absolute victimhood. In the most successful narratives, this develops a tension between the agency of the industry and the agency of the sufferer. Some shift the history of industrial exposure to the background; others complicate the sufferer's knowledge or participation in their exposure. Many subordinate this conflict to other endemic concerns of late modernity, like precarious work practices, climate change or the rise of religious or identitarian fundamentalism. Although these strategies are aimed at the narrative content, they have a reciprocal impact on the form of the narrative. As they vacillate between favouring open or closed endings, these narratives develop alternative forms of subjectivity by either radiating out from the disease to its place within a wider socio-economic context or burrowing into the statistical, metaphysical or theological meanings to be uncovered within a sustained regard of the disease itself. Where, in my previous chapter, the salamander offered the means to mediate asbestos's liveliness, here I want to consider how writers draw on epistemic resources closest to hand to mediate the liveliness of asbestos diseases. Insofar as this tendency approximates a narrative tradition, it is in using whatever epistemic resources one has as the means to make sense of one's illness. In this regard, my aim for this chapter is perhaps more modernist in sentiment than in content, recalling the aim of Virginia Woolf's 1926 essay, 'On Being Ill'.

Modernism and the Illness Narrative

Woolf's essay is often read as a call to legitimate illness narratives, which, Woolf apparently claims, have been hitherto neglected: 'Novels, one would have thought, would have been devoted to influenza; epic poems to typhoid; odes to pneumonia, lyrics to toothache. But no."[1] This has certainly marked its critical trajectory within Illness Narrative scholarship. Reviewing this trajectory, Sarah Pett has noted that, contrary to this consensus, Woolf's concern is more with received modes of reading and writing. Since there are numerous examples of illness in literature predating the essay, Woolf can't simply be calling for more novels about illness. Rather, Pett shows, the essay posits a critique of a certain tradition that excludes the illness narrative as worthy of scholarly attention. This much accords with existing scholarship. Pett goes further, however, reading the essay as a creative manifesto to 'develop modes of writing that actively deconstruct the habits and preconceptions that readers bring to certain images and themes, and in doing so to open up the scope of meaning with which they are associated.'[2] Pett's recovery of Woolf's essay acts as a foil to the rest of this chapter, which, in a sense, does seek out novels devoted to mesothelioma, poems to pleural plaques and odes to asbestosis. The challenge that faces asbestos illness narratives is their lack of a tradition. Many of the works I discuss rely on historical, medical and legal narratives about asbestos-related diseases; they don't see themselves as contributing to a literary tradition. While some do make use of conventional illness narratives, they do so in ways that frequently elide the specific, and several, challenges of ARDs. While I point to trends within these narratives, they are, by and large, written in isolation from each other. Each is forced to craft their own tradition. In a sense, then, this chapter seeks to grasp these narratives together, the better to present a set of 'habits and preconceptions' for subsequent writers to 'deconstruct'.

When I first planned this chapter, I had thought the best way to present such a tradition would be through a sequence of sections about the primary asbestos diseases – asbestosis, mesothelioma, pleural plaques and lung cancer – and their associated texts. At first glance, their different etiologies do demand different narrative approaches. After all, asbestosis, an inflammatory response to the lacerations and scarring of the lung by asbestos fibres, develops over periods of prolonged exposure. As such, it depends upon the amount of asbestos inhaled and is progressive and irreversible. By contrast, there is no minimum threshold linked to the development of mesothelioma or asbestos-related lung cancers. Mesothelioma, a cancer that affects the lining of the lung and abdomen, is almost entirely associated with asbestos exposure, while asbestos-related lung cancers, like other lung cancers, are complicated by any history of, or exposure to, smoking. Asbestos-related pleural diseases, including pleural plaques, effusions and thickenings, are generally asymptomatic signs of asbestos exposure, connoting the possibility of lung cancer or mesothelioma. Finally, while asbestosis tends to develop in concert with exposure to asbestos, often manifesting as a progressive and debilitating dyspnea exacerbated by other factors, like age or smoking, mesothelioma and lung cancer have long latency periods (15–50 years, post-exposure) followed by a precipitous mortality soon after the illness manifests (people typically die nine months after diagnosis).

But, in the vast majority of narratives about asbestos-related diseases, the concern is not with the physiology of the disease itself so much as the ways in which the disease alters one's understanding of life. Havi Carel has said of illness generally that it changes how the ill person, and those close to them, experiences the world and inhabits it.[3] Carel's focus on breathlessness makes her work particularly appropriate for asbestos-related disease, where shortness of breath is often the first and primary symptom. For Carel, breathlessness alters the social and physical geographies that face the subject: the accusing look when caught coughing on a bus, for instance, or the flight of stairs, once easily navigated, that turns into an impassable barrier. Glynnis, the metalworking artist who develops mesothelioma in Lionel Shriver's *So Much For That* (2009), finds herself breathless as she 'gropes upstairs': 'Breathing – somehow whenever she inhaled these it was too late. The breath was too late; she had needed the air in this breath in the breath before."[4] Glynnis's air hunger, like her pain 'which had assumed an elevated position of awesome sanctity', provides a physical explanation for Shriver's actual concern: that, for Glynnis, 'all matters were of the same importance. So there was no longer any such thing as importance' (375). Her symptoms are less important than what they imply: a disconnection from her previous life. Shriver emphasises this disconnect with capitalised Befores and Afters, to highlight the attrition of interest that accompanies Glynnis's symptoms: the failure of feeling where once feeling seemed so important. The true resonance with Carel's work, then, lies in a concern with psychosocial impacts that might be generic to the narration of all illnesses.

Carel's work resonates with much of the early scholarship on illness narratives. For all their differences, scholars like Arthur Kleinman, Anne Hunsaker Hawkins and Arthur W. Frank shared a tendency to understand narrative as the means of ordering an otherwise unmanageable experience.[5] So, Kleinman notes that narrative helps to construct meaning, and Hawkins finds existing myth structures permeating these responses, while Frank develops a taxonomy of quest, restitution and chaos narratives to schematise different ordering strategies. Despite their undeniable significance in opening up a hitherto unrecognised field, these earlier, more schematic approaches tended to simplify narrative closure by opposing temporal experience to narrative order. The schema does not, as one might first imagine, caricaturise narrative, so much as the complex workings of temporality that narrative seeks to resolve. Ann Jurecic has addressed this complexity directly, by considering how illness narratives negotiate the difficulties of living with statistical risk, with the prognosis of an illness, and in pain.[6] This temporal focus resonates in particular with my concern with the relation between asbestos diseases and a phenomenology of time. Nevertheless, Jurecic's primary interest is in the generic: those qualities of illness narratives generalisable beyond the constraints of particular illnesses.

My approach needs to bridge this divide between the generic and the concrete, in ways that complicate the opposition, now quite conventional in illness narrative scholarship, between treating the ill person as a 'case' and as a singular individual.[7] 'A case', responds Adam Phillips to John Forrester's seminal *Thinking in Cases* (2017), 'holds, confines, protects and travels; it also categorizes and exemplifies.'[8] The experiences of Kershaw and the Northern Cape residents were turned into cases by Cooke (1924) and Wagner et al. (1960), as they became the medically acknowledged bases for asbestosis and mesothelioma. But, when people with asbestos diseases present as cases, they aren't just 'confined' by the case-based thinking of medical epistemology, they are also mobilised by anti-asbestos activists, company obfuscationists and policy makers for political purposes. The absolute singularity of each person's encounter with death, already defamiliarised by the diseases' 'slow violence', is doubly alienated: first, by medical knowledge structures, and then by political expediency.

These concerns can hardly be disentangled, as demonstrated in the legal, medical and political consequences that accompany the different forms of defamiliarising slowness taken by the different diseases. The gradual attrition of lung capacity suffered through asbestosis means that the asbestosis-suffering body will have made various, barely conscious accommodations, perhaps over years, in preparation for this moment. Mesothelioma, on the other hand, is regularly thought of as 'coming out of the blue', an unsuspected threat that, frequently, is only made knowable by a consultation with a physician, a test and a confirmatory diagnosis. While the temporalities associated with mesothelioma and lung cancer have more in common with each other than, say, asbestosis, they are distinct illnesses with distinct social and legal implications. If mesothelioma grants its victims an absolute moral and legal claim against the predations of profit-mongering asbestos companies, such claims are complicated for sufferers of lung cancer, where social stigma and shame around smoking affect clear-cut cases of culpability. Since industrial contexts frequently 'naturalise' expectations of occupational health problems, not even asbestosis, which clearly demonstrates the culpability of employers, enjoys the moral exceptionalism of mesothelioma. It remains a highly contested area of law whether pleural plaques should be compensated. Although benign, they present an increased risk of a subsequent, more harmful asbestos disease developing. By auguring a future where this development has become a distinct possibility, they do, in effect, cause damage, as has been recognised by the French and Scottish legal systems: people diagnosed with pleural plaques may develop chronic anxiety disorders. The differences that attend to these moral, political and economic implications indicate how difficult it is to formulate a generic narrative response to asbestos-related disease. The time frames of illness (exposure, manifestation, diagnosis and outcome) and narrative (exposition, complication, exacerbation, climax and resolution), the narrative setting (the place of exposure, the place of diagnosis, the place of treatment and the place of cure or death), and the moral concerns of the characters and their readers (including affective dimensions such as anger, blame, responsibility, shame and stigma); all these change according to the differing conditions of the diseases described, certainly, but the more so by the narrative strategies their authors use to organise their experience in or out of alignment with legal agency.

Gendered Exposures

The stakes of this examination emerge as particularly fraught in the story of Alice Jefferson, who, like my grandfather, worked for Cape Asbestos, albeit some 7,500 miles away in Hebden Bridge, in the north of England. Jefferson was the subject of a Yorkshire Television documentary by John Willis, *Alice – a Fight for Life* (1982).[9] Although a general indictment on the asbestos industry, the principal focus of *Alice* was on Jefferson's personal life after her diagnosis with diffuse pleural mesothelioma at 47. The cause of her mesothelioma was traced to a nine-month period when Jefferson, then 17, worked at Cape Asbestos's Acre Mill factory. The film depended upon a stark contrast between the profound life-altering, and life-ending, effects of mesothelioma and the relative remove of its cause, the initial exposure to asbestos.

Such a stark contrast risks the narrative disconnection that emerges in all asbestos illness narratives, since exposure is so removed from time and consequence. The film resolves this dilemma by attending in detail to the effects in Alice's life, relegating the cause to the small, but absolutely necessary, medically and historically endorsed fact that she was exposed at the factory. In Geoffrey Tweedale's summary, the film followed Alice in 'the misery of what was left of her daily life, on her tortuous short walks, lying sick in bed, sitting morosely in an ambulance, attending court, through to the final scenes in a hospice.'[10] This emphasis on the quotidian marked a deliberate change in strategy from previous efforts to raise awareness about the asbestos disease story, in documentaries like *The Dust at Acre Mill* (1971) and *The Killer Dust* (1975).[11] The earlier exposés had framed their narratives as responses to corporate malfeasance, with much of the attention focused on conditions at the mill. Testimonies, given in formal or semi-formal interviews in a set location, generally appear as background context. *Alice* was different, insofar as the documentary centred on Alice's experience, and moved with her through different contexts, highlighting the manifold ways in which the disease had affected her life. It emphasised the disease as a curtailment of her future as a result of temporary work in her past. This curtailment was all the more tragic because Alice had a teenage son and 5-year-old daughter when she was diagnosed. If *Alice* relied heavily on the sentiment that accrues around a blameless mother-victim, Jefferson herself became all the more effective as a figure because of her unstinting honesty. She is honest about feeling bitter, about hating Cape, and about feeling disappointed that she won't see her children grow up. She even worries if this disappointment is selfish: 'I don't know whether it's a selfish thing or not, but I think every mother wants to watch her kids develop and I'd have like to have been there and watched over them.'

Alice repeats temporal concerns that characterise other mesothelioma narratives. But, by emphasising Alice's current identity as a mother-victim and dampening her connection to her previous work at the mill, it also created a normative narrative that translated asbestos effects from the factory into the home. This might explain why it generated such an overwhelming effect on public perception about asbestos in the United Kingdom and elsewhere. *Alice*, declared Tweedale twenty-five years after it was first broadcast, 'remains one of the most harrowing documentaries ever made and also one of the most effective.' The director, John Willis, notes that 5.8 million people watched it when it was first aired and that the Rochdale-based asbestos company, Turner & Newall, lost £60 million pounds on its share price overnight.[12] These figures bear witness to the success of *Alice* in generating what James Jasper calls 'moral shock', 'when an unexpected event or piece of information raises such a sense of outrage in a person that she becomes inclined toward political action.'[13] As an activist document, *Alice*'s success marked an important turning point in public perceptions about asbestos. By signalling that there was a market for such narratives, it anticipated subsequent texts, which, consciously or not, have resorted to the same figure of the blameless mother-victim, often to the detriment of the character's agency.

Works focused on women's experiences of mesothelioma have tended to dwell on their roles as mothers, rather than imagining them as workers. To consolidate this distinction, these narratives frequently use paraoccupational asbestos exposure, those instances of exposure when asbestos dust was brought home by working spouses or parents on clothes or uniforms. The term effectively differentiates between the work of the spouse and the para-work of the victim, usually female, since exposure often happened when the victim washed the spouse's work clothes. Ross Raisin's *Waterline* (2011), for instance, opens just after the funeral of the protagonist's wife, Cathy, who has died of mesothelioma caused by paraoccupational exposure to asbestos.[14] Cathy is mobilised as a blameless victim, for whose death the protagonist, Mick, feels acutely responsible. When he considers whether or not to make a claim for compensation, he decides against it because 'it was him brought the stuff in the house. And he should have known' (65). Mick resists what he calls a 'windfall' because he feels he made the house unsafe. His self-recrimination is caustic: 'Him that brought it into the house and handed her the overalls to wash and here's two hundred grand, pal, take it, it's yours – you deserve it' (66). Mick's shame at having failed to protect Cathy plays an important role in his subsequent decline, which, in turn, will permit Raisin to explore the material conditions of precarity in post-industrial Britain. But by using paraoccupational exposure in this way, he recapitulates the pernicious tendency to eradicate any recognition of Cathy's domestic labour as labour. Not only does this downplay the agency of women in the labour history of asbestos, it imagines the asbestos disease sufferer as absolute victim, a reified condition further distorted by a legal system that, of necessity, uses the term for sufferers. Cathy becomes a sublime victim, denied even the ghostly agency permitted to male workers.

Given the tendency to reify female asbestos disease sufferers as absolute victims, it is unsurprising that 'mesowarriors', or activists living with mesothelioma, have adopted a powerful agency narrative, often in response to the moral shock that accompanied their diagnoses. In some ways, this agency parallels the 'positive thinking' found in the 'Pink Ribbon Culture' of breast cancer survivors and criticised by Barbara Ehrenreich in *Smile or Die*.[15] Following her own diagnosis with breast cancer, Ehrenreich wrote a scathing critique of her encounter with 'cancer culture', which she found to be 'an ideological force [. . .] that encourages us to deny reality, submit fully to misfortune, and blame only ourselves for our fate' (44). But, despite obvious parallels with Pink Ribbon Culture, mesowarriors remain distinct from it, and for reasons that often overlap those given by Ehrenreich. For mesowarriors, blame lies with companies who advocated the use of asbestos, rather than with themselves. The notoriously poor prognosis for mesothelioma means that, for many, the best that can be hoped for is a slight extension of time. This means that while many mesowarriors embrace the positivity of pink ribbon culture, they do not shy away from Ehrenreich's caustic realism. In the case of mesothelioma, and asbestos diseases more generally, the emphasis is not, then, on Ehrenreich's distinction between positivity and negativity, but on vulnerability and resilience.

Asbestos disease narratives tend to sediment this emphasis in one of two ways. Either asbestos disease sufferers are victims, without agency, whose condition demands a response from the main character (caring for, hurting, ignoring, avenging, remembering or forgetting) or they are 'heroes', who operate with excesses of will, commitment and compassion, exerting themselves to greater and greater achievements, even as their health begins to fail.[16] There are gender and racial inflections to this binary, but it remains markedly consistent as a schema, even across national, linguistic and generic divisions. Similar concerns emerge for the Australian miners of Tim Winton's *Dirt Music* (2003) and Michelle Johnston's *Dustfall* (2018), the Scottish shipbuilders in Anne Donovan's 'All that Glisters' (2001) and Suhayl Saadi's *Joseph's Box* (2009), the Italian pipefitter of Alberto Prunetti's *Amianto* (2012), the South African shopkeeper in François Loots's *Die Jakkalsdans* (2011), or the Canadian artist in Louise Penny's *The Long Way Home* (2014).[17]

The Poetics of Causality

I want to contrast this case-based schema with some examples where people with asbestos-related diseases use their knowledge, their 'epistemic resources', to mediate relations between their 'selves', their disease and their social conditions. Effectively, they reflect on the tension between their position as 'cases' and the absolute singularity of the fate that awaits them. To keep the stakes fairly low, I take a fictional character as my first example: in one of the episodes of Margaret Drabble's *The Dark Flood Rises* (2016), Teresa, who is dying of mesothelioma, finds solace in the language of theology and houses.[18] Drabble's novel unfolds as a series of vignettes on the matter of aging and the approach of death, 'the dark flood' of the novel's title. Links between sections are developed structurally and thematically, which is to say, by creating relations with characters already introduced, rather than by developing a noticeable causal or linear sequence (i.e. a conventional plot). All characters are placed in a network that revolves around, but does not centre on, Fran, the character who appears first and most frequently through the novel. This networked sociological approach, combined with the use of the literary present, a present tense used to recapture the essence of a story in retrospect, suggests to the reader that, at any moment in the narrative, one of the aging characters might be carried off. Fran's childhood friend, Teresa, is one such character:

> Teresa is dying of mesothelioma. At first she told Fran she was dying of lung cancer, an allied affliction, and as we all now know, commonly caused by smoking. Mesothelioma, in contrast, is a cancer of the lung and chest walls, and almost always caused by exposure to asbestos. Exposure often dating back many decades. Teresa had not wanted her newly found old friend to scroll back through time, as Teresa herself has been doing, in search of causation. She has been re-reading the past, trying to identify the source of the asbestos which has been at first slowly and secretly, but now not so slowly and very visibly and surely, destroying her. The school buildings, the semi-detached suburban houses [. . .] the council estate [. . .] the school in Canada, the house in Vermont [. . .] Who can say? She is not an industrial casualty, as were so many miners and shipbuilders. But she is a casualty. Of something. (158–9)

Note how Teresa introduces the less well-known asbestos-related disease via the more commonly repeated story that she told Fran: that she is dying of lung cancer. Drabble draws on a tradition, a sedimented understanding of the story of lung cancer, as the base from which to develop her innovation, her discussion of mesothelioma. Rhetorically, 'we all now know' and 'commonly' help Drabble's reader find their bearings in things she presumes 'we' know, 'in contrast' with this strange word, mesothelioma, which is a technical term, and, accordingly, demands denotative and literal language (i.e. language that explains). Because of the fixed coordinates of what is already known (lung cancer), and what can definitively be told (mesothelioma), the reader is prepared for the true challenge the passage presents for writing about exposures 'dating back many decades': the challenges uncertain demarcations of past, present and future pose for narration. Again, fixed geographies help to navigate the spatial aspects of this uncertainty: the buildings where Teresa might have been exposed. These act as concrete referents to Teresa's task: to scroll back through time in search of causation, or, in the words of Paul Ricoeur, 'to read time itself backwards, as the recapitulation of the initial conditions of a course of action in its terminal consequences.'[19] Clearly, however, narrative attempts to order her chaotic experience of causality and casualty render the aporias inherent within it all the more glaring.

> The extraordinary arbitrary nature of this particular affliction. It can be caused, apparently, by the inhalation, many years ago, of a single fibre, as well as by years at the coal face. A school teacher, pushing a drawing pin into a classroom partition, can release particles that, if inhaled, can kill. A single one of them can kill. Cause and effect seem to have no moral connection, no possible meaningful relationship.[20]

This is not simply a matter of a reversal that Teresa must experience before a final resolution. After all, Teresa is already well aware of her condition. Such easy appeals to narrative causality, such as those found in earlier responses to Illness Narratives, are here rendered meaningless by Teresa's challenge to the causality of narrative structure itself, which has 'no moral connection, no possible meaningful relationship'. Teresa's narrative distends across multiple possible sites of exposure in buildings from as far afield as Canada, the UK and the US, and at multiple points in the past. No single point of focus can corral it back into coherence; indeed, not even the degree of exposure can provide any correlative order. Moreover, as a discrete, if interrelated, fragment within a novel that is already episodic, the specific conditions of this vignette cannot even be placed in proportion to the larger narrative structure, since the novel already puts causality under pressure.

To explain the causality of mesothelioma, Teresa turns to theology:

> Had God ordained, when Teresa was born [. . .] that she should inhale this particular fibre? Had the unknown and unknowing agents who had installed the asbestos in the wall been directly or indirectly or morally responsible for the now imminent consequence of her death? [. . .] It is an interesting conundrum. Teresa has always been attracted to such conundrums, and the casuistry with which priests and philosophers seek to explain them. Catholic though she be, after her fashion, she is also attracted to the more contemporary ethical notion of moral luck [. . .] (159–60)

Moral luck is offered as one way to order this experience. Others include God's ordination and the unknown and unknowing agents. But these substantively different strategies are less important, I think, than their appearance in a series. Drabble creates a narrative connection based less on the lived continuity of Teresa's life (as, for instance, *Alice* did with Jefferson), than on the discursive continuity between the conundrum and its corresponding casuistry. Teresa's problem is rendered narratively understandable by the resources afforded by the discourse of scholastic theology, not because any one theological response is adequate, but because it orders the problem within the tradition of such responses. This is clearest when she alludes to perhaps the most famous example of casuistry: that parody of scholastic angelology asking how many angels can dance on the head of a pin.

> Teresa is fascinated by the example of the drawing pin. A pin is so small, so innocent. How many angels dance upon the head of a pin? How many invisible fibres did the pin release?
> And would those hypothetical builders have felt guilty, or even sorry, if they knew they had killed Teresa Quinn with a drawing pin?
> And all for the want of a horseshoe nail.
> Teresa feels sorry for the unwitting killer builders [. . .] and wishes exonerate them from any suspicion of blame. [. . .] She has learned not to blame.
> She has learned the hardest lesson, which is not to blame herself.
> Fran finds this mindset fascinating, and wonders what it may have to do with religion and faith in God.
> Nobody is to blame, but God. (160)

Like the sophistry of the innocent pin, the proverb, 'the kingdom was lost for want of a horseshoe nail' builds a chain of causality that registers large effects from very small causes. The want of the nail affects the horse, which throws the rider, who loses the battle, which loses the kingdom. But this chain of causality also throws up the aporia inherent in such chain narratives: when causal origins are too small or distant to be determinate, no poem, proverb or syllogism will order their effects. Butterflies may cause hurricanes, but who can say without the butterfly to prove it.

Teresa's solution to this problem – not to blame – does not simply exonerate mortal beings at the expense of the eternal. In this respect, it is not, as Fran thinks, simply a deferral of blame onto God. If God here stands in for the eternal, the relation Teresa sketches, between her 'luck' and God's ordination, may be better understood as a complementary relation between time and the eternal. Thought as a complementary relation, the eternal offers itself as a pole against which to measure the temporalities that emerge for Teresa, when she contrasts the uncertainties of her exposure with her scholastic efforts to reconcile these uncertainties. Accordingly, Teresa's descriptions of different chains of causality, and their accompanying distressing distentions, do serve as a lesson in 'not blaming': they 'fascinate' her, which is to say, hold her attention to particular structures of spatiality and temporality.

All Drabble's examples of 'conundrum' and 'casuistry', up to and including the proverb, recognise a latent absurdity in proportional causality. Individually inadequate at explaining mesothelioma's 'extraordinary arbitrariness', their coherence develops as Drabble grasps them together. Taken together, they configure a tradition of thought about unexpected consequence and improbable cause that extends from medieval scholasticism to the present. Making sense of mesothelioma's temporal absurdity is not about finding a single correct explanation: as Teresa shows us, each is as easily dismissed as raised. These inadequate responses combine to form a tradition of thinking that accommodates the failure to find satisfactory causality. Causality in the case of asbestos exposure is always, on some level, casuistry: arbitrary and liable to disruptive distentions. Teresa is not immune to such disruptions because she has deflected her blame onto God, but because she has access to a tradition that shows causality itself is characterised by aporia.

Now, there are very good reasons to be suspicious of this conclusion. After all, behind Teresa's hypothetical builders sit corporate entities that did know the effects of asbestos, and pursued its dissemination regardless, as is well-evidenced by history. Drabble's novel itself seems to have reached an impasse with Teresa's resolution 'not to blame herself'. First, it returns to Fran as focaliser, who immediately shifts the blame to God, thereby effectively obscuring the earlier, more complex interplay of temporalities. Shortly thereafter, the novel moves away from the matter of mesothelioma altogether. The two subsequent sections that deal with Teresa will adopt more conventional approaches to narrating her illness, emphasising instead the distortions of time that accompany her experience of pain and developing disability. Teresa's experience of time distends into what Alison Kafer has called 'crip time', a time that reimagines 'our notions of what can and should happen in time' and recognises 'how expectations of "how long things take" are based on very particular minds and bodies'.[21] Of course, Teresa's experience is not just liberatory. Like those more alienating aspects of crip time, described by Ellen Samuels variously as broken, sick and vampiric, Teresa's meditations on religious despair and physical distress, her dreams of escaping her body, all serve to undermine the sense of stoical acceptance evoked in her observations about causality.[22] These passages show that the conditions of mesothelioma are not quite so sanguine as the earlier section suggests. In so doing, they also turn away from the specific concerns of mesothelioma to more generic concerns with death and dying, displaying formal features similar to those described by Jurecic, Kafer and Samuels. What distinguishes the first section, then, is its effort to open up the aporia of causality to scrutiny. Drabble shows the substantive explanations of causality are, perhaps, less important on their own terms than in their being formally 'grasped together' and sedimented into a tradition. The problem of causality presents its own poetics, which I discuss in relation to three exemplary non-fictional accounts of mesothelioma by Stephen J. Gould, Jesús Mosterín and Christina Sharpe.[23]

THE MESOTHELIOMA NARRATIVE

Stephen J. Gould wrote 'The Median isn't the Message' two years after he was diagnosed with peritoneal mesothelioma, to tell 'a personal story of statistics, properly interpreted, as profoundly nurturant and life-giving'. Playing on Marshall McLuhan's oft-quoted phrase, 'the medium is the message' from *Understanding Media: The Extensions of Man* (1964), the essay contrasts Gould's immediate impression of his statistical chances of survival to his more measured response to the information the statistics actually conveyed.[24] At the time, the median figure for the period from diagnosis to death was eight months. But this median, or central tendency, was, Gould understood, inadequate to describe his own experience, which was subject to variation. Statistics, Gould notes, tend to be reified, treated as 'hard "realities"', whereas 'the variation that permits their calculation [is viewed] as a set of transient and imperfect measurements of this hidden essence'. In fact, the contrary is true: 'variation itself is nature's only irreducible essence. Variation is the hard reality, not a set of imperfect measures for a central tendency. Means and medians are the abstractions.' In an expanded version of the essay, written for his popular science book, *Full House*, Gould explains the differences between the three major measures for central tendency, mean, mode and median: 'the mean, or average obtained by adding all the values and dividing by the number of cases'; 'the mode, or most common value'; and the median, 'the halfway point in a graded array of values. In any population, half the individuals will be below the median, and half above' (49). 'The median correctly informs us that half the afflicted population dies within eight months of diagnosis', but if you do not fall into that first half, the tailing off period after eight months may 'extend out forever, or at least into extreme old age' (49). The message apparently conveyed by the median – you will die in eight months – was therefore not true, or at least unlikely, for Gould, since his variable factors all pointed to his position in the long tail. Indeed, Gould died some twenty years after his diagnosis, and from a different cancer.

In a sensitive critique of the essay, Jurecic notes it may be 'one of the most widely read risk narratives of the twentieth century' and that it 'appears on many cancer-support Websites', but that it tends to be misread.[25] Gould's positive outcome obscures his argument about statistics: 'although the point of Gould's essay is that he recognized that the particularities of his case meant his individual outcome was unlikely to fall within the median range, readers generalize from his experience to their own. The essay's message becomes: if Stephen Jay Gould can beat the odds, so can I' (36). Jurecic is right to note that the essay's iterations, as an anecdote that supports a generalised hopefulness, runs counter to the comfort statistical knowledge brought Gould as an individual. The essay has certainly been decoupled from its specific account of mesothelioma statistics: versions of the essay appear on websites related to kidney cancer, alternative medicine, graphic sociology, radiation oncology and science advocacy. But it is perhaps reductive to claim, with Jurecic, his 'narrative allows readers to avoid the full complexities of living with risk and in prognosis' (36), since such a claim denies the elusive irresponsibility inherent in the medium Gould uses to communicate his 'median': the essay.

The essay form is primarily an exploration of the self, conducted in public. Jonathan Franzen suggests the essay is 'something hazarded, not definitive, not authorative', but that it may be judged by its attempt to take the measure of the writing self and invest the complexities of that self with substance.[26] By addressing the essay form more explicitly, Jurecic might have expanded on the space that exists between 'the point' of Gould's essay and its wide misreading. For Gould writes the essay to connect his own immediate, visceral reaction to the median outcome – 'I sat stunned for about fifteen minutes' – to his later search for solace in statistical variation. By reading Gould's essay for its 'promise' of beating the odds, other survivors misread their own potential salvation as Jurecic argues. But Jurecic does not consider how Gould's message of promise measures itself against his essay's primary interlocutor: a 'mesothelioma discourse' marked by grim finality and corporate victimhood in the medical, legal and historical scholarship about the disease. Gould's statistical insight challenges the tone of finality in this discourse because, in his case, it does not apply. In asserting an agentive response to statistics, moreover, Gould implicitly attacks another actor in mesothelioma discourse: the implicit loss of agency associated with a diagnosis of mesothelioma. When mesothelioma sufferers speak of the anger they feel towards the asbestos companies, in part they are referring to the experience of a loss of agency to those corporate interests that disseminated the disease-causing asbestos. Gould's silence about corporate interests notwithstanding, his essay offers an alternative to either activism or victimhood by suggesting alternatives for asserting agency: in his case, through more reading. Gould introduces a distinctive mesothelioma discourse into generic illness narrative, while also opening up an alternative multimedia narrative to the story of ARDs. The median may not be the message, but the medium certainly has something to tell us.

In *Understanding Media*, McLuhan identifies a medium as 'any extension of ourselves' (7). So, in addition to the expected litany of media – television, film, books, newspapers and radio – he includes cars, language and the light bulb. The expository power of this move is to be found in the comparatively straightforward shift in focus: if most media, conventionally understood, distract us with their content, by expanding the definition to include media 'without content' that, nevertheless, create new environments (like light bulbs), media does not simply offer an alternative to the message, but the message itself. McLuhan overextends his analysis, by considering even the content of transmissions to be relics of older media – television transmits, as its message, radio; radio, print; and print, the written form – and by reifying media itself without due regard for its parts, whether semiotic, technological or ideological. But his work offers a point of connection between the solutions that statistics present for Gould or tradition for Drabble, and what Ricoeur calls the prefiguration, configuration and refiguration of the pre-narrative, or anticipated, story, its narration, and its reception by readers. Or, in other words, mediation. There is something in the mediation of the essay form itself that lends solace to the meditating subject.

This solace is perhaps clearer in an essay written by the philosopher Jesús Mosterín about his own mesothelioma diagnosis, 'Una cita con la parca [A date with Death]' (2015). Like Gould, Mosterín uses the essay to open up a space between the grim discourse he faces – the 'six months' expected of a biphasic mesothelioma diagnosis – and his disposition to that discourse. Whereas Gould sought reassurance in statistical variation, Mosterín contemplates the philosophical solace offered by the knowledge of his 'cita' or appointment. Although we never know when we might die, Mosterín begins, we receive our 'first idea' about how long we might expect to live from the deaths of our parents, 'in the absence of accidents, infections and surprises'. His own expectations were set by his parents living to their nineties. 'But, a few months ago, a surprise happened.'

The surprise, unsurprisingly for my reader, was mesothelioma. Mosterín, however, delays this revelation. Instead, he tells us, he received warning of a predisposition to deep vein thrombosis from the genetics testing company, 23andMe. As expected, he developed a thrombosis, which was operated upon, thereby avoiding 'a pre-ordained death'. But it was during his stay in hospital that he was diagnosed with mesothelioma – the surprise – which leads him to consider the fragile uncertainty of good health, and of knowing one's date with fate, and, eventually, to advocate for euthanasia, the essay's main point.

As in many such accounts, Mosterín recalls his previous exposure to asbestos, which, in his case, happened while playing near a factory in Begaño, a suburb of Bilbao, some sixty years before, and again during a 1992–1993 research trip to MIT in Cambridge. This attempt to locate the significant moment of exposure from other, less significant moments seems, at first reading, a deviation from the point of the essay, and one likely, as in so many accounts of mesothelioma, to end in failure or fiction. However, it sets up a pattern for thinking about mesothelioma as a condition that subverts the rational expectations offered by genetic inheritance, not simply in its effects but in its causes.

Not only are there two possible sites, themselves separated by decades, but there was a further contingency to his MIT exposure that he explores in some detail. That his building at MIT still contained large amounts of asbestos was an exception, rather than the norm; its demolition had been opposed by Noam

Chomsky for aesthetic reasons. Mosterín does not explain his reasons for giving these facts, but they do implicate Chomsky's love of the building in his own possible exposure, diagnosis and, later, death (Mosterín died of mesothelioma in 2017). Against this concern with contingency, Mosterín will set the certainties of genetic inheritance, repeating in his closing paragraph, 'Our genes carry on in our descendants (mine, in my seven grandchildren), but that is their path, not ours, and even this lineage's days are numbered.' Mosterín hopes that some certainty might be extracted from the genetic – this much is structurally encoded in his repeated return to matters of inheritance – despite the very evacuation of certainty by the 'surprise', which is not an 'accident' or an 'infection'.

For all the neatness of its conclusion – that one should accept death as natural – the dialectic that forms between the inevitable and the contingent in the structure of Mosterín's essay is never really resolved. I know that Gould and Mosterín had mesothelioma principally because they both wrote essays about it. As established academics with proven skills in discursive writing, they could reasonably expect a platform (*El País*, where Mosterín's essay appeared, is the second most circulated daily newspaper in Spain). Like Gould, Mosterín turns to his academic discipline, in this case philosophy of science, for intellectual ballast against the apparent senselessness of his diagnosis. Unlike Gould, Mosterín does at least engage with his circumstances of exposure. But he, like Gould, leaves the socio-economic conditions that dictated these circumstances largely underexplored.

This begs the question how other thinkers give voice to its embeddedness within a socio-economic context. In her seminal meditation on Blackness and Being, *In the Wake* (2016), Christina Sharpe, writing of her brother, Stephen, and his mesothelioma diagnosis, reflects on how 'the damage from one summer's work forty-five years earlier at a local insulation company in Wayne, Pennsylvania, when he was fourteen years old could suddenly appear, now, to fracture the present.'[27] While Sharpe's work is not an essay by a sufferer, she, like Gould and Mosterín, uses her discipline to make sense of Stephen's diagnosis. But, where Gould and Mosterín respond to their fears and concerns by zeroing in on discursive contradictions (whether in the language used to convey medical statistics or the arguments against euthanasia), Sharpe expands her account of his suffering into a larger reflection on the ongoing structural violence of slavery on Black bodies: 'To be *in* the wake is to occupy and to be occupied by the continuous and changing present of slavery's as yet unresolved unfolding' (13–14). Following Saidiya Hartman's consideration of the 'autobiographical example', Sharpe explains that she wants 'to connect the social forces on a specific, particular family's being in the wake to those of all Black people in the wake; to mourn and to illustrate the ways our individual lives are always swept up in the wake produced and determined, though not absolutely, by the afterlives of slavery' (8). Stephen's story relates to the wider story of slavery as 'one's own formation [does] as a window onto social and historical processes', with the aim 'to tell a story capable of engaging and countering the violence of abstraction'.[28] His work for the insulation company links to the wider legacy of slavery not because he endured slavery, but because both are only apparently past: their effects always threaten to erupt in the present, thereby ripping away their illusory security of pastness, or being in the past. Or, as Sharpe writes, 'in the wake, the past that is not past reappears, always, to rupture the present' (9). Like Drabble, Gould and Mosterín, Sharpe observes the refusal of asbestos temporalities to heed conventions of past, present and future (the non-past that ruptures the present and, potentially, the future). But her response to this is closer to Drabble's than either Gould's or Mosterín's, since her recourse is not to narrate oneself to a cognitive solution, but to 'sit with it' as a narrative dilemma.

Sharpe 'sits with it' in the time she spends with Stephen as he is dying. This, she realises, is work: 'hard emotional, physical and intellectual work that demands vigilant attendance to the needs of the dying, to ease their way, and also to the needs of the living' (10). For Sharpe, 'sitting with' describes the 'important work of sitting (together) in the pain and sorrow of death as a way of marking, remembering and celebrating a life' (10–11). But it also includes Sharpe's family's more pragmatic resistance to a common experience for Black patients, who are treated as if they feel less pain and are therefore rationed or denied palliative medicine. Sharpe understands the need to dwell with the problem that legacy raises, without rushing to resolve it or covering over its disproportionate affects for some people as opposed to others.

To imagine this legacy in a continuous present, to sit with it and 'do the work' of vigilant attendance without simply seeking a solution or a resolution, Sharpe turns to breath, the embodied expression of presence. Like many sufferers of mesothelioma, Stephen's first symptom is 'difficulty breathing' (9). When he died, surrounded by his family and friends, Sharpe writes, 'Stephen sat up, he looked at us, he tried to speak, a tear ran down his face, he exhaled, he lay back down, and he died' (10). When Sharpe describes Stephen's final moments, she anticipates her later discussion of slavery as many instances of Black life being refused the right to breathe. To keep and put 'breath back in the Black body in hostile weather', Sharpe considers the 'violent and life-saving' affordances of aspiration, which describes 'the withdrawal of fluid from the body *and* the taking in of foreign matter (usually fluid) into the lungs with the respiratory current, *and* as *audible breath* that accompanies or comprises a speech sound' (113; 109). Aspiration ties the individual sufferer to a larger socio-political legacy by involving them in a set of relations: to foreign matter (through a taking out and a taking in), to speech (through phonetic emphasis), and to opportunity (through desire for what are perceived to be achievable ambitions), although Sharpe eschews this last implication. But, because these ties are mediated by aspiration, as a process but also as a polysemic term, their relations remain necessarily indirect. Terms cannot simply stand in for each other: the individual cannot be reduced to a two-dimensional representation of the context, nor can the context be flattened into a mere backdrop for a particular person's story. Breath isn't just a mediator that insulates the individual and the context from sliding into each other's remit; it also ensures that our concerns remain materially focused on actual breathing people.

Although Sharpe's concern with Stephen centres on his all too easily occluded Blackness, her work can also open up new ways of discussing gender and class inequalities in the asbestos illness narratives I have raised in this chapter. These are not simply discursive categories, but concerns with real physical impacts on racialised, gendered and classed bodies. Sharpe and Drabble both remind us of mesothelioma's punishing effects on the body. Alice challenges the reductive victimisation of Raisin's Cathy by giving voice to her experience. By contrast, Gould and Mosterín exclude descriptions of their physical sensations from their accounts. Insulated by their epistemic resources, supported by class, race and gender privilege, they perhaps feel free of the need to describe their sensations in simple terms. Seemingly, they become the two figures in my analysis most at risk of perpetrating a 'violence of abstraction'.

Conversely, I think their material privilege keeps them too insulated. If they perpetrate a violence of abstraction, it is against themselves. Gifted with the epistemic resources to explain how they think about their illness, Gould and Mosterín do not bring themselves to the limits of those resources, where thinking breaks down in the face of bodily vulnerability. Whether or not they *should* is, for my purposes here, immaterial; what matters is how closely a writer reconciles an attempt to reconstitute their agency, using whatever epistemic resources they have at their disposal, in light of causal conditions that rob them of this agency. By claiming to make sense of their illness, Gould and Mosterín deny conditions that make it, by necessity, senseless.

If it seems that bodily immediacy is the only response to the violence of abstraction, then this misses the point, made by Sharpe, Drabble and others, that bodily immediacy is always mediated: most obviously in textual form, but even in those scenes where the audience sees Alice (in bed, at the kitchen table, walking down her street). The point is not to avoid the strategies, adopted by Gould and Mosterín, to use epistemic resources to mediate the illness experience; rather, it is to realise that a certain mediated incomprehension is not only useful, but necessary, when faced with asbestos's temporal distentions.

Notes

1. Virginia Woolf, 'On Being Ill', 4 (1) *The New Criterion* (1926), p. 32.
2. Sarah Pett, 'Rash Reading: Rethinking Virginia Woolf's On Being Ill', 37 (1) *Literature and Medicine* (2019), pp. 44–5.

3. See Havi Carel, *Phenomenology of Illness* (Oxford: Oxford University Press, 2016).
4. Lionel Shriver, *So Much For That* (London: HarperCollins, 2010), p. 389.
5. Arthur Kleinman, *The Illness Narratives: Suffering, Healing, and the Human Condition* (New York: Basic Books, 1988); Anne Hunsaker Hawkins, *Reconstructing Illness: Studies in Pathography* (West Lafayette: Purdue University Press, 1991); Arthur W. Frank, *The Wounded Storyteller: Body, Illness, and Ethics* (Chicago: University of Chicago Press, 1995).
6. Ann Jurecic, *Illness as Narrative* (Pittsburgh: University of Pittsburgh Press, 2012).
7. See John Forrester, *Thinking in Cases* (Cambridge: Polity Press, 2017).
8. Adam Philips, in Forrester, *Thinking*, p. xv.
9. *Alice: A Fight for Life*, dir. John Willis (ITV Yorkshire, 1982).
10. Geoffrey Tweedale, 'Alice: A Fight for Life – The Legacy', 67 *British Asbestos Newsletter* (2007). Accessed 23 February 2021: https://www.britishasbestosnewsletter.org/ban67.htm
11. *The Dust at Acre Mill*, dir. John Sheppard (Granada Television, 1971); *The Killer Dust* (BBC, 1975).
12. John Willis, 'Alice – A Fight for Life: 25 Years On', 67 *British Asbestos Newsletter* (2007). Accessed 23 February 2021: https://www.britishasbestosnewsletter.org/ban67.htm
13. James M. Jasper, *The Art of Moral Protest: Culture, Biography, and Creativity in Social Movements* (Chicago, IL: University of Chicago Press, 1997), p. 106.
14. Ross Raisin, *Waterline* (London: Penguin Books, 2011).
15. Barbara Ehrenreich, *Smile or Die: How Positive Thinking Fooled America & the World* (London: Granta Books, 2010).
16. To this tendency, Shriver's novel provides a welcome exception.
17. Tim Winton, *Dirt Music* (London: Picador, 2003); Michelle Johnston, *Dustfall* (Crawley: University of Western Australia Press, 2018); Anne Donovan, *Hieroglyphics and Other Stories* (Edinburgh: Canongate, 2001); Suhayl Saadi, *Joseph's Box* (Ullapool: Two Ravens Press, 2009); Alberto Prunetti, *Amianto: Una storia operaia* (Rome: Edizioni Alegre, 2014); François Loots, *Die Jakkalsdans* (Cape Town: Umuzi, 2011); Penny, *Long*.
18. Margaret Drabble, *The Dark Flood Rises* (Edinburgh: Canongate, 2016).
19. Ricoeur, *Time 1*, p. 68.
20. Drabble, *Flood*, p. 159.
21. Alison Kafer, *Feminist, Queer, Crip* (Bloomington: Indiana University Press, 2013), p. 27.
22. Ellen Samuels, 'Six Ways of Looking at Crip Time', 37 (3) *Disability Studies Quarterly* (2017),.
23. Stephen Jay Gould, *Full House: The Spread of Excellence from Plato to Darwin* (Cambridge, MA: Harvard University Press, 1996); Jésus Mosterín, 'Una cita con la parca', *El País*, 23 March 2015; Christina Sharpe, *In the Wake: On Blackness and Being* (Durham: Duke University Press, 2016).
24. Marshall McLuhan, *Understanding Media: The Extensions of Man* (Cambridge: MIT Press, 1994), p. 7.
25. Jurecic, *Illness*, pp. 34, 36.

26. Jonathan Franzen, *The End of the End of the Earth: Essays* (London: 4th Estate, 2018), p. 3.
27. Sharpe, *Wake*, p. 9.
28. Saidiya Hartman, *Lose Your Mother: A Journey along the Atlantic Slave Route* (New York: Farrar, Straus and Giroux, 2008), p. 7.

5

COMPENSATING FOR FRANZ KAFKA

On 27 November 1910, a young lieutenant in the reserves, Karl Hermann, married Elli Kafka, daughter of Hermann Kafka and sister of the writer, Franz Kafka. Karl, short of funds, wanted to use Elli's dowry to open the first asbestos factory in Prague, which, he proposed, would provide fireproofing to various industrial concerns. But this direct use of the dowry seemed risky to Hermann Kafka. The compromise was to pass the funds on to Franz, who would be a silent partner in the enterprise. In November 1911, the company, Prager Asbestwerke Hermann & Co. was formed. If the enterprise was ultimately short-lived, its closure in 1917 can be attributed at least as much to the shortage of asbestos caused by the war as any managerial incompetence. During the First World War, asbestos became an important material for the war effort, meaning supplies to civilian enterprises, such as Hermann & Co., were limited. The biographical consensus is that this closure was a relief: Kafka experienced his role, originally envisaged as merely that of silent partner, as onerous. When Kafka mentions the factory in his diaries and letters, these references vary from the curtly factual to the hyperbolic. In a diary entry for 28 December 1911, he complains of 'the torment that the factory causes me', while he recalls to Max Brod, 'after writing well Sunday night [. . .] I had to stop for the following reason: my brother-in-law, the manufacturer, this morning left for a business trip.'[1] These frustrations may explain why Kafka did not probe for problems at Prager Asbestwerke Hermann and Co., despite drafting documents about the risks of industrial injury at the Workers Accident Insurance Institute.[2] By 1911, studies of English (1899), French (1906) and Italian (1908) factories signalled problems associated with dust exposure, even if the first German language publication on asbestos-related pneumoconiosis only emerged in 1914.[3] However, I am less interested in developing a tendentious argument around what Kafka could or should have known, than in the potent image the asbestos factory offers for thinking about causation, compensation and justice.

In this chapter, I recover Kafka's coincidental relationship with asbestos to imagine how it might affect our understanding of compensation and justice, even if this risks clichés about aporias in bureaucracies and judicial processes. Importantly, the coincidence recalls a moment in 'legal modernism' when, as Ravit Reichman has argued, the experimentalism of modernist literature collides with changing attitudes about tort and compensation.[4] 'Law and narrative', Robert M. Cover reminds us, 'are inseparably related. Every prescription is insistent in its demand to be located in discourse – to be supplied with history and destiny, beginning and end, explanation and purpose.'[5] For Cover, 'Law may be viewed as a system of tension or a bridge linking a concept of reality to an imagined alternative – that is, as a connective between two states of affairs, both of which can be represented in their normative significance only through the devices of narrative' (9). Here, I want to think about how Kafka's style might bridge the real and the imagined to make the link between asbestos exposure and its diseases narratively observable. We might find Kafka's approval in his diary entry on 'a literature whose development is not in actual fact unusually broad in scope' more famously referred to as 'minor literature' written soon after the opening of the factory. There Kafka offered 'the acknowledgement of literary events as objects of political concern' in his enumeration of the benefits offered by literary activity.[6] But, as Kafka warned in the same entry, a writer's influence may 'take the place of their writings': 'One speaks of the latter and means the former, indeed, one even reads [their writings] and sees only [their influence]' (132). To address the significance of the writings themselves without simply 'clinging to political slogans', it seems, leads us to an impasse between the work, which appears to anticipate the dilemmas facing the asbestos victim, and the history, where no such anticipation seems plausible.[7] Rather than attempt to elide this impasse by reading Kafka allegorically, I propose to foreground it by considering works that have 'recovered' Kafka as a modernist forebear, with the explicit purpose of representing the crisis of recognition endured by asbestos victims.

Recovering Kafka

This recovery of Kafka by two British writers, Alan Bennett and James Kelman, is not simply a matter of filiation or intertextuality, although these concerns are also present; the writers compensate for Kafka's historical ignorance about asbestos by relying on their own, idiosyncratic appropriations of Kafka's style.

Bennett (b. 1934) and Kelman (b. 1946) are themselves perhaps as different as two near contemporary white British writers might be. Bennett, an Oxford-educated playwright, brought to fame by his collaboration with Peter Cooke and Dudley Moore in *Beyond the Fringe*, seems to stand for all those aspects of whitewashed Englishness that Kelman, a Glaswegian born in a tenement and an early exponent of Scottish kitchen sink dialecticism, claims to despise. Nevertheless, they share, or shared, a fascination with Kafka that seems to coalesce around what Isak Winkel Holm has identified as Kafka's stereoscopic style, 'the style with which he emulated the doubled vision of the stereoscope'.[8] The stereoscope is a device that provides separate, two dimensional images to the left and right eyes. When looked at together, the perceiver sees a fused, three-dimensional image. Following Kafka's encounter with a stereoscope in Friedland some nine months before the factory was opened, he began to develop a style based on the juxtaposition of 'two dissimilar images of the same object' (7). Here, I want to track a similarly stereoscopic style in Bennett and Kelman that, whether or not it is owed to Kafka, permits us to consider 'the dual vision of a legal and political community' as it relates to asbestos victims like Kershaw (9). In parallel, I want to consider how aligning Bennett and Kelman on the relation between Kafka and asbestos can produce a further stereoscopic image for the critic. Bennett's use of Kafka the asbestos factory owner as a figure in his play, *The Insurance Man* (1985), presents an autobiographical figure that counterpoints Kelman's appropriation of Kafka's style, when he writes about compensation seekers in his Booker prize-winning novel, *How Late it Was, How Late* (1994).[9] As a consequence, it considers two alternative ways for recovering the work of Kafka for the present.

To those familiar with recovery projects, such dual visions will be nothing new, although the recovery method, developed to understand the revival of obscure writers marginalised by structural racism or classism, seems strangely at odds with a writer of Kafka's stature.[10] By contrast, I would suggest that the plenitude of scholarly material has provoked calls for a recovery project. In 1987, Bennett would write of 'the perils in writing about Kafka', imagining there to be 'a Fortress Kafka' 'garrisoned by armies of critics' whose 'admission' demands 'a certain high seriousness'.[11] 'More secondary works have now been written about him,' Kelman ends his dissertation on Kafka, 'than any other writer aside from Shakespeare and Goethe.'[12] But, for Bennett, 'there is something that *is* English about Kafka',' and, for Kelman, his place 'is within the tradition known as "the existential".'[13] Whatever these claims might mean, their reconstitution of Kafka in terms the writers find usable suggests some kind of recovery process at work. 'Although recovery,' according to Leif Sorenson, 'sets out to restore a voice to the voiceless and to reunite what was has been fragmented, it frequently exacerbates both of these situations [. . .] the desire that drives recovery fragments the recovered figure and renders the recovered artist and text untimely.'[14] For all their awareness of Kafka scholarship, Bennett and Kelman both commit to creative projects that rely on understanding his work as a unity in order to restore what they feel to be overlooked aspects of Kafka's voice. These projects don't just fragment our understanding of Kafka; they render our understanding of the history of his involvement with asbestos untimely, 'alter[ing] conventional understandings of causality'. Whereas 'timely, linear histories employ periodization to compose a narrative in which the past helps us understand how we arrived in the present', 'untimely, nonlinear histories find moments in the past that disturb the common sense of the present with the hope of producing an alternative future' (14). So, when Bennett and Kelman recover Kafka for the present, they open up the possibility of an untimely reading of his encounter with asbestos as a resource for an alternative future, understood as an 'affective projection that retrospectively reconstructs the conditions of its own possibility' (14). In other words, they permit a critical stereoscope that juxtaposes the conditions of the history of the factory with those of the aesthetic possibilities it opens up.

Prager Asbestwerke Hermann & Co.

In my introduction, I anticipated this stereoscopic reading by considering what happens when Kafka's case is read alongside that of Nellie Kershaw. Here, I want to explore another coincidence: Nellie Kershaw is a historical figure who corresponds, more or less directly, with the unnamed female figures who populate Kafka's most extensive recollection about the factory. Recorded in a diary entry dated 5 February 1912, the passage focuses not on his frustrations about the factory, but its deformative effects on his female employees:

> Yesterday in the factory. The girls, in their unbearably dirty and untidy clothes, their hair dishevelled as though they had just got up, the expressions on their faces fixed by the incessant noise of the transmission belts and by the individual machines, automatic ones, of course, but unpredictably breaking down, they aren't people, you don't greet them, you don't apologize when you bump into them, if you call them over to do something they do it but return to their machine at once, with a nod of the head you show them what to do, they stand there in petticoats, they are at the mercy of the pettiest power and haven't enough calm understanding to recognize this power and placate it by a glance, a bow. But when six o'clock comes and they call it out to one another, when they untie the kerchiefs from around their throats and their hair, dust themselves with a brush that passes around and is constantly called for by the impatient, when they pull their skirts on over their heads and clean their hands as well as they can – then at last they are women again, despite pallor and bad teeth they can smile, shake

their stiff bodies, you can no longer bump into them, stare at them, or overlook them, you move back against the greasy crates to make room for them, hold your hat in your hand when they say good evening, and do not know how to behave when one of them holds your winter coat for you to put on.[15]

The passage has played an important role in scholarly recognition of Kafka's asbestos factory, not least in biographies by Reiner Stach and Nicholas Murray.[16] His biographers imply a retrospective historicism, if not anachronism, when they comment upon it. 'It is not the linear, discrete world of electric motors that Kafka is depicting here,' writes Stach, 'but the grimy mechanization of the nineteenth century, a greasy and noisy technology that was constantly breaking down' (37). Stach extends this internal anachronism – the factory's datedness – to the problem of the asbestos it produced. Taking 'the vantage point of a century later,' he declares that 'it appears macabre that Kafka of all people, who by profession championed the rights of the working class, exposed "his" workers to highly carcinogenic material' (37). Similarly, Nicholas Murray takes it to be 'a profound irony' that Kafka sponsored an asbestos factory, adding hyperbolically, 'by dying so young, Kafka, a man with a deep compassion for the hardships faced by industrial workers, was at least spared the anguish and guilt he would certainly have felt if he had lived to see the facts about asbestos come to the fore' (94). Both Stach and Murray appeal to Kafka's sense of justice, either by virtue of his profession or his sensibility. Stach refers to Kafka's work at the Workers' Accident Insurance Institute, where it was Kafka's responsibility to establish the cost of insurance for companies by measuring their accident records against their implementation of safety procedures and protocols, while Murray, more sentimentally, appeals to an affective reading of Kafka the man. They coincide in appealing to a situation where Kafka's treatment of people in 1911 is placed in opposition to a monstrous sense of his ignorance in the present.

Holm presents a more nuanced, 'stereoscopic' reading of the passage in *Kafka's Stereoscopes*.[17] He observes that the passage is split into two clear sections divided by a temporal marker ('six o'clock'): one where the workers are dehumanised, and another where they are "transformed" back into women. When the sections are fused together, they demonstrate a problem less for time, than for judgment over 'the social situation in which politeness as such is either relevant or irrelevant' (42). First, Kafka presents a conventional narrative of human recognition, as following a pattern of social rules, albeit subverted by being cast in the negative: 'they aren't people, you don't greet them' etc. Then, as the relation between the manager, 'you', and the 'women [Frauen]', changes to reflect a new-found recognition of the latter's civic status, he develops a second, contrasting image of the same community. The consequence is not simply that the stereoscope allows for two disjunctive images of the same person or object; rather, 'Kafka's stereoscopes afford us a dual image of the basic shape of a given community' (41). In this way, the passage exemplifies Holm's larger project: to show how Kafka's stereoscopic style 'prompts a kind of political thinking endowed with a world-building force' that, following Hannah Arendt, aims to break with 'a petrified order of things and recreate the foundation of communal life' (13). For this project, Holm develops three theses about Kafka's literary stereoscopes that I translate to Bennett and Kelman. First, the content of these stereoscopic passages is the configuration of a community, based upon a shared 'social imaginary' or 'a repertoire of figures, metaphors, symbols, narratives, and other forms of imagination with which people represent the order of things' (14). The 'unbearably dirty and untidy clothes' of the 'girls' may be a description, but it figures them within a shared social understanding. Second, their form 'is defined by the juxtaposition of images from the same community', which 'triggers a process of comparison' (14). So the 'girls' become 'women' as they change their clothes, which challenges the reader 'to move back and forth between the orderly and disorderly image' (14). Finally, this functions 'to bring about a reconfiguration of a community' to 'restructure and reshape the image of communal life' (14). While their circumstances change, the women remain denied the means to speak to Kafka (first through his poor treatment of them, then through his embarrassment around them): the fateful hour of six does not mark their liberation, but simply their different roles as objects of capitalist exploitation and as subject-targets of commodity fetishism. For Holm, stereoscopic style offers 'a technical apparatus' that 'makes the reader ready for political thinking'; it is, in his gloss on the diary entry about minor literature, 'a *Besprechungsmöglichkeit*', or an opportunity to negotiate or discuss something (16). For the immediate purposes of my analysis, it offers a concrete technical device from Kafka that is 'recovered' in Bennett and Kelman. More generally, however, it offers a schema for understanding how Bennett's historical Kafka might be juxtaposed with the Kafka figures that populate Kelman's novels.

Holm's analysis focuses on the passage's configuration of community. His interest is less 'asbestos' than the 'factory': for Holm, the deformations of the women resonate more with capitalist exploitation than anticipatory illness. Stach and Murray are more attentive to the changing status of asbestos, but are, if anything, laxer about its consequences for reading Kafka, preferring to diagnose a general 'irony' about the situation. Holm, Murray and Stach insist on Kafka's ignorance about asbestos diseases. Therefore, their more rigorous fidelity to his work makes it necessary to bracket out a historical appreciation of things that would have appeared incidental to him. These timelier approaches to Kafka's relationship with the factory offer a foil to the untimely recovery presented by Bennett and Kelman, to which I now turn.

THE INSURANCE MAN

Bennett explicitly responds to Kafka's relationship with the factory in *The Insurance Man*, a television play where Kafka's biographical involvement in asbestos production becomes the backdrop for a story about a young man in the process of applying for compensation from the Workers Accident Insurance Institute.[18] Bennett's interest in imagining the effects of asbestos is evident from the play's opening. It begins with an establishing shot of an elderly man walking in 'a foreign city. A body hangs from a lamp-post.'[19] It then cuts to an x-ray image of a pair of lungs. They are, the audience discovers, under examination by a doctor, for the elderly man, Franz. The year is 1945, the place is Prague, and Franz's condition is 'a fibrous condition of the lungs' (90). Repeated references to the man's 'breath' in the dialogue and the image of his lungs emphasise his illness as lung-related, but, from the opening, it is overshadowed by the hanged man and the context of the Second World War: 'In peacetime you might call it pain,' remarks Franz, 'these days illness is a luxury' (89). 'You have to live long enough to be able to die,' considers the doctor, 'you could be lucky and live to be hung from a lamp-post' (90). Even though illness is the core concern of the play, it is always framed by historical context. Indeed, the doctor's attention to Franz's occupational history will stimulate the flashback which makes up much of the action. For, although Franz at first remembers only his work for the railway, when pressed by the doctor he recalls he once worked for a dyeworks, in 1910.

In the flashback, young Franz suffers from a dermatitis, or skin condition, apparently caused by the dye. He seeks compensation from the Workers Accident Insurance Institute. In his pursuit of compensation, he is forced to navigate the labyrinthine processes by which the Institute establishes whether he has a case, whether dermatitis may be considered 'accidental'. In this navigation, he encounters Dr Franz Kafka, who, unable to award him compensation, suggests that he 'may be able to help' by offering him a job in his factory (128). 'So what is it you're producing here?' asks Franz. 'Building materials. Mainly asbestos,' answers Kafka. 'Thank you. You saved my life,' responds Franz, with due dramatic irony (130). At this point, the play returns to its historical present, Prague 1945. Bennett uses the juxtaposition to infer that asbestos must be the cause of old Franz's lung condition. 'It's so long ago. But you think it may have been that factory?' wonders Franz. 'It's possible,' muses the doctor. 'Who knows?' Neither the doctor nor Franz might know, but, Bennett implies, the 1985 viewer should. Franz, in 1945, shows symptoms of mesothelioma because he inhaled asbestos when he worked in the factory.

The entire narrative arc of the play depends on the significance of this passing reference to asbestos. Without it, the sequence becomes an episodic literary biography: Kafka's actual Institute rendered as if it were the attic courts of *The Trial* or the bureaucracy of *The Castle*, loosely connected by Franz's dermatitis, and with little or no relation to the play's 1945 frame. With it, one can retrospectively trace a network of breath- or lung-related allusions and metaphors that integrate this narrative at the level of local aesthetic conceits. It is the paradox, Bennnett says, 'at the heart of the play. Kafka does Franz a favour by giving him a job in his factory, but since the factory turns out to make asbestos this good turn leads in the end to Franz's death' (78).

It is worth noting that this integration also produces surprisingly uncomfortable effects. Not only does the play anticipate Kafka's historical death, from tuberculosis, with anachronistic references to his 'coughing', but, and perhaps more dangerously, Bennett parallels occupational asbestos exposure and the gas chambers of the Holocaust (129; xxv). Franz recalls, 'he worked there too, Doctor Kafka, part-time, so I suppose the same thing could have happened to him' and, later, adds 'I've a feeling he died. But he was a Jew, so he would have died anyway' (130; 131). The doctor bridges these two reflections on Kafka's potential morbidities – Kafka's possible asbestos-related disease, as opposed to his historically more certain death, either by the tuberculosis that actually killed him or the Nazi death camps that might have – by remarking, 'You weren't to know. He wasn't to know. You breathed, that's all you did wrong [. . .] You breathed in the wrong place' (131). The avoidance of agency is, and should be, troubling. If breathing 'in the wrong place' is all that either Franz or Kafka might have done wrong, then, by extension, mere 'not knowing' seems to exculpate potential perpetrators, Kafka included. The callousness of this expression arises, I think, from Bennett's decision to draw parallels between discrete histories of lethal exposure to airborne substances: whether the tuberculum bacillus, asbestos, or Zyklon B. But if Bennett's play risks dissembling discrete histories of culpability, particularly by paralleling the asbestos industry and the camps, this dissemblance also affords a solidarity of the breathless, fostered by a clearer sense of potential morbidities as they impact across bodies in general. This is not to excuse the liberties Bennett takes with the Shoah, nor to legitimate Franz's utterance as a matter of historical accuracy: rather, Bennett's play usefully advances the possibility of solidarity for victims of breathlessness across sites of respiratory affliction that struggle to be recognised.

The Insurance Man is concerned with the civil procedures that accumulate around accidents, broadly thought of as recognised moments of realised risk, when the individual is caught up in conditions larger than themselves and therefore beyond their control. In my introduction, I considered how asbestos exposure might usefully be thought about through Nixon's 'slow violence'. It should not surprise us, then, that Bennett's Kafka will refer to Franz's exposure to the dye as 'a long slow accident' (127). Just before this comment, Miss Weber cynically remarks that the people applying for compensation would 'rather have our health *and* our money' (126). Taking her comment more seriously than it is intended, Kafka responds that it calls for 'a justice that doesn't exist in the world' (126). It requires, Kafka suggests, a whole new way of understanding 'accidents':

> Take this millworker. No beam has fallen on his head. No bottle has exploded in his eye. He has not got his shirt caught in the shaft and been taken round. All that has happened is that he has been inhaling cotton dust for some years. And day by day cotton dust has crept into his lungs, but so slowly, so gradually that it cannot be called an accident. But suppose our lungs were not internal organs. Suppose they were not locked away in the chest. Suppose we carried our lungs outside our bodies, bore them before us, could hold and handle them, cradle them in our arms. And suppose further they were not made of flesh but of glass, or something like glass, not yet invented, something pliable. And thus the effect of each breath could be seen, the deposit of each intake of air, calculated, weighed even. [. . .]
>
> And if we were able to magnify each inhalation, see under the microscope each breath, capture the breath that killed the cell, register the gasp that caused the cough that broke the vein that atrophied the flesh. Wouldn't that be an accident? A very small accident? This man has no claim because he is suffering from a condition. But isn't a condition the result of many small accidents that we cannot see or record? (127)

Even though the case at hand uses the millworker's lungs as a cipher for Franz's dermatitis, Bennett has Kafka use the indeterminacy associated with long-term lung damage because it serves his ultimate purpose: to address the insufficiency of 'accident' to describe long tail asbestos diseases. The diminishing returns of infinite regression produce the representation of the accident that would otherwise remain inexistent ('Not applicable,' interrupts Miss Weber, 'Neither of them. Not accidents.') (127). In order to represent this accident, Bennett formulates it through a series of stereoscopic images. First, he proposes a series of recognisable accidents that might have affected the millworker, only to subvert this series by casting them in the negative. He juxtaposes these non-accidents with the image of cotton dust 'creeping' into the millworker's lungs. Then, he invokes the lungs' containment within the body, again in the negative, only to contrast it with a notional set of lungs made of clear plastic and cradled in one's arms. Finally, he considers how the progression of the dust might indeed be the correlative of the falling beam or exploding bottle, were each breath magnified to follow the 'small accidents' they cause. Although Bennett's explicit content is not the community seen in Holms's Kafka, it relies on a shared social understanding of the accident, which it presents in formally disjunctive images, to restructure that understanding in a more expansive way.

Bennett makes the 'slow violence' of the dust narratively comprehensible, and therefore compensable. Compensation, as is demonstrated by the succession of farcical cross-cuts of claimants at the Institute, requires the employer to be responsible for a verifiable accident that causes an observable injury. As such, it requires not just this narrative atomisation, it also requires some sort of evidence. But, in this world devoid of spirometry, there is no means of showing injury sustained through the breath.[20] To evoke an alternate reality, where such damage might be observed, Bennett's Kafka draws out the image of pliable, transparent lungs, able to be handled or cradled, like trees in the snow that might appear to be simply 'resting' on the snow's surface. The image, designed to produce a response ('what would we say . . . ') to the injustice of this slow violence, ultimately fails to convince Kafka's colleagues: Pohlmann responds that it 'still wouldn't be an accident' (127). Indeed, even the paradoxical inertia fails: 'So is living,' Pohlmann says, 'Or dying. There is no alternative but to breathe' (127). What both offer, however, is a narrative compensation, which, after all, is what Franz wants: 'I don't want money. I want it to be given a name. How can I ever get rid of it if it doesn't have a name?' (124). Or, as Bennett frames it in his introduction, 'this kind of quest, where what is wanted is the name of the illness as well as compensation for it, has something in common with Joseph K's quest in *The Trial*. He wants his offence identified but no one will give it a name; this is his complaint' (xvi). Compensation, yes, but first, recognition.

Bennett's Kafka offers us two images for understanding accidents: an atomised rendition of the process by which dust destroys the lungs, and a fantastic image of these lungs themselves, made of transparent material and carried outside the body. Both draw on breath conceits, the better to develop an association with the play's central paradox: the conditions leading to Franz's asbestos-related disease. The ultimate purpose of these techniques for understanding accident is not, as it may seem, to expand the recourse to compensation, but to draw out a 'name' for the condition. This might explain why the play treats compensation as a paradox that, much like the hanged man, is most dangerous to those it seems to support: 'his refuge turns out to be his doom' (78). Bennett and Kelman both intimate a basic inadequacy in compensation. 'Justice is not money', wrote James Kelman in 1992 of the fight for more ample recognition of asbestos-related diseases.[21] But Kelman's understanding of this phrase differs significantly from Bennett's. For Kelman, compensation is not simply 'where limbs become commodities and to be given a clean bill of health is to be sent away empty-handed', as Bennett describes it (125). 'Obviously for any victim of asbestos abuse, compensation must come into it,' responds Kelman, 'there is no choice about that. But it is also about Justice' (209). In *The Insurance Man*, the scalar deformations associated with asbestos, historically, histologically and epistemologically, are too great for 'justice' to be possible. The historical lag between Franz's exposure and his illness manifesting is too long, the damage to his lungs too gradual and incremental.

Bennett's Kafka is no Manichean capitalist. Rather, he is the victim of historical circumstance. Ultimately, in order to maintain Kafka's historical affability, Bennett must ignore his participation, his conscious participation, in exploiting his workers, who, he sees, transform at six o'clock from the less than human to the human. Bennett's play tells the story of Kafka's biographical connection to asbestos, as a way of recovering (his own reading of) Kafka's work to address asbestos exposure. But his work is ultimately limited by the need to recognise the limits of historical Kafka's knowledge. It is Franz who must bear the shocking consequences of being sentenced 'not only in innocence, but also in ignorance'. Kelman's prose, with its more direct representation to interior monologue, offers a necessary counterpoint to Bennett's drama.

The Claimant

To supplement Bennett's explicit engagement with Kafka within the constraints of his own historical moment, I turn to a more direct engagement with the challenges facing compensation claimants: Kelman's *How Late it Was, How Late*, a novel in Glaswegian dialect about a small-time huckster, Sammy Samuels, who is mysteriously struck blind and finds himself at the mercy of the Welfare State. It is easy to read *How Late* as an account of 'a fight against bureaucracy'. The novel closely follows Sammy through encounters with various authorities: from his prison cell at the police station, through the offices of the Department for Social Services and the rooms of a medical practitioner to his conversations with his 'rep', Ally. Nonetheless, it may appear a strange intertext for continuing our argument about Kafka and Bennett, since, unlike Bennett's play, it does not explicitly engage with Kafka or factories, and it has only one passing reference to asbestos. When raising the question of Kelman, Kafka and asbestos, the emphasis necessarily shifts from Kafka's biography to Kelman's. For, if Bennett's focus was the historical Kafka's involvement with the asbestos trade, Kelman's interest in Kafka is largely stylistic. There is no written evidence that he was aware of Kafka's involvement in the asbestos industry.

On the other hand, anyone familiar with Kelman's biography knows that he was exposed to asbestos when he worked for the major British asbestos firm, Turner & Newall. For all the links to Kafka that follow, it may be that the most resonance comes in a factory exposure scene. In Kafka's diary, the factory exposure dehumanised the female workers, as seen by the owner. In Bennett's play, again it is Kafka that sees the exposure, but in his capacity as an insurance claims clerk. Here, Kelman tells the story from the perspective of the worker himself.

> The best dressed guy on the floor was a Jamaican whose name I think was Danny. He worked directly beneath me on the spreading table. The asbestos and cement came from Lithgow to me. [. . .] When I was learning

> I erred and forgot to put in the cement element of the composition. Danny released the chute and out splashed a tidal wave of asbestos paste. I had forgotten to put in the solidifier. I looked over the rail to apologise. He was covered in stuff, wiping it out of his eyes and mouth.[22]

In their comments on this passage, Mitch Miller and Johnny Rodger hypothesise that this incident (both his exposure and his hand in someone else's) may account for Kelman's commitment to the asbestos cause: 'Kelman's motives for direct action are grounded in direct experience and sympathetic imagination [. . .] while causes are important and ideologies can have their value, these constructs exist to redeem, illuminate, enrich and redress the personal history of the individual.'[23] Kelman has spent more than thirty years in conversation with the trials and tribulations of asbestos victims, most notably in work for the Clydeside Action on Asbestos.[24] 'Those who don't understand the struggle talk about justice,' he wrote in his 2015 submission to the Scottish Parliament on the question of compensation for Pleural Plaques related to asbestos exposure.[25] But, he continues, 'justice cannot happen. The reality is that people are being compensated because there IS no justice. It is too late. Their health has been taken and cannot be returned. They have to cope with a further horror. Their health, and in far too many cases their very lives, have been taken through criminal negligence and those responsible are not being held to account.' Justice, in Kelman's assessment, is impossible for 'victims of asbestos abuse'. No amount of pleading, conniving or strategising will grant them access to the law, since their sentence ('their health has been taken') has already been passed ('it is too late') and they have no recourse to hold 'those responsible' to account. There is no process by which justice may happen.

Comparing Kelman's reading of Kafka with that of Gilles Deleuze and Felix Guattari in *Kafka: Toward a Minor Literature* (1973), Miller and Rodger note common features in their interest in 'entrapment and the meditation on escape from suffocating social formations [. . .] Sammy Samuels (in *How Late it Was, How Late*) blindly groping his way out from the bureaucratic determinations of his existence' (77). But Miller and Rodger also see a technical interest in Kelman's Kafka that they do not find in Deleuze and Guattari: 'technical aspects of how a "reality" is introduced into Kafka's fiction; in questions about what is reality on the one hand, and what is the character's interior reflection on reality on the other [. . .]' (77). Not only does this turn to technique avoid the political sloganeering in *Toward a Minor Literature* criticised by Stanley Corngold, but it also frames Kelman's engagement as a technical response to 'the problem of how to introduce an environmental "reality", context or history, without recourse to an omniscient narrator [. . .]'.[26] For Miller and Rodger, both Kafka and Kelman 'go to great pains to avoid posing an external authority between the action and the reader' (77–8). It is here that Miller and Rodger resolve the contradiction many see in his work, 'between his insistence, in his fiction, on the freedom of the individual, and his stress, in some critical and political writings, on social action', since both insist on the deconstruction of authority, whether the narrator, the subject or the state (79). This deconstruction does not naïvely imagine an end to authority. Rather, it challenges authorities to recognise moments of injustice (and their role in perpetrating these moments). As Kelman himself says, 'to win a campaign is simply to have acknowledged by those in authority that a miscarriage of justice has occurred.'[27] Kafka's legacy to Kelman is, then, a style that permits him to address this lacuna: not, as in Bennett, by creating a visual effect, but instead, by developing a narrative voice that challenges the reality-claims of an overarching authority.

How, then, does Kelman draw on this narrative voice in relation to asbestos? Kelman scholarship acknowledges the importance of his asbestos activist work, but it has remained a footnote in literary analyses, serving as but one example of Kelman's broader interest in social justice. Even Miller and Rodger's *The Red Cockatoo*, arguably the most thorough engagement with Kelman's activist work to date, does not present links between the work itself and asbestos, even if it notes Kelman's personal engagement with the Clydeside Action. Discussions of *How Late it Was, How Late*, for instance, have tended to focus on the politics of, variously, dialect, class and the divide between high and lowbrow literature. This oversight is remarkable because Kelman has repeatedly tied the novel to asbestos-related issues. In 2015, a feature on Kelman's asbestos work in Glasgow's *Evening Times* acknowledges that 'he has not written explicitly in novels about the plight of asbestos victims' but 'while writing his Booker winning novel he was a campaigner and the subject provided inspiration for a scene in the book.'[28] It quotes Kelman: 'In one section of that novel there is a semi-parody of the horrific situation a victim of asbestos experiences in trying to get an actual diagnosis from a "medical expert".' This was by no means the first time Kelman linked the novel to asbestos and compensation. As early as 1995, Kelman would make an explicit connection between Sammy and asbestos activism. Responding to a question by Pat Kane, about the vulnerability of Sammy, 'an ex-con, skint, and blind', in a 'police-dominated society', Kelman suggests a comparable vulnerability might be experienced by 'an ordinary member of the public [. . .] who's a victim of asbestos'.[29] Later in the interview, Kelman ties this directly to Kafka and compensation. When Kane suggests the novel has some ephemeral relation to the Kafkaesque, Kelman insists on the 'reality' of the bureaucracy in Kafka's world: 'he was faced with a situation where these layers and layers of bureaucracy, structured in such a way that you could never get to the person who was actually responsible for doing something' (20). In 2001, Kelman suggested the furore that arose when the novel won the Booker might explain why the political dimensions of asbestos and compensation had been overlooked:

> The way Sammy is treated is the same as the way any asbestosis victim is treated by the British state, which is very convenient for them. The burden of proof is on the victim to prove that you are a victim. You have to prove yourself innocent. But people found a way of not talking about the politics in the book. Questions such as 'surely this is not something that happens to people in UK society?' never arose. Instead there was a red-herring debate about language. It was a quasi-political response to what could have been a much more political discourse in relation to welfare. The pseudo political thing to go after was the language, and I can see that might be the case again with the new book.[30]

Instead of addressing the 'burden of proof' laid on Sammy, the novel gave rise to a 'pseudo political thing' about language. Later, I will return to the 'semi-parody' of the encounter with the medical expert, which, alongside conversations with the disability rep, Ally, and the Department for Social Security personnel, constitute the novel's engagement with compensation. For the moment, however, I want to recall the debate that Kelman refers to, which ensued when members of the panel that decided to award *How Late* the Booker Prize excoriated the novel on public record. In this regard, his defenders were as problematic as his detractors, since the overwhelming urge was to 'redeem' Kelman as a highbrow writer, whose works transcended such vulgar concrete realities as class or compensation. Even before *How Late* won the Booker, Kelman was wrestling with this tendency to deify him as a latter-day modernist. In an interview leading up to the award, Anthony Quinn noted, 'in the portrait of Sammy as an ordinary man baffled by bureaucracy one can detect the pale shade of Josef K.', going on to add that 'Kelman admits that a spell doing tribunal work for asbestos victims had a parallel in Kafka's career as an insurance clerk, but he's wary of the "accepted wisdom" that sees Kafka as a fantasist.'[31] Kelman's response was to identify Kafka as a 'supreme realist': 'the establishment reading wants to see it as parable or metaphor, divorced from realism, whereas I would regard Kafka as a supreme realist. On a common sense level, his work suggests as much, the idea of him working for a law firm and dealing with workers' compensation claims. There's so much in Kafka that derives from that fight against bureaucracy.' 'The fight against bureaucracy' that motivates Kelman's Kafka is perhaps out of keeping with the historical Kafka's work as a bureaucrat, given in *Diaries*, *Letters* and *The Office Writings*, but it is an image of Kafka perpetuated by both Kelman and Bennett. Bennett, however, must reconcile the anti-bureaucrat

Kafka with the historical Kafka because he invokes the biographical method. Kelman's interest in Kafka's style, as a realist representation of an individual's entanglement with bureaucracy, does not suffer the same burden of historical proof. Indeed, Kelman himself will write approvingly of critical work on the writer that does not 'extend the story into Kafka's biography'.[32] Instead, 'in the world of Joseph [sic] K., Franz Kafka has presented the existence of horror as a fact about [that society], and if we do not "see" horror as a fact then we are ignoring important things that are going on in the novel'. (302)

Kelman's comments on Kafka's style echo *How Late*'s concerns with physical sight, blindness, bureaucratic knowledge and ignorance; elsewhere, he writes that Kafka 'refers to a space which then fills with a crowd of things that either don't exist, or maybe don't exist. He fills the page with absences and possible absences, possible realities.'[33] Similarly, Sammy must negotiate a Glasgow that, stripped of visual stimuli, seems constituted mostly of possible realities, ruled by bureaucratic judgments about what is and is not relevant. This is most obvious in Sammy's encounters with the various officials of the DSS (86–111), the receptionist and medical expert at Health & Welfare (122–5; 217–25) and Ally (214–16; 226–44; 292–315). Although dense description introduces and navigates these scenes, they mostly rely on dialogue interactions, which consist in pages of clipped refinements of previous statements. So, for instance, the encounter with the medical professional mentioned by Kelman in the 2015 interview:

> Aye, sorry for interrupting doctor but see when you say 'alleged'?
> Yes?
> Are ye saying you dont really think I'm blind?
> Pardon?
> Ye saying ye dont think I'm blind?
> Of course not.
> Well what are ye saying?
> I told you a minute ago.
> Could ye repeat it please?
> In respect of the visual stimuli presented you appeared unable to respond.
> So ye're no saying I'm blind?
> It isnt for me to say. (225)

This interaction stages the medical expert's failure to deliver a judgment that may be translated into legal compensation, whether through 'a diagnosis', 'an opinion', or 'a referral' (228). Here, Kelman presents medical caution about linking observation to a definitive, compensable diagnosis as the failure to make common sense judgments. Since Kelman ties this failure to the doctor's obstruction of the claim, it is a moral failing. What, under different circumstances, might be termed scientific discretion, here becomes a frustrating intransigence about identifying symptoms ('visual stimuli') as conditions ('blindness'). It sets up two diverging images of the medical encounter, whose juxtaposition renders their incommensurability all the more absurd. Stereoscopic passages like these demonstrate how difficult it can be for the victim to establish a link between experience and problem, not to mention between cause and compensation.

These encounters with bureaucracy usefully illustrate Kelman's stereoscopic inheritance, but they risk distracting us from the internalised antipathy Sammy himself feels to the processes of compensation. Like Bennett's more farcical rendition of the same kinds of bureaucratisation, the dialogue highlights an opposition to external authority. And yet, Kelman's debt to Kafka is most apparent when he projects this anxiety not in an external conflict with authority, but in the character's internal antagonism with his own interpellated desires and compulsions, or what Aaron Kelly calls 'unfree direct discourse'.[34] Kelly recasts Hugh Kenner's classic definition of free indirect discourse – 'the normally neutral narrative vocabulary pervaded by a little cloud of idioms which a character might use if he were managing the narrative' – as *unfree* direct discourse to describe the collision in Kelman's work between

> a narrative and a character that are not only heterogeneous and unreconciled to one another but also to themselves. No shared, overarching focalization is possible whereby the discourse may move freely across subject positions. There is only the direct impacting of discourses that are unfree or bounded by their situatedness in hierarchical registers of language and a society stratified by inequality. (92)

This unfree indirect discourse is evident in Sammy's inconsistent feelings about compensation. When Sammy says goodbye to Ally after they meet at Health & Welfare,

> Sammy took out the prescription and the referral and crumpled them up. But he didnay fling them away; he was about to but he stopped and stuck them back in his pocket. Ally might have been watching from along the street. No that it mattered cause he had nay intention of going anywhere the morrow morning. He had nay intention of using a rep either. He had nay intention of doing fuck all except what he felt like. [. . .] Ye do yer crime ye take yer time. (245)

Glossing this passage as an illustration of Kelman's poetics, Scott Hames notes that 'in Kelman's fiction, personal integrity can never survive its mediation by representative regimes (such as parliament, political parties, or trade unions).'[35] Sammy's equivocation about, and ultimate rejection of, Ally, the representative, fits into a broader pattern that Hames, and others, identify in Kelman's work: 'Not only does his fiction generally eschew moments of collective identification, it goes out of its way to scramble and corrode them, pulling at their internal torsions and modelling a wary detachment from pre-given modes of "community" and voice' (197). But Sammy's attack is not merely on representation, as such. His expletives direct their violence at both the other and himself. This violence appears in response to an internal contradiction, between the reflexive concern that 'Ally might have been watching' and the subsequent defiant claim not to care. The double image seems consistent with Sammy's claims to personal accountability, but the certainty is entirely at odds with the form this accountability takes three pages later:

> He was the cause of the sightloss, him himself. That was obvious. If they needed the arguments he would supply them. Hope doesnay spring eternal. Ally tried to give him hope but there was nay hope. So why fucking bother? You wind up the loser; ye get double-fuckt. Ye just play the game for as long and as much as ye need to. It wins ye breathing space. Breathing space is what he was giving to Charlie. Maybe. Who knows. (248)

By this point, the narrative of personal accountability has been sidelined by a more existential universal guilt. No longer a strict correspondence between action and consequence (the 'crime' and the 'time'), the outcome is inevitable, and inevitably a loss. The best one can hope for is 'breathing space' between the fiction of hope and the reality of hopelessness. Again, Sammy finds no reason to use a 'rep', but whereas before he asserted a rugged individualism – doing what he felt like and getting himself out of trouble – now it is because the situation is hopeless.

This recapitulates the sense of 'smothering' captured by the accusative 'you' that opens the novel:

> Ye wake in a corner and stay there hoping yer body will disappear, the thoughts smothering ye; these thoughts; but ye want to remember and face up to things, just something keeps ye from doing it, why can ye no do it; the words filling your head: then the other words; there's something wrong; there's something far far wrong; ye're no a good man, ye're just no a good man. (1)

Kelman's 'ye [you]' interpellates Sammy, through the accusative, into an ideology of individual responsibility that, as the later passages show, maps inconsistently across the narrative. Since compensation relies on forms of representation, whether the state or private claimant, that Kelman's fiction adamantly rejects (as Hames has argued), we might hypothesise that applications for compensation violate those conditions for existential responsibility that Kelman's characters prize most. Given our paratextual material, however, this hypothesis appears odd. Compensation may not be a sufficient condition for justice for Kelman, but it remains necessary. Sammy's direct discourse is manifestly 'unfree' because his refusal to accept the possibility of compensation stems not, as he claims, from his existential guilt or his rugged individualism, but from his inconsistent internalisation of both value systems. Sammy's 'smothering' thoughts throughout the novel suggests that this imperfect internalisation produces anxiety. It is this breathlessness that returns us most clearly to asbestos, because the only direct mention of asbestos in the novel happens when Sammy calms himself with a breathing exercise:

> A guy once showed him the ropes. It was based on breathing exercises. Especially good if ye were a smoker cause it helped clear yer lungs at the same time: what ye did was ye breathed out as far as ye could go then ye held it for a wee while, then blew out again; then ye breathed in slow, through yer nose [. . .] and ye carried on til ye forgot all about it. Good for awkward situations. It wasnay even a guy in the poky telt him it was somebody he laboured with on a building site. Stoor everywhere. Fucking clouds of it; auld asbestos man everything. Up yer nose and down yer throat. When ye spat up first thing in the morning it came out like a lump of fucking dross. But it was to calm ye down, that was the real reason ye done it, so ye dinnay lose yer temper. (159)

The 'real reason ye done it' is so that Sammy can calm himself in the cell. But, before that real reason, Sammy remembers a more material, if apparently less pressing, reason: to clear the lungs. Like the women in Kafka's factory, or the millworker in Bennett's play, Sammy has been breathing in dust or 'stoor' ('clouds of it'). But the consequences are productively different. Dust affords Kafka's women the opportunity to dust themselves off, a process whereby their inhumanity before six may be contrasted with their humanity after. This process is dialectical, but it is where the dust sits, or doesn't, that matters for the human/inhuman relation. Focussing on the movement of the dust, and its consequences, as visual phenomena whose temporal aspect must be slowed down, Bennett tracks the inhalation of the dust as it comes to rest within the body by attending to the microscopic frame of the dust. Visualising phenomena in this way is, of course, useful, but it hardly represents the experience of the millworker. Rather, it draws out the historical Kafka's interest in modelling the schematics of workplace accident through his stylistic use of paradoxical tropes. Kelman's rendition of Sammy's workplace breath rituals are far more attuned to the ways in which workers respond to dust, as a whole phenomenon ('auld asbestos man everything') that strikes the worker at once. If Kelman, like Bennett, attends to the dust's dynamics, he is not concerned with how it comes to sit in the lungs, which embodies an actuarial problem. Rather, he is concerned with expelling, exhaling, the dust, however insufficient or palliative such an intervention might seem. Performing the breath rituals, whether diegetically as a description or non-diegetically in the recitation of that description, become a way of accommodating conditions that exceed the control of Kelman's narrator, a brief stasis allowed amidst his unfree direct discourse.

While *The Insurance Man* is ultimately concerned with visualising the torturous path taken by the claimant, *How Late* burrows into the mind of the claimant himself, who, in an ironic inversion of Bennett's technique, no longer accesses the visual at all. The two are bound together by their suspicion of compensation, a suspicion in part developed through their respective engagement with Kafka's stereoscopic style, as Holm has more recently called it. Bennett juxtaposes contrasting images of accidents, thereby allowing him to visualise the very small and very gradual effects of dust on the lungs. For Kelman, Kafka is a supreme realist who turns horror into fact. Less concerned with trying to visualise actual interactions with asbestos, Kelman considers how the compensation process challenges the asbestos victim's sense of autonomy. What each 'reading' of Kafka presents, then, is a different response to the asbestos environment, coproduced in interactions between both response and environment. To understand why it matters that one 'sees' the gradual deterioration, over time, presented by Bennett, I needed to frame these changes against the stark division between institutions and individuals, presented by Kelman. Understood thus, compensation becomes about something more than just paying costs or giving a condition a name: it also involves a catalogue of injustices rendered against working victims that extends beyond their identity as workers. When Nellie Kershaw found that her identity as a worker actively impeded her rights as a working victim, her case presented a *differend*, a wrong that arises from incommensurable discourses. I realise this when I look at Kershaw's situation stereoscopically: that is, as two mutually exclusive images of the same person. This realisation threatens to remain schematic, if I don't also understand how internalised assumptions about autonomy, contradictory though they may be, can also obstruct the desire for compensation or other forms of help, as demonstrated by Kelman. Only then may I begin to recover from Kafka an understanding of compensation that may be seen and is just.

NOTES

1. Franz Kafka, *The Diaries: 1910–1923*, ed. Max Brod, trans. Joseph Kresh and Martin Greenberg (with the cooperation of Hannah Arendt) (New York: Schocken Books, 1976), p. 138; Franz Kafka, *Letters to Friends, Family, and Editors*, ed.

Max Brod, trans. Richard and Clara Winston [1959] (New York: Schocken Books, 1987), p. 126.
2. See the essays collected in Franz Kafka, *The Office Writings*, ed. Stanley Corngold, Jack Greenberg and Benno Wagner (Princeton, NJ: Princeton University Press, 2009).
3. See Lucy Deane, 'Report on the Health of Workers in Asbestos and Other Dusty Trades', in *HM Chief Inspector of Factories and Workshops: Annual Report for 1898* (1899), pp. 171–2; Étienne Auribault, 'Sur l'hygiene et la securite des ouvriers dans la filature et tissage d'amiante', *Bulletin de l'inspection du travail* (1906), pp. 120–32; L. Scarpa, 'Industria dell'amianto e tubercolosi', in *XVIIe Congresso della Società italiana di Medicina interna*, ed. L. Lucatello (1908), pp. 358–9. T. Fahr, 'Kristallbildung in der Lunge', 30 *Deutsche Medizinische Wochenschrift* (1914), pp. 1548–9.
4. Ravit Reichman, *The Affective Life of Law: Legal Modernism and the Literary Imagination* (Stanford: Stanford University Press, 2009), p. 7.
5. Robert M. Cover, 'Nomos and Narrative', 97 (1) *Harvard Law Review* (1983), p. 5.
6. Kafka, *Diaries*, p. 131. Translation adapted in Stanley Corngold, 'Kafka and the Dialectic of Minor Literature', 21 (1) *College Literature* (1994), p. 92.
7. Kafka, *Diaries*, p. 133. Translation adapted in Corngold, 'Kafka', p. 96.
8. Isak Winkel Holm, *Kafka's Stereoscopes: The Political Function of a Literary Style* (London: Bloomsbury, 2020), p. 1.
9. Alan Bennett, *Two Kafka Plays: Kafka's Dick and The Insurance Man* (London: Faber & Faber, 1987); James Kelman, *How Late it Was, How Late* (London: Minerva, 1995).
10. For excellent critiques of the politics of recovery projects, see Leif Sorenson, *Ethnic Modernism and the Making of US Literary Multiculturalism* (New York: Palgrave Macmillan, 2016); Natalia Cecire, *Experimental: American Literature and the Aesthetics of Knowledge* (Baltimore, MD: Johns Hopkins University Press, 2019).
11. Bennett, *Plays*, p. ix.
12. James Kelman, '*And the Judges Said . . .': Essays* (Edinburgh: Polygon, 2008), p. 335.
13. Bennett, *Plays*, p. ix; Kelman, *Judges*, p. 268.
14. Sorenson, *Modernism*, p. 140.
15. Kafka, *Diaries*, p. 179.
16. Reiner Stach, *Kafka: The Decisive Years*, trans. Shelley Frisch (Princeton, NJ: Princeton University Press, 2013); Nicholas Murray, *Kafka* (London: Little, Brown, 2004). See also Hans Gerd Koch and Klaus Wagenbach, *Marbacher Magazin: Kafkas Fabriken*, No. 100 (2002).
17. Holm, *Kafka*, Chapter Two.
18. See Neil Cornwell, *The Absurd in Literature* (Manchester: Manchester UP, 2006), p. 198.
19. Bennett, *Plays*, p. 89.
20. Even if spirometry was readily available, its in-built biases might compromise the results. See Lundy Braun, *Breathing Race Into the Machine: The Surprising Career of the Spirometer from Plantation to Genetics* (Minneapolis: University of Minnesota Press, 2014).
21. Kelman, *Judges*, p. 204.

22. James Kelman, *An Old Pub near the Angel* (Edinburgh: Polygon, 2007), p. 168.
23. Mitch Miller and Johnny Rodger, *The Red Cockatoo: James Kelman and the Art of Commitment* (Inverness: Sandstone Press, 2011), p. 107.
24. See James Kelman, *Some Recent Attacks: Essays Cultural & Political* (Stirling: AK Press, 1992) and *Judges*.
25. James Kelman, 'Compensation, Not Justice A Discussion Paper on Asbestos Abuse read to the Scottish Parliament', *Christie Books*, 20 October 2015. Accessed: 27 September 2021. https://christiebooks.co.uk/2015/10/compensation-not-justice-a-discussion-paper-on-asbestos-abuse-read-to-the-scottish-parliament-by-james-kelman/?doing_wp_cron=1632735657.9196989536285400390625
26. Miller and Rodger, *Kelman*, p. 77. See also Corngold, *Dialectic*.
27. Kelman, *Judges*, p. 11.
28. Stewart Paterson, 'Asbestos Victims Treatment is a Scandal says James Kelman', *Glasgow Evening Times*, 19 September 2015.
29. Pat Kane, 'Underclass, Under-what? Fictions and Realities from Glasgow to Prague: an Interview with James Kelman', 7 *Regenerating Cities* (1995), p. 18.
30. Kelman qtd Nicholas Wroe, 'Glasgow Kith', *The Guardian*, 2 June 2001.
31. Anthony Quinn, 'Category A Literature in Glasgow: How does a Literary Outsider become the Booker Favourite? Anthony Quinn meets James Kelman', *Independent*, 7 October 1994.
32. Kelman, *Judges*, p. 299.
33. Kelman, *Some Recent Attacks*, p. 6.
34. Aaron Kelly, '"I Just Tell the Bloody Truth, as I See it": James Kelman's *A Disaffection*, the Enlightenment, Romanticism and Melancholy Knowledge', 12 *Études écossaises* (2009), p. 79–99.
35. Scott Hames, '"Maybe Singing into Yourself": James Kelman, Inner Speech and Vocal Communion', in *Community in Modern Scottish Literature*, ed. Scott Lyall (Leiden: Brill, 2016), p. 199.

PART III
TRANSFORMING ASBESTOS

In the closing chapter of *Il sistema periodico* [*The Periodic Table*] (1975), Primo Levi imagines telling 'the story of an atom of carbon.'[1] Levi follows this atom, as it is extracted from the ground, passes through a falcon, is absorbed by a leaf, becomes wine, goes around the world three times and, eventually, ends up in a glass of milk that Levi drinks. From there, it works its way to Levi's brain, where it 'guides this hand of mine to impress on the paper this dot, here, this one' (223). Levi has, the reader realises, brought together the time of the narrative (the story) and the time of narration (his act of telling the story) at the moment, and the sign, of its terminus: 'this dot' describes his final full stop. The story of the carbon atom fits into a longer genealogy of it-narratives, dating back to the eighteenth century, where they 'taught readers the rules governing cash and credit [or, circulation] in a commercial society.'[2] Levi's narrative expands this tradition not so much in his observation of a thing the size of an atom – which is anticipated in Lucretius's *De rerum naturae* – or his recognition that it is the story that marks an otherwise identical atom as exceptional – 'so identical that only the fiction of the story permits me to distinguish them' – but in his insistence that 'this completely arbitrary story is nevertheless true. I could tell innumerable other stories and they would all be true [. . .] the number of atoms is so great that one could always be found whose story coincides with any capriciously invented story.'[3] Since chance determines where an asbestos fibre will land in the lung or the gut, and therefore whether a particular fibre causes, or does not cause, mesothelioma, survivors must grapple with the destabilising sense of randomness and chaos in the world. Unlike Levi's carbon atom, only a single, unknowable story tells the truth of a fibre that kills. Nevertheless, Levi models how an atom or fibre accumulates stories as it passes through different places. In what follows, I draw out the story of the asbestos fibre from the places through which we follow it. In earlier chapters, I tried to reconstruct the movement of asbestos across different epistemic sites. To get at its cultural meaning, I compared its use in popular genres: the utopia, the mystery novel and the horror story. As I discussed these genres, I came to the conclusion that asbestos retained some irreducible kernel that evades its use-value, whether it appeared as utopian infrastructure or mysterious device. By returning to its longer cultural history, I found a way to mediate this remainder by resuscitating, first, asbestos's animacy, then the epistemic categories most immediate to a survivor's field of knowledge, and, finally, the problem of causation for compensation and justice. Literary asbestos was thus transformed into an object of knowledge for, variously, science, medicine and law. I tracked these transformations through a comparison of modernist and contemporary literatures: bringing the undiagnosed use of asbestos in modernism together with contemporary literature's affective realism.

In Part 3, I want to refigure my understanding of asbestos, by combining asbestos's configurations, explored in Part 2, with its prefigurations in Part 1. Levi's efforts to follow the carbon atom anticipate my own attempt to follow the fibre's life-cycle. This, I argue, can help us to understand asbestos as a commodity, a locus of meaning and an actor. To translate the dynamic process of following a fibre to a schema more appropriate to the localised problem of literary reading, I focus on the literature that has developed around four generic sites: extraction at the mine, manufacture in the factory, distribution and consumption in the built environment, and abatement or disposal in the dump or, metaphorically, the court room. In cultural geography, such 'followings' aim to uncover the relations disguised by a commodity's dislocations, while building on earlier work that sought to track changes in an object's value that occur as it drifts in and out of the commodity chain. But processes of emplotment and interpretation add a further layer of complexity to these relative values. Not all asbestos novels draw the same conclusions, or attribute the same meaning, to the asbestos they contain.

What soon becomes clear is that literary asbestos sites, unlike their real-world equivalents, frequently depict asbestos as an object that obstructs or interferes with its own production process. In this regard, they continue the trend, noted in the previous Part, where asbestos is a fetish that halts, rather than permits, the circulation of commodities. This is particularly 'modernist'. Thought of as an obstruction, literary asbestos displays that 'feeling of regard' that Douglas Mao identifies as 'one of minor trademarks' of the twentieth century, and modernism in particular: 'for the physical object as object – as not-self, as not-subject, as most helpless and will-less of entities, but also a fragment of Being, as solidity, as otherness in its most resilient opacity.'[4] If this risks identifying all literary representations of asbestos as modernist, clearly this depends upon an interpretative frame that keeps its eye on the object, despite the movements of the narrative. So, while I do distinguish descriptions of these sites in modernist, late modernist and more contemporary texts, I also try to make a stronger claim here: that I can firm up my sense of a distinct asbestos literature by reading it as if it were such.

As I begin to navigate the different sites where asbestos appears as a commodity, I adopt a more interventionist approach, using my reading practice to foreground social concerns that generally motivate the practice of thing following. While not all the texts support or warrant these readings, I justify this practice as approximating the manifestly political concerns that must, ultimately, determine my understanding of the place asbestos occupies in the world. In Chapter 6, for instance, I read literature about the asbestos mine as a form of 'covert pastoral', adapting William Empson's term for proletarian literature. Converting qualities that Empson identifies in the pastoral into methodological points of focus, I demonstrate how the figure of the expert changes in literature about the asbestos mine between the 1930s and the 2010s: a change which reflects a growing suspicion about the partiality of engineering and medical expertise. As Chapter 7 moves from the mine to the factory, I expand my method of 'reading for the pastoral' to incorporate a more sustained attention to the role of anger. Here, again, I don't simply identify moments of anger in texts about asbestos factories; I develop a method of 'reading for anger', to foreground the importance of the emotion in understanding the factory space. These reading techniques, ultimately, cannot explain the covert ways that asbestos insinuates itself into our lives, when it reaches our homes. So, in Chapter 8, I move from things that signal asbestos as a more overt presence to those that incorporate it in increasingly subtle ways. This method counterpoints the atomisation experienced when asbestos is encountered in the home with the ostensible collectivities that formed around asbestos in the workplace, in my previous two chapters. Finally, I conclude the book by turning to the dump. Perhaps the most recognisable endpoint of asbestos, I use the dump to show how the techniques of literary reading, developed through the book, can uncover the political expediency in real cases of asbestos abatement.

Notes

1. Primo Levi, *The Periodic Table*, trans. Raymond Rosenthal (New York: Schocken Books, 1984), p. 225.

2. Leah Price, *How to Do Things with Books in Victorian Britain* (Princeton, NJ: Princeton University Press, 2012), p. 110.
3. Levi, *Periodic*, p. 228; 232.
4. Douglas Mao, *Solid Objects: Modernism and the Test of Production* (Princeton, NJ: Princeton University Press, 1998), p. 4.

6

THE MINE

'All mines are magical per se,' Primo Levi writes in *The Periodic Table*, 'and always have been. The entrails of the earth swarm with gnomes, kobolds (cobalt!), *nickel* [. . .] many are the minerals whose names have roots that signify 'deception, fraud, bedazzlement'."[1] At the same time, Balangero, the asbestos mine Levi describes in 'Nickel', reminds him of nothing so much as 'the schematic representations of Hell in the synoptic tables of Dante's *Divine Comedy*' (64). For Levi, the language of folklore and theology present a resource for imagining the mine, in both its deceptive offerings and its infernal associations. Equally, one might say that Levi's descriptions displace prosaic descriptions of the mine's workings with a language that similarly 'deceives, defrauds and bedazzles'. Here, I want to suggest that Levi's language is no simple distraction; rather, it folds asbestos's animacy, developed in Part 2, into the sociology of its use, anticipated in Part 1 and developed here in relation to the asbestos mine and its community.

For, while it *appears* that the mine originates, operates and ends according to rational principles of discovery, extraction and exhaustion, this *ignores* the roles played by magical thinking, political theology and deception at the beginning and the end of asbestos mining operations. Asbestos, unlike gold, silver or even coal, presents no immediate exchange value to the local markets of the miners themselves. For its discovery to be economically significant, there must be a world market, which, in turn, demands a capitalist mode of production, where value depends on a labour-power alienated from its work. Value is not intrinsic to the material; it emerges from its interactions with the labour that extracts it. At the same time, asbestos never loses its malignant properties, which, after all, arise in the interaction between flesh and fibre. This means it refuses easy categories of mine closure and rehabilitation. 'Notwithstanding human attempts to sequester and contain it,' Nicky Gregson writes,

> asbestos is endlessly potentially recurring, dispersed, and dissipated, and as such touches us all. Asbestos signals the advent of a politics whose site is no longer purely that of the territory of the nation-state, of the laboring body made political through occupational health, or even the environmentally exposed body of public health. Rather, this is a form of materialist politics that enacts a radical network ecology.[2]

At the beginning, asbestos must be made valuable by finding a use for it, while no fixed point may be taken as its end. And yet, asbestos is treated as if it has intrinsic value and as if it can be contained. These insights aren't commonly thought of as forms of magical thinking, because they are underwritten by the expert, a figure often invoked when announcing a mine's value or its closure and rehabilitation. The expert limns the line between realism and folklore.

To address the mine's prosaic and fantastical elements, I track the mediating figure of the expert through modern and contemporary narratives about asbestos mines from Australia, Canada, Italy, the USA and the USSR. In these texts, the expert supports the discovery or exploitation of the deposit by correctly identifying the material and, critically, informing both the finder/miner and the reader of its significance. Likewise, they assert moments of ending for asbestos's ongoing 'materialist politics'. If these are the expert's generic functions, the nature of their intervention changes, depending on the place a text is written, its narrative mode, which ranges from the realistic to the folkloric, and on the relationships the expert makes with people around the mine. Accordingly, I develop two techniques for registering this change. To compare narrative modes, I pair texts that examine the same general area using either realist or mythopoetic description. At the same time, I model the relationships the texts describe on a dynamic that William Empson calls 'Covert Pastoral'.

In his opening chapter to *Some Versions of Pastoral* (1935), William Empson notes that 'good proletarian art is usually Covert Pastoral.'[3] Two qualities of the pastoral, in particular, underpin this identification for Empson: the 'pastoral process of putting the complex into the simple' and, by extension, 'a double attitude of the artist to the worker, of the complex man to the simple one ("I am in one way better, in another not so good")' (25; 19). Pastoral plots bring together representatives of different classes, high and low, to show the basic workings of complex societies. To do this, they rely on an author who elevates the worker's profound simplicity above her own more modern sensibility, while discretely acknowledging that this elevation demands a recognition that only the author is able to provide. Here, I adapt Empson's description of actual proletarian literature of the 1930s into a necessarily contingent method for approaching literature about the asbestos mine.

Even as I focus on the differences between the realist and mythopoetic modes of description, I approach the plots of these texts as if they were covert pastorals, where the complex is put into the simple. What emerges from this forceful reading is an inversion of the authority claimed in the pastoral proper. When read as a tradition that develops over the twentieth century, asbestos mining texts demonstrate a tendency to undermine, rather than covertly assert, the figure of the expert. Although these experts cannot be said to map exactly on to their authors, their gradual humiliation offers a suggestive corollary to a growing cultural awareness of the need for greater humility about the unforeseen consequences of interventions like asbestos.

If someone is needed to explain the value of the deposit, if something lasts after it is gone, when, exactly, are the moments of discovery and closure? I begin by locating two discovery moments in *Lost Farm Camp* (1912), a prospecting novel by Henry Herbert Knibbs, and 'Spaceships have Landed' (1994), a short story by Alice Munro.[4] Standing on either end of the twentieth century, these texts introduce two modes for telling a mine's origin story: the realistic and the mythopoetic. These claims are further confirmed by two further pairings of mythopoetic and realist accounts. So I bring together two texts about the USSR's primary source of asbestos, Asbest: Walter Arnold Rukeyser's travel memoir, *Working for the Soviets* (1932), and Pavel Bazhov's folktale, 'Šëlkovaja gorka [Silk Mountain]' (1947).[5] Then I turn to Italy's Balangero mine in the 1940s and 1950s, paralleling Levi's autobiographical account of his time in the mine in 'Nichel [Nickel]' (1975) with Italo Calvino's reportage on a miners' strike, 'La Fabbrica nella Montagna [The Factory in the Mountains]' (1954).[6]

Read in sequence, these texts map a declining belief in the authority of the expert. This is echoed in a comparable attrition of belief in the mine doctor, as this figure is presented in André Langevin's *Poussière sur la ville* [*Dust over the City*] (1953), Jim Williams's *Rock Reject* (2012) and Michelle Johnston's *Dustfall* (2018).[7] Importantly, these processes of attrition are linked not to knowledge about asbestos, as such, but to the subordination of scientific and medical authority to the interests of capital. This culminates in the distrust evinced in Tim Winton's *Dirt Music* (2003), where the formal destruction of Wittenoom by authorities cannot eliminate its unfinished business.[8]

FOUNDING THE MINE

Set against the backdrop of a place called 'Lost Lake', somewhere north of Boston and south of the Canadian border, *Lost Farm Camp* presents a fictional account of the discovery of asbestos at Belvidere Mountain in Northern Vermont. The novel takes place on a smallholding where Hoss, an old lumberman, and his daughter, Swickey, supply food to the lumberjacks of the local timber industry. The arrival of David, an apprentice logger improbably wealthy and educated, triggers a series of events that will see Hoss discover an asbestos deposit on his land. Barney Axel, another lumberman, informs them of 'a fortune of money [. . .] layin' right on the ground waitin' for him to come and find it' (40). When they look in the place, they find 'nothing [. . .] except stone' (51). When David shreds the stone to 'a white fibre' and tests it against a flame, he realises it is asbestos (51). David and Avery then go into partnership to develop the deposit as a mining concern.

Structurally, David, the expert, is necessary if Avery is to understand the latent value of his land, just as Avery is necessary if David is to have some excuse to provide his expertise. In order for these roles to appear more than merely instrumental, Knibbs explains both David's presence at the farm and the friendship he cultivates with Avery through the processes of simplification and double attitude found in Empson's covert pastoral. Upon David's return to Boston, his aunt responds to a poorly written letter by Avery: 'My goodness! And that's your friend at Lost Farm. No wonder he wants you to teach his daughter, David. Do you really enjoy living with such people? (120). David responds: 'It isn't just the people, Aunt Bess. It's the place, the surroundings, the simplicity of everything – and it's big. Boston isn't big, it's just complex' (121). And yet, while the 'bigness' of this simplicity means 'there's room to breathe in up there', their entire venture is premised upon a complex process of deferral (121). Crucially, Avery and David are shown asbestos that others have already discovered. Like many uneasy settler narratives, the novel ultimately asserts Avery and David's moral legitimacy through legally recognised land ownership rather than discovery.[9] It covers over the complexities of this act of original violence by displacing the conflict to a more immediate battle between the prospecting landowner and the big city folks who want to cheat him out of his land. But it also relies on the complex explanations of the expert and the abstractions of the world market, all in the name of simplicity.

That the bare bones of this story still operate some eighty years later can be seen in the opening pages of 'Spaceships have Landed'. Munro begins this tale about rape and alien abduction by replaying the origin story of Asbestos, Quebec. A man responding to 'a call of nature [. . .] sees this stuff laying around. Sheets of it, laying around. If that isn't the very thing. Laying all over, in sheets. So he picks it up and stuffs it in his pockets and thinks, Plenty for the next time' (226; 227). When the man gets 'back to camp', a 'lumber camp. Away up north in the Province of Quebec,' the storyteller continues, 'somebody sees what he's got. What's that there? Well, he says, I don't know. Where'd you pick it up? It was just laying around' (227). It turns out the substance was asbestos, 'and on the spot they developed the biggest asbestos mine in the entire world. And from that mine came a fortune!' (227).

Where Knibbs describes the discovery moment *in situ* through a romance-inflected realism, Munro gives the story a mythic quality, describing the protagonists in vague, archetypic terms, as part of a folktale tradition. This accounts for the segment's discrete separation from the rest of the story: indeed, these pages were excised when another version of the story was published in *The Paris Review*.[10] As a result, the discovery account can itself be read as one of the open secrets that gives Munro's collection its name: 'something not startling until you think of trying to tell it' (160). The opening paragraph introduces the story's protagonist, Rhea, seated in a bootlegger's house (Monk's) with her boyfriend, Billy Doud. Then, the tale-within-a-tale of Asbestos begins with the aforementioned storyteller revising his language – 'a call of nature, then, let's say a call of nature' – because Rhea, a woman, is present. The end of the segment brings the reader full circle, to hear, with Rhea, someone say 'watch your language' and, in response, 'the call of nature' repeated (232). There is a sense, then, that these six pages function semi-autonomously, necessary for the rest of the story but not, in themselves, needing the rest of the story to carry their full significance.

W. R. Martin and Warren Ober are perhaps the only critics to devote much attention to this section, which, they note, 'diverges from its point and is interrupted by misunderstandings, irrelevancies, non sequiturs, and even a discussion of which expressions are appropriate in the presence of women.'[11] Two interruptions, in particular, suggest the origin of Asbestos is an open secret, which startles in the telling. First, when the storyteller performs the questions asked about the substance the man has picked up, one of the listeners mistakes the question as one aimed at the audience: '"Sounds a lot like asbestos," said another man [. . .] a former teacher [. . .] "Asbestos," said the man who was telling the story, not pleased' (227). The former teacher's interruption has robbed the storyteller of his reveal. But, on a diegetic level, the interruption helps us call into question a common narrative sequence: the progression from discovery to identification to exploitation and, finally, to fortune. The discovery of asbestos is not, as the storyteller likes to imagine, a story never before heard: the former teacher knows the tale well enough to scupper the storyteller's attempt at creating suspense. Like the history of the discovery itself, the narrative continuity of the story's performance is marred by demonstrations that the story is already known, and little believed.

This disruption to the sequence is, perhaps, even clearer in the second interruption. When the storyteller gushes about the fortune of the 'biggest asbestos mine', he is interrupted by Dint Morgan, who qualifies this: '"Not for the fellow that found it, I bet you it wasn't. It never is. It never is a fortune for the fellows that found it." "It is sometimes," said the man telling the story. "Never is," Dint said.' (227). Discovery, Dint Morgan observes, never accrues benefit to the discoverer, no matter that their narratives imagine it happens 'sometimes'. If story and teller believe that discovery brings personal riches, the crowd interrupts, declaiming this as never happening.

I have already remarked on how gold and silver are already given wealth: their exchange value as a commodity readily conflates with their relation to money, the universal equivalent. Since asbestos needs to be sold to a manufacturer and then turned into a product to appreciate its worth, this conflation doesn't happen: its commodity value has to be either explained or it must be understood, as an open secret. This may be why writers describe what asbestos does, or what it is, before marking a discovery story as a discovery. The discovery itself seems inscribed in the allocutory domain, pleading for a specific moment in time to be acknowledged above, say, the processes that discovery actually demands: the erasure of Indigenous presence, the confirmation of a find through a legal claim and the creation of a market. This creates a spurious narrative all too easy for Munro's hecklers to deconstruct. By the 1990s, the expert no longer seems quite so able to occupy a position of 'epistemic virtue' as David can in 1912. More people are likely to question the attempt to simplify the complex ways in which such discoveries actually play out or the potential for asbestos to be simply translated into ready wealth.

Asbest, The Urals 1929–1947

The realist and mythic narratives adopted by Knibbs and Munro reveal different attitudes to the discovery moment: the first prefers to establish the conditions of the moment, whereas the second presents a more generalised account that incorporates discovery and its consequences. But the historical distance between the two writers complicates this claim, infecting it with a supplementary concern: the growing distrust of the expert. To show how the realist and mythic narratives diverge in more proximate conditions, I want to consider two responses to Asbest, in the Urals. Not only do these texts also demonstrate concerns about expertise, they emphasise the need for a capitalist mode of production for asbestos mining to make sense.

In my preface, I introduced Walter Arnold Rukeyser, an asbestos engineer whose work for Uralasbest at the Asbest mine in the Urals from 1929 to 1931 gave him the opportunity to witness the first Five Year Plan in action. Then, I turned to Rukeyser to explain the pride that I imagine my grandfather felt about working with a substance as challenging to mine as asbestos. Rukeyser's raptures about calling asbestos mining an art rather than a science explained, though it did not excuse, the way in which the industry's scientific challenges might have blinded its engineers to some of its more pernicious effects. Rukeyser finds a parallel excitement in the larger purpose of his account: to celebrate the role his 'comparatively small industry' would play in 'a laboratory which experimented not only with iron and steel, stresses and strain, but with a hundred and fifty or sixty million human guinea pigs [. . .] where a sociological and human result was the primary stake' (8; 9–10). Rukeyser addresses this most grand, and destructive, of modern projects with a double attitude: at one and the same time, the book celebrates both the 'Russian character' of the enterprise and Rukeyser's ability to discern this character, with all its flaws and foibles. Rukeyser's account of the first Five Year Plan, like his account of the asbestos industry itself, demonstrates a palpable excitement not simply at their modernising potential, but at his own ability to see and understand this potential. If hindsight proves how limited his understanding actually was, this affective response helps to explain the collective investment in the asbestos story.

Rukeyser's emphasis on modernisation in his account of Asbest presents only one side of a dialectic at work in accounts of asbestos mining from Cassiar to Wittenoom. If asbestos mining was proof of a fast-moving modernity, it often relied upon the evocation of a lost or distant past, where individual ingenuity had helped to 'discover' asbestos's use. This explains the distinction between the realistic and mythopoetic accounts. To appreciate the other side of this dialectic, I turn to Pavel Bazhov's folk tale about the origins of the asbestos industry in Russia, 'Silk Mountain'. First published by Bazhov in the newspaper, *Uralsky Rabochy*, in November 1947, 'Silk Mountain' is a comparatively late, lesser-known addition to Bazhov's *Malakhitovaya Shkatulka* [*The Malachite Box*], a collection of tales from the Urals he compiled between 1936 and 1945 as part of the Party's general commitment to record folklore in the 1930s. At the First Congress of the Soviet Writers in 1934, Maxim Gorky had declared that 'the art of words begins with folklore'. Bazhov's collection exemplifies both this commitment and the ideological burdens it carried.

The tale attempts to correct two historical misapprehensions about the original discovery of asbestos at Asbest, and of the origins of asbestos weaving, more generally. Asbestos weaving is said to begin with Eleni Perpenti, an Italian seamstress who sewed an asbestos collar for Napoleon. Not so, asserts the frame narrator, who, as in all of Bazhov's tales, is Grandfather Slyshko: the arche-seamstress is a peasant woman, Marfusha Zubomoyka. Not only is Marfusha responsible for finding a way of weaving asbestos stone into fabric, she also knows that the eponymous 'silk mountain' is where these stones may be found. For her pains, Marfusha is written out of history, when a bourgeois family, the Demidovs, takes credit for her discoveries. But the origins of Asbest, and its industry, do not lie with the Demidovs. The story has restored to Marfusha a posthumous acknowledgment of her invention; 'in all respects,' it concludes, 'by blood, by work, by invention.'

In the 1930s, Soviet writers looked to folklore as a possible precursor for Maxim Gorky's socialist realism. In this milieu, Bazhov's tales were particularly important, argues Mark Lipovetsky, because they identified a proletarian, rather than simply peasant, past, where the bourgeoisie took credit for the inventions and innovations of workers.[12] At the same time, as Lipovetsky, Rebecca Hurst and others have made clear, Bazhov's tales themselves can be read as coded references to the Great Terror of 1937.[13] Hurst, in particular, has shown how mining in *The Malachite Box* may be understood as both a literal reference to proletarian practices in the Urals and as an allegorical means, used by Bazhov, to critique Stalinism (94). The fabulous underworlds of *The Malachite Box* gesture, obliquely, to that which cannot be said, as do the secret histories they tell. If the stories' double levels map onto the surface and subterranean purposes of the tales, this presents parallels, argues Hurst, with Bazhov's own reluctance to be identified as the author. He is, rather, the collector of stories, as told to him by Grandfather Slyshko (162).

Empson's covert pastoral is hard at work in Rukeyser and Bazhov. Their narratives don't simply position themselves as both better and worse than their proletarian subjects, they simplify the complexities of the Soviet system in ways that make it acceptable as travelogue or allegorical narrative. Both writers make a concerted effort to deflect attention away from themselves: Rukeyser repeatedly asserts the specificity of his own experience, amidst the spectacular immensity of the sociological project that is the Five Year Plan, while Bazhov is at pains to separate himself from his tales by calling himself a collector, rather than an author, and by inserting a framing narrator.

It is clear, however, that neither folktale nor travelogue is entirely adequate to the task of describing Asbest, nor of putting the complex in the simple. Although Marfusha is uncovered as the true inventor of asbestos weaving, this does not explain why history passed over the Demidovs in favour of the Italian Perpenti, nor how it was that Marfusha herself came to know that the stones on Silk Mountain produced flax. By doubling history's occlusions (first Demidov, then Marfusha), the tale can, at a stroke, tell the stories of Russia's systematic marginalisation within a European imaginary and of the marginalisation of the proletariat by the bourgeosis. But, in the context of the folktale, a genre whose historical truth is often subordinate to its mythic function, this serves less to set the record straight than to imagine the possibility of still prior claims to discovery. The puzzle in Bazhov's folktale is that Marfusha already appears to know about the asbestos stones; this, in turn, impacts directly upon the origin story of Asbest. Here, the prior existence of the stones, and the concomitant need to discover them, obscures the point of origin in what otherwise serves as a story of proletarian invention.

Asbestos, when understood as an obstruction in Rukeyser's account, conceals a much darker purpose. When Rukeyser comes to describe the processes that make asbestos mining an art rather than a science, it arises as an apologia for why his own insights proved superior to those of the technical director of Uralasbest, despite the older man's extensive experience in the coal industry. Rukeyser must make this apologia, his reader learns, because his criticisms of the director do not, as 'in the capitalistic world', simply result in 'a loss of [his] position', they 'result in disaster': by the end of the book, the technical director has been imprisoned because of Rukeyser's comments.[14] The closest Rukeyser comes to acknowledging responsibility is when he reflects on the need for the foreign consultant to be careful of his criticisms. To this acknowledgment, however, the apologia becomes a counterpoint. In other words, the difficulties of working with asbestos provide Rukeyser with a defence against the consequences of his actions.

Developed more or less in parallel, the two stories appear to present contrary visions of Asbest, as a place of either collective progress, rapid development and modernisation or mysterious origins and magical properties harnessed to serve individual ingenuity. Read together, however, they bear an uncanny resemblance to many of the trade texts that would appear between the 1880s and 1950s, in particular those of Robert H. Jones (1888), Leonard Summers (1922) and Oliver Bowles (1948), where an enumeration of asbestos's 'modern' uses was often prefaced with a short, quasi-mythic history of its appearance in Greek and Roman legend, medieval doxology and Early Modern Science. In other words, the progress narrative is often found in lockstep with the mythologising narrative. This lockstep is understandable when related to the political economy at work in both texts. The fervour with which Rukeyser writes about the first Five Year Plan as a large-scale sociological experiment finds its parallel in the nationalist purpose of Bazhov's folktales (if not their subversive subtext) precisely because asbestos, in these narratives, can never be explained by simple economics; it serves a nationalist (or internationalist) purpose, which grants it a political significance that continues into the present.

Balangero, Piedmont 1941–1954

If the stories of Asbest are about uncovering that which has been disguised by capitalist propaganda, the political economy of Balangero in Northern Italy must negotiate its own veil of secrecy. When first mentioned, the mine in Primo Levi's 'Nickel' is abstracted as 'some place' where '2 percent of some useful material' is taken, leaving '98 percent of some sterile material' wherein 'there was some nickel' (62). This cryptic location only gradually becomes 'localized in space' as Levi meets other people working there. Even this localisation is left somewhat incomplete, since Levi leaves the mine unnamed throughout the story. Our best clue to its identity comes three pages later, when he remarks: 'it wasn't difficult to figure out that the final purpose of that gigantic labor was to extract a miserable 2 percent of asbestos' (65). Asbestos production means it is not difficult to identify the mine as Balangero. But if identification solves the problem of location, it misses, I think, Levi's purpose in leaving Balangero unnamed.

When Primo Levi arrives at Balangero, his work is marked by 'a double seal of secrecy' (62). His job will be to assess whether commercially viable amounts of nickel might be synthesised from its tailings. The job is provisional on Levi keeping two secrets: knowledge of his Jewish identity and of the project's aim. Levi mirrors this secretive narrative with a similarly enigmatic narration about the identity of Balangero. This emerges through Levi's proleptic realisation, given at the end of 'Nickel', that, had his investigations been successful, the nickel produced would have supplied Italian and German Fascism with 'armor plate and artillery shells' (77). Until this moment, the reader has been 'dazzled' by Levi's hunt for a method to synthesise nickel from the mine's tailings, which he characterises as a choice between 'success and failure, to kill the white whale or wreck the ship' (75). Swept up by the injunction not to 'surrender to incomprehensible matter', Levi's readers will him to succeed, only to find themselves mired in the dilemma that science often faces when its political obligations are made manifest.

Levi's text offers a prescient warning about how short-term benefits in scientific advancement can blind people to their long tail consequences. Unlike Rukeyser, for whom such blindness offers an exculpation, Levi reflects on the need to balance scientific pride with ethical caution. By recognising, albeit belatedly, the potential future harm of his discovery, Levi challenges his earlier assumption that chemistry's truths provided an 'antidote' to the lies of Fascism, that it was 'clear and distinct and verifiable at every step, and not a tissue of lies and emptiness, like the radio and the newspaper' (42). If chemistry offers Levi an immediate veracity lacking in Fascism, it also produces a desire for knowledge that overlooks potential political repercussions. This knowledge tends to be revealed as time passes, with its full contours only revealed, as for Levi's nickel experiment, in retrospect. Levi's narration performs this belated revelation, in turn, by delaying our knowledge of 'some place' until it has already been marked by its strangely Dantean landscape and by the political intimations of its community. In other words, Levi wants to make the mine's primary economic purpose – to extract that miserable two per cent of asbestos – secondary to his own lonely, Dantean dilemma: his temptation by the epistemic (rather than economic) rewards of success, and his recognition of its consequences.

This warning calls into question Levi's reliability as a narrator. Levi is not caught in a lie, because he does acknowledge his own blindness to the consequences of his actions. As if to distance his biographical self, who was obsessed with nickel at the time, from his narrating self, more aware of its consequences, Levi spends much of the story on descriptions of the mine and anecdotes about its workers. Although doubtless the product of his observations at the time, this parallel, episodic narrative distances him, as a narrator, from his errors in judgment, made as a character. As a consequence, community relations come to dominate our understanding of the mine, over and above its purpose: the production of asbestos.

The overall effect sets up oppositions that echo those found in Bazhov's folktale. Levi opposes the knowledge of a worker with that of the mine management. When there is a blockage in the mine, it causes a dam to form which the worker knows will eventually burst. The managers ignore him. The manifest opposition is between the worker and the managers, but the story depends on a further opposition between the compromises of social relations and the uncompromising 'nature' of physical forces. This explains the recurring oppositions between animate and inanimate matter. The community of the mine, like the trees of the valley, 'feel the heat and the frost, enjoy and suffer, are born and die,' unlike the 'hostile, extraneous hardness' of 'the green serpentine of the Alpine foothills' (74). This community is characterised by a 'gossipy and easygoing atmosphere' where 'all fifty of the mine's inhabitants had reacted on each other, two by two, as in combinatorial analysis' (68). The liveliness of the mine's people is presented in opposition to the hostile deadness of its product. And yet, it is this hostile deadness that motivates Levi's Ahab-like obsession in 'Nickel'. The opposition between mineral and living matter that characterises his anecdotes, therefore, underscores the *political* consequences that resolve the story's plot: the problem is not merely that Levi will be aiding the Axis war effort; his quest implicitly violates an already established allegiance between living beings against the passive hostility of mineral nature.

This opposition is not yet a matter of asbestos disease, but that complication would not take long to develop. Only thirteen years after Levi's time at Balangero, but some twenty years before the publication of *The Periodic Table*, Italo Calvino could already observe how the asbestos was affecting both the people and the environment in the area:

> But there are no hares in the wood, no mushrooms grow in the red earth from chestnut urchins, no wheat grows in the hard fields of the surrounding villages; there is only the grey asbestos dust from the quarry that burns leaves and lungs where it lands; there is the quarry, the only one in Europe, their life and death.[15]

Written for *l'Unita* (the official newspaper of the Italian Communist Party) as a report on the 1954 Balangero strike, Calvino's essay describes a present absence – a semantic erasure of possible life physically eclipsed by the asbestos and the quarry – comparable with Rachel Carson's 'A Fable for Tomorrow' in *Silent Spring* (1962).[16] However, Calvino's counter to the silent environment is not, as for Levi, the labouring scientist inured to his work's possible catastrophic consequences. Rather, after a brief first paragraph that describes the view of the mountain from 'the car' after it 'turned the last curve among the chestnut trees', Calvino describes the action of the miners in the negative: 'Everything was still, in that grey: for thirty five days, no gunmen went up, armed with shovel, spike and crowbar, neither did the drill rigs buzz against the wall, nor did the mine-men shout and light their fuses' (192). This absence of action contrasts with the action that happens later in the essay: a meeting between the striking miners and the company representative, where the representative, at first confident that his complex explanations will perplex and overwhelm the miners, is gradually humiliated by their more concrete and sophisticated understanding of the issues at stake. The subsequent demonstration of knowledge counters the view that, just because such places present themselves as 'a world unto itself', 'away from the world of stock packages, of dividends, of boards of directors', that nothing happens there, or that such places are disconnected from the economic particulars in more established metropolitan hubs (193). But the earlier enumeration of activities that are not taking place serve as a reminder of the labour that has been absented by the strike: it affirms these actions as absent presences.

Levi and Calvino provide complementing visions of Balangero as a place where human intervention has changed the natural environment. These interventions do not lead to an opposition between the natural and the man-made, so much as a situation whose conditions call into question whether such a transformation can be justified. For Levi, this provides the backdrop for his concern with the bewitching allure of research, where the excitement of discovery erases a more ethical awareness of its possible political consequences. For Calvino, it tests the conditions of the strike action of its workers. Both Levi and Calvino challenge scientific authority that seeks to exempt itself from inclusion within the political context in which it appears: Levi through an autocritique of his claim to be a disinterested chemist and Calvino through a satiric dialogue between the representative and the much more knowledgeable miners. To highlight the concrete need for this inclusion, Levi and Calvino rely upon physical descriptions that extract the mine from its situation, to mark it as distinct from the surrounding environment, even if its effects are not so easily contained. This, then, serves to underscore the distinctiveness of the community, as bound by a common purpose, whose understanding of their locality extends to an understanding of their health conditions and their political circumstances.

In this sense, asbestos dust offers a material effluvia of this purpose. Its ubiquity throughout the mining area, and its propensity to spill over into the surrounding environment, give purpose to the collective labour of the mine, its workers and its machinery, while also detracting from the real magic of the processes Levi and Calvino are interested in observing. As Levi observes, 'there was asbestos everywhere, like ashy snow' (66). Even as it acts as the material marker of common purpose, however, it also frames those spaces where, when that purpose is conspicuously absent and the asbestos itself is absent, the relations that actually interest Levi and Calvino are free to emerge. As Levi continues, 'if you left a book for a few hours on the table and then picked it up, you found its profile in negative' (66). Asbestos frames something 'in negative' by being either absent or out of place. This framing is made possible over time, those 'few hours' the book spends on the table: *where* the asbestos is not is also *when* it is not. When it is not, precisely, is when communities come to speak of themselves and their relations. By presenting experts that only seem to know the consequences of their actions, Levi and Calvino create social situations where their disabusement can be enacted, either before readers, who can register the misplaced priorities at work, or before workers, who prove to him that he does not know what he is talking about. At the same time, it demands a Levi or a Calvino to be there, to witness this humiliation of the expert.

Levi and Calvino reproduce stories as told by the miners and their families to contrast these views with those of the mine authorities, whether the managers or the doctors and scientists that support them. In these clashes between different social classes, the worker is demonstrated to have a better sense of the mine's dangers, a stance that effectively presents the writers as allies to the workers against the bosses. Yet, this allyship also begs the question of the validity of their own judgments, a validity, moreover, that Levi explicitly challenges. Both Levi and Calvino must position themselves, on the one hand, as characters who develop and learn from their encounters with the miners, and, on the other, as narrators who, writing in retrospect, are able to understand the miners intimately. To alleviate the tension this creates, the mine must be presented as an *unproductive* space, whose obstructions can, in effect, distract us from the writer's 'double attitude' by foregrounding the conflicts of these communities with management or nature. By opposing the community to the bosses and to the mine itself, the writer elides his own contradictory position as both authority and observer, since calling into question the one role comes to rely, implicitly, on our trust in the other. Levi's mistake, therefore, becomes a testament to his honesty as an observer, which is borne out by his patient recapitulation of the miners' stories.

Excursus: Doctors in Quebec, Cassiar and the Pilbara 1953–2018

When figured in fiction about asbestos mines, medical doctors often assume the role of protagonist or narrator. Like Rukeyser's engineer or Levi's chemist, they provide a credible, literate subject, with the necessary expertise to diagnose the problems that lurk within the mine and at the centre of the novel. So, again, we see the double attitude that can marvel at the miners, while also pitying them. In this excursus, I want to link together three texts that depend upon doctor protagonists: André Langevin's *Dust over the City* (1953), Jim Williams's *Rock Reject* (2012) and Michelle Johnston's *Dustfall* (2018). These novels are significant, insofar as they call the credibility of the doctor into question: over the course of each novel, the doctor protagonists are, or come to be, disgraced because of a perceived error in medical judgment. In asbestos histories, doctors are usually heroes (Irving Selikoff), villains (Anthony Lanza) or heroes that become villains (Richard Doll). For all their trials and tribulations, it is their stance on asbestos that threatens their standing with the profession. Conversely, in these three asbestos novels, the error, and the associated feelings of guilt and shame, do not relate to the industry, or at least not directly: their victims are frequently children or women during childbirth.

In Langevin's *Dust over the City*, a doctor, Alain Dubois, and his wife, Madeleine, move to Macklin, a fictional mining town modelled on the asbestos mining community at Thetford Mines, Quebec. Like her literary forebear, Emma Bovary, Madeleine soon begins an affair, in this case with one of the miners. At the same time as the affair challenges his social standing, Alain's medical authority is called into question when he makes a number of decisions perceived to be errors, most notably an emergency operation on a child with hydrocephalus and a diagnosis of a serious heart condition in an older patient. As Julie Robert observes of the latter, 'rather than disclosing his diagnosis, explaining it, and prescribing a course of treatment, Dr Dubois performs the process in reverse.'[17] Effectively, this means that Alain undermines his own authority, not because his diagnoses are wrong, but because he doesn't reinforce them with the social performance expected of the diagnostic situation.

Robert reads Langevin's novel in a broader tradition of 'medico-national allegories in Quebecois fiction' wherein it appears that 'the sick character's body becomes a figure for the sick nation' (5). 'Appears' because, as Robert explains, the profusion of ill characters in Quebecois fiction, like the dominant motif of medical diagnostic language in social commentary of the time, actually emerge when Quebec's health system shows signs of notable improvement. Rather than making claims about Quebec's moral, political or bodily health, these 'illness narratives are a response to change, particularly to the kinds of change that occasion collective anxieties about the social, political and cultural status of the nation' (14). Within this broader canon, *Dust* offers itself as an allegory of the difficulties facing any authorities attempting to diagnose this change.

Here, asbestos plays a not inconsequential role, even if Langevin's descriptions of the substance itself figure it as simply obdurate: 'the rain and the asbestos dust combined to produce a sort of third dimension in the air.'[18] *Dust* is often taken as an allegory for the 1949 Asbestos Strike, where miners in Asbestos and Thetford Mines resisted efforts by the Quebec government, led by Maurice Duplessis, to cow them back into work for foreign companies, like Johns Manville. The strike, in turn, was diagnosed by liberal reformers, most notably Pierre Trudeau, who later became Prime Minister, as the sign of Quebec's imminent modernisation: 'a violent announcement that a new era had begun.'[19] If so, it is less overtly marked by Quebecois nationalism than the other major Quebecois novel about the asbestos industry of the time, Jean-Jules Richard's *Le Feu dans l'amiante* [*The Fire Over Asbestos*] (1956).[20] Indeed, Robert's point is that, when Alain refuses to accede to the social and medical niceties required to cloak his diagnoses with authority, Langevin resists any straightforward allegorical attempt to cast his character as a liberal reformer. Insofar as the novel has any allegorical message at all, it may be found in its criticisms of conflating medical-expert and socio-political claims to authority, which gives the medical diagnosis a socio-political force that, reciprocally, turns the diagnostic act into a socio-political performance, over and above what is medically necessary. Its allegorical target in the Asbestos Strike would be precisely politically motivated experts, like Trudeau, who, in presuming to speak on behalf of the miners, turned the Strike into a foundational event for modern Quebec. As Jessica Van Horssen has shown, the demands of the miners were local, pragmatic, and largely ignored in subsequent political economic analyses.[21] When the Strike ended after five months, the health concerns over dust control that had fueled the strike action had to be abandoned in the name of job security.[22] The desire to turn the Strike into an Event, while successful as a socio-political declaration, voided the actual conditions facing the returning workers.

This reading of *Dust over the City* serves to diagnose some of the naïve reformism lurking in Jim Williams's *Rock Reject* (2012). Set in Cassiar, British Columbia, during the 1970s, Williams's novel tells the story of Peter, a former Toronto-based medical student who flees to the Stikine River area when his wife dies from complications related to an illegal abortion. Peter's shame causes him to turn away from his education and engage in behaviour that, given his learning, can only appear to be self-destructive. Nevertheless, an abiding sense of justice provokes him to find medical evidence that will correct the worst health and environmental problems produced by the mine. His knowledge ('I am in one way better') provides the impetus for his advocacy for better conditions for the miners and the local Indigenous community, while his shame ('in another not so good') explains his presence at the mine in the first place. Indeed, it is the mystery of his shame and the desire to discover its source that supports the reader through the iterations of his day-to-day experience of the mine and provides, in other words, the novel with its other plot. Although his knowledge grants the union some leverage in improving conditions, ultimately his intervention seems as futile as his work returning ore spill to a conveyer belt: a Sisyphean job, he is confidently told, that is 'futile and hopeless' (28). The spill, here, constitutes the fall out of the dust, which 'floated in the cold air, so thick that the view beyond fifty feet was obscured in the haze' (28). Here again, asbestos dust seems to obstruct the functioning of the mine, but it also might as well describe the limits of Peter's vision: he ends the novel not as a reformer or a campaigner, but firm in the commitment to return to medical school to specialise in lung conditions. However unwittingly, *Rock Reject* resolves itself by returning to the same socially imbued authority that *Dust over the City* sought to deconstruct.

The complicity, or at least quietism, on the part of the company doctors, does not mean that the social authority of doctors should be universally called into question. However, it does problematise a conflation, made by Peter at the end of *Rock Reject*, between the moral purpose of the doctor ('first, do no harm') and their social authority. This is at least hinted at by Peter's sometime love interest, Susan, who notes the similarity between the Physician's Oath, when Peter pledges himself 'to consecrate my life to the service of humanity' and the Company's brochure, which advertises asbestos's virtues as 'in the service of mankind' (248). The rhetoric of medical selflessness, it appears, has been thoroughly debased by the Company's cynicism. But a possible alternative emerges in Michelle Johnston's *Dustfall* (2018), which shifts the emphasis on a doctor's 'social authority' from authority to social.

Dustfall weaves together two narratives about disgraced doctors against the backdrop of Wittenoom, an abandoned mining town in Western Australia's Pilbara region. The novel opens with a narrative about Lou Fitzgerald, who goes to the all-but-abandoned Wittenoom for 'a bit of space' in the 1990s (8). In parallel, alternating chapters, it presents the story of Raymond Filigree, whose appointment at the Wittenoom clinic shortly precedes the mine's closure in 1966. Raymond's narrative recreates a contemporary account of an asbestos town, while Lou's sets this account against its long-term consequences, but both narratives are pulled together by similar medical errors, haunting both Raymond and Lou: both missed clear signs of parental abuse in child patients who subsequently died.

Notwithstanding the oscillating descriptions of the past and the present, clear parallels emerge between Peter's story and those of Raymond and Lou. Because of a failure to act, both Johnston's doctors have taken up posts in remote locations. Their presence in Wittenoom, therefore, speaks to a shame that is equivalent to Peter's, even if the causes are very different. At the same time, this expertise permits them to make some kind of positive intervention in the life of the community: Raymond helps to reveal the dangers of asbestos, while Lou reconciles Dave, a Wittenoom resident, with his dying father. Both Raymond and Lou are presented with a double attitude of shame and privilege that is, again, explained through the double plot of medical disgrace and environmental catastrophe. But, by juxtaposing the two stories, Johnston reflects two dimensions of the story that Williams does not: the long-term effects on places contaminated with asbestos and how, with these long-term effects, the role of the doctor shifts from diagnostic intervention to palliative care. In *Dustfall*, the crucial intersection between the parallel stories does not occur in some kind of transhistorical meeting between Raymond and Lou; it happens through Lou's encounter with Dave's father, an ex-miner, who is dying of mesothelioma. Johnston's doctors are humiliated, then humbled, and, finally, find a new social purpose in a commitment to social, rather than strict medical, care.

What Might have Happened in Wittenoom, 1963–Present

Asbestos mines, in literary texts, are characterised by challenges to authority that seem to undercut the very author-figure upon which literature functions. One of these challenges can be found when I interrogate the mine's origins and endings, which, as I already hinted in my discussion of Bazhov, can be a latent obstruction to authoritative claims. If asbestos mines have questionable beginnings in Bazhov and Munro, often relying upon the covert pastoralism of an expert to identify the worth of the claim, political and economic decisions about when these mines 'end' are often undercut by endemic contamination and commitment to community. Perhaps the best-known example is Wittenoom. When mining ceased in 1963, the town swiftly shrank. By last report, the town consisted in three people. Wittenoom is the most well-known case of a former asbestos town wished away by national government. I have already mentioned how Jon Ford aimed 'to remove all signs of the town's existence and wipe it off the map'. Given this effort toward a violent extinction that registers at least as strongly in text as in reality, Wittenoom has produced a range of cultural responses to rival those of Asbestos, Quebec, including at least three novels, two poems (one lyric, the other a digital responsive artwork), a mini-series, and even a song, not to mention numerous documentaries and travel shows.[23] However, where the principal affect related to Asbestos was nationalist pride, Wittenoom, in both the national discourse and the art objects that challenge it, tends to reflect the same national shame about its existence that led to its obliteration.

Although little of Tim Winton's *Dirt Music* (2003) actually takes place in Wittenoom, its brief appearance ties the town to Western Australia's ongoing engagement with the extractive industry, a sign that, despite being 'off the map', Wittenoom continues to exercise a significant pull on the Australian national imaginary. *Dirt Music* follows Luther Fox, a fishing poacher who lives alone just outside a small town, and his love affair with Georgie, girlfriend to the town's most successful fisherman. At first, then, the extractive industry most in evidence is the West Australian fishing industry. However, Fox's isolation from the rest of the community is not solely on account of his poaching; he has also removed himself over his shame that his family died in a car accident, after he allowed his brother to drive drunk.

When Georgie's boyfriend discovers their affair, Fox decides to travel to Wittenoom, a decision the novel anticipates in an earlier conversation about the death of Fox's father. Fox replies: 'Mesothelioma. I was seventeen. He was at Wittenoom before we were born. Mining asbestos' (96). Georgie, a nurse, responds, 'I probably nursed his mates. Him, even' (96). 'All dead,' Fox muses, 'He was dyin our whole life. But we didn't even know it' (96). It is a leitmotif of asbestos narratives generally, that dying extends back into a time before knowing, a latent effect whose latency is realised only in retrospect. Later, as

Luther approaches Wittenoom, accompanied by the surfer, Rusty, he is asked, 'Why Wittenoom? [. . .] Fox tells him about the old man and the asbestos mine. The mesothelioma and the monumental bastardry of the cover up' (229). Rusty then recalls 'a Midnight Oil song', a reference to Midnight Oil's *Blue Sky Mine* (1990). Fox's response, however, turns from existing corporate histories to the visceral impact of mesothelioma on the body:

> Fox nods. He doesn't mention the dying, the actual way he went [. . .] Lying there like a man being held down in a tub of water [. . .] But he was drowning anyway. [. . .]
>
> For revenge, says Rusty, I could understand it. But from what I've heard there's nothin there, no one. (229)

Revenge is impossible because nothing and no one remains at Wittenoom, which, in any event, Rusty only recalls as a reference to a song. Fox, on the other hand, must bear the memory of 'the actual way [his father] went', an experience of 'drowning' paralleled with other moments of drowning during the novel, whether his own or Georgie's. The passage sets up an opposition between Fox, for whom Wittenoom implies all the physical consequences of mesothelioma 'the falling down and liquid shitting and desperate respiration', and Rusty, who receives his knowledge about the mine through a protest song and for whom the mine merely signifies an example of generic environmental injustice without visceral consequence (229).

Critically, these reflections on Wittenoom are almost entirely absent when they reach 'gorge country [. . .] mostly it's just empty streets and health warnings' (234). The passages set in the town are resolutely devoid of any significant action, a matter that Rusty, who expects 'revenge' or protest, finds ridiculous: 'That's it? You come this far and that's all you wanna see? This is the place that killed your father and five minutes and a dose of hippy piss is all he gives it?' (235). But, of course, the meaning of Wittenoom in *Dirt Music* is given in its failure to provide closure, to render meaningful either the death of the father or the wanderings of the son.

Threaded through these literary accounts has been a more or less critical reflection about the need to substantiate claims to authority that the asbestos industry, with its deliberate cultivation of doubt and ignorance, have called into question. This was possible through the double attitude, offered by the covert pastoral, but, since the double attitude itself relies upon an implicit authority, the challenge to authority also proved undermining for the structures of the mining fictions themselves. This might be why, in the end, the most acute diagnoses of the asbestos mining situation needed to come from short vignettes lodged within longer narratives. The fictions diagnose the problems about authority that swirl around the asbestos story. They figure asbestos itself as an obstruction, which serves to remind us that, as a concrete material, it has damaging effects that exceed those generic structural or slow violences committed by capitalism in the name of all commodities. But, having disclosed these problems, what is literature to do? Instead of offering awareness as a palliative, I might follow Johnston's doctors in assuming a kind of epistemic humility about what literature can do, without simply dismissing as impossible any notion that it can effect change.

NOTES

1. Levi, *Periodic*, p. 64.
2. Nicky Gregson, 'Asbestos', in *Making Things International 2*, ed. Mark B. Salter (Minneapolis, MN: University of Minnesota Press, 2016), p. 271.
3. William Empson, *Some Versions of Pastoral* (Harmondsworth: Penguin Books, 1966), p. 5.
4. Knibbs, *Lost Farm Camp*; Alice Munro, *Open Secrets* (London: Vintage, 1995).
5. Rukeyser, *Working with the Soviets*; Bazhov, 'Šëlkovaja gorka'.
6. Levi, *The Periodic Table*; Italo Calvino, 'La Fabbrica nella montagna', intro. Francesco Carnevale and Stefano Silvestri, 18 *Epidemiologia e prevenzione* (1994), pp. 191–3.
7. André Langevin, *Dust over the City*, trans. John Latrobe and Robert Gottlieb (Toronto: McClelland and Stewart Ltd, 1974); Williams, *Rock Reject*; Johnston, *Dustfall*.
8. Winton, *Dirt Music*.
9. In keeping with such novels, there is also a repressed Indigenous presence, registered through the offensively named 'Injun Pete'.
10. Alice Munro, 'Spaceships have landed', 131 *The Paris Review* (1994). Accessed online: 14 September 2021. https://www.theparisreview.org/fiction/1797/spaceships-have-landed-alice-munro
11. W. R. Martin and Warren U. Ober, 'Alice Munro as Small-town Historian: "Spaceships have landed"', 66 *Essays on Canadian Writing* (Winter 1998), p. 140.
12. Mark Lipovetsky, 'Pavel Bazhov's Skazy: Discovering the Soviet Uncanny', in *Russian Children's Literature and Culture*, eds Marina Balina and Larissa Rudova (New York: Routledge, 2008), pp. 242–83.
13. Rebecca Hurst, *Digging Deep: the Enchanted Underground in Pavel Bazhov's 1939 Collection of Magic Tales*, The Malachite Casket (Manchester, University of Manchester PhD Thesis, 2018).
14. Rukeyser, *Working*, p. 58.
15. Calvino, 'Fabbrica', p. 192.
16. Rachel Carson, *Silent Spring*, intro. Linda Lear (Boston: Houghton Mifflen Co., 2002).
17. Julie Robert, *Curative Illnesses: Medico-National Allegory in Québécois Fiction* (Montreal: McGill-Queen's University Press, 2016), p. 78.
18. Langevin, *Dust*, p. 33.
19. Pierre Trudeau, 'Epilogue', in *The Asbestos Strike*, ed. Pierre Trudeau, trans. James Boake (Toronto: James Lewis & Samuel, 1974), p. 329.

20. Jean-Jules Richard, *Le Feu dans l'amiante* (Montréal: Réédition Québec, 1971).
21. Jessica Van Horssen, *A Town Called Asbestos: Environmental Contamination, Health, and Resilience in a Resource Community* (Vancouver: UBC Press, 2016), p. 89.
22. Van Horssen, *Town*, p. 115.
23. Tim Winton, *Dirt Music* (2004); Michelle Johnston, *Dustfall* (2018); Lois Murphy, *Soon* (2017); *Tropic of Cancer* with Simon Reeve; Jason Nelson, *Wittenoom: Speculative Shell and the Cancerous Breeze* (2010); *Devil's Dust* (ABC, 2011); John Kinsella, 'Blue Asbestos at my Bedhead' in *Sack* (2014); Midnight Oil, 'Blue Sky Mine'.

7

THE FACTORY

ANGER IN THE FACTORY

On Friday, 30 November 2001, Chilean activist and Communist Party member Eduardo Miño Pérez walked into the plaza in front of the Palacio de la Moneda, the official residence of the President of Chile in Santiago. He handed out flyers condemning the Chilean asbestos company, Pizarreño, its Mutual Aid programme, the doctors supporting them, and the government, for their failure to care for Pizarreño's workers. The flyers, written in the form of a letter, also explained his subsequent actions as a protest against what might be called general conditions of the neo-liberal Chilean state: sanctioned unemployment, support for the military industrial complex, US-oriented imperialist globalisation, and attacks against the Communist Party. Then, having declared in print that his actions were done in sound mind and body 'to impress upon the conscience of the guilty the weight of their criminal misdeeds', Miño stabbed himself in the abdomen and set himself alight.[1] Despite hospitalisation, he died of his injuries the next day. He concluded his letter: 'My soul, which overflows with humanity, can no longer endure such injustice' (7). Miño's story introduces anger as an important lens for thinking about asbestos. But it also shows how dangerous anger can be, when mobilised as the basis for a larger political project. For all that Miño's letter justified his auto-da-fé in cogent, rational terms, his action was dismissed as incomprehensible by Pizarreño, the Chilean Government and even his former colleagues in the Chilean Communist Party.

Anger is present as a transnational constant across the asbestos story, even if it is seldom expressed as absolutely as Miño's. 'It is the fury that flashes', recalls Gideon Haigh of his meeting with the anti-asbestos activist Bernie Banton in *Asbestos House* (2006), Haigh's 'secret history' of the Australian asbestos producer James Hardie.[2] Banton developed asbestosis, pleural plaques and peritoneal mesothelioma from his work in James Hardie's factory, and, subsequently, his work with James Hardie products. Like Miño, his anger expands outwards from his own condition to incorporate Hardie's larger role in fostering ignorance about asbestos, despite knowing of its harmful effects. 'The only reason Hardie's is a successful company,' Banton famously lambasted Hardie's chief negotiator,

> is the thousands of lives they put at risk when they knew it was a dangerous product. They knew what was going on and did nothing about it. So don't you tell me what a great company Hardie's is. You're a lot of grubs. I don't know how you can look at yourselves in the mirror. How dare you! This is a despicable company with no morals whatsoever. (8)

Banton's anger attaches itself to the company because of a prior knowledge and negligence ('they knew what was going on and did nothing'). This condition of past culpability registers in the present as a moral failure ('this is a despicable company with no morals whatsoever') that deserves to be shamed, through the diminution of its managers to the state of insect life ('you're a lot of grubs').

Relying upon appeals to morality, shame and knowledge, the urgency of Banton's diatribe hardly invites me to pause and examine the qualities of his anger itself. And yet, when I do pause, it is readily apparent how difficult it is to know where this anger is best directed. In this regard, Banton's shift from third to second person is not just striking, but factually correct, since, as Haigh reminds me, the *dramatis personae* of Hardie have all changed over the long history of the company. Or, as Alice Jefferson, who I introduced in Chapter 4, asks herself during *Alice – A Fight for Life* (1982): 'What do I think about Cape [Asbestos]? I hate them. I bloody hate them. And I don't know why I hate them, because Cape is just a word.' Jefferson articulates the problem with simply hating the company. The hatred is necessary, but, she recognises, it becomes illogical when a company is 'just a word'. Whereas Miño included the crimes of the Chilean state into his protest and Banton conflated Hardie's management past and present, Jefferson questions the sense of such expansive reference. Of course, a company is more than just a word. It remains liable for a history of gross negligence, even if its current management are not personally responsible (at least, legally speaking). But Jefferson makes an important point that risks being missed, perhaps, in the more targeted language of Miño and Banton. If Cape is 'just a word', the anger that Jefferson feels is no longer 'caused' by Cape; instead, it 'attaches' to Cape, as it might to any other object. This might explain why anger tends to move in anti-asbestos discourse, whether expanding to condemn state policy and medical infrastructure (Miño) or honing in on particular executives (Banton). Anger's ability to attach to different objects is not unique to the asbestos story, nor are its movements within anti-asbestos discourse illogical. Nevertheless, its presence, even dominance, when thinking about asbestos demands some kind of theoretical examination.

For this chapter, I want to consider the role of anger, and its relation to other affects, in thinking about the asbestos factory space. Historically, it was observations of factory workers that led to the first public health investigations of asbestos-related diseases. As early as 1898, Lucy Deane had observed the evil effects of asbestos dust on workers, and from there the histories follow a linear trajectory from Auribault (1906) to Merewether and Price (1930). Here, I would like to adopt a different approach; instead of repeating the history of the asbestos factory, I want to concentrate on how aesthetic works attempt to corral the rage it provokes, either by dissimulating it, in service of company interests, or by magnifying it, as prompted by activism. These comparisons will rely, again, on the four qualities of asbestos proletarian literature, mentioned in the introduction to Part 3.

I also return to the idea that asbestos relies on a capitalist mode of production. In Chapter 6, I unpicked assumptions about the material's intrinsic value by connecting asbestos discovery narratives, the world market and capitalism. Then, I hinted at the role Marx grants labour under capitalism: workers alienated from the benefits of extracting asbestos while suffering the health consequences for doing so. Labour in Marx's *Capital* is not, as is generally thought, a transhistorical reference to human production; instead, Moishe Postone argues, it needs to be understood as a historical category determined by capitalism itself. This means that conventional approaches to emancipation – ending private property and the social distribution of wealth – fail to address the problems inherent in labour as a productive process: 'the social character of labor as a productive activity structurally becomes an attribute of the totality – which, although constituted by social practice, is opposed to, and dominates [. . .] its concrete dimension.'[3] My relative freedom to choose my place of work (the 'concrete dimension' of my labour) is conditioned a system of social necessity (its 'abstract dimension') that determines I should work, whether I want to or not. How I understand my labour is not external to capitalism; it is entirely imbricated within it. When labour's circumstances favoured unions (collectivised work patterns, shared or adjacent accommodations), this distinction was less important, since collective action (often conflated with labour power) helped to offset the imposition of labour's 'abstract dimension' (its 'social character') in peoples' lives. However, when deindustrialisation and globalisation diminished the power of local unions, the distinction resurfaced, evidenced by 'choices' like zero-hour contracts and precarious work conditions.

The rise and fall of the asbestos industry paralleled the rise and fall of workers' unions. This parallel points to a historical difference in the treatment of worker action by the texts I look at. Whereas texts from the 1930s invoke worker union to great effect, in texts from the end of the twentieth century the call to union action often results in failure. As a consequence, I try to look for new sites of collectivity on the asbestos question. Indeed, these sites are found where there is a shared anger at other injustices, past and present, where, in other words, an economics of rage takes hold. 'In the case of rage,' writes Peter Sloterdijk,

> there is no complex inner life, no hidden psychic world, no private secret through which the hero would become understandable to other human beings. Rather, the basic principle is that the inner life of the actor should become wholly manifest and wholly public.[4]

Rage, then, is not an expression of the actor's inner life, but presents 'an energetic supplement' that flows through the person who 'contains' it. Such containment is not passive: 'the guardian of rage also has to create a conscious relationship to this rage' (11). For Sloterdijk's Plato, the 'organ' that allows for this regulated passage is 'thymos' – 'the impulsive center of the proud self [that] also delineates the receptive sense' – which, alongside *nous* (reason) and *epithumia* (appetite or desire), forms a tripartite human *psyche* (11).

Thymos serves Sloterdijk as the means for translating rage from the poetry and philosophy of Ancient Greece to the contemporary moment. For it is through the civilising of *thymos* that rage does acquire some semblance of an inner life: as *thymos* comes to be associated with striving to live up to one's expectations (in Plato) and for recognition from others (in Hegel), so the frustration of this striving, and the shame this provokes, manifests as rage, against the self or the other. But it is also this civilising process that eventually relies on a dissimulation or deferral of rage: first in Stoicism, then in Christianity. Sloterdijk argues that this resulted in a 'transcendent bank of vengeance', whereby a wrathful God avenges present harms in the future promised by the after-life. The bank metaphor is crucial to Sloterdijk's argument, since he wants to align *thymos* with a present-day psychopolitics, imbricating economic considerations with affective forces like rage, pride, and shame.

Sloterdijk's framework suggests how the moral guilt of the asbestos industry and the anger it causes might be translated into economic terms. Compensation does not just offer the victim a figure based on their projected future earnings; it does so because of moral guilt about a past failure. Both guilt and debt 'make sure that the lives of those they affect remain bound by a knot created in the past' (30). This relentless balancing of the books leads to resentment, Sloterdijk worries, where nothing can be gotten for free and everything must be paid back to the last penny. An alternative economy calls into question this dependency on the equals sign by focusing on *thymos*'s potential to prioritise a thinking of 'unequal values'. The economic version of this may be found when people 'invest their resources to satisfy their pride and to attest to their good fortune'; the moral equivalent is the gesture of forgiving someone who is guilty: 'wherever this happens, the chain of revenge, the economy of payback, is broken' (30).

Certainly, Sloterdijk's description of the thymotic economy explains why activism aims to shame industries into changing its practices, and why, when combined with institutional oversight, they succeed. He is right to note that undue emphasis on equivalence can generate feelings of resentment and revenge. After all, when James Kelman declared that compensation was not justice in Chapter 4, he proposed that criminal prosecution should accompany any payout because compensation was not sufficiently an equivalent. And yet, I am unwilling to concede to Sloterdijk that philanthropic forgiveness offers the only alternative to a politics of quid pro quo resentment. To this end, I want to consider how the asbestos story might mobilise a thymotic force of its own, a righteous anger modelled upon, but not equivalent to, the implicit resentment that, rightly or wrongly, constrains Kelman, Banton and Miño.

Miño expands our range of accusation to a larger neo-liberal engine that facilitated injustice, while Jefferson acknowledges the incongruity of being angry with companies that are 'just a word'. In order to consider how such a force might be generated, I want to shift our focus from the meaning factory exposure might have for the activist-sufferer to its broader implication for readers, spectators and audiences who are not so immediately implicated in the asbestos story. By shifting our attention to our reception of the text, I of course follow the companies and their dissenters who competed for this attention, a competition I see play out in two contrasting Modernist texts that take very different approaches to representing the conditions of the factory worker: a series of illustrations by William Heath Robinson and a poem by Edwin Rolfe. Then, I turn to more contemporary texts – Patxi Irurzun's *Ciudad Retrete* [*Toilet City*] (2002) and Alberto Prunetti's *Amianto: Una storia operaia* [*Asbestos: A Worker's Story*] (2012) – that negotiate the asbestos factory space within the larger context of deindustrialisation. Finally, I find new possibilities for thinking about the homes of these workers in Nasser Hashmi's *A Fistful of Dust* (2015) and Yolanda Wisher's ongoing poetry project, *Maple Street Rag*.

Modernism's Factory

In 1930, the artist William Heath Robinson was commissioned to produce a set of six illustrations by Asbestos Cement Building Products Ltd, a distributor for, among others, Turners Asbestos Cement. The resulting promotional book, 'finely printed by photogravure on heavy, deckle-edged paper and tied in embossed card covers with a silk ribbon', 'portrayed the various processes of manufacture in his own inimitable way.'[5] Geoffrey Beare notes at least one occasion when a lecture on asbestos cement products, given in 1932 to Canterbury and Districts' Ironmongers' Assistants' Association, concluded with the 'highly diverting series of Heath Robinson Cartoons' (26). By this point, Robinson was already famous for drawing elaborate machines that performed simple functions. Stylistically, the asbestos machines resemble Robinson's other commercial work, which included drawings for Hovis, Johnny Walker and Oxo.

Like those of his US counterpart, Rube Goldberg, these elaborations are frequently dismissed as whimsy. And yet, like Goldberg, there is something in their conscious exaggeration of cause and effect that, even as it replicates the machinic logic of the conveyer belt, grants their observer the means to view, in sequence, the steps by which a cause realises its effects. Even as they 'reduce human beings to the muted status of side effects', as Aaron Jaffe argues, these Robinson/Goldberg variations remind us 'about the missing bits of surplus work programmed into things.'[6]

The diagrams provide a schematic reassurance that mechanical stages in developing an outcome can still provide sites of wonder. As gimmicks, in Sianne Ngai's sense of the word, they perform this function as 'both a wonder and a trick. It is a form we marvel at and distrust, admire and disdain'.[7] In producing wonder, Robinson's asbestos machines certainly do not present anger. They rely, if anything, on a 'disinterested spectator' whose feelings about the asbestos industry will not overcome their 'momentary anaesthesia of the heart.'[8] In this, they serve as a useful opposition to my second text: Edwin Rolfe's 1933 poem, 'Asbestos', wherein 'a stunning, if gruesome, conceit transforms a worker's body into his deathbed'.[9] As with many works written by poets of the literary left in the 1930s, Cary Nelson argues, it 'combines sharp social critique with a sense of revolutionary expectation', seeks 'to define a new politics and to help bring about the changes it evokes' and forms part of 'a collaborative rhetorical action' (738). Rolfe's poem contrasts the enthusiasm of Robinson's characters with the grim future that awaited the asbestos factory worker. Where Robinson foregrounded the amazing machinic processes associated with modernism, Rolfe wanted to address the deleterious consequences of mechanisation on workers' bodies. Robinson and Rolfe present two views on the asbestos factory that set up an affective dialectic between indifference and anger.

Such indifference seems hardly incidental. In 1932, around the same time that UK-based Asbestos Cement published Robinson's prints in their promotional trade book, Dr Anthony Lanza of Metropolitan Life found that an astonishing 87 per cent of US-based Johns Manville workers with more than fifteen years' work experience displayed signs of asbestosis in chest X-rays. Despite this, the standard response by Johns Manville was, in the words of Kenneth Smith's infamous memo: 'As long as the man is not disabled, it is felt that he should not be told of his condition so that he can live and work in peace, and the company can benefit by his many years of experience.' Or, as Charles Roemer later recalled of a conversation with Lewis Brown, Johns Manville's president: 'I said, "Mr. Brown, do you mean to tell me you would let them work until they dropped dead?" He said, "Yes. We save a lot of money that way."'[10] As Geoffrey Tweedale has shown, similar insights proliferated in the UK as well. In 1937, Turner & Newell director, Robert H. Turner, wrote to W. H. Rooksby that

> All asbestos fibre dust, whether it arises in a factory or elsewhere, is a danger to lungs . . . [however], if we can produce evidence from this country that the [asbestos cement] industry is not responsible for any asbestosis claims, we may be able to avoid tiresome regulations and the introduction of dangerous occupation talk.[11]

Coming after the death of Nellie Kershaw, the findings of the Merewether and Price report, not to mention earlier concerns with dust exposure, the private correspondence of senior executives of both Johns Manville and Turner & Newell demonstrates the significant efforts made to disavow knowledge that asbestos exposure led to asbestosis. The active construction of strategic ignorance characterised a general strategy of the asbestos industry – as Tweedale, McCulloch and others have shown – but it adopts a particular inflection in the case of Robinson's prints.

The six images figure a series of cross-sections to track the movement of asbestos through the mine, and through the factory, where the fibre is mashed, mixed with cement, cast into sheets, and cut into tiles. In the mine image (Fig. 7.1), Black mineworkers are contrasted with white overseers, who are presented in various positions of surveillance.

Overly pronounced racialised features in some of the miners suggests that Robinson, in part, was drawing on contemporary racist grotesquery. The seriousness of the labour involved is undercut by the equipment the miners use: a corkscrew to extract the asbestos ore, plates to carry small amounts of ore to a bicycle-powered train, a toasting fork to transfer the ore to a bucket system one piece at a time. The only indication that Robinson might harbour some ambivalence about the extraction process is suggested in his inclusion of a bar underground. While the suspicious barrel might contain water, the implication is that its white barkeep is discharging alcohol: a visual reminder of the South African *dop* or tot system, where workers were paid in alcohol. The mine image displays clear racist overtones. When compared with the other images, moreover, the superficial similarity between the workers, who, white or Black, are slightly overweight, taciturn men, belies the industriousness with which white workers carry sacks; pedal, push or wind pullies; pump bellows; or climb ladders. The relative languor of the Black miners acts as a foil to this industriousness, emphasising the convivial commitment of the white workers in Figures 7.2–7.5.

Figure 7.1 The Mining and Transport of Raw Asbestos
(© the Heath Robinson Museum)

Figure 7.2 Patent double-action grinder (© the Heath Robinson Museum)

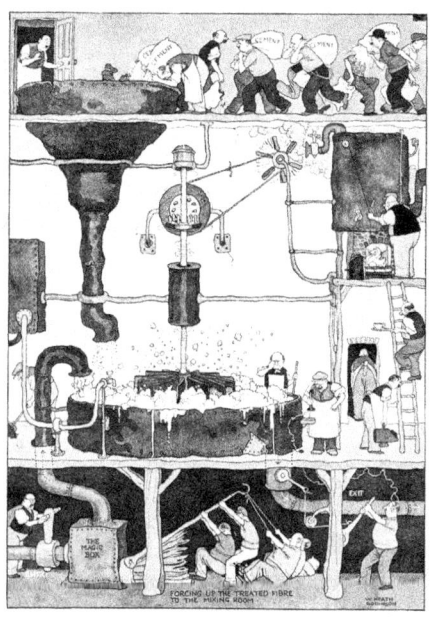

Figure 7.3 Mixing treated asbestos fibre with cement
(© the Heath Robinson Museum)

Figure 7.4 Powerful machinery (© the Heath Robinson Museum)

Figure 7.5 In the finishing departments (© the Heath Robinson Museum)

This contrast may explain why Robinson included a mining image in a promotional book for what was essentially a factory operation. Comparing the working conditions of white workers in the factory with those of Black workers in the mine relativizes the preferable conditions of the former, deflecting attention away from divisions between workers, overseers (who are often receiving cups of tea), and owner-observers (wearing suits and top hats) by subtly insisting on the white workers' superior commitment. Like many instances of racial capitalism, Cedric Robinson's term for the derivation of social and economic value from a person's racial identity, the Black miners are explicitly racialised in order to subvert any solidarity developing between labour from the mines and in the factory.[12]

The prints present a factory, where machines are powered by human labour. While the public health literature about asbestos factories raised concerns about dust exposure, the atmospheres of the prints are clear. Whereas reports detailed the punishing work by men and women wearing masks, Robinson's pictures are peopled solely by men, whose efforts seem comically out of proportion to their minimal production. Given the furious attention paid to the asbestos factory in the 1920s and 1930s, Robinson's images seem nothing so much as a particularly effective form of propaganda, designed to dissimulate precisely the rage that so many subsequent works about asbestos have sought to raise.

Robinson's work serves, then, as a useful foil to historical documentation about the dusty factory: the aesthetic equivalent of a cover-up. When considering how, or why, they are so effective in this cover-up, we might recall a distinction that both Adam Gopnik and Geoffrey Beare draw between Robinson and Goldberg. Goldberg, formerly an engineer for the San Francisco Department of Water and Sewage, was a self-taught cartoonist; Robinson had trained at the Islington School of Art and the Royal Academy. For Gopnik, this distinction is reflected in the more practical (and therefore more sinister) machines of Goldberg, which lack the 'fantasy and whimsy and cosiness' of Robinson's; for Beare, 'Robinson's inventions are beautifully rendered, often set in finally depicted landscapes or townscape and need no explanation. The humour depends on the fact that there is no hint of the comic in the way they are drawn.'[13] This combination of cosiness, whimsy and artistic seriousness serves to defuse strong emotions about the workers. Its insidious effect is not, then, simply to turn the workers into amusing caricatures, in order to create a sanitised image of the factory; it is to dampen the affective range of our response to the situation as a whole.

Activist responses to asbestos tend to focus on the industry's greed to incite a righteous indignation or rage on the part of its victims. Accordingly, when the private correspondence exposes the preference for profits over people, reading this should provoke feelings of shock. That this does not always occur may, perhaps, be explained via Robinson's whimsical prints. Activism relies on an intensification of affective response on both sides of the opposition: the rage of the workers finds its counterpart in the malicious actions of the industry. But Robinson's work suggests that industry's response is not to deny the claims (although they may do that as well) so much as to dampen the affective response, diminishing the site of concern into an object of gentle humour. It prompts us to reframe the emotional opposition between activism and industry. Whereas both develop emotionally-charged communication to help their cause, it was in the industry's interests to downplay such emotions, while activism seeks to heighten them. Their opposition can better be described as divided between the intensification or dampening of affect.

Now, I want to contrast Robinson's comic factory with one of the few modernist literary works to condemn the treatment of asbestos factory workers: Rolfe's 'Asbestos'. Rolfe's poem is made up of four quatrains. The first two quatrains introduce us to a worker, John, who, 'like a workhorse', 'cements the granite tower' with his 'sweat'. But this introduction is, if anything, fractured. The likeness to the workhorse only arises in the second quatrain. By then, the speaker has introduced John through two parenthetical allusions framed in the negative: 'Knowing (as John did) nothing of the way / men act when men are roused from lethargy, / and having nothing (as John had) to say / to those he saw were starving just as he / starved.' In not knowing or having something to say, John suffers from what John Marsh calls a 'circumscribed political consciousness.'[14]

Then, at the beginning of the third quatrain, the tense changes from the habitual past to the simple present, as the speaker introduces the effects of this circumscription: 'John's deathbed.' Where enjambment, or run-on lines, connected stanzas one and two ('as he / starved'), and three and four ('now serves / his skullface'), a full stop at the end of the second stanza emphasises this caesura, or break, in the poem's focus. According to Marsh, the poem shifts from 'John's false consciousness to his decaying, "embedded" body': 'Whereas before the workers' body structured "the granite tower," it now constructs, rather gruesomely, his own death bed.' Or, in the words of Cary Nelson, 'The exploitation of workers literally impresses itself on their bodies. Those bodies are the fulcrum, the point of application in which their lives are embedded.'[15] The conditions of John's work morph into the domestic scene of John's bed, made, as it is, of the viscera – the posts, bones; the springs, nerves; the mattress, bleeding flesh – of other workers. By combining the generic qualities of the popular ballad (a hero named John; an *abab* rhyme scheme) with this disturbing central conceit, the poem, in Nelson's reading, echoes popular form to emphasise the exploitation that its culture tends to disavow.

Rolfe first published the poem as 'The 100-percenter' in *The Daily Worker* in 1928. When it was republished in the collection *We Gather Strength* (1933), the only change Rolfe made was to the title. When considering the 'grim, admittedly anachronistic historical irony' in Rolfe's decision to change the poem's title, Marsh cites Rolfe's 'prescience' in linking the poem to a substance that, at the time, 'had only barely (and reluctantly) been acknowledged as even a *potential* threat to workers' bodies'. While useful to our purpose, Marsh's determination to clarify links between the poem and historical documentation risks eliding two competing concerns. On the one hand, whether or not Rolfe could have 'known' about the specific diseases related to asbestos, this specialist knowledge should be distinguished from a more general awareness that all dusty industries carried added risks of respiratory illness, a recurrent concern for workers whose traces can found throughout Karl Marx's *Capital*. The poem supports a more general consideration of respiratory illness than that offered by Marsh, when the 'infinite air, / compressed from dizzy altitudes, now serves / his skullface as a pillow'. John's 'pillow' of compressed infinite air might simply support his head, but the odd compound, 'skullface', with its evocations of a skeletal 'death's head', suggests the service the pillow provides is more ambivalent than first meets the eye. If the air covers John's 'skullface' then the pillow seems more likely to smother – a feeling that frequently accompanies advanced fibrosis – than support. Less likely, but suggested by the compression of air, the service and the face, this 'pillow' could refer to an oxygen mask, given the recent advances in oxygen therapy.

On the other hand, fixing the poem to these historical contexts misses perhaps its most useful function: its play on knowing and not knowing to stimulate interest and stoke anger. Tellingly, the analyses of neither Nelson or Marsh (compelling as they are) address the strange effect of the parenthetic introduction to John in lines 1 and 3. The obvious synonym to 'knowing nothing' is a passive 'not knowing'. However, when the phrase is split by the parenthesis '(as John did)', it inflects 'not knowing' with activity and agency: John actively knows nothing as opposed to John passively does not know anything. The delay provided by the parenthesis is vital to displacing our received understanding of 'knowing nothing'. Again, this delay serves Rolfe well, when the parenthesis '(as John had)' follows 'having nothing'. Although the completed sentence refers to John having nothing to say to (i.e. no solidarity with) his fellow workers, the pause creates a useful double entendre on 'having nothing' whether to eat or at all. These syntactic operations underline the readings of Nelson and Marsh, and so, perhaps, seem secondary to the point of the poem. Their use to my argument lies in their opening up a speculative third space between knowing and not knowing, a site that might reconcile having nothing and having nothing to say. My discussion of strategic ignorance in the introduction finds, here, its poetic salve in a syntax that registers how actively certain people might pursue the will not to know.

The final stanza returns to the concern about knowledge raised in the opening line: 'A vulture leers in solemn mockery, / knowing what John had never known: that dead / workers are dead before they cease to be.' For Marsh, the vulture represents the doctors and industry leaders who were already 'in the know' about asbestos. Alternatively, the vulture embodies that speculative position already suggested by the parenthetic intervention: the position of knowledge that can determine what, and to what extent, John does not know: 'dead workers are dead before they cease to be'. Vulture-like, the poem's listeners know not just what it is that John does not, but where the borders lie between his lack of knowledge and his choice not to know. This is perhaps made clearer when I introduce Rolfe's clear intertext for the rather archaic phrase 'before they cease to be': John Keats's 'When I Have Fears' (1818).[16]

Keats's poem begins 'When I have fears that I may cease to be' and proceeds to enumerate the writing and loving that his death would leave undone. The poem's resolution is not action, however; it leaves him standing alone 'on the shore / Of the wide world', thinking 'Till Love and Fame to nothingness do sink'. Contemplation of mortality leads the poetic subject to an impasse; his priorities ('Love and Fame') fall away. Excessive reflection upon mortality, Keats warns, interferes with action. When Rolfe recasts the phrase in the third person, it contrasts Keats's knowing speaker to the unknowing workers, who are dead 'before' they can indulge in such meditations. Ceasing to be, for Keats, combines with death a curtailed future made up of the life that might have been but wasn't. The workers, rendered into what Giorgio Agamben calls 'bare life' by their absorption into 'the granite tower' and the 'deathbed', have no such future, curtailed or otherwise.[17] The extravagant possibilities, which Keats's speaker offers up – his writings, tracings and lovings – as that future which his death will peremptorily erase, never occur to John, the worker who shares Keats's name.

The poem's links to Keats suggests that the structure of the poem might echo not simply the popular ballad (as observed by Nelson), but the sonnet form of 'When I Have Fears'. While Keats's regular 14-line sonnet follows a similar *abab* for three quatrains before ending in a rhyming couplet, Rolfe's poem continues for two more lines, which effectively repudiates the closure offered by the couplet: a 'mockery' that scorns his fear that he will 'cease to be'. This admittedly tendentious reading is strengthened by the contrasting rhythms of the two works. 'When I Have Fears' interrupts its iambic pentameter only to emphasise two caesuras, to break the monotony with two spondees, and to miss a stress in the final line as a gesture to the falling away of 'nothingness'. The first two quatrains of 'Asbestos' struggle towards a regular trochaic metre to match Keats's iambs; similarly, the final two aspire to an iambic pentameter that only the description of John's bed achieves. 'Struggle' and 'aspire' because, from the first parenthesis, Rolfe robs us of Keats's rhythmic certainty: the establishment of a trochaic regularity with 'knowing nothing', which might have overcome the anapestic inclinations in 'of the way', is altogether disrupted by '(as John did)'. Rolfe further wrong-foots his listener with the other parentheses, the trailing 'lethargy', and the enjambment, all of which contribute to a sense of uncertainty about what is, or should be, happening rhythmically in the poem. While Keats exploits variations in rhythm to highlight certain areas of concern or interest, Rolfe undermines the very basis of rhythmic expectation to challenge the listener's secure sense that she knows what is what.

The connection between Keats and Rolfe is less strange than it might first appear: after all, a friend of Rolfe's remembered him as 'a Jewish replica of Keats'.[18] In *A Poetics of Global Solidarity*, Clemens Spahr notes that Rolfe's 1935 poem, 'To My Contemporaries', rewrites a line from Keats's 'Ode to a Nightingale', drawing on the spiritual conflict enshrined in the latter to better understand the historical moment of the former.[19] Keats is often dismissed as exemplifying an individualising poetry that 'projects an idealistic self' inimical to the project of revolutionary politics. But, Spahr argues, Rolfe turns Keats into a means for mediating a collective form of subjectivity that co-opts, rather than excludes, the fiction of the self. Rolfe's use of Keats alludes to the possibilities available to Romantic subject, demonstrates that the conditions of capitalism deny these possibilities to the worker, and suggests how the lyric voice might 'remain present in a higher collective form of subjectivity' as 'the basis of a poetics of engagement' (37). Spahr's observation that Rolfe draws a revolutionary potential out of Keats in his later work may be seen even at this early stage.

I could dwell on this comparison a bit longer: considering, for instance, how the habitual drag of time on John, 'older every hour', resonates with Keats's more ephemeral 'fair creature of an hour'; or how the poem's 'vulture' revisits the optical positioning of Cortez's 'eagle eyes' in 'On First Looking into Chapman's Homer'. But its chief value lies in showing how Rolfe conceptually, structurally and rhythmically reworks Keats to develop a relation between death and ignorance quite different to that conventionally associated with the speculative Romantic subject. What John knows is less important to Rolfe than informing his listeners that their furnishings are made with 'John's' viscera. Likewise, worker knowledge about the dangers of asbestos should be immaterial; Rolfe calls on his readers to attend to the harm inflicted by companies *and their implication in this process*. This reading works because it trades on tensions in the poem, replayed throughout the asbestos story, between knowing, not knowing and ignorance. This is no mere philosophical puzzle, however: Rolfe makes the distinction deeply unsettling in three different ways. First, the listener adopts the same position as the observing vulture, overlooking the conditions of John's life and death. John, by contrast, has no knowledge about his condition; further, he doesn't even know that he doesn't know. The listener looms over the unsuspecting John as a potential beneficiary of his demise. If these two images of exploitation implicate the listener, there is no easy reconciliation to be found in the rhythmic and syntactic disruptions that structure the poem. If Rolfe's poem advocates outrage, it is not targeted at activists like Miño, workers like Banton, or victims like Jefferson (even if these individuals engage with all three identities), but at ourselves: the unwitting beneficiaries of the asbestos industry.

By turning away from the rage of activists, workers and victims, objectively represented, towards a poetics that might inspire the reader to share these feelings, I want to mark an important refiguration of my argument about both Robinson and Rolfe: presenting these works, side by side, sets up a dialectic between the responses they each attempt to engender in their viewers or listeners. For Robinson, the humorous, lighthearted depiction of the factory worker provides a (racialised) optic that defuses the emotional investment of his viewer. For Rolfe, the fractured presentation of ignorance as variated not between what is known and what is unknown, but between who knows and who doesn't, prompts an uneasiness about the situation that, if not rage itself, may well be its precursor.

On Asbestos Snow and the Long Downturn

The dynamic I have developed in my response to Robertson and Rolfe, between innocence and experience, can be traced in the juxtaposition of white asbestos and snow. As chrysotile dust billows about, it looks like snow. This is why it was used as a snow substitute in Hollywood films, like *The Wizard of Oz* (1939) and *Citizen Kane* (1941). In the 1940s, James Hardie's in-house magazine would make light of this, captioning a cartoon about their Adelaide factory: 'Birkenhead, the only place in South Australia where it snows every day.'[20] When, in Stephen Blanchard's novel about growing up in Hull in the early 1960s, *Gagarin and I* (1996), a bus driver drops off the protagonist, Leonard, and his mother to visit Leonard's father, the driver sardonically refers to the area as 'Little Lapland': the factory where Leonard's father works – 'to make *asbestos*', his mother exclaims, 'it's saved thousands of lives in the world. An asbestos house will never burn' – makes him think 'it's snow sometimes [. . .] You can pretend it is Christmas all year.'[21] Blanchard, writing at perhaps the height of public awareness about asbestos diseases, leaves the irony unexplained: he notes in passing how the asbestos fibres 'tickle' Leonard's throat and cause his father to spit, but he does not explicate how the association between snow and asbestos should be less a cause for play than for outrage (203).

Similar memories about factories in Ambler in Pennsylvania, Glasgow's Clydeside area, or Leeds in West Yorkshire, have been mobilised to insist upon the innocence of workers and provoke outrage at their unknowing exploitation. Asbestos snow appears in plays that feature the surroundings of asbestos factories, like *The White Mountains* (2018), a collection of community theatre compositions written about the Keasbey & Mattison waste dumps in Ambler, Frances Poet's *Fibres* (2019), a play that recalls the factories beside the Clyde river in Glasgow, Alice Nutter's radio drama *Snow in July* (2008) and Ken Yates's *Dust* (2009), both about the Turner & Newall factory in Armley, West Leeds. These dramatic works use the associations between snow, play and innocence to emphasise the malevolence behind the companies' gross malfeasance. 'Snow in July?' Eileen asks her husband, Maurice, in Nutter's play, on seeing a photo of his friend, Roy.[22] 'It's not snow,' Maurice responds, 'it's dust, used to blow across. If you spat on it, you could make little balls, snow that never melted . . . not even when you swallowed it.' 'It's snowing,' begins Poet's *Fibres*, 'And he says it like he's a seven-year old or something.'[23] Lucy, whose parents will both die of mesothelioma over the course of the play, begins by exalting in the snow. Soon, however, she realises 'this isn't snow?' 'Just looks like snow,' her father, Jack, responds, 'Not the real thing [. . .] you breathe it in and it takes hold of you [. . .] kills you from the inside' (11). The scene ends with Lucy desperately trying to stop her mother, Beanie, from shaking the 'snow' off Jack's jacket. The innocence associated with playing in the snow becomes the vehicle for engendering a protective response on the part of the audience, which, in turn, galvanises audiences to action.

Asbestos snow highlights the risk courted by texts mourning deindustrialisation and the decline of the welfare state: the tendency to collapse into melodrama. Clydeside Glasgow narratives have shown how useful asbestos is in allegorising an ambivalence about deindustrialisation nostalgia.[24] Anne Donovan's 'All that Glisters' (2001), Suhayl Saadi's *Joseph's Box* (2009) and Ross Raisin's *Waterline* (2011) each evoke nostalgia for industry, where present-day melancholia counterpoints memories of greater security, camaraderie and satisfaction in the lost world of the factory developed through narratives of *bildung*. To temper this nostalgia, they acknowledge these affective and financial securities, or 'freedoms from care', were bought and paid for with toxic exposure that compromised the health of workers and their families, and created greater concerns for the present and future. But where Donovan and Saadi ultimately shy away from the melodrama of the asbestos victim, by mediating their experience through a child narrator (Donovan) or by demonstrating the victim was no innocent (Saadi), Raisin reifies the already deceased Cathy into something of a secular saint. By 'using' asbestos to sacralise Cathy, he conflates it with all that was difficult, unsatisfactory or negative about industrial life, a process that allows one to externalise it, and thus preserve, untainted, an idyllic understanding of proletarian life.

When cultural works recreate working conditions mimetically, only to twist these dirty realist descriptions to fit melodramatic plots based on polarising forms of innocence and ignorance, they sacrifice social and aesthetic nuance. In *Some Versions*, Empson mentions melodrama in connection with the covert pastoral, to suggest that, in melodrama too, efforts to convey the complex through the simple frames the worker as both better and worse than their writer. In this regard, Bill D'Agostino's contribution to *The White Mountains* collection, 'The Hill', warns us about the problems inherent in overemphasising innocence in the conflation of asbestos and snow.[25] In a conversation between Lulu and her grandmother, the grandmother notes that, while it is true that they used to slide down the 'hills' of asbestos with sleds, if they had not, she would never have met the girl's grandfather. The hills were not simply sites where the innocent were exposed; they provided important points of social and communal exchange. This is why the grandmother advocates not for their eradication, but their rehabilitation into a park.

The dialectic developed through our reading of Robinson and Rolfe usefully introduced the factory space as either a space of congenial, if boring, opportunities to celebrate human work or as an exploitative space, slowly killing its participants. While this stark opposition served in the midst of the industrialised 1930s, subsequent changes to functional 'collective labour' have eclipsed this dialectic. Thus, when the 'deindustrial' novel seizes upon asbestos as an evil product of industrialisation, it effectively elides earlier tendencies to present workers as agents as well as victims. Moreover, the rise in a general awareness linking capital to toxic events – from Rachel Carson's *Silent Spring* (1962) to the catastrophic events associated with the names Chernobyl,

Bhopal or Love Canal – mean that simple claims to innocence ignore the real and ongoing contributions of activist thinking. When it comes to the contemporary proletarian novel, like Patxi Irurzun's *Ciudad Retrete* [*Toilet City*] (2002) or Alberto Prunetti's *Amianto: Una storia operaia* [*Asbestos: A Worker's Story*] (2012), the earlier reliance on proletarian solidarity dissipates as the workers, themselves, adjust to increasingly precarious labour practices. *Ciudad Retrete* follows a union of workers who occupy their factory, POZAL S.A., when they learn that their company plans to use a labour integration programme to expand the workforce. They worry, rightly, that this will make their positions more precarious. Because of their subaltern status (in 'grupos marginales'), the workers already work in unsafe conditions with materials that contain 'agents harmful to their health,' 'like the asbestos in the wagons used to load and unload porcelain at the kiln.'[26] Indeed, 'everything began,' Javier Rípodas writes in the first of his 'diary' sections, 'the day, after so much time, I began to pee blood again' (13). As if to emphasise their treatment as human waste, the factory manufactures toilet bowls: 'They were used and sacrificed as dehumanized raw material in service of the city's economy, which is completely dependent on POZAL S.A.' (11–12). Importantly, the prologue informs us that the workers' occupation lasted almost the whole of April 1986, that it ended with a 'famously fatal eviction in which two of them lost their lives', and that the events became the subject of an investigation of a newspaper, *La Calle* [*The Street*] (11). By enclosing the narrative, at the start, with the circumstances of its conclusion, the novel shifts the site of suspense from what happens to how the workers, themselves, tell the story of what happens. So, like Indra Sinha's *Animal's People*, it communicates a media story from below, by drawing on transcripts of a character's recorded interviews (also called Animal), the diary of another, and the love letters of a third. Not only do these provide 'antidotes to boredom and discouragement', but they 'testify [. . .] to the circumstances, the facts that determine lives that someone judged as useless [inservibles], but that, in the end, teach us about values like solidarity and dignity, so devalued today' (12).

The solidarity in this union provides a striking contrast to Renato, the protagonist of Prunetti's *Amianto* and the author's father, who was a '*transferista*, a rootless and specialized worker who was always on the road, traveling from one site to the next'.[27]

> As a specialized worker, he was part of the aristocracy. He and his colleagues were content with their higher paychecks and were less rebellious than the masses of workers who came of age in the 1960s and 1970s, who leaned more towards absenteeism and sabotage, and who were critical of work ideologies. (36)

For all that Renato's relative individualism appears at odds with the solidarity of the workers in *Ciudad Retrete*, both texts are deeply enmeshed in the changing conditions for labour in the 1980s and 1990s. *Amianto* is a memoir about Renato's life and work. More exactly, it is an attempt to reconstruct Renato's life after his death from mesothelioma, when Prunetti must decide whether to pursue compensation or not. This becomes a gradual accounting for those moments when Renato, a welder, might have been exposed to the fibres that finally killed him:

> Small crystalline darts. Invisible shards that find their way into the esophagus or lungs, that stick to the pleura for twenty, thirty, even forty years, and that cause a wound that the body can't heal or eradicate, triggering a process of cellular degeneration. A tumor. (29)

At the same time, it is a resurrection not simply of his father's work and death, but of their way of life: his father's encounter with a famous actress; the football games he played as a child. As Prunetti observes, the book 'is a scar, a scar that was healed by the suture thread of writing'.[28]

The personal anecdotes are as important as the more obvious engagement with Renato's disease, death and compensation proceedings, since they perform much the same function as the diary, the recording and the letter in *Ciudad Retrete*. Formally intimate, these devices turn workers, who frequently appear as mere embodiments of their labour, into people. Monica Jansen and Enrico Cesaretti have noted of *Amianto* that it aims to turn private events into a collective 'resistance against capitalism', to 'expand the act of narration into that of cultural activism'.[29] But it does not do so by, as in Rolfe's poem, arousing our anger about a general mistreatment of workers. Indeed, if Jansen is correct, it manifests through an 'affective realism', which Lauren Berlant associates with 'the attrition of a fantasy, a collectively invested form of life, of good life'.[30] The attrition of individual fantasies reflects the more sustained attrition of the collective fantasies that underpinned the 1930s proletarian novel, as labour conditions changed over the twentieth century. But, since such fantasies originate from the collective, I can complete the hermeneutic circle by aligning *Amianto* with *Ciudad Retrete*, where the ostensible collectivity of the workers, proposed by the prologue, is supported by the individual, private voices of Javi, Animal and Juan Fante, aka Corbalancito.

We can differentiate the melancholic attitude to deindustrialisation in Ross Raisin from that in Irurzun or Prunetti. Raisin's work is already post-industrial: it can no longer find possibilities for workers to excise themselves from their circumstances. The best they can manage is a change in attitude. For Prunetti and, to a lesser extent, Irurzun, such changes are insufficient, not only because they try to historicise deindustrialisation as an ongoing process (rather than something already completed), but because the author, as a figure, is also imbricated in this narrative of precarity. Prunetti calls himself a 'precarious cognitive worker' (107).

At the same time, it is clear that, within the circumscribed conditions of both *Ciudad Retrete* and *Amianto*, anger is rendered impotent. The strike has already failed at the beginning of Irurzun's novel; Prunetti's memoir emerges not from collective action, but as the biographical supplement needed when applying for state-sanctioned compensation. While there are ample expressions of rage within the narratives (exemplified in Animal's frequent, Tourette's-driven expletives), their agitations fail, ultimately, to produce meaningful, long-term political consequences. This is exemplified in 'Like Steve McQueen', the chapter Prunetti added to *Amianto*'s second edition. Alluding to the famous actor who died of mesothelioma aged 50, the chapter, according to Jansen, offers a kind of mythopoesis, wherein Renato and his fellow victims might be inscribed into 'the collective myth of cinematic outcasts and rebels'.[31] Prunetti, however, is more ambivalent about this, as his epigraph to the chapter makes clear: 'Damn bastards . . . I'm still alive! Papillon, with more bark than bite [con più rabbia che denti]' (210). These are McQueen's final lines in *Papillon*, as the film closes on him floating away on a pile of coconuts. McQueen's 'rabbia', here, is not the confident anger of *The Great Escape*; it is a last gasp of defiance, barely heard, as the camera takes its leave of the title character, losing sight of him in a rolling Caribbean sea.

This impasse seems to reflect Martha Nussbaum's view that anger inevitably leads to a dead-end, harming both the wrongdoer and their victim.[32] Although not quite so impotent as for McQueen's Papillon, anger for Nussbaum can neither repair the damage caused nor lead to the betterment of society. At best, one might hope for a 'transition-anger', to protect 'dignity and self-respect', 'taking the wrongdoer seriously' and 'combatting injustice' (6). But, it remains of 'limited usefulness' and 'normatively problematic' (6). Forgiveness too, when it is transactional and conditional, fails to correct the imbalance. Only 'unconditional love and generosity', with their emphasis on intimate human relations in the personal, social and political spheres, can move 'beyond the whole drama of anger and forgiveness to forge attitudes that actually support trust and reconciliation' (13). For all that their methods are different, even contradictory, Nussbaum's conclusions resemble Sloterdijk's, who also advocates unconditional generosity to discharge excesses of rage and anger. But do such ideals continue to hold, when I pass from the factory to the home, as asbestos 'travels' there on workers' clothes?

New Worksites

I have mentioned Raisin, who uses these histories to develop a sentimental disregard for his protagonist's wife, Cathy. Now, I want to turn to Frances Poet's play, *Fibres* (2019), to consider how the same device might disclose richer, more complex ways of addressing domestic labour as an important form of work in its own right. *Fibres* parallels the stories of Jack and Beanie, a couple who both develop mesothelioma, their daughter Lucy, who is struggling in the wake of their deaths, and Pete, Lucy's love interest. Relying, for the most part, on expository monologue, the play's dynamism develops from rapid scene changes rather than dialogue or action. These vignettes serve to juxtapose conditions, whose decades of separation make the development of asbestos diseases so difficult to track. To concretise the connections between these diverse scenes, the play leans heavily on imagery of fibres: the characters are connected by asbestos fibres, fibre optic cables (Lucy and Pete work for a telecommunications company), and even clothing fibres.

Importantly, Beanie's exposure happens, as does Cathy's, when she launders Jack's asbestos-contaminated clothing (he was an electrician). Poet's success in the play lies in taking the neglected act of laundry and centralising it. Even Beanie's mesothelioma comes to be understood through the metaphor of laundry: 'my washing machine "cell" is so buggered up by the overalls that it doesn't turn off and ends up flooding the whole damn house. My carpets, my machine, everything ruined because of Jack's dirty bloody overalls' (15). Beanie's laundering of Jack's 'bloody overalls' crosses over into myth, as 'Beanie' explains that her nickname is based on the 'bean nighe', a Scots omen of death that takes the shape of a washerwoman, washing bloody clothes in a stream. The relation thus set up between laundry and death has repercussions for Lucy, who finds herself incapable of cleaning her parents' clothes, or even starting a relationship with Pete (she fears she will have to do his washing). The play resolves itself with Pete taking it upon himself to clean the clothes, which frees Lucy from her anxiety about laundry while also showing her that he loves her.

Laundry is the cause of illness, a mythic omen of death, and the central conceit around which love is shown and conflicts are resolved. Why? In Social Reproduction Theory, a particular theoretical development in Marxist Feminist analyses of domestic labour, the household plays an integral role in reproduction of class society. Domestic labour, like laundry, goes unpaid, and therefore undervalued, in capitalist economies. On first glance, Poet's conceit seems to push for a more equitable redistribution, where laundry is recognised as labour. When exposure to asbestos in domestic settings happens as a result of one's domestic labour, it becomes an occupational illness. Instead of appeals for sympathy, as if for innocents, asbestos exposures through domestic labour should provoke calls for labour justice.

Within Social Reproduction Theory, there are criticisms of this wholehearted celebration of domestic labour; certainly, it has and should have value, but insofar as it is 'a key input into the reproduction of capitalist society', domestic labour functions hand in glove with capitalist society's 'attendant social misery and environmental destruction'.[33] When Beanie's domestic labour is intentionally conflated with her work in a laundromat, it does not just highlight the domestic as a sphere of work, it signals a continuity between waged and unwaged labour. The distinction between these two forms of labour, Lucy realises at the end, is based on love: 'it wasn't just poison they shared. It was love' (51). But if unwaged labour is done for love, then love enters into an exchange relation with unwaged labour. Love, Poet obliquely suggests, has been co-opted into the capitalist economy. So, when Jack suggests their travails have at least helped them realise 'how much we loved each other', Beanie insists that 'the people responsible' 'stole years from us' (50). For such people, who 'put profit over life', only money matters; therefore, the only just response is to 'chip away at their bonuses, their nest eggs, their private health care, their retirement cruises' (51–2). Beanie's point is not that money can truly compensate for the time stolen from them; it is that, within the miserable conditions of a capitalist economy, money becomes the only available means to acknowledge the hidden cost of working with asbestos, waged or unwaged, in the home or out of it. If, on the face of it, laundry seems to be a way of communicating love, it is, under the conditions of capitalism, a sign of how love itself becomes reified, commodified, and tied to labour practices.

For Nussbaum, the uses of anger and conditional forgiveness are limited because they fracture intimate relations between individuals, societies and polities. But if love is compromised by capitalism, it is similarly compromised in resolving anger. If anything, the conditions Beanie describes demand a kind of angry love. Perhaps, then, the relation is not between Nussbaum's key terms: anger and forgiveness, or resentment, generosity or love? What if, as Audre Lorde writes, anger's counterpart is hatred: 'Hatred is the fury of those who do not share our goals, and its object is death and destruction. Anger is the grief of distortions between peers, and its object is change.'[34] Anger, in this situation, is transitionally useful, insofar as it takes 'the grief of distortions between peers' as the basis for political change. This is not so incompatible with Nussbaum's argument as it might appear. Nussbaum opens her book by reflecting on the transformation of the Furies into Kindly Ones at the end of Aeschylus's *Oresteia*. Importantly, Nussbaum argues that their previous 'unbridled anger' [hatred] undergoes 'a profound inner reorientation, going to the very roots of their personality', changing to 'a mindset of common love' (2; 3). To resurrect this transformation from hatred into anger, a new proletarian literature cannot simply trade on old forms of solidarity: while cognizant of their usefulness as models, Irurzun and Prunetti show us that these approaches are already foreclosed. Instead, it must try to relate these older injustices to current and ongoing forces of hatred in the present. In this regard, two of the most interesting responses to the asbestos factory can be found in a novel by Nasser Hashmi, about the Turner Brothers' Factory in

Rochdale near Manchester, and the ongoing poetry project of Yolanda Wisher, about the Keasbey & Mattison factory in Ambler, Pennsylvania, since they both relate the legacy of asbestos exposure not just to forms of angry love but to two forms of ongoing hatred: Islamophobia in the United Kingdom and Anti-Black racism in the US.

Notwithstanding the novel's abrupt style, Hashmi's *A Fistful of Dust* (2015) offers an important, and all too rare, response to South Asian experiences in UK asbestos factories.[35] His protagonist, Shah Rafiq, begins the story with a diagnosis of asbestosis. Rafiq is a widower, who lives with his daughter and has been hiding the signs of his illness for some time. When he describes the Turner Brothers factory, it follows in the tradition of Rolfe: his workmates were 'gobbled up [. . .] and spat out with ferocious regularity'; the work has 'taken my house, my health and my dignity'; it relied on a choice between 'work and get ill or no work at all. It wasn't much of a choice' (11; 17; 21). If this recalls the proletarian tradition, Hashmi's innovation is to parallel the trajectory of Rafiq's illness with his journey to rescue his grandson, who has joined a fundamentalist group in Iraq. Rafiq decides to follow him, to persuade him to return. And, over the course of some weeks, persuade him he does. When Wasim returns, he throws himself into the organisation of his grandfather's compensation case. Ultimately, however, the police arrest him for terrorism; he is tried, convicted and sentenced to twelve years. The novel closes with Rafiq's death, shortly after, 'Hope for Wasim – if not for me. There was only one martyr in this family' (328).

The novel presents a strange and unsatisfying parallel: the fibres that are killing Rafiq seem to demand a corollary that all too easily falls on the idea that people like Wasim present a threat to the British body politic. At Spotland Road, the site of the old Turner Brothers factory, Rafiq wonders at the comparison: 'I [. . .] imagined both pavements packed with exhausted workers [. . .] they knew what mattered: to provide and be responsible [. . .] So [. . .] how did a boy from this town get involved in the dead-end of jihad?' (323). Anticipating familiar critiques of failed cultural immersion, Rafiq notes the 'hundreds' who aren't immersed, but 'weren't interested in "saving" their "brothers and sisters"' (323). At the end of this reflection, Rafiq observes that 'this raw, irritable line of thinking subsided' as he moves away from the factory. Like the fibres in his lungs, it is the line of thinking that proves raw and irritable to Rafiq. In a similar manner, then, the proper targets of Hashmi's metaphor about asbestos fibres appear to be ideas, not people: not least, those ideologies that imagine that jihad and cultural immersion offer mutually exclusive solutions to the problems facing the migrant and those posed by the figure of the migrant. Rafiq's 'line of thinking' subsides as he offers one prayer that a new development on the site of the old Turner Brothers factory will bring much needed jobs to the area and another for Wasim. Certainly, more equable distribution is rather more likely to work to undercut radicalism than ideological warfare, but the force of the novel is not to be found in Rafiq's ideas. Rather, it seems to be in his belief in fostering human relationships: as when Wasim channels his fundamentalist hatred into an anger about compensation, or when Rafiq goes to fetch him in Iraq.

A comparable project of relationship building emerges in Yolanda Wisher's *Maple Street Rag*, named for the street in Ambler where her grandmother lived.[36] In the US, Ambler was once regarded as 'the asbestos capital of the world' because of the Keasbey & Mattison factory based there. More recently, it is known as the site of two Superfund sites. The first, declared in 1986, tried to rehabilitate the 1.5 cubic tonnes of discarded asbestos that made up an area known as the 'White Mountains'. The second, declared in 2009, included the nearby BoRit factory. It is unsurprising, then, that Wisher mordantly calls one of her poems 'My Grandmama's House Is Now The EPA.'[37] Importantly, the concluding refrain – 'see, them doctors can't save you, but your grandma may' – presents in condensed form what seems to me a key concern for Wisher's project: the resurrection of kinship as the means to salvage intimate bonds, whilst not dismissing the clear grounds for anger.

Wisher explores this concern in the poem 'Hiraeth', which reflects on home-finding in the broader context of anti-Black violence in the United States. 'Hiraeth', which takes as its title the Welsh word describing homesickness for a place that never existed, tells the story of Wisher's family moving from Ambler to North Wales, some five miles away:

> We left Ambler and were safe from asbestos, family drama, low country beginnings, 'til he started beating us and drinking, or did he start drinking and then beating us, and the one floor house was full of pus no one could see [. . .]

If the new home is an escape from Ambler, it offers no escape from the residue of anti-Black hatred, a 'pus no one could see' whose vitriolic effects are cathected through alcohol and violence. Paradoxically, it is back in Ambler where a home can be found:

> We would get dropped off at Ambler with trash bags full of clothes for a week, while something in our house got excommunicated [. . .] [Gram's] house was a fortress against thunderstorms.

Wisher is attentive to the ambivalent protections of this fortress, however, which she parses from sweets to watermelons to mesothelioma: 'The melons we imbibe leave us pregnant with mesothelioma, Hodgkin's.' This, she explains, comes from the 'two feet of vegetation between us and earth's most insidious minerals'. But, in a place where 'slumlord more powerful than the borough', the contingencies of environmental contamination become inevitable when building a home. Importantly, there is no escape, even when you leave. As Wisher writes, 'I walk around like there's a tropic rain breeze in my lungs, but I'm from there.' Hiraeth may offer the illusions of a home, but to Wisher, who is 'from there', it sounds like 'a noose', evoking the long and traumatising history of anti-Black lynching. To write about Ambler, while attending to the twinned histories of environmental contamination and anti-Black violence, demands more than mere protective gear; it calls for Lorde's 'grief of distortions between peers'. Or, in Wisher's words, 'Looking back through poison requires more than a mask, you might need a blowtorch.' And yet, there is hope in the kin-making relations that might be formed. After all, 'They left home, to remake it in their children.'

Both Hashmi and Wisher return to the power of familial bonds as the means to form intimate relations that can weather the forces of an anger that is necessary and justified. They appreciate that, with the withering of previous forms of labour solidarity, it may be that the family offers the best site where such work might begin. But, and this is crucial, neither Hashmi nor Wisher return to the heteronormative, nuclear family. Rather, they imagine this relation through grandparents and grandchildren: directly linked genetically, certainly, but generationally removed. These relations offer potential places of sanctuary that develop through the ongoing and persistent efforts of the people involved: the grandfather in Hashmi's case; the grandchild in Wisher's. Importantly, the relations are tried and tested through an acceptance of the other's anger that bypasses agreement, legitimation or ratification.

When the factory turns from a site of contested labour practice to a site of environmental contamination, labour loses the collectivity it needs to offer any meaningful form of defiance. Having no site to be staged nor clear target, the anger that erupts is liable to become a kind of hatred that might as easily be turned against the self as any actual perpetrator. Nevertheless, this anger is necessary; without it, one can easily retreat into a nostalgia for an industrial past that, despite its equivocations, finds more satisfaction in past injustice than changing conditions in the present. Resurrecting the past, as a site of contestation, can provide useful models, but only if their usefulness is tied to a hermeneutic process of understanding, rather than a dialectical process of overcoming. These models can inspire, but they cannot provide example. Amidst the withering of labour solidarity, new sites of possible solidarity have emerged, at the intersection between racial violence and environmental contamination. Such sites are risky, insofar as they depend on a few, who, having suffered both racial violence and environmental contamination, must become the figureheads for this new solidarity. But they are also offer new possibilities for large, coordinated action, provided that people can build the relationships necessary to bear each other's anger.

Notes

1. Eduardo Miño, qtd. in Francisco Báez Baquet, *Amianto: Un genocidio impune* (Málaga: ediciones del Genal, 2014), p. 7.
2. Gideon Haigh, *Asbestos House: The Secret History of James Hardie Industries* (Melbourne: Scribe Publications, 2006), p. 7.
3. Moishe Postone, *Time, Labor, and Social Domination* (Cambridge: Cambridge University Press, 1994), p. 350.
4. Peter Sloterdijk, *Rage and Time*, trans. Mario Wenning (New York: Columbia University Press, 2010), p. 9.
5. Geoffrey Beare, *Heath Robinson's Commercial Art* (London: Lund Humphries, 2017), p. 27.
6. Jaffe, *Way*, p. 49.
7. Ngai, *Gimmick*, p. 54.
8. Henri Bergson, *Laughter: An Essay on the Meaning of the Comic*, trans. Cloudesley Brereton and Fred Rothwell (New York: The Macmillan Company, 1911), p. 3.
9. Edwin Rolfe, *Collected Poems*, eds Cary Nelson and Jefferson Hendricks (Chicago: University of Illinois Press, 1997), p. 62; Cary Nelson, 'Lyric Politics: The Poetry of Edwin Rolfe', 38 (3) *Modern Fiction Studies* (1992), p. 738.
10. Charles Roemer, qtd in Paul Brodeur, *Outrageous Misconduct: The Asbestos Industry on Trial* (New York: Pantheon Press, 1985), pp. 276–7.
11. Robert H. Turner, qtd in Tweedale, *Magic*, p. 23.
12. See Cedric Robinson, *Black Marxism: The Making of the Black Radical Tradition* (Chapel Hill: University of North Carolina Press, 1983), Chapter 1.
13. Adam Gopnik, 'Introduction', *The Art of Rube Goldberg* (New York: Abrams Comicarts, 2013), p. 17; Beare, *Heath*, p. 10. Interestingly, the opening sketch of *The Art of Rube Goldberg*, relating an invention of a Professor Butts, relies on using asbestos bags to catch cigarette butts.
14. John Marsh, '"Dead Before They Cease to Be": On Edwin Rolfe's "Asbestos"', *Modern American Poetry Site*, 2001. Accessed 23 February 2021: http://www.modernamericanpoetry.org/criticism/john-marsh-asbestos
15. Nelson, 'Lyric', p. 739.
16. John Keats, *The Complete Poems*, ed. Jack Stillinger (Cambridge, MA: Belknap Press, 1982), p. 166.
17. Giorgio Agamben, *Homo Sacer: Sovereign Power and Bare Life*, trans. Daniel Heller-Rozen (Stanford: Stanford University Press, 1998), p. 4.
18. Alan M. Wald, *Exiles from a Future Time: The Forging of the Mid-Twentieth-Century Literary Left* (Chapel Hill, NC: University of North Carolina Press, 2002), p. 12.
19. Clemens Spahr, *A Poetics of Global Solidarity: Modern American Poetry and Social Movements* (Basingstoke: Palgrave Macmillan, 2015), p. 37.
20. Matt Peacock, *Killer Dust: James Hardie Exposed* (Sydney: HarperCollins, 2011), Ebook.
21. Stephen Blanchard, *Gargarin and I* (London: Vintage, 1996), p. 201; 202; 203.
22. Alice Nutter, *Snow in July*, BBC Radio 4, 8 January 2008.
23. Poet, *Fibres*, p. 9.

24. Phil O'Brien presents a more sympathetic account of deindustrialisation in Chapter 4 of *The Working Class and Twenty-First-Century British Fiction: Deindustrialisation, Demonisation, Resistance* (London: Routledge, 2019).
25. Bill D'Agostino, 'The Hill', in *The White Mountains*. Accessed 23 February 2021: https://reachambler.sciencehistory.org/theplay
26. Patxi Irurzun, *Ciudad Retrete* (Tafalla: Txalaparta, 2002), p. 11.
27. Alberto Prunetti, 'Asbestos: The Story of a Tuscan Welder', trans. Oonagh Stransky, 41 (2) *New England Review* (2020), p. 34.
28. Alberto Prunetti, *Amianto: Una storia operaia* (Rome: Edizioni Alegre, 2014), p. 161.
29. Jansen, 'Asbestos', p. 23; Cesaretti, *Elemental*, p. 146.
30. Berlant, *Cruel*, p. 11.
31. Jansen, 'Asbestos', p. 22. For an account of the confusion caused when McQueen's diagnosis and subsequent, nontraditional treatment plan became conflated with his onscreen and offscreen personae as the rebel outsider, see Barron Lerner, *When Illness Goes Public: Celebrity Patients and How We Look at Medicine* (Baltimore, ML: Johns Hopkins University Press, 2006), Chapter 7.
32. Martha Nussbaum, *Anger and Forgiveness: Resentment, Generosity, Justice* (Oxford: Oxford University Press, 2016).
33. Kirstin Munro, '"Social Reproduction Theory," Social Reproduction, and Household Production', 83 (4) *Science & Society* (2019), p. 454.
34. Audre Lorde, 'The Uses of Anger', 9 (3) Women's Studies Quarterly (1981), p. 8.
35. Nasser Hashmi, *Fistful of Dust* (Kibworth Beauchamp: Matador, 2015).
36. Yolanda Wisher, 'Performance with the Afroeaters', *Kelly Writers House*, 5 September 2017, Pennsound, Accessed 23 February 2021: https://writing.upenn.edu/pennsound/x/Wisher.php
37. Yolanda Wisher, 'My Grandmama's House Is Now The EPA', *Jacket2: Solidarity Texts*, edited by Laynie Browne, 13 April 2018. Accessed 23 February 2021: https://jacket2.org/poems/grandmamas-house

8

THE HOME

Gas-fires and Talcum Powder

In Samuel Beckett's *Murphy* (1938), asbestos plays a small, supporting role in servicing Murphy's gas-fire. After Murphy replaces his associate Ticklepenny at the Magdalen Mental Mercyseat, a mental asylum loosely modelled on the Bethlehem Royal Hospital (Bedlam) in South London, Ticklepenny helps him move into a garret at the top of the building. They set up an asbestos radiator to heat the room. The radiator is jury-rigged to the gas supply in the bathroom below. But it lacks an asbestos nozzle to regulate the flow. Eventually, this causes one of the more desultory of gas explosions in literary history, blowing up both Murphy and garret: 'Soon his body would be quiet, soon he would be free. The gas went on in w.c., excellent gas, superfine chaos. Soon his body was quiet.'[1] Despite playing an instrumental role in Murphy's 'dehiscence', the radiator has occasioned little mention in Beckett criticism. Not even Chris Ackerley's exhaustive *Demented Particulars* picks up on its asbestos aspect. Perhaps rightly. As Murphy himself says, 'I should have thought that the radiator was secondary to the gas' (108). Still, this 'tiny old-fashioned gas radiator', whose 'crazy installation' by Ticklepenny 'develops from the furthest fetched of visions to a reality that would not function', does provide Murphy the creaturely comfort of heating (108). And it seems to have a life of its own: 'rusty, dusty, derelict, the coils of asbestos falling to pieces, it seemed to defy ignition' (108). If the asbestos falling to pieces might strike us as presciently dangerous, there is something surprisingly animate about it as an object. Not only does it 'defy' ignition, but it plays on the need to be fed: the gas reaches the radiator through a series of 'discarded feeding tubes'. Finally, it is quite easily embarrassed – 'the radiator lit with a sigh and blushed with as much of its asbestos as had not perished' (109).

Readings of *Murphy* often focus on Murphy's attempts at retreating from consciousness, noting Murphy's efforts to surrender his attachment to the Big World. Much like the act of reading a novel, Murphy's retreats are transitory, although, again like a novel, they can be curtailed or lengthened depending on the length of the narrative, how it grips the reader or how slowly they read. In this tenuous allegorical reading, Murphy's radiator stands in for those ways in which asbestos was always meant to insulate us from the dangers of the Big World, so that we might better enjoy the little worlds of our foamy home environs. But it fails to insulate Murphy. Murphy's radiator is embarrassed not so much for being made of asbestos, as for the parts that have perished, and thus failed in their duty as an insulator. Looked at it in this way, the grand narrative about asbestos as something inflicted upon an unknowing public seems to have missed something out. Unable to insulate us from all the consequences of our disavowed attachments, asbestos had, even in its heyday, already fallen short of its promise.

Murphy is not the only modernist character whose sighing fire depends upon asbestos or signals immiseration. In Patrick Hamilton's *Hangover Square* (1941), Netta, the love interest of Hamilton's protagonist, George Harvey Bone, stares into her gas-fire as she waits 'to go out and get lit up again': 'That gas-fire – what sinister, bleak misery emanated from its sighing throat and red, glowing asbestos cells! To those whom God has forsaken, is given a gas-fire in Earl's Court.'[2] Hamilton's gas-fires generate a desperate sense of loneliness in his characters, because, James Bainbridge suggests, gas-fires offered 'the means of solitary life, and as such, became an emblem of this in the literature of the early twentieth century.'

> [G]as-fires seem to have been taken up particularly in tenement accommodation and other multiple-occupancy buildings. The great advantage that the gas-fire had was its cleanliness; for this group of people it meant that there was no longer the need for the daily visit of the charwoman, meaning that flats could for the first time become completely private spaces.[3]

This privacy means that George can kill Netta and her lover, Peter, in relative peace. Later, when George decides to kill himself, he will do so by turning on the gas in his locked room. Gas, the creator of privacy and loneliness, will euthanise George: as he loses consciousness, he remembers having an operation 'under gas [. . .] under chloroform'. If, like Murphy's, George's death is characterised by becoming simultaneously 'free' and 'quiet', the two deaths operate at the two extremes of gas's potentially devastating consequences: the one, explosive force; the other, suffocation. Where gas afforded the means for privacy in modernist literature, asbestos provided its material infrastructure.

Hence, in John Rodker's 1920 poem, 'Gas Fire', 'the sparse blue flame / pulses and pours / through salamander asbestos / annulated like arteries'.[4] Or, for that matter, John Updike's 1973 poem, 'Phenomena', where, 'In a cave of asbestos a vivid elf / went *dancy, dancy, dancy*'.[5] If, for both Rodker and Updike, the interest is in the roaring gas fire, which, in the words of Rodker's 1914 poem, 'The Gas Flame', offers 'a tale of Arcady', they recognise this flame needs to be contained and channelled (6). Indeed, it is probably a testament to the invisible efficacy of asbestos that it disappears in Bainbridge's other examples, from Stevie Smith, George Orwell and A. S. J. Tessimond.

If the gas-fire signals the role of asbestos in heating modernism's built environment, talc provides a sign of its presence as a more portable object. A brief survey of *McClure's* from the early 1900s will bring up numerous advertisements for 'Floral Cluster Talc Powder', 'Colgate's Violet Talc', or 'Williams' Talcum Powder'. By then, talcum powder was already an established business: the Mennen Company was founded in 1878 by Gerhard Heinrich Mennen to sell powdered talc, and in 1894 Johnson & Johnson began to market it as a baby powder. An 1898 Mennen advert offers 'a positive relief for Prickly Heat, Chafing and Sunburn'. So established was Mennen's in particular that it could be used as an illustration in the 1914 farce about advertising, *It Pays to Advertise* by Roi Cooper Megrue and Walter Hackett, where when one character disputes another's argument that his opinions are nothing more than evidence of the power of advertising, the second responds: 'What do you know about Mennen's Talcum Powder? Nothing, except that it has the picture of the homeliest man in the world on the box and it's so impressed your imagination, you just mechanically order Mennen's.'[6] Peale's point is useful not simply because it establishes talcum powder as a commodity that becomes, essentially, subnarrated, but because it also raises, however unintentionally, the spectre of future deaths caused by what went 'nondetected' in this pervasive ordinariness.

What was not generally known about talcum powder, Mennen's or otherwise, became public knowledge on 23 June 2020, when the Missouri Appellate Court upheld a decision to award twenty women some $2.1 billion in compensation for the ovarian cancer they developed from using Johnson & Johnson talc-based baby powder. This award, the largest to date, presented only the most recent instance of a long history of talc-based claims. Talc, itself, is not yet thought to be a carcinogen, but it often occurs in close proximity to tremolite or anthophyllite, two types of amphibole asbestos. This means that, as the talc is extracted, it is often contaminated by trace amounts of asbestos. These trace amounts were often billed by the industry as nondetected; as its defence, J & J held that there was 'no detected asbestos'. However, as David Rosner et al. have demonstrated, the decision to claim the product had 'no detected asbestos' was strategic, adopted over the blatantly incorrect claim 'asbestos free'.[7] By using optical microscopy and X-ray diffraction as their methods of detection, the industry could plausibly argue that they could not find significant amounts of asbestos. Arthur N. Rohl argued as early as 1974 that 'very large numbers of asbestos fibers may be present in talc end products, yet they remain undetected if only [these methods] are used'.[8] When the same samples are considered using electron microscopy, a far higher fibre count was registered. 'Nondetected', in the industry parlance, shifted the statement from a matter of being ('is or isn't') to a matter of knowledge ('can or can't find it'). It provides a compelling instance of how significant language use (and abuse) was, and still is, in the asbestos story. It also serves as an unsettling reminder of the many ways in which asbestos enters the home, in modernism and after.

In the texts that follow, I turn to more fundamental asbestos infrastructures: roofs, walls and waterpipes. These infrastructures testify to a common aspiration in a globalised modernity: access to affordable housing. This aspiration is qualified by the materials available. Before asbestos even accumulates its disastrous health connotations, it is disparaged as cheap and lower class. For the purposes of this chapter, I want to consider not simply the aspirations that came to be associated with asbestos, but how they were positively or negatively inflected by concerns that range beyond those of health. This can explain why contemporary use of asbestos is not simply explainable through uneven stages of development, or what Ernst Bloch called 'the simultaneity of the nonsimultaneous'.[9]

Bloch, writing in Germany in the 1930s, used the phrase to describe the co-existence, at the same time, of industrial and peasant labour, with their comparable discrepancies in social mores, political ideals and cultural interests. As Peter Osborne notes, it derives from Marx's own notion of unequal development, where less developed countries lag behind more developed capitalist partners.[10] Simultaneous with the collapse of the asbestos market in the West was a 'nonsimultaneous' parting of ways, as 'developing' nations invested in asbestos infrastructure and 'developed' nations devested. The present, then, is constituted by the simultaneous existence of two nonsimultaneous attitudes to asbestos, roughly divided into the Before and After to which I have so often turned.

This explanation ignores two important facts. With the collapse of Western markets, asbestos companies invested heavily in selling their products to developing nations, where their attendant risks were to be accepted as a necessary price to pay for development, and in funding political elites, who would then support these sales. These endeavours were implicitly endorsed by successive Canadian and American governments, who refused to ratify international protocols like the Rotterdam Convention (1998). Far from demonstrating unequal, nonsynchronous development, asbestos use in these texts can be understood as the manifestation of economic and political soft power in action. The simultaneity of nonsimultaneous testifies less to stages of economic development than to discrepancies in the relative autonomy of nations to authorise bans.

If this simply recapitulates an all-too-familiar scene that opposes developed and developing nations, I resist this narrative by recalling the centrality of the so-called peripheries to anti-asbestos knowledge, from the pioneering work on mesothelioma by Wagner et al. in South Africa's Northern Cape to the robust anti-asbestos activism of Mahasweta Devi and the Roro asbestos miners in Jarkhand, Eastern India.[11] Moreover, the concrete particularities of asbestos offer a compelling material counterpoint to the simultaneity of the nonsimultaneous. After all, the asbestos infrastructure described in the earlier texts of modernism still exists in some form or another today: some 80% of UK schools and 94% of NHS Trusts still contain significant amounts of asbestos. However nonsimultaneous one's political development might be, the reality of asbestos has inverted. Where, once, it described the nonsimultaneity of the simultaneous, where healthy people could sit side by side survivors with asbestos illnesses without understanding the risks posed by the material, now it creates the possibility for such people to anticipate in present exposure the possibility of future illness, or a new simultaneity of the nonsimultaneous.

Asbestos Roofs

In a short but compelling 1978 essay, on the ways that design comes to be accepted as tradition, the Sri Lankan architect, Roland Silva, considered the birth and growth 'of a tradition of the so-called "American style roof"' in Sri Lanka.[12] 'The two ingredients of a tradition,' Silva continues, '"accumulated experience" and "continuous usage", have been established with the asbestos "American style roof" [. . .] Some consider the "American style asbestos roof" to be a good tradition, but these are value judgements [. . .]' (251). Designs, which, according to Silva, fluctuate within three dimensions – Time ('a stratified cultural sequence'), Place ('geographical identity') and Person ('in the same sense as an autographed painting') – 'accumulate' as traditions through experience and use. Silva performs this accumulation in his iterative description of the asbestos roof: simply an American style roof when first mentioned, asbestos qualifies the 'American style roof' when next it is referred to, and, by Silva's third iteration, it has been included in quotes, becoming fully integrated into the object. No longer a mere American roof, or an American roof made from asbestos, the 'American style asbestos roof' encloses its substantive link to asbestos as a defining element.

Silva's discussion of time, place and person offer a framework against which to observe asbestos's accumulative inclusion into matters of everyday infrastructure.

For, the 'asbestos roof' has become sedimented in fictional landscapes of both the Global North and Global South. Asbestos, in the texts that follow, becomes a device against which to register the personal relations of characters, the geographical concerns of locations, and stratified cultural sequences in time. To illustrate this, I first show how location, character and sequence can be brought together through the simple image of rain falling on an asbestos roof. As if to demonstrate the success of the 'American style asbestos roof', I briefly present the image repeated in texts purposefully cherry-picked to demonstrate a chronological and geographical diversity. Then I want to consider how asbestos as a matter of physical infrastructure, in roofs and elsewhere, comes to act as a plot mechanism, or textual infrastructure. Focussing my discussion on the effects of asbestos infrastructures on persons (as an interaction of weather, rather than illness), geographies or times, I successively examine individual responses to existing or future infrastructures, the presentations of asbestos in collective infrastructures, and, finally, the affects that emerge when asbestos is eliminated from the environment.

The origins of Silva's 'American style asbestos roof' can be found in roofing catalogues as early as 1868, where folded pamphlets celebrated the 'Improved Roofing, Asbestos Roof Coating & Cement' of H. W. Johns. Henry Ward Johns founded H. W. Johns & Co. in 1858 to produce roofing materials. In 1868, he patented 'a new and Improved Composition of Matter for Roofing', made by 'compounding the fibrous mineral known as asbestus [sic] with pigments, oil, coal-tar, mineral-pitch or asphaltum, wood-tar, resin, varnish, and the like'.[13] Granting a tough elastic quality to the compound, due to its fibrous qualities, Johns noted that, unlike animal or vegetable fibers, 'the asbestus is fire-proof, imperishable, and not soluble in Water, nor liable to undergo any chemical change under ordinary circumstances. It is therefore the only fit ingredient of a fibrous flexible nature for roofing' (1). 'Heretofore asbestus [sic] was but little known to the arts,' Johns expounds, 'but by my invention this anomalous mineral, so abundant in nature, is utilized and made to conduce to the Welfare of man' (1). Notwithstanding the evident historical irony, a measure of Johns's 'conducivity' may be found in the increasingly elaborate designs of these catalogues, which, by the 1880s, had become books of some thirty pages. These earlier catalogues uniformly open with a description of asbestos that avows its links to the classics, Enlightenment science and nineteenth-century industry. Johns's patent was to be the basis for the success of H. W. Johns & Co. and, after its merger with the Manville Covering Co. in 1901, H. W. Johns Manville & Co. or simply, Johns Manville.

Asbestos cement, patented in 1900 by Ludwig Hatschek, provided a second revolution in asbestos roofing. By combining asbestos with Portland cement, Hatschek created a durable, weatherproof, heat resistant and fireproof slurry that, when cast and dried, could be moulded into various forms. When Keasbey & Mattison began producing Hatschek's 'fibre cement' in

1907, it set the scene for 'American style asbestos roofs' by producing shingles and tiles, for domestic dwellings, and 'the corrugated sheet idea of roofing and siding factory buildings, warehouses, train sheds, etc.'[14] More sober and serious publications, oriented to industry, showed factory parks roofed with corrugated asbestos, which offered 'comparative lightness, ease of application, weather- and fire-proof qualities, pleasing appearance and permanence' (3). Meanwhile, by the mid-1920s, the catalogues of Johns Manville, Keasbey & Mattison and Eternit had begun to sport full colour images of houses roofed with asbestos shingles, to 'enable the architect and the owner to visualize the many distinctive colour combinations which are possible through the use of these shingles'.[15] As *Selecting Your Roof*, a 1928 Eternit trade publication begins, 'the roof you buy should have these four qualifications. It must have color, vivid color – permanent, lasting color. It must be a roof than cannot burn. It must give you years of service – life-long service. And sell at a price your purse can afford."[16]

The emphasis on the possibilities of colour – as a marker of individuality and taste – also gave rise to class distinctions, framed through the competing discourses of shingle and slate. According to *From Rock to Roof*, a 1930 publication by Pennsylvania Slate Institute, the 'air of handcraftsmanship' offered by slate had a 'charm' that was 'natural' and 'distinguished' in 'this day of machine-made products'.[17] Asbestos cement, the publication went on, offered a 'semi-permanent roofing', by which 'we mean the factory-made imitations of natural rock and slate' (5). Whereas asbestos catalogues emphasised how closely their products matched the natural products they imitated, producers of wood shingles or slate insisted that such 'semi-permanent roofing' would reveal itself as mere imitation. Far from contradicting the narratives in the asbestos trade literature, however, this antagonism between appearance and reality provided the asbestos producer a compelling, even Postmodern, basis for favouring the mimetic over the real. For the trade literature often emphasised differences between asbestos products and those materials it imitated: appearance offered social ease when making decisions on the basis of cost, durability and safety.

But where does the asbestos roof appear? Everywhere, it seems. In Amos Oz's *To Know a Woman* (1989), set in Tel Aviv, Israel, Yoel Ravid listens to 'the even, unexpressive rain beat at the shutters and drummed drearily on the asbestos awning'.[18] For Michael Moorcock's transplanar detective, Jerry Cornelius, 'rain rattled on the corrugated asbestos roof' in a neo-colonial 'Simla'.[19] James, a servant trapped by the rain in Yvonne Vera's short story, 'Crossing Boundaries' (1992), interpellates the sound into music as he listens to Nora, his white boss, play her piano: 'As the rain hit violently against the asbestos roof, he wondered how much of her own music she gathered from the commotion.'[20] Rain again accompanies music in Rosemary Manning's *The Chinese Garden* (1962) when 'on the asbestos roof of the chapel the rain beats incessantly a monotonous and dismal accompaniment to our childish orisons'.[21] Set in Somerset, England, *The Chinese Garden*'s description of the school chapel, 'a long, low asbestos erection', suggests the image of rain on an asbestos roof crosses divisions between the Global North and South. Rain conditions the entire narrative of Angela Arney's detective novel, *Old Sins, Long Memories* (2014), set in the quasi-fictional English village of Stibbington. The murder that opens the novel is possible because the victim cannot hear his murderer: 'the garage, built in the 1930s, was a single-walled brick affair with an asbestos roof, and the heavy rain thudding down drowned all noise inside and out' and, after the murder, 'the sound of rain drummed out the pattern of death with a rhythmic tom-tom beat on the asbestos roof'.[22] In Sue Everett's account of Lutz Eichbaum—Australian internee and Dunera boy—heavy falling rain wakes Lutz "like rapid drum beats hammering down onto the asbestos roof."[23] 'The rain', in the Akure, Western Nigeria, of Chigozie Obioma's *The Fishermen* (2015), 'dragged [. . .] and pummelled zinc and asbestos roofs until sunset when it weakened and ceased.'[24] Obioma returns to the image of rain on an asbestos roof in his second novel, *An Orchestra of Minorities* (2019), when the narrator, Chinonso's *chi* or spirit, waits for his host to awake: 'I had watched, helpless, as rain poured down on his laundry until the drumming on the asbestos roof woke him.'[25]

These incidents, geographically and stylistically disparate as they are, bear witness to the sedimentation of the asbestos roof in built environments across the World Market. They repeat a concern with misplaced rhythm, its monotony critically out of step with the dynamic encounters occurring beneath the eaves. This discordance presents a useful, if completely coincidental, resonance with this book's refrain that relations with asbestos are marked by misapprehensions and missteps. There is nothing to suggest asbestos itself is significant, since the image of rain beating upon roofs is by no means specific to this material. But, this insignificance is itself a useful feature of what one might call reliance, the acceptance of asbestos in the built environment. For the moment, I also want to brush over the obvious 'nonsimultaneity', wherein asbestos roofs are, for the Global North, of a particular time (Arney's 1930s garage), whereas they continue to proliferate in the Global South. Instead, I want to think about how the asbestos roof links to aspiration, whose toxic effects retrospectively turn this aspiration into a form of cruel optimism.

Aspiration and the Asbestos Roof

When Obioma, in *The Fishermen*, first mentions the 'rusting roofing sheets – leftovers from when the house was built in 1974 – piled against the fence at our mother's backyard tomato garden', these might be the unused partners of those zinc roofs the novel will batter with rain (43). Later, as his narrator negotiates the garden, now planted with corn, he 'had almost reached the end of it – where the old asbestos sheets lay piled against the wall' (201). The sheets play no significant role in the narrative, which explains their parenthetical appearance, and perhaps deserve little attention. But why mention they are leftovers from when the house was built in 1974? Asbestos does not rust – this, together with its resistance to acid, fire and other forms of decomposition, is an important reason why it is used. So, are these the same sheets? Since they can be used to pull diverse strands of the narrative together, they have to be. The inconsistency may be a literary mistake, or it may reflect a mineral alteration of roofing materials that parallels the more expected transition in the garden's vegetable produce from tomatoes to corn, or some even more esoteric explanation. My own interest in it remains in the image – the importance implied in storing asbestos sheeting.

Responding to a similar image in Buhera, Eastern Zimbabwe, Jens A. Andersson notes that the accumulation of asbestos sheets is a sign of urban success. Whether or not it carries the same weight in Akure, South Western Nigeria, it signals the plans of Andersson's informant, George Zvarevashe, to add three rooms to his house: 'new asbestos roof sheets are stored in the living room, next to the big television and stereo set'.[26] 'In rural Buhera,' Andersson explains, 'a brick-built house plastered with cement and roofed with asbestos or iron sheets reflects urban success' (99).

Success is contingent not merely where it happens, like Buhera, but also when it happens. The roofing sheets in *The Fishermen* and Buhera testify to historical moments (1974; 2001) when asbestos roofs still demonstrated success. But they also rely on conflicting interpretations: in *The Fishermen*, the roofing sheets are presented as ignored leftovers, while for Andersson they demand an explanation. Ruth Prawer Jhabvala's *A Backward Place* (1965) captures both sides of this conflicting narrative impulse.[27] Jhabvala's narrator sees 'nothing interesting' in Judy's home in Delhi (7). Nevertheless, she continues to note a number of architectural features including 'a sort of cooking-shed, covered with an asbestos roof' (7). The narrator's surprising decision to enumerate what 'wouldn't be interesting or unusual' means the reader must simultaneously note the asbestos as present and dismiss it as uninteresting (7). Effectively, the asbestos roof becomes subnarrated.

Returning to Zimbabwe, we find the subnarrated asbestos roofs of Thandanani Street, Makokoba, in Yvonne Vera's *Butterfly Burning* (1998), represent both the promise of containment and the failure of that promise.[28] After her husband sells her for the value of a bicycle wheel, 'a woman' stands 'on that asbestos roof with no clothes at all to cover her own body and announced loud and clear that she preferred two bicycle wheels to one, and if anyone had two bicycle wheels [. . .] she would leave' (91). Grace Musila has linked the 'woman of 62 Thandanani Street' to Phephelaphi, the novel's protagonist, who will later set herself on fire, in the one room house she shared with Fumbatha, her lover, made of 'asbestos and cement' (47). Both seek, through madness or self-murder, to reclaim a control over their bodies that their lives cannot but cede to the men of Makokoba. Phephelaphi, Musila argues, chooses physical death over other forms of social or spiritual death because she 'symbolically rejects their lifestyles, and implicitly refuses to be limited to the prostitution that seems to be the destiny of all women in Makokoba'.[29] So, when Zandile, her mother's friend, offers her a dress in preparation for a life of prostitution, Phephelaphi refuses because 'she has already concluded that Zandile is like a spider; she wants her caught in a web' (129). Like the spider that hangs from asbestos ceilings in Vera's final novel, *The Stone Virgins* (2002), Zandile is a survivor who also knows 'that love cannot be founded on mercy but that mercy can be founded on love' (84). Zandile's choice to prostitute herself, conforming to the system, has enabled her to build 'my own house in Makokoba not out of asbestos sheets, but out of brick and cement. It is one room, but it is my own solid shelter' (129). The solidity of Zandile's shelter is marked by its not being constructed of asbestos sheets, which immediately sets it apart from the porous 'asbestos and cement' dwelling that Phephelaphi and Fumbatha share, where the 'thin distance between their breathing and the next room' means the neighbours 'witness what they never tired of hearing', the sound of the two lovers' intercourse (48; 49). The novel does not systematically link its preoccupation with fire to these asbestos roofs, even if the 'candle burning beside' the woman of Thandanani street, like the 'sunset' that 'cascad[es] over the asbestos roofs like angry flame' while Phephelaphi and Fumbatha make love, anticipate the moment when Phephelaphi will self-immolate (48). And yet, even if asbestos isn't 'of interest' to Vera, its presence is associated with the aspiration to contain fires that eventually burst this container's bonds.

Asbestos's 'uninteresting presence' does not just index inadequate containment; it also becomes a health concession made for practical or political reasons. Vimbai, the narrator of Tendai Huchu's *The Hairdresser of Harare* (2010), makes just such a concession when she notes of her parents' house that it 'was the same pink bungalow with an asbestos roof that I'd grown up in. I've heard that asbestos can make you sick, but nearly every house in the neighbourhood had an asbestos roof.'[30] She then returns to the ostensible point of her visit: the memorial for her brother, Robert. Asides like this are a stylistic feature of Huchu's novel. At other moments, she will observe that 'the air hung thick with woodsmoke. No one could afford paraffin, if you could find it that is' or 'we had breakfast by the pool. Bacon, eggs, beans and toast, a whole other meal again. The shortages obviously did not mean anything to the Ncubes' (32; 148). Vimbai's asides appear to be symptomatic of an absence the reader is compelled to notice: they mostly respond to the availability (or not) of goods or services in Zimbabwe in the wake of the 2003 international sanctions and the presidential elections of 2008. Read in this light, the 'but' in 'but nearly every house in the neighbourhood had an asbestos roof' suggests a pragmatic fatalism about the realities of the housing situation. Vimbai is not taking issue with the possibility that asbestos causes illness: the ubiquity of the asbestos roof does not, after all, disprove the claim that it 'makes you sick'. Rather, it is an indictment of contemporary Harare, where concessions are expected for all but the privileged. No one can afford paraffin but the Ncubes can still have bacon and eggs. Asbestos represents but one instance in a general consideration of those concessions expected of some but not others.

Still, the concession in *The Hairdresser of Harare* remains a matter of ironic ambivalence. In other examples, such concessions are more openly a matter of force. In *Red Sun: Travels through Naxalite Country* (2008), Sudeep Chakravarti's account of his year-long investigation of Naxalism, or Indian Maoism, Chakravarti notes that Salwa Judum, an illegal anti-Naxalite militia, forced villagers in the Chhattisgarh region to relocate.[31] In order to facilitate resettlement, the families were given 'Rs 12,000 for the house, and a supply of asbestos roofing sheets on purchase that replaces local thatch, wood and palm leaf with a dangerous composite that will bake anyone inside' (82). Chakravarti notes elsewhere that, in such relocations, displaced persons tend 'to be "rehabilitated", if at all, in tin-and-asbestos slums on barren land' (123).

In his memoir, *My Father's Fortune* (2010), Michael Frayn responds to asbestos in a way that will bring together Vera's imperfect container, Jhabvala's narrative indifference, and the concessionary aspirations of Huchu and Chakravarti. Frayn recalls a fence made of 'sheets of TAC roofing' that his father built to keep ducks away from the lupins in their garden during the Second World War.[32] Like Vera's roofs, this container proves imperfect. 'Ducks, however, rather like holes in the ground, turn out to behave in ways that my father has not foreseen. They fly' (95). This is not the only thing that Frayn's father has not foreseen. 'TAC' first appears in the memoir in Chapter Four. Then, the child, Michael, understands it merely as the 'printed headings' of his father's company stationery (65). 'What else?' Frayn recalls, 'My father writes reports. Reports on what? His sales, I assume, now I come to think about it, though I never did at the time. Reports are simply reports. They're the things my father writes' (65). The tautology recalls our earlier discussion of Kafka, not simply because the reports become their own justification, but because, TAC, Frayn reveals in Chapter Six, 'stands for Turners Asbestos Cement' (100).

This revelation, made two fifths of the way through the memoir, will be the fixed point upon which Frayn's narrative irony will turn. The hitherto 'uninteresting' TAC develops narrative significance. Still, Frayn recalls how important TAC was in realising his father's aspirations. This is why he goes to some lengths to equivocate on the substance itself. Writing of TAC's role in the Second World War, he explicitly introduces asbestos via an ekphrastic account of 'the firm's logo', which shows a female figure in Greek robes doing rather what my father's doing as Fire Captain. She's confronting a sea of flames, armed not with a stirrup-pump or a long-handled shovel but a shield made of asbestos. This is the great selling point of the product, particularly now that the Luftwaffe's attempting with some success to repeat the effects of the Great Fire of London: unlike wood and various forms of wood substitute it's non-inflammable [. . .] asbestos has no vices. (100–1)

The personification of Asbestos, depicted in the classical style, is primarily concerned with protecting people from fire-related harm. If Frayn grants 'there's something profoundly dreary about its lifeless greyness', it seems a worthy compromise for something so immediately protective (101).

Figure 8.1 Lady Asbestos

Frayn equivocates over asbestos in another way too. His father's interactions with asbestos always parallel his Uncle Sid's interactions with cigarettes. Shortly after asbestos is introduced, Frayn will recall his Uncle Sid, who 'keeps bringing the cigarettes', who comes 'to relax in the health-giving cigarette smoke and asbestos dust of the Surrey Hills', and whose 'modest part' in the War Effort is 'levelling the bricks and mortar of Germany', while Frayn's father's part is 'raising the asbestos roofs and pipes of Britain' (102; 103). Frayn indulges in a stratagem familiar to those who have filed compensation claims, where defence teams of asbestos companies parallel the harms of tobacco and asbestos, then conflate them, and finally dismiss the claim for lacking sufficient clarity of cause. Frayn uses it to more salubrious effect: to resurrect the flawed but likable figure of his father, place his belief in asbestos in historical context and demonstrate how this belief was itself a manifestation of his father's aspirations.

Nevertheless, he concedes that these aspirations came at a price. 'He was a rotten father', recalls Frayn's sister, Gill.

> Whatever my sister meant by her dismissal of our father, it's true that he did play a part in leaving her and the world at large a terrible legacy.

> Thirty-three years after he died she begins to suffer from shortness of breath [...] mesothelioma [...] The only asbestos she can recall ever being exposed to was in the samples that my father used to bring home [...] A hand has reached out the remote and innocent past. (250–1)

His sister's death from mesothelioma is preempted by the succession of other cancers experienced by the family, including 'Phil [who] wheezes on into his seventies and Doris, who loyally sewed in Phil's cigarette smoke, continues into her mid-eighties' (247). This hand 'out of the past," Frayn realises, may reach out for him: 'I may yet go the same way myself' (251). While the memoir is written, as Frayn concludes, to bear his father 'out of the ashes of the past [like] Aeneas bore his father Anchises on his back out the ashes of Troy', this writing happens against a backdrop of latent, or potential, consequence – an asbestos hand reaching out of the past to snatch the author, like it snatched his sister (251). What makes narrative irony of this tension is the memoir's reliance that Frayn's reader will equivocate in their judgment of his father, and, by extension, contingently accept that he believed in the substance that ultimately kills his daughter. Frayn's contingent exculpation of asbestos, as a product whose success must be registered in its specific historical moment, expresses a moment of detachment from both the industry's Manicheanism and the product's harmful effects. This moment permits Frayn's readers to imagine the utopian possibilities of asbestos, while also pointing us to the ways it failed to live up to these ideals, even on its own terms.

The Age of Asbestos Housing

The equivocations about using asbestos demonstrate intersecting anxieties that are not simply tied to disease, but also to aspirations about class mobility, independence and security. To reinforce this argument, I briefly want to compare the use of fibrocement in Patrick Chamoiseau's *Texaco* (1992) with that of Patrick White in *The Tree of Man* (1955).[33] Chamoiseau frames his epic history of the Texaco township, just outside Martinique's Fort-de-France, as a sequence of ages. As in Hesiod's *Works and Days* or Ovid's *Metamorphoses*, these ages are identified by certain substances whose use characterises the space and time under discussion. Hesiod and Ovid blur distinctions between those ages characterised by symbolic association (like gold or silver) and those where the relation depends upon concrete use (bronze or iron). Chamoiseau's ages foreground this blurring. Their names correspond to the literal materials with which Texaco is built (straw, crate wood, fibrocement or asbestos cement, and concrete), but the ages themselves, like 'The Age of Asbestos', evidence a 'jostling of epochs [...] with straw, crate wood, tin sheets for the roof, and these new slabs brought here by the bekes [white people], which gave the illusion of a cement house' (266). The new slabs, made of Hatschek's fibrocement, show development to be combined and uneven. The 'hutches', or shacks, of Texaco are situated in the same time and space, but their materials imply different stages of development in the trajectory of modernity. At the same time, the coincidence of these different materials challenges the sequence delineated in Chamoiseau's table of contents or the works of Hesiod or Ovid, wherein the trajectories of materiality, if not modernity, are imagined as linear. Straw and crate wood do not simply give way to asbestos, even as asbestos does not simply give way to concrete. The novel is too attentive to the ways in which these materials blend together. Moreover, asbestos is not treated as unambiguously positive: it is brought by the bekes and only gives the 'illusion' of a cement house. Indeed, it remains highly fragile. Nevertheless, it does bring with it a certain commodity value that remains inextricably linked to its use value. The novel, narrated for the most part by Marie-Sophie Laborieux to an interlocutor named Oiseau de Cham (Cham's bird, or Chamoiseau), records Marie-Sophie's excitement at encountering asbestos: '*Mmmmm dear Lordy . . . ! asbestos . . .* to leave the straw and the crate wood and the white tin plate, for a home in cement! That was everyone's hymn! [. . .] It was a real joy. Your job's money would vanish in those fragile slabs' (266). The fragility of the asbestos also produces craftsmen able to handle it: 'Nelta knew how to nail the asbestos without shattering it', a skill he teaches Marie-Sophie (266).

If the Age of Asbestos begins by heralding the potential uses of asbestos, it ends with the destruction of large portions of the new settlement that has sprung up around Marie-Sophie's hutch: 'as soon as they emptied a hutch, the soulless-blackmen would go at it with crowbars, smashing the crate wood, splintering the asbestos' (306). For if asbestos offers new opportunity, it proves fickle and fragile, unable to protect the hutch dwellers from the depredations of the police: 'we could only [. . .] hang on to our so precious tin sheets, to our asbestos slabs whose every crack broke our hearts' (307). Asbestos is a state of elevation in the novel, but it is a vulnerable state, without security. So, Marie-Sophie will 'sometimes [. . .] manage to raise my hutch up to the point of asbestos, but it would be destroyed as soon as I'd turned my back' (310). Asbestos might provide the semblance of permanence, even as it functions as a marker of relative success or opulence, but these attributes do not, ultimately, persevere. Asbestos remains friable, brittle and fragile, easily destroyed, despite its solid appearance.

Texaco's Ages provide a structure for Bloch's simultaneity of the nonsimultaneous, where 'jostling' stages of development, represented by the houses of wood, asbestos and concrete, are brought into a spatial simultaneity. This parallels the post-war development of Australian suburbia, where 'fibro', as it was called, 'was the boom material of the 1950s'.[34] As in the Martiniquan slums, fibro offered working-class Australians the opportunity to build a home of their own in rapidly expanding suburbia. Here, too, this aspiration proved fragile, not just in terms of the substance, but to the harsh judgments of their neighbours.

In Part Four of White's *The Tree of Man*, his novel about the Parker family's life in the Castle Hill suburb of Sydney, White describes a similar jostling in the house-building that has gone on around the Parkers' property. The 'landscape' has 'taken possession' of 'old inconsiderable wooden houses', while 'the waterproof brick ones' are 'in possession' (394).

> There was also another kind, which caused resentment, and against which it was hoped the Council would revise its policy. There were the homes in fibro-cement. These were to be found in outcrops, of a different stratum. It was in their favour, of course, that they could last only a little while. But for how long? In the meantime human beings went through the motions of living in them. Young couples locked their doors and left their homes as if they were not open. A child had kicked a hole in one, for fun. And at night the fibro homes reverberated, changed their shape under the stress of love or strife, changed and returned, standing brittle in the moonlight, soluble in dreams.[35]

Jostling with one another are wooden, brick and fibro houses in simultaneous appearances of nonsimultaneous stages of development. Brigid Rooney observes that the wood houses and the brick describe two layers of settlement: the semi-rural wooden buildings a precondition for the brick suburbia that replaces them, while also presenting an Edenic counterpoint to the suburban sprawl of brick.[36] This fits into a larger trend of anti-suburban rhetoric in Australian writing over the long twentieth century. But the subsequent inclusion of fibro appears to complicate this narrative, and not simply because it is 'attuned to life' as Rooney states (61).

Like the houses in Vera's Makokoba or the hutches in Chamoiseau's Texaco, White's fibro homes may accommodate the concertina effects of love and strife, but they scarcely mask those dramas from their neighbours or provide the security that their residents imagine they do. What is more, these homes, like their residents, are 'of a different stratum', where people only go through the motions of living. If the permanent possessiveness of the brick upsets the delicate ecology wrought by the wooden buildings, the fibro homes breed only resentment and the 'soluble' dreams of permanence, security and the good life.

White returns to fibro in his memoir, *Flaws in the Glass* (1981), when he recalls how his mother despised the asbestos church of his childhood 'for aesthetic reasons: "I'd burn it down if it would burn." If she were alive today she might have got some satisfaction from reading that we are being poisoned by asbestos.'[37] The aesthetic reservations of White's mother in 1923 herald a critical, and classist, reaction to fibro through Australian literature to 'the fibro-belt' of A. L. McGann's *Subtopia* (2005) and the 'fibro cottages' of Felicity Castagna's *No More Boats* (2017). The 'little while' White anticipates extends, then, almost 100 years. In the end, they would become as 'possessed by' the built environment as the wooden buildings he so prefers.

This gestures to a process of physical sedimentation; its narrative equivalent may be gleaned from Rian Malan's *My Traitor's Heart* (1989), simply by juxtaposing his successive references to asbestos roofs in former township areas of Apartheid South Africa. Malan imagines 'a normal Soweto house – a cement hut, really, with an asbestos roof'.[38] The one becomes many, when, a few pages later, Malan describes Soweto as 'a desolate gray landscape. The houses are gray; their asbestos roofs are gray; the wastelands are strewn with gray ash and rubble. The roads are clogged with morose men streaming home from the railroad in cast-off gray overcoats' (97). When describing the township of Bekkersdal, Malan will refer to 'a sea of small asbestos-roofed houses' (307). Likewise, Frayn writes: 'everywhere we go my father can point to great grey corrugated cliffs and hillsides of asbestos cement [. . .] there's something profoundly dreary about its lifeless greyness [. . .] but at least it will remain grey and not go charcoal-black or mouldy-green or rust-red.'[39] Both Malan and Frayn turn an asbestos built environment into a natural landscape, whether 'a wasteland', 'a sea', 'a cliff' or 'a hillside'. Such naturalism is not, perhaps, common across all references to asbestos, but that mistakes the meaning of the metaphor. Malan and Frayn refer to an asbestos proliferation across the built environment, not because these spaces are 'natural', in the rather antiquated sense of the word, but because the asbestos itself is no longer dissociable from this environment.

Asbestos is undeniably a toxicant, but it is important to understand the significance it comes to have, outside discourses of capitalist apologia and health disaster. This is not to ameliorate the substance's use; rather, it serves to address the matter of its use as a complex engagement with uneven opportunities pursued in relation to space-time. *Texaco*'s form illustrates this better than any reference to asbestos in the novel: in order to recuperate those users of asbestos from their status as pure victims or perpetrators, an Age of Asbestos – implying a particular space-time-use relation – must necessarily complicate the presence of asbestos in the built environment.

Asbestos Pipes

At some critical moment, then, asbestos fails to live up to the promise that it will secure or contain the subject. In these cases, this failure is not because it constitutes a threat in itself. Rather, asbestos fails to live up to its promises even when taken on its own terms. Nowhere is this more evident than in asbestos water pipes. From the 1930s, asbestos cement pipes began to replace cast iron in water supply systems. A 1988 report to the UK Department of the Environment explains this use, which peaked in the 1950s and 1960s, as 'a result of being cheaper and easier to handle [. . .] and its claimed resistance to corrosion attack'.⁴⁰ However, as the authors note, asbestos cement does deteriorate, especially when carrying 'soft' water, which leaches the calcium hydroxide from the cement matrix (9). Even in 1988, the authors observed that such 'potentially aggressive environments' where the pipes were laid could 'lead to either premature failure or progressive release of asbestos fibres' (126). At the date of the report, some 37,000 miles of asbestos cement piping carried water to an estimated 12 million people in the United Kingdom. Significantly, a subsequent 2002 report for the Drinking Water Inspectorate found 'no concern for the health of consumers receiving the water and [. . .] no programmes to replace asbestos cement pipe for this reason'.⁴¹ This may account for why as recently as 2017, newspaper articles continued to use the same 1988 estimate of UK piping: a more recent estimate could not be found. There is a scientific debate about whether or not asbestos in drinking water causes mesothelioma or other cancers, even if the precautionary principle demands we err on the side of caution.⁴² But the fact that such decaying infrastructure seems to occasion the concern only of activists testifies to the way that asbestos remains nondetected, even today.

Campaigns to remove asbestos water pipes are particularly interesting because they 'detect' the consequences of letting public infrastructure fray and decay and then translate these consequences into the home. In this respect, a particularly salient example emerges in the United States and Canada, where some 600,000 miles of asbestos cement piping continue to channel water. In 1985, as Woodstock, once the symbol of the 1960s counterculture movement, began to be affected by gentrification, a local scandal over the asbestos in the water went regional. Francine Prose's 1986 *New York Times Magazine* exposé, 'Woodstock: A Town Afraid to Drink the Water' and its fictional counterpart, Barbara Bond's *Everyday Enemies* (2011), both try to activate anxieties about the home.⁴³ For the residents of Woodstock in 1985 and 1986, asbestos is hardly nondetectable. 'Clumps of blue fibrous material came out of showerheads,' Bond writes, 'The stuff tangled in Dorothy Johnson's hair' (6). She juxtaposes this with the scientific study Cassie is reading: 'Disintegrating asbestos-cement water pipes are releasing asbestos into our water. Tests reveal more than 300 million fibers per liter' (6). But, as both Prose and Bond realise, the most effective point-counterpoint comes by highlighting the exposure as itself a nondetected act. Here, Bond's heavy-handed foreshadowing dominates the opening paragraphs of *Everyday Enemies*. 'Early that morning,' the novel begins, 'before parents learned they were poisoning their kids microscopic bit by bit, Cassie Duncan served her sons one last, strong dose at breakfast' (2). The weather forecast plays on a radio 'that would soon warn of Woodstock's toxic water' (2). '[U]naware of the toxin in the juice, [Cassie] served it to her boys' (2). In the midst of this, Cassie's only suspicions are, rightly, of her husband, Brian, who, it later turns out, is having an affair: 'she silently wondered, not for the first time, what he did on snowy nights in the state capital' (2). Whether the repeated emphasis on Cassie's transitory ignorance is necessary for a Kindle quick read or stylistic clumsiness, it illustrates the need to place the emotive force of the crime in what goes on unknown in the home.

The asbestos roof, like the gas-fire, permits new configurations of privacy and independence in situations of straitened circumstances. But it is easy enough to skim over these instances as concerns for over there ('Third Worldism') and over then ('technical obsolescence'). Although 80 per cent of British schools and 9 out of 10 NHS trusts still contain substantial amounts of asbestos, despite the 'hidden epidemics' of asbestos-related diseases amongst teachers and healthcare professionals, awareness about asbestos in infrastructure seems to have deteriorated in the years following the successful public health campaigns of the 1970s, 1980s and 1990s. Scandals around asbestos demand a double move, highlighted in Bond's excessive use of the device: to ascertain what exposure is happening, while disavowing knowledge. Again, it trades on sentiment that, like the pipes they are set upon, fray and fall apart with use. So, to conclude this chapter, I want to consider how we might circumnavigate such sentimentality, attending and discarding it according to its use.

In this chapter, I have shown that almost everyone might be included as allies, by virtue of their own possible exposure to the harms of asbestos. This, then, provides an answer to a question Osborne raises in a review of Max Tomba's *Marx's Temporalities*, where Osborne takes both Bloch and Tomba to task for failing to anticipate how situations of nonsimultaneity impede the possibility of political action. If shared political subjectivity relies on shared goals or agendas, it needs its participants to intersect at some moment in time. 'From within which time(s),' Osborne challenges Bloch and Tomba, 'does the political agent/subject of politics act?' (46). For Bloch, the answer lay in an articulation that blended the 'simultaneous' structural concerns of capitalism with the 'nonsimultaneous' interests of proletarian groups. For Tomba, who develops the nonsimultaneous as a defence against the market synchronisation of global capital, it is less clear who the articulating subject should be. But, perhaps, asbestos points to a contradiction within market synchronisation itself: that the simultaneity of the nonsimultaneous is measured in the actual and perceived effects of asbestos on our bodies, a danger, moreover, that constitutes a real and persistent basis for international solidarity.

NOTES

1. Samuel Beckett, *Murphy*, ed. J. C. C. Mays (London: Faber & Faber, 2009), p. 158.
2. Patrick Hamilton, *Hangover Square*, introduced by J. B. Priestley (London: Penguin Books, 2001), p. 49.

3. James Bainbridge, 'Tuesday, 28th May, 2013', *JWRB.me Blog*, Accessed 23 February 2021: https://jrwb.me/tag/tessimond/
4. John Rodker, *Poems and Adolphe 1920*, ed. Andrew Crozier (Manchester: Carcanet, 1996), p. 78.
5. John Updike, 'Phenomena', *The New Yorker*, 24 February 1973, p. 38.
6. Roi Cooper Megrue and Walter Hackett, *It Pays to Advertise* (New York: Samuel French, 1917), p. 29.
7. David Rosner, Gerald Markowitz and Merlin Chowkwanyun, '"Nondetected": The Politics of Measurement of Asbestos in Talc, 1971–1976', 109 (7) *American Journal of Public Health* (2019), p. 969–74.
8. Arthur N. Rohl, 'Asbestos in Talc', 9 *Environmental Health Perspectives* (1974), p. 130.
9. Although the phrase was only coined in *Heritage of Our Times* (1935), Bloch explores the idea of nonsimulaneity (or nonsynchronicity) in Ernst Bloch, 'Nonsynchronism and the Obligation to Its Dialectics', trans. Mark Ritter, 11 *New German Critique* (1977), pp. 22–38.
10. Peter Osborne, 'Out of Sync: Tomba's Marx and the Problem of a Multi-layered Temporal Dialectic', 23 (4) *Historical Materialism* (2015), p. 42.
11. See Wagner et al., 'Diffuse' and Devi, 'Sabbath' and 'Countryside'.
12. Roland Silva, 'Traditional Design and Modern Architecture', in *Senarat Paranavitana Commemoration Volume*, eds Johanna Engelberta Lohuizen-De Leeuw, Karthigesu Indrapala, Leelananda Prematilleka, Senarat Paranavitana (Leiden: Brill, 1978), p. 251.
13. Henry W. Johns, 'Improved Compound for Roofing and Other Purposes' (United States of America Patent, 1868), p. 1.
14. *Ambler Asbestos Corrugated Roofing* (Ambler, PA: Keasbey & Mattison, 1918), p. 3.
15. *The Book of Roofs* (New York: Johns-Manville Co., 1923), p. 2.
16. *Selecting Your Roof* (Boston: Eternit, 1928), p. 3.
17. *From Rock to Roof: What You Need To Know About Slate* (Pen Argyl, PA: Pennsylvania Slate Institute, c. 1930), p. 3.
18. Amos Oz, *To Know a Woman*, trans. Nicholas de Lange (London: Vintage, 2011), p. 142.
19. Michael Moorcock, *Jerry Cornelius: His Lives and His Times* (London: Orion, 2018), p. 22.
20. Yvonne Vera, 'Crossing Boundaries', *Why Don't You Carve Other Animals?* (Toronto: Tsar, 1992), p. 3.
21. Rosemary Manning, *The Chinese Garden* (New York: The Feminist Press, 2000), Ebook.
22. Angela Arney, *Old Sins, Long Memories* (London: Robert Hale, 2014), Ebook.
23. Sue Everett, *Not Welcome: A Dunera Boy's Escape from Nazi Oppression* (np: Port Campbell Press, 2010), Ebook.
24. Chigozie Obioma, *The Fishermen* (London: Pushkin Press, 2015), p. 183.
25. Chigozie Obioma, *An Orchestra of Minorities* (London: Little, Brown, 2019), Ebook.

26. Jens A. Andersson, 'Reinterpreting the Rural-Urban Connection: Migration Practices and Socio-Cultural Dispositions of Buhera Workers in Harare', 71 (1) *Africa* (2001), p. 90.
27. Ruth Prawer Jhabvala, *A Backward Place* (London: Abacus, 2013).
28. Yvonne Vera, *Butterfly Burning* (New York: Farrar, Straus and Giroux, 2000).
29. Grace Musila, 'Embodying Experience and Agency in Yvonne Vera's *Without a Name* and *Butterfly Burning*', 38 (2) *Research in African Literatures* (2007), p. 60.
30. Tendai Huchu, *The Hairdresser of Harare* (Glasgow: Freight Books, 2013), p. 33.
31. Sundeep Chakravarti, *Red Sun: Travels in Naxalite Country* (London: Penguin Books, 2009).
32. Frayn, *Fortune*, p. 95.
33. Patrick Chamoiseau, *Texaco*, trans. Rose-Myriam Réjouis and Val Vinokuro (New York: Vintage International, 1998); Patrick White, *The Tree of Man* (London: Penguin, 2010).
34. Charles Pickett, *The Fibro Frontier: A Different History of Australian Architecture* (London: Lund Humphries, 1999), p. 98.
35. White, *Tree*, p. 394.
36. Brigid Rooney, *Suburban Space, the Novel and Australian Modernity* (London: Anthem Press, 2018), p. 61.
37. Patrick White, *Flaws in the Glass: A Self-Portrait* (London: Vintage, 2013), p. 17.
38. Rian Malan, *My Traitor's Heart* (New York: Grove Press, 1990), p. 92.
39. Frayn, *Fortune*, p. 101.
40. J. Mordak and J Wheeler, 'Deterioration of Asbestos Cement Water Mains', *Final Report to the Department of the Environment* (Wiltshire: Water Research Center, 1988), p. 1.
41. John K. Fawell, 'Asbestos Cement Drinking Water Pipes and Possible Health Risks: Review for DWI', *Report for Contract 70/2/135* (Devizes: FaberMaunsell Ltd, 2002), unpag.
42. Agostino Di Ciaula and Valerio Gennaro, 'Rischio clinico da ingestione di fibre di amianto in acqua potabile', 40 (6) *Epidemiologica e prevenzione* (2016), pp. 472–5.
43. Francine Prose, 'Woodstock: A Town Afraid to Drink Water', *New York Times*, April 13, 1986; Barbara Bond, *Everyday Enemies* (np: Barbara Bond, 2012).

CONCLUSION: THE DUMP

This book has, for the most part, explored the changing significance of asbestos through literature of the nineteenth, twentieth and twenty-first centuries. Nowadays, most asbestos finds its way, eventually, to a dump. It would be a fitting end, then, to think about asbestos waste in cultural texts; for instance how, in his 2001 horror film, *Session 9*, Brad Anderson uses asbestos abatement in an abandoned psychiatric hospital to link a crew's material disturbance of the building to their psychic disturbance by it.[1] Or, the giant dumpsite in North East New England/South West Quebec that David Foster Wallace imagines in *Infinite Jest* (1996), in a coded reference to the Jeffrey Mine in Asbestos.[2] Or the asbestos shipbreaking featured in Jonathan Raban's *Waxwings* (2003) and Paolo Bacigalupi's *Ship Breaker* (2010), the flytipping in John Kinsella's 'See that Gully' (2015) and the illegal survey in Maria Flook's 'Asbestos' (1991).[3] Waste, after all, highlights questions of use by considering objects brought to the very limits of their usefulness. How fitting, then, to end an interrogation of asbestos's uses by thinking about how these fictions reuse and recycle this apparently decommissioned material.

To think of waste's endtimes, Will Viney reframes Mary Douglas's famous formulation for dirt – 'dirt is matter out of place' – as a 'matter out of time' whose use has passed.[4] Of course, as the entire field of Discard Studies testifies, waste can be, and is, big business; few more so than asbestos abatement. But the problem with asbestos abatement, Nicky Gregson observes, is that asbestos's problems are ongoing, even after it becomes waste, even after it becomes a banned substance. 'Bans,' she argues,

> perform fictions. They allow sequestration to appear as erasure. The spatiality of sequestration, however, repositions asbestos. It moves it from a regime of global governance to position it within territorial boundaries, and within a regulatory framework characterized by the political techniques of remediation and disposal.[5]

For, while a ban ostensibly ends all future trade in a substance, it cannot undo the processes of extraction, production or construction I have followed in Part 3. Nor does asbestos lose its horrific effects when consigned to the pit: it sits, inert but waiting, a latent threat to any who uncover it. Depending on how or where the asbestos is rendered as 'waste', it might easily be 'recycled' as a new object, 'remodelled' or sealed into a building, or 'remediated', removed and disposed of. But none of these resolve the problem of asbestos, which is unending. Until such time as we achieve total remediation, we must work out ways to endure asbestos time.

To endure asbestos time is to mediate the various temporalities associated with asbestos through our experiences, our knowledge, and our understanding of our social conditions.[6] My reflections on the literary examples in this book have attempted to testify to this mediation. To play this book out with further literary examples would, however, miss my aim in writing it: to use literary criticism to think seriously about asbestos's use. What, then, might I say in my imagined conversation with my grandfather that might convince him, an engineer with a fondness for Shakespeare but no stake in Shakespeare criticism, that this was useful? First, I would observe that, for many, the story of asbestos has been prefigured by the genre in which this story is told: utopia or dystopia; mystery, detective or horror story. Second, I would offer a new configuration for these assumptions by focussing on particular sites of incommensurability: asbestos's apparent animacy, when and how its diseases are noticed, and compensation for these illnesses. To acknowledge they represent interrelated problems, I might observe that the anxiety over whether asbestos is animate or not translates into an anxiety about the threat it poses to our own liveliness, a threat which generates forms of narrative compensation that, like their material equivalents, can only ever approximate a just response. The names I have given to the stages in this sequence were the salamander, the diagnosis and Kafka's factory, though others, like the dice game found in Cassie Bérard, might work as well. Third, I would argue that these problems differ according to the contexts where asbestos was mined, produced, used or dumped. The context manifests the problem in different ways, to different ends. In the mine, humbling the expert serves to express a desire for greater humility on the part of expertise. In the factory, anger raises the possibility of an emotional redress between equals. And, in the home, the apparent nonsimultaneity of our exposures may open up into a much more passionate declaration of their simultaneity. Literary criticism shows us how the problem of asbestos has been framed. It offers us names for asbestos's underappreciated effects. And, perhaps most importantly, it advocates for a change in approach: the tendency to *individualise* asbestos's effects needs to give way to a greater *communalising* of our response.

For this conclusion, I want to think how these reflections on literary criticism might address three real-world examples, where an uncritical attitude to asbestos's mediation allowed the supposedly admirable task of asbestos abatement to be twisted to particular political ends. These examples show how important it is to be aware of asbestos's role as a mediator. But they also alert us to intersections between asbestos and larger issues related to mass migration, climate change, plastic proliferation, racial injustice and toxic legacies. This is not to highlight the intractability of these problems, but new possibilities for their resolution: for, if asbestos seems a niche issue to researchers of migration, climate, plastic and toxicity, it is precisely its relative containment that has produced a sophisticated jurisprudence, a complex epidemiology and a globally integrated, committed network of activists. These provide sources of translatable knowledge and places to meet potential comrades. Where once asbestos's precautionary lesson was its unforeseen toxic effects, we can reframe this lesson as a set of legal, medical and activist advances that herald tried-and-tested strategies for handling the challenges ahead. If this seems, to those concerned with asbestos, an unnecessary distraction, then consider how this new-found solidarity might recentre debates about asbestos that have receded into history. Here, too, one can find political models in those communities who have already developed new forms of mediating their relationship with asbestos.

An uncritical relationship to asbestos abatement finds its shocking denouement in the murder of Phikolomzi Ignatius 'Igo' Mpambani on Tuesday, 20 June 2017, gunned down at the intersection of South Road and Bowling Avenue in Sandton, Johannesburg. Some years before, Mpambani's company, 605 Consulting Solutions, had entered into an agreement to help another company, Blackhead Consulting, 'procure contracts'. Mpambani's political contacts would help Blackhead Consulting and a third company, Diamond Hill Trading 71, secure a joint tender for the 'assessment [and] audit of houses roofed using asbestos material'.[7] The resulting contract, a R255 million deal awarded by the Free State Department of Human Settlements, permitted Blackhead and Diamond to appoint a fourth company, Mastertrade, to compile the report, for which it was paid R44 million. In turn, Mastertrade subcontracted a fifth company, the Ori Group, to perform the actual audit, which cost a little over R21 million. In the words of Pieter-Louis Myburgh, the journalist who broke the story, 'it took just three months for them to complete a report that, at fifty-three pages, cost taxpayers nearly R5 million a page' (243). It is likely the work was unnecessary. 'Old houses with asbestos roofs are usually concentrated in the same area in each township,' one source told him, 'and the municipalities have records of where those houses are located' (243). Certainly, the report itself contained duplicate pictures of the same houses: 'You would see a picture of house number 20 in a certain township, and, a few pages later you would again see the same house' (244). There were further irregularities in the monies paid for the audit (which were paid per house inspected, rather than per house contaminated with asbestos) and in the projected sums for subsequent abatement (R36,000).

This story forms the substantive empirical evidence of Myburgh's larger argument, which implicates Ace Magashule, the Secretary General of the African National Congress, South Africa's ruling party, in state capture, crony capitalism, and tenderpreneurism. As might be surmised from his book's title, *Gangster State*, Myburgh's aim to write an exposé of Magashule, and, by extension, the network of state capture made visible during the presidency of Jacob Zuma and after. As such, the asbestos audit and abatement scandal simply provide the means by which this particular instance of 'raiding' occurred: its concrete particulars matter only insofar as they expose the extent of the corporate malfeasance. But the Mpambani tender generates a particular resonance because it foregrounds the ongoing presence of asbestos roofing materials in areas designated for disenfranchised Black South Africans during Apartheid. Asbestos, here, stood in as the material legacy of particular Apartheid practices, wherein marginalised groups suffered not just exclusion and neglect, but outrightly harmful building practices.

Asbestos roofs, for instance, still protect many houses in former townships, a circumstance replicated in different sites across the country. These roofs tell a story of Apartheid-era neglect, cost-cutting, and short-termism, which it has been the task of the ANC, as the party of liberation, to try to correct. We can acknowledge the insurmountable nature of the problem without defending the crony capitalism of leading figures in the party. Indeed, such cronyism has thrived in part because of the conflation of acknowledgment and defence. But we should also recognise that asbestos abatement proves to be a particularly useful site for such cronyism, especially in the South African context, because abatement, in itself, seems morally unimpeachable.

A similar example can be found in right-wing news stories about 'The Jungle,' the most publicised informal settlement outside Calais between January 2015 and October 2016. *The Daily Mail*, a British newspaper notable for its demonisation of migrants, ran a number of stories over the period that, surprisingly, seemed concerned with the well-being of The Jungle's inhabitants, after asbestos was discovered in their informal shelters. The underlying message, however, remained ideologically consistent: the migrants needed to be removed and the settlement destroyed. Now, however, the removal might be done in good conscience and without abandoning a moral superiority; it needed to be done for the good of the migrants themselves. Asbestos became the means by which an already entrenched ideological position might retrospectively justify itself.

My third example is from Noam Leshem's account of urban resilience in Israel/Palestine. In *Life after Ruin* (2016), Leshem shows how asbestos abatement sometimes leads to more complex problems.[8] He considers the case of Dudi Balasi, whose house's gradual sinking is interrupted by its demolition for a private development contract. Before the house was demolished, Balasi reported, 'the city council won't even allow me to replace the asbestos roof. Any improvement in the house is automatically seen as a breach of the law and an excuse for them to tear it down' (6). Even if the house were not doomed to destruction for capitalist expansion, the removal of the asbestos roof would, by improving the property, render it illegal and subject to destruction. If accounts of The Jungle raised the asbestos problem as the basis for destroying the settlement, here solving the asbestos problem would, paradoxically, have the same effect. These contrasting examples show how the pressures of asbestos abatement may be exerted to ideological ends. The matter of asbestos waste is no mere waste matter.

At this point, when the loss of authority, the impossibility of containment and the persistence of the fibre have been convincingly demonstrated, I want to identify the activist work of the Asbestos Interest Group (AIG) of Kuruman in the Northern Cape as a possible site where this slow destruction might galvanise action, and where, by extension, the literary problematic of mediation comes to be bound to an activist praxis. John Trimbur has delivered an exceptional account of the AIG's formation and its activities.[9] In 2003, an out-of-court settlement between South African plaintiffs, represented by Richard Spoor, and the Griqualand Exploration and Finance Company (Gefco), General Mining Corporation (Gencor), Msauli, African Chrysotile Asbestos Limited (ACA) and Hanova Mining Holdings, led to the formation of the Asbestos Relief Trust (ART). Unlike a parallel 2003 settlement, between the Concerned People Against Asbestos (CPAA) group in Prieska and Cape Plc, which, as a class action suit, resolved itself by paying out compensation to all signatories, the ART set itself up as a fund for future, and ongoing, claims for compensation. To support its efforts, in publicising the compensation available, building relationships with the local community and offering palliative care, the ART turned to an organisation that had been critical for community mobilisation in making the case against Gefco et al.: the AIG.

However, rather than simply act as a mouthpiece for the ART, the AIG developed a sophisticated set of tools for liaising between local communities and ART. At the same time as the AIG liaised with the ART with a degree of formality that sought to mimic the paper trails that had proved so crucial to the law case, it also created a set of cartoons for local communities to communicate how asbestos exposure happens, drawing on the community's rich visual literacy, rather than relying upon purely textual information. In one cartoon, discussed by Trimbur, a set of panels track the life and death of a woman, exposed to the dust on her partner's work clothes. By juxtaposing different scenes in the woman's life, the AIG translated material information into a visual narrative that communicated the pattern of causation to local communities. These efforts to mobilise diverse corporate and community-facing literacies to its cause demonstrate how the AIG eluded attempts by the ART to position it, as within a covert pastoral, as the simple figure in one sense better and in another worse. The mines, the AIG prove, are not places where the complex can be stated simply. Indeed, as Trimbur shows, the case of the AIG challenges the tendency to see the asbestos mining community as isolated or peripheral to the world-system, when they are absolutely central to this system's functioning.

Cases like the AIG help us understand ways in which literary mediation might effect larger change. We might follow the AIG's lead in thinking how such narratives might best be translated into visual narratives that might serve a wider purpose. But this mistakes use for basic instrumentality. Instead, I want to suggest that the place where the AIG and the literary narratives intersect is not simply in helping those of us who do not live in Kuruman or Prieska, Asbestos or Cassiar, Wittenoom or Asbest, to develop a little epistemic humility about our unfairly dampened expectations about such places. Rather it shows how living with asbestos contamination is living with a constant obstruction, a thing that stubbornly gets in the way of our flourishing.

This, after all, is what the Resources for Education and Action for Community Health (REACH) project in Ambler found, when it worked with local communities on matters of history, literacy and cultural identity: that a rich culture was inextricably linked with the community's toxic legacy. Jessica Van Horssen observes the same complexities in her cultural history of Asbestos, while Agata Mazzeo has noted comparable community developments in the site of the old Eternit factory at Casale Monferrato in Northern Italy and the Sao Félix Mine at Bom Jesus da Serra in Bahia.[10] So, if community efforts to re-mediate their understanding of legacy serve as incitements to further thinking, the role such communities should play in developing just reparation demands more immanent reworking.

It is clear that all of these sites suffer from their position on capitalism's periphery: the source of asbestos's wealth, they are still denied just reparations, making do, instead, with compensation and remediation. Compensation itself remains a wasteful practice that imagines individual solutions to community level problems. In his analysis of the asbestos litigation process in the US, Jeb

Barnes notes three historical conditions that have obstructed more efficient processes of asbestos compensation: 'drift' ('the shift in the impact of programs on social life through changing circumstances'), 'conversion' ('the reinterpretation of existing rules and programs'), and 'layering' ('the adding of new institutional arrangements without eliminating old ones').[11] As asbestos litigation became more and more necessary, the relative inability of compensation programmes to 'drift' left claimants without the legal means to apply for damages. Litigation rushed to fill in the gap, as existing laws were 'converted' to address the lacuna in case precedent. When compensation programmes were developed, these were simply 'layered' over existing case precedent, giving claimants multiple possible avenues to seek redress.

Barnes's account may be reframed as a consideration of the historical mediating factors that determined the wastefulness of the current system. But, the actions of the AIG, the community work of REACH Ambler, the resilience of other single resource towns in Brazil, Canada and India also teach us that such mediations demand the pressures of robust, community responses. Making this a community issue demands, reciprocally, community funding. These moneys might come from asbestos trusts, but these were often left relatively impoverished when companies like Johns Manville, Cape Plc, James Hardie, W. E. Grace and others set them up to divest themselves of their moral and financial responsibilities. It is clear, then, that such divestment must be reversed, for the sake of those communities in whose name the companies so cynically sold their products. These companies were absolutely instrumental in the development of these communities, and that it was these communities they abandoned. It is as communities that demands for compensation are best mediated, and as communities that decisions should be made as to how best to distribute this money for the common good. Pursuant on this precedent, we could imagine the asbestos story spearheading a much larger network of allied movements seeking reparations for historical injustices: slavery, endemic pollution, plastic contamination and climate change. If, in some small way, this book mobilises us towards such thinking, then it might have found a use.

Notes

1. *Session 9*, dir. Brad Anderson (USA Films, 2001).
2. David Foster Wallace, *Infinite Jest* (London: Abacus, 1996). I explore this allegory in 'Asbestos Populism in David Foster Wallace's *Infinite Jest*', 21 (3) *Safundi* (2020), p. 339–54.
3. Paolo Bacigalupi, *Ship Breaker* (London: Hatchette, 2010); Jonathan Raban, *Waxwings* (London: Picador, 2003); John Kinsella, 'See that Gully: The Ghost I Have Become in a World of Asbestos', 74 *Meanjin Quarterly* (2015), p. 44–50; Maria Flook, 'Asbestos', 30 (4) *Michigan Quarterly Review* (1991), pp. 667–82.
4. Will Viney, *Waste: A Philosophy of Things* (London: Bloomsbury, 2014), pp. 1–2.

5. Nicky Gregson, 'Asbestos', *Making Things International 2*, ed. Mark B. Salter (Minneapolis, MN: University of Minnesota Press, 2016), p. 264.
6. For an account of disaster temporalities, to which I am greatly indebted, see Kasia Mika, *Disasters, Vulnerability, and Narratives: Writing Haiti's Futures* (London: Routledge, 2019).
7. Pieter-Louis Myburgh, *Gangster State: Unravelling Ace Magashule's Web of Capture* (Cape Town: Penguin Books, 2019), p. 224.
8. Noam Leshem, *Life After Ruin: The Struggles Over Israel's Depopulated Arab Spaces* (Cambridge: Cambridge University Press, 2016).
9. John Trimbur, *Grassroots Literacy and the Written Record: A Textual History of Asbestos Activism in South Africa* (Bristol: Multilingual Matters, 2020).
10. Van Horssen, *Asbestos*; Mazzeo, *Dust*.
11. Jeb Barnes, *Dust-Up: Asbestos Litigation and the Failure of Commonsense Policy Reform* (Washington, DC: Georgetown University Press, 2011).

BIBLIOGRAPHY

Abbott, H. Porter, *Real Mysteries: Narrative and the Unknowable* (Columbus, OH: Ohio State University Press, 2013).
Agamben, Giorgio, *Homo Sacer: Sovereign Power and Bare Life*, trans. Daniel Heller-Rozen (Stanford: Stanford University Press, 1998).
Ahmed, Sara, *What's the Use? On the Uses of Use* (Durham, NC: Duke University Press, 2019).
Alaimo, Stacy, *Bodily Natures: Science, Environment, and the Material Self* (Bloomington: Indiana University Press, 2010).
Alder, Emily, *Weird Fiction and Science at the Fin de Siècle* (London: Palgrave Macmillan, 2020).
Alice: A Fight for Life, dir. John Willis (ITV Yorkshire, 1982).
Ambler Asbestos Corrugated Roofing (Ambler, PA: Keasbey & Mattison, 1918).
Anand, Nikhil, Akhil Gupta and Hannah Appel, *The Promise of Infrastructure* (Durham, NC: Duke University Press, 2018).
Andersson, Jens A. 'Reinterpreting the Rural-Urban Connection: Migration Practices and Socio-Cultural Dispositions of Buhera Workers in Harare', 71 (1) *Africa* (2001), pp. 82–112.
Appadurai, Arjun, 'Commodities and the Politics of Value,' in *The Social Life of Things: Commodities in Cultural Perspective*, ed. Arjun Appadurai (Cambridge: Cambridge University Press, 1986), pp. 3–63.

Arboleda, Martín, *Planetary Mine: Territories of Extraction under Late Capitalism* (London: Verso, 2020).
Arney, Angela, *Old Sins, Long Memories* (London: Robert Hale, 2014).
'Asbestos Fest', *Schitt's Creek* (CBC, 23 January 2018).
Asbestos . . . A Matter of Time (U.S. Bureau of Mines with Johns-Manville Corporation, 1959).
Asbestos.com, https://www.asbestos.com/asbestos/
Augustine, Aurelius, *The City of God, Volumes I & II*, ed. and trans. Marcus Dods (Edinburgh: T&T Clark, 1871).
Auribault, Étienne, 'Sur l'hygiene et la securite des ouvriers dans la filature et tissage d'amiante', *Bulletin de l'inspection du travail* (1906), pp. 120–32.
Bacigalupi, Paolo, *Ship Breaker* (London: Hatchette, 2010).
Báez Baquet, Francisco, *Amianto: Un genocidio impune* (Málaga: ediciones del Genal, 2014).
Bainbridge, James, 'Tuesday, 28th May, 2013', *JWRB.me Blog*, Accessed 23 February 2021: https://jrwb.me/tag/tessimond/
Barad, Karen, *Meeting the Universe Halfway: Quantum Physics and the Entanglement of Matter and Meaning* (Durham, NC: Duke University Press, 2007).
Barnes, Djuna, 'Fireman Michael Quinn: 40 Years a Flame Fighter', *Brooklyn Daily Eagle*, 2 November 1913, Part 4, p. 22.
Barnes, Jeb, *Dust-Up: Asbestos Litigation and the Failure of Commonsense Policy Reform* (Washington, DC: Georgetown University Press, 2011).
Barnes, Joanne, 'Pleased to Meet You', *Asbestos Awareness and Support Cymru*, Accessed 23 February 2021: http://a-a-s-c.org.uk/wp-content/uploads/2012/01/pleased-to-meet-you.pdf
Bartrip, Peter, *Beyond the Factory Gates: Asbestos and Health in Twentieth Century America* (London: Continuum, 2006).
Bartrip, Peter, *The Way From Dusty Death: Turner and Newall and the Regulation of the British Asbestos Industry 1890s–1970* (London: The Athlone Press, 2001).
Bass, Rick, 'With Every Great Breath: Living and Dying in Lincoln Country', Box 24, Folder 4, *Rick Bass Papers, 1986–2013 and Undated*, Southwest Collection/Special Collections Library, Texas Tech University, Lubbock, Texas.
Bazhov, Pavel, 'Šëlkovaja gorka', *Uralsky Rabochy*, 7 Nov 1947.
Beare, Geoffrey, *Heath Robinson's Commercial Art* (London: Lund Humphries, 2017).
Beckett, Samuel, *Murphy*, ed. J. C. C. Mays (London: Faber & Faber, 2009).
Bellamy, Edward, *Looking Backward from 2000–1887*, ed. Matthew Beaumont (Oxford: Oxford University Press, 2009).

Bennett, Alan. *Two Kafka Plays: Kafka's Dick and The Insurance Man* (London: Faber & Faber, 1987).
Benjamin, Walter, 'Franz Kafka: On the Tenth Anniversary of His Death', *Selected Writings 2, 1927–1934*, eds M. W. Jennings, H. Eiland and G. Smith, trans. R. Livingstone et al. (Cambridge, MA: Belknap Press, 1999), pp. 794–818.
Bérard, Cassie, *Qu'il est bon de se noyer* (Montréal: Éditions Druide, 2016).
Bergson, Henri, *Laughter: An Essay on the Meaning of the Comic*, trans. by Cloudesley Brereton and Fred Rothwell (New York: The Macmillan Company, 1911).
Berlant, Lauren, *Cruel Optimism* (Durham, NC: Duke University Press, 2011).
Bird-David, Nurit, '"Animism" Revisited: Personhood, Environment, and Relational Epistemology', 40 (1) *Current Anthropology* (February, 1999): S67–S91, S69.
Blackwood, Algernon, *John Silence: Physician Extraordinary* (New York: Brentano's, 1910).
Blanchard, Stephen, *Gagarin and I* [1995] (London: Vintage, 1996).
Blanchot, Maurice, *The Space of Literature*, trans. Ann Smock (Lincoln, NE: University of Nebraska Press, 1982).
Bloch, Ernst, *Heritage of Our Time*, trans. Neville and Stephen Plaice (Cambridge: Polity Press, 1991).
Bloch, Ernst, 'Nonsynchronism and the Obligation to Its Dialectics', trans. Mark Ritter, 11 *New German Critique* (1977), pp. 22–38.
Bloch, Ernst, *The Principle of Hope: Volume 1*, trans. Neville Plaice, Stephen Plaice and Paul Knight (Oxford: Blackwell, 1986).
Bluemel, Kristin and Michael McCluskey, *Rural Modernity in Britain: A Critical Intervention* (Edinburgh: Edinburgh University Press, 2018).
Boggio, Andrea, *Compensating Asbestos Victims: Law and the Dark Side of Industrialization* (Abingdon: Routledge, 2013).
Boltanski, Luc, *Mysteries & Conspiracies* (Cambridge: Polity, 2014).
Bond, Barbara, *Everyday Enemies* (np: Barbara Bond, 2012).
Bonnefoy, Yves, *L'Improbable et autres essais* (Paris: Gallimard, 1980).
Bonnefoy, Yves, *On the Motion and Immobility of Douve*, ed. Timothy Mathews, trans. Galway Kinnell (Hexham, Bloodaxe Books, 1992).
The Book of Roofs (New York: Johns-Manville Co., 1923).
Borges, Jorge Luis, 'Kafka and his Precursors', *The Total Library: Non-Fiction 1922–1986*, trans. Eliot Weinberger (London: Penguin, 2001), pp. 363–5.
Bowen, Elizabeth, *Eva Trout; or Changing Scenes*, intro. Tessa Hadley (London: Vintage, 2011).
Bowles, Oliver, *Asbestos: The Silk of the Mineral Kingdom* (np: Ruberoid Co., 1946).
Boyd, Damien, *Death Sentence* (Seattle: Thomas & Mercer, 2016).

Braun, Lundy, *Breathing Race Into the Machine: The Surprising Career of the Spirometer from Plantation to Genetics* (Minneapolis: University of Minnesota Press, 2014).
Braun, Lundy, 'Structuring Silence: Asbestos and Biomedical Research in Britain and South Africa', 50 (1) *Race & Class* (2008), pp. 59–78.
Braun, Lundy and Hannah Kopinski, 'Causal Understandings: Controversy, Social Context, and Mesothelioma Research', 13 *Biosocieties* (2018), pp. 557–79.
Braun, Lundy and Sophia Kisting, 'Asbestos-Related Disease in South Africa: The Social Production of an Invisible Epidemic', 96 (8) *American Journal of Public Health* (2006), pp. 1386–96.
Braun, Lundy et al., 'Scientific Controversy and Asbestos: Making Disease Invisible', 9 (3) *International Journal of Occupational and Environmental Health* (2003), pp. 194–205.
Breathless, dir. Daniel Lambo (np: Storyhouse Film, 2018).
Brodeur, Paul, *Outrageous Misconduct: The Asbestos Industry on Trial* (New York: Pantheon Press, 1985).
Brody, Richard, 'The Real Problem with *Peter Rabbit*'s Allergy Scene', *The New Yorker*, 14 February 2018.
Brooks, Maria Gowen, *Zóphiël, or the Bride of Seven* (London: R. J. Kennett, 1833).
Brown, Nicholas, *Autonomy: The Social Ontology of Art Under Capitalism* (Durham, NC: Duke University Press, 2019).
Browne, Clare, 'Salamander's Wool: The Historical Evidence for Textiles Woven with Asbestos Fibre', 34 (1) *Textile History* (2003), pp. 64–73.
Browne, Thomas, *Pseudodoxia Epidemica* (1646/1672). *Sir Thomas Browne*, Accessed 24 September 2019: http://penelope.uchicago.edu/index.html
Browning, Elizabeth Barrett, *Poetical Works: Volume 3* (London: Chapman Hall, 1866).
Bryant, Marsha, 'Polymers: Fantastic Plastics in Postwar America', *Impact of Materials on Society*, eds Sophia Krzys Acord, Kevin S. Jones, Marsha Bryant, Debra Dauphin-Jones and Pamela Hupp (Gainesville: Library Press @ UF, 2021).
Burchell, William J., *Travels in the Interior of Southern Africa: Volume 1* (London: Longman et al., 1822).
Büttner, Jan Ulrich, *Asbest in der Vormoderne: Vom Mythos zur Wissenschaft* (Münster, Waxmann Verlag GmbH, 2004).
Calvino, Italo, 'La Fabbrica nella montagna', intro. Francesco Carnevale and Stefano Silvestri, 18 *Epidemiologia e prevenzione* (1994), pp. 191–3.
Carel, Havi, *Phenomenology of Illness* (Oxford: Oxford University Press, 2016).
Carson, Rachel, *Silent Spring*, intro. Linda Lear (Boston: Houghton Mifflen Co., 2002).

Castleman, Barry, *Asbestos: Medical and Legal Aspects*, 5th ed (New York: Aspen Publishers, 2005).
Cesaretti, Enrico, *Elemental Narratives: Reading Environmental Entanglements in Modern Italy* (University Park, PA: Penn State University Press, 2020).
Cesire, Natalia, *Experimental: American Literature and the Aesthetics of Knowledge* (Baltimore, MD: Johns Hopkins University Press, 2019).
Chakravarti, Sundeep, *Red Sun: Travels in Naxalite Country* (London: Penguin Books, 2009).
Chamoiseau, Patrick, *Texaco*, trans. Rose-Myriam Réjouis and Val Vinokuro [1994] (New York: Vintage International, 1998).
Chang, Ruth, 'Incommensurability (and Incomparability)', in *The International Encyclopedia of Ethics*, ed. Hugh LaFollette, (Malden, MA: Wiley-Blackwell, 2013), pp. 2591–604.
Charon, Rita, *Narrative Medicine: Honoring the Stories of Illness* (Oxford: Oxford University Press, 2006).
Cheah, Pheng, *What is a World?* (Durham, NC: Duke University Press, 2016).
Chen, Mel Y., *Animacies: Biopolitics, Racial Mattering, and Queer Affect* (Durham, NC: Duke University Press, 2012).
Cohen, Jeffrey Jerome, *Stone: An Ecology of the Inhuman* (Minneapolis: University of Minnesota Press, 2015).
Cohen, Ralph, 'Introduction: Theorizing Genre', 34 (2) *New Literary History* (2003), pp. iv–xiv.
Cooke, W. E., 'Fibrosis of the Lungs due to the Inhalation of Asbestos', 2 (3317) (1924), pp. 140–2; 147.
Cooper Megrue, Roi, and Walter Hackett, *It Pays to Advertise* (New York: Samuel French, 1917).
Corngold, Stanley, 'Kafka and the Dialectic of Minor Literature', 21 (1) *College Literature* (1994), pp. 89–101.
Cornwell, Neil, *The Absurd in Literature* (Manchester: Manchester University Press, 2006).
Cover, Robert M.,'Nomos and Narrative', 97 (1) Harvard Law Review (1983), pp. 4-68.
Culler, Jonathan, *Theory of the Lyric* (Cambridge, MA: Harvard University Press, 2015).
cummings, e. e., *The Enormous Room* (London: Jonathan Cape, 1928).
D'Agostino, Bill, 'The Hill', in *The White Mountains*. Accessed 23 February 2021: https://reachambler.sciencehistory.org/theplay
Deane, Lucy, 'Report on the Health of Workers in Asbestos and Other Dusty Trades', in HM *Chief Inspector of Factories and Workshops: Annual Report for 1898* (1899), pp. 171–2.
Devi, Mahasweta, *Dust on the Road* (Kolkata: Seagull Books, 2000).
Devil's Dust, dir. Jessica Hobbs (ABC, 2011).

Di Ciaula, Agostino and Valerio Gennaro, 'Rischio clinico da ingestione di fibre di amianto in acqua potabile', 40 (6) *Epidemiologica e prevenzione* (2016), pp. 472–5.

Doctorow, Cory, *Walkaway* (London: Head of Zeus, 2017).

Doll, Richard, 'Mortality from Lung Cancer in Asbestos Workers', 12 *British Journal of Industrial Medicine* (1955), pp. 81–6.

Donovan, Anne, *Hieroglyphics and Other Stories* (Edinburgh: Canongate, 2001).

Doolittle, Hilda (H. D.), *Tribute to Freud*, intro. Adam Philips, Afterword by Norman Holmes Pearson (New York: New Directions, 2012).

Doolittle, Hilda (H. D.) and others, *Analyzing Freud: Letters of H. D., Bryher, and their Circle*, ed. Susan Stanford Friedman (New York: New Directions, 2002).

Drabble, Margaret, *The Dark Flood Rises* (Edinburgh: Canongate Books Ltd, 2016).

Durrell, Lawrence, *The Black Book* [1938] (New York: Dutton & Co., 1960).

The Dust at Acre Mill, dir. John Sheppard (Granada Television, 1971).

Ehrenreich, Barbara, *Smile or Die: How Postive Thinking Fooled America & the World* (London: Granta Books, 2010).

Empson, William, *Some Versions of Pastoral* [1935] (Harmondsworth: Penguin Books, 1966).

Epps, Tracey, *International Trade and Health Protection* (Cheltenham: Edward Elgar, 2008).

Everett, Sue, *Not Welcome: A Dunera Boy's Escape from Nazi Oppression* (np: Port Campbell Press, 2010).

Ewald, François, 'The Return of Descartes's Malicious Demon: An Outline of a Philosophy of Precaution', trans. Stephen Utz, in: *Embracing Risk: The Changing Culture of Insurance and Responsibility*, eds Tom Baker and Jonathan Simon (Chicago, IL: University of Chicago Press, 2002), pp. 273–301.

Fahr, T., 'Kristallbildung in der Lunge', 30 *Deutsche Medizinische Wochenschrift* (1914), pp. 1548–9.

Fairchild v Glenhaven Funeral Services Ltd [2002] UKHL 22

Fawell, John K., 'Asbestos Cement Drinking Water Pipes and Possible Health Risks: Review for DWI', *Report for Contract 70/2/135* (Devizes: FaberMaunsell Ltd, 2002).

Fein, John M., *Toward Octavio Paz: A Reading of His Major Poems, 1957–1976* (Lexington: The University Press of Kentucky, 1986).

Ferns, Christopher S., *Narrating Utopia: Ideology, Gender, Form in Utopian Literature* (Liverpool: Liverpool University Press, 1999).

Fischer, J. Alfred, 'The Mining, Manufacture and Uses of Asbestos', *Transactions of the Institute of Marine Engineers* (1892–93), pp. 5–22.

Fitzgerald, F. Scott, *Fie! Fie! Fi-Fi: A Facsimile of The 1914 Acting Script and Musical Score* (Columbia, SC: University of South Carolina Press, 1996).

Fitzgerald, F. Scott, 'The Diamond as Big as the Ritz', 68 (2) *Smart Set* (June 1922), pp. 5–29.

Flook, Maria, 'Asbestos', 30 (4) *Michigan Quarterly Review* (1991), pp. 667–82.

Forrester, John, *Thinking in Cases* (Cambridge: Polity Press, 2017).

Frank, Arthur W., *The Wounded Storyteller: Body, Illness, and Ethics* (Chicago: University of Chicago Press, 1995).

Franzen, Jonathan, *The End of the End of the Earth: Essays* (London: 4th Estate, 2018).

Frayn, Michael, *My Father's Fortune: A Life* (London: Faber & Faber, 2010).

Freedgood, Elaine, 'Ghostly Reference', 125 (1) *Representations* (2014), pp. 40–53.

From Rock to Roof: What You Need To Know About Slate (Pen Argyl, PA: Pennsylvania Slate Institute, c. 1930).

Garuba, Harry, 'Explorations in Animist Materialism: Notes on Reading/Writing African Literature, Culture, and Society', 15 (2) *Public Culture* (2003), pp. 261–85.

Gilman, Charlotte Perkins, *What Diantha Did*, intro. Charlotte J. Rich (Durham, NC: Duke University Press, 2005).

Ginzburg, Carlo, 'Clues: Roots of a Scientific Paradigm', 7 (3) *Theory and Society*, pp. 273–88.

Giraud, Eva Haifa, *What Comes After Entanglement?* (Durham, NC: Duke University Press, 2019).

Godden, Richard, 'A Diamond Bigger than the Ritz: F. Scott Fitzgerald and the Gold Standard', 95 (3) *ELH* (2010), pp. 589–613.

Gopnik, Adam, 'Introduction', *The Art of Rube Goldberg* (New York: Abrams Comicarts, 2013), pp. 15–18.

Gould, Stephen Jay, *Full House: The Spread of Excellence from Plato to Darwin* (Cambridge, MA: Harvard University Press, 1996).

Green, Louise, 'Thinking Outside the Body: New Materialism and the Challenge of the Fetish', 5 (3) *Cambridge Journal of Postcolonial Literary Inquiry* (2018), pp. 304–17.

Gregson, Nicky, 'Asbestos', *Making Things International 2*, ed. Mark B. Salter (Minneapolis, MN: University of Minnesota Press, 2016).

Gregson, Nicky et al., 'Inextinguishable Fibres: Demolition and the Vital Materialisms of Asbestos', 42 (5) *Environment and Planning A: Economy and Space* (2010), pp. 1065–83.

Gulddal, Jesper, Stewart King and Alistair Rolls, eds, *Criminal Moves: Modes of Mobility in Crime Fiction* (Liverpool: Liverpool University Press, 2020).

Gumbrecht, Hans Ulrich, 'How (if at all) can we Encounter what Remains Latent in Texts?', 7 (1) *Partial Answers* (2009), pp. 87–96.

Haigh, Gideon, *Asbestos House: The Secret History of James Hardie Industries* (Melbourne: Scribe Publications, 2006).
Hall, Stuart, 'Encoding/Decoding', in *Media and Cultural Studies: Keyworks*, eds Meenakshi Gigi Durham and Douglas M. Kellner (Oxford: Blackwell, 2006), pp. 163–73.
Hames, Scott, '"Maybe Singing into Yourself": James Kelman, Inner Speech and Vocal Communion', in *Community in Modern Scottish Literature*, ed. Scott Lyall (Leiden: Brill, 2016), pp. 196–213.
Hamilton, Patrick, *Hangover Square* [1941], intro. J. B. Priestley (London: Penguin Books, 2001).
Harremoës, Poul et al., *Late Lessons from Early Warnings: the Precautionary Principle, 1896–2000, Environmental Issue Report 22* (Copenhagen: European Environment Agency, 2001).
Hartley, Daniel, *The Politics of Style: Towards a Marxist Poetics* [2016] (Chicago: Haymarket Books, 2017).
Hartman, Saidiya, *Lose Your Mother: A Journey along the Atlantic Slave Route* [2006] (New York: Farrar, Straus and Giroux, 2008).
Hashmi, Nasser, *Fistful of Dust* (Kibworth Beauchamp: Matador, 2015).
Hawkins, Anne Hunsaker, *Reconstructing Illness: Studies in Pathography* (West Lafayette: Purdue University Press, 1991).
Hayot, Eric, *On Literary Worlds* (Oxford: Oxford University Press, 2012).
Health and Safety Executive, 'Why is Asbestos Dangerous?', *Health and Safety Executive*. Accessed 24 September 2019: http://www.hse.gov.uk/asbestos/dangerous.htm
Hollin, Gregory, Isla Forsyth, Eva Giraud and Tracey Potts, '(Dis) Entangling Barad: Materialisms and Ethics', 47 (6) *Social Studies of Science* (2017), pp. 918–41.
Holm, Isak Winkel, *Kafka's Stereoscopes: The Political Function of a Literary Style* (London: Bloomsbury, 2020).
Horn, Eva, *The Future as Catastrophe: Imagining Disaster in the Modern Age*, trans. Valentine Pakis (New York: Columbia University Press, 2018).
Houser, Heather, *Infowhelm: Environmental Art and Literature in an Age of Data* (New York: Columbia UP, 2020).
Hubble, Nick, *The Proletarian Answer to the Modernist Question* (Edinburgh: Edinburgh University Press, 2017).
Huchu, Tendai, *The Hairdresser of Harare* [2010] (Glasgow: Freight Books, 2013).
Hurst, Rebecca, *Digging Deep: the Enchanted Underground in Pavel Bazhov's 1939 Collection of Magic Tales, The Malachite Casket* (Manchester: University of Manchester PhD Thesis, 2018).
Hutchison, Hazel, *The War that Used Up Words: American Writers and the First World War* (New Haven: Yale University Press, 2015).

International Ban Asbestos Secretariat, http://ibasecretariat.org
Iovino, Serenella, *Ecocriticism and Italy: Ecology, Resistance, and Liberation* (London: Bloomsbury, 2016).
Irurzun, Patxi, *Ciudad Retrete* (Tafalla: Txalaparta, 2002).
Jaffe, Aaron, *The Way Things Go: An Essay on the Matter of Second Modernism* (Minneapolis: University of Minnesota Press, 2014).
Jameson, Fredric, *Archaeologies of the Future: The Desire Called Utopia and Other Science Fictions* (London: Verso, 2007).
Jameson, Fredric, *The Political Unconscious: Narrative as a Socially Symbolic Act* [1981] (London: Routledge, 2002).
Jameson, Fredric, 'The Vanishing Mediator: Narrative Structure in Max Weber', 1 *New German Critique* (1973), pp. 52–89.
Jansen, Monica, 'The Uses of Affective Realism in Asbestos Narratives: Prunetti's *Amianto* and Valenti's *La Fabbrica del Panico*', *Encounters with the Real in Contemporary Italian Literature and Cinema*, eds Loredana Di Martino and Pasquale Verdicchio (Newcastle: Cambridge Scholars, 2017), pp. 3–28.
Jarrell, Randall, 'Thoughts about Marianne Moore', 19 (6) *The Partisan Review* (1952), pp. 687–700.
Jasper, James M., *The Art of Moral Protest: Culture, Biography, and Creativity in Social Movements* (Chicago, IL: University of Chicago Press, 1997).
Jeremy, David J. 'Corporate Responses to the Emergent Recognition of a Health Hazard in the UK Asbestos Industry: The Case of Turner & Newall, 1920–1960', 24 (1) *Business and Economic History* (1995), pp. 254–65.
Jhabvala, Ruth Prawer, *A Backward Place* [1965] (London: Abacus, 2013).
Johns, Henry W. 'Improved Compound for Roofing and Other Purposes', (United States of America Patent, 1868).
Johnson, Ronald and Arthur McIvor, *Lethal Work: A History of the Asbestos Tragedy in Scotland* (East Linton: Tuckwell, 2000).
Johnston, Michelle, *Dustfall* (Crawley: University of Western Australia Press, 2018).
Jonas, Hans, *The Imperative of Responsibility. In Search of an Ethics for the Technological Age* (Chicago, IL: University of Chicago Press, 1984).
Jones, Robert H., *Asbestos, Its Production and Use: With Some Account of the Asbestos Mines of Canada* (London: Crosby Lockwood & Son, 1888).
Jurecic, Ann, *Illness as Narrative* (Pittsburgh, PA: University of Pittsburgh Press, 2011).
Justice, Daniel Heath, *Why Indigenous Literatures Matter* (Waterloo: Wilfrid Laurier University Press, 2018).
Kafer, Alison, *Feminist, Queer, Crip* (Bloomington: Indiana University Press, 2013).
Kafka, Franz, *Letters to Friends, Family, and Editors*. ed. Max Brod, trans. Richard and Clara Winston [1959] (New York: Schocken Books, 1987).

Kafka, Franz, *The Diaries: 1910–1923*, ed. Max Brod, trans. Joseph Kresh and Martin Greenberg (with the cooperation of Hannah Arendt) (New York: Schocken Books, 1976).
Kafka, Franz, *The Office Writings*, ed. Stanley Corngold, Jack Greenberg and Benno Wagner (Princeton, NJ: Princeton University Press, 2009).
Kafka, Franz, *The Trial* [1925], trans. Breon Mitchell (New York: Schocken Books, 1998).
Kane, Pat, 'Underclass, Under-what? Fictions and Realities from Glasgow to Prague: an Interview with James Kelman', 7 *Regenerating Cities* (1995), pp. 18–20.
Keats, John, *The Complete Poems*, ed. Jack Stillinger [1978] (Cambridge, MA: Belknap Press, 1982).
Kelly, Aaron, '"I Just Tell the Bloody Truth, as I See it": James Kelman's *A Disaffection*, the Enlightenment, Romanticism and Melancholy Knowledge', 12 *Études écossaises* (2009), pp. 79–99.
Kelly, Aaron. *James Kelman: Politics and Aesthetics* (Oxford: Peter Lang, 2013).
Kelman, James, *An Old Pub Near the Angel* [1973] (Edinburgh: Polygon, 2007).
Kelman, James, *'And the Judges Said . . . ': Essays* [2002] (Edinburgh: Polygon, 2008).
Kelman, James, 'Compensation, Not Justice A Discussion Paper on Asbestos Abuse Read to the Scottish Parliament', Christie Books, 20 October 2015. Accessed: 27 September 2021. https://christiebooks.co.uk/2015/10/compensation-not-justice-a-discussion-paper-on-asbestos-abuse-read-to-the-scottish-parliament-by-james-kelman/?doing_wp_cron=1632735657.9196989536285400390625
Kelman, James, *How Late it Was, How Late* [1994] (London: Minerva, 1995).
Kelman, James, *Some Recent Attacks: Essays Cultural & Political* (Stirling: AK Press, 1992).
Kermode, Frank, *The Sense of an Ending: Studies in the Theory of Fiction* [1966] (Oxford: Oxford University Press, 2000).
Key, Laura E. B., '"A Love-Hate Relationship": F. Scott Fitzgerald, Money Management and "The Diamond as Big as the Ritz"', 95 (6) *English Studies* (2014), pp. 654–73.
Khanna, Ranjana, *Dark Continents: Psychoanalysis and Colonialism* (Durham, NC: Duke University Press, 2003).
The Killer Dust (BBC, 1975).
King, Stephen, *Danse Macabre* [1981] (New York: Gallery Books, 2010).
King, Stewart, 'The Reader and World Crime Fiction: The (Private) Eye of the Beholder', in *Criminal Moves: Modes of Mobility in Crime Fiction*, eds Jesper Gulddal, Stewart King and Alistair Rolls (Liverpool: Liverpool University Press, 2019), 195–210.
Kinsella, John, *Sack* (London: Picador, 2014).

Kinsella, John, 'See that Gully: The Ghost I Have Become in a World of Asbestos', 74 *Meanjin Quarterly* (2015), pp. 44–50.

Kirouac-Massicotte, Isabelle, 'L'horreur comme littérature-monde, le cas de la littérature québécoise: *Mort-Terrain* de Biz et *Qu'il est bon de se noyer* de Cassie Bérard', 53 (3) *Journal of Canadian Studies* (2019) pp. 555–76.

Kleinman, Arthur, *The Illness Narratives: Suffering, Healing, and the Human Condition* (New York: Basic Books, 1988).

Knibbs, Henry Herbert, *Lost Farm Camp* (New York: Grosset & Dunlap, 1912).

Koch, Hans Gerd, and Wagenbach, Klaus, *Marbacher Magazin: Kafkas Fabriken*, No. 100 (2002).

Kotelchuck, David, 'Asbestos: The Funeral Dress of Kings', in *Dying for Work: Workers' Safety and Health in Twentieth-Century America*, eds David Rosner and Gerald Markowitz (Bloomington, IN: Indiana University Press, 1987), pp. 192–207.

Kreienbrock, Jörg, *Malicious Objects, Anger Management, and the Question of Modern Literature* (New York: Fordham University Press, 2012).

Kuhlenbeck, Britta, *Re-writing Spatiality: The Production of Space in the Pilbara Region in Western Australia* (Münster: Lit Verlag, 2010).

Kunzmann, Richard, *Salamander Cotton* [2006] (London: Pan Macmillan, 2007).

Labban, Mazen, 'Deterritorializing Extraction: Bioaccumulation and the Planetary Mine', 104 (3) *Annals of the Association of American Geographers* (2014), pp. 560–76.

Langevin, André, *Dust Over the City* [1955], trans. John Latrobe and Robert Gottlieb (Toronto: McClelland and Stewart Ltd, 1974).

Latour, Bruno, 'Love Your Monsters', 2 *Breakthrough Journal* (2011). Available at https://thebreakthrough.org/journal/issue-2/love-your-monsters

Latour, Bruno, *Politics of Nature: How to Bring the Sciences into Democracy* (Cambridge, MA: Harvard University Press, 2004).

Latour, Bruno, *We Have Never Been Modern*, trans. Catherine Porter (Cambridge, MA: Harvard University Press, 1993).

Laufer, Berthold, 'Asbestos and Salamander, an Essay in Chinese and Hellenistic Folk-Lore', 16 (3) *T'oung Pao* (1915), pp. 299–373.

Leacock, Stephen, *Nonsense Novels* (London: The Bodley Head, 1914).

Legends of Asbestos (Ambler, PA: Keasbey & Mattison, 1940).

Lerner, Barron, *When Illness Goes Public: Celebrity Patients and How We Look at Medicine* (Baltimore, ML: Johns Hopkins University Press, 2006).

Leshem, Noam, *Life After Ruin: The Struggles Over Israel's Depopulated Arab Spaces* (Cambridge: Cambridge University Press, 2016).

'Letter of Prester John', *Selections from the Hengwrt Mss. Preserved in the Peniarth Library*, ed. and trans. Robert Williams, London, Thomas Richards, 1892. Reproduced at *Celtic Literature Collective*, Accessed 24 September 2019: http://www.maryjones.us/ctexts/presterjohn.html

Levi, Primo, *The Periodic Table* [1975], trans. Raymond Rosenthal (New York: Schocken Books, 1984).
Levitas, Ruth, *Utopia as Method* (Basingstoke: Palgrave Macmillan, 2013).
Lipovetsky, Mark, 'Pavel Bazhov's Skazy: Discovering the Soviet Uncanny', in *Russian Children's Literature and Culture*, eds Marina Balina and Larissa Rudova (New York: Routledge, 2008), pp. 242–83.
Litvintseva, Sasha, 'Asbestos: Inside and Outside, Toxic and Haptic', 11 (1) *Environmental Humanities* (2019), pp. 152–73.
Lomas, Herbert, 'On the Motion and Immobility of Douve by Yves Bonnefoy', trans. Galway Kinnell, *132 Ambit* (1993), pp. 70–1.
Loots, François, *Die Jakkalsdans* (Cape Town: Umuzi, 2011).
Lorde, Audre, 'The Uses of Anger', 9 (3) *Women's Studies Quarterly* (1981), pp. 7–10.
Luckhurst, Roger, *The Mummy's Curse: The True History of a Dark Fantasy* (Oxford: Oxford University Press, 2012).
Lyotard, Jean-François, *The Differend: Phrases in Dispute*, trans. Georges Van Den Abeele (Minneapolis: University of Minnesota Press, 1988).
McAleer, Samantha, 'Is Using Asbestos a "Bad Lifestyle Choice!?"', *Thompsons Solicitors Scotland Blog*, Accessed 23 February 2021: https://www.thompsons-scotland.co.uk/blog/28-disease-compensation-claims/2847-is-using-asbestos-a-bad-lifestyle-choice
McCulloch, Jock, *Asbestos Blues: Labour, Capital, Physicians and the State in South Africa* (Bloomington: Indiana University Press, 2002).
McCulloch, Jock, 'Saving the Asbestos Industry, 1960 to 2006', 121 (5) *Public Health Reports* (2006), pp. 609–14.
McCulloch, Jock, 'Science Is Not Sufficient: Irving J. Selikoff and the Asbestos Tragedy', 17 (4) *New Solutions: A Journal of Environmental and Occupational Health Policy* (2008), pp. 293–310.
McCulloch, Jock and Geoffrey Tweedale, *Defending the Indefensible: The Global Asbestos Industry and its Fight for Survival* (Oxford: Oxford University Press, 2008).
McGoey, Linsey, *The Unknowers: How Strategic Ignorance Rules the World* (London: Zed Books, 2019).
McLuhan, Marshall, *Understanding Media: The Extensions of Man* (Cambridge: MIT Press, 1994).
Maher, Ashley, *Reconstructing Modernism: British Literature, Modern Architecture, and the State* (Oxford: Oxford University Press, 2020).
Maines, Rachel, *Asbestos and Fire: Technological Tradeoffs and the Body at Risk* (New Brunswick, NJ: Rutgers University Press, 2013).
Malan, Rian, *My Traitor's Heart* (New York: Grove Press, 1990).
Manning, Rosemary, *The Chinese Garden* [1962] (New York: The Feminist Press, 2000).

Mao, Douglas, *Solid Objects: Modernism and the Test of Production* (Princeton, NJ: Princeton University Press, 1998).
Marsh, John, '"Dead Before They Cease to Be": On Edwin Rolfe's "Asbestos"' *Modern American Poetry Site*, 2001. Accessed 23 February 2021: http://www.modernamericanpoetry.org/criticism/john-marsh-asbestos
Martin, W. R. and Warren U. Ober, 'Alice Munro as Small-town Historian: "Spaceships Have Landed"', 66 *Essays on Canadian Writing* (Winter 1998), pp. 128–46.
Mason, Dancy, '"Another Armored Animal": Modernist Prosthesis and Marianne Moore's Posthumanist Animiles', 1 (3) *Feminist Modernist Studies* (2018), pp. 318–35.
Masson, Thomas L., 'A Pilgrim's Progress in France', *New York Times Book Review*, 28 May 1922, pp. 10, 23.
Mazzeo, Agata, *Dust Inside: Fighting and Living with Asbestos-Related Disasters in Brazil* (New York: Berghahn, 2020).
Mazzeo, Agata, 'The Temporalities of Asbestos Mining and Community Activism', 5 (2) *The Extractive Industries and Society* (2018), pp. 223–9.
Merewether, E. R. A. and C. W. Price, *Report on Effects of Asbestos Dust on the Lungs and Dust Suppression in the Asbestos Industry* (London: HMSO, 1930).
Mesothelioma + Asbestos Awareness Centre, https://www.maacenter.org/asbestos/products/
Midnight Oil, *Blue Sky Mine*, Accessed 23 February 2021: https://www.youtube.com/watch?v=Ofrqm6-LCqs
Mika, Kasia, *Disasters, Vulnerability, and Narratives: Writing Haiti's Futures* (London: Routledge, 2019).
Miller, Elizabeth Carolyn, *Extraction Ecologies and the Literature of the Long Exhaustion* (Princeton: Princeton University Press, 2021).
Miller, Mitch and Johnny Rodger, *The Red Cockatoo: James Kelman and the Art of Commitment* (Inverness: Sandstone Press, 2011).
Moorcock, Michael, *Jerry Cornelius: His Lives and His Times* [1976] (London: Orion, 2018).
Moore, Marianne, 'Humility Concentration, and Gusto', in *The Norton Anthology of Modern and Contemporary Poetry, Volume 1*, eds Jahan Ramazani, Richard Ellmann, Robert O'Clair (New York: Norton, 2003), pp. 994–1000.
Moore, Marianne, 'Marianne Moore: Poet', in Mary Austen, *Everyman's Genius* (Indianapolis, The Bobbs-Merrill Company, 1925).
Moore, Marianne, *New Collected Poems*, ed. Heather Cass White (New York: Farrar, Straus & Giroux, 2017).
Mordak, J. and J. Wheeler, 'Deterioration of Asbestos Cement Water Mains', *Final Report to the Department of the Environment* (Wiltshire: Water Research Center, 1988).

Moretti, Franco, 'The Slaughterhouse of Literature', 61 (1) *MLQ* (2000), pp. 207–27.
Mosterín, Jésus, 'Una cita con la parca', *El País*, 23 March 2015.
Muños, José Esteban, *Cruising Utopia: The Then and There of Queer Futurity* (New York: New York University Press, 2009).
Munro, Alice, *Open Secrets* [1994] (London: Vintage, 1995).
Munro, Kirstin, '"Social Reproduction Theory," Social Reproduction, and Household Production', 83 (4) *Science & Society* (2019), pp. 451–68.
Munro, Alice, 'Spaceships have landed', 131 *The Paris Review* (1994). Accessed 14 September 2021. https://www.theparisreview.org/fiction/1797/spaceships-have-landed-alice-munro.
Murphy, Lois, 'On Writing "Soon"', *Kill Your Darlings*, 9 November 2017. Accessed 7 September 2021. https://www.killyourdarlings.com.au/2017/11/november-first-book-club-lois-murphy-on-writing-soon/
Murphy, Lois, *Soon* (Yarravile: Transit Lounge, 2017).
Murray, Robert, 'Asbestos: A Chronology of Its Origins and Health Effects', 47 (6) *British Journal of Industrial Medicine* (1990), pp. 361–5.
Murray, Nicholas, *Kafka* (London: Little, Brown, 2004).
Musila, Grace, 'Embodying Experience and Agency in Yvonne Vera's *Without a Name* and *Butterfly Burning*', 38 (2) *Research in African Literatures* (2007), pp. 49–63.
Myburgh, Pieter-Louis, *Gangster State: Unravelling Ace Magashule's Web of Capture* (Cape Town: Penguin Books, 2019).
Naughton, John T., *The Poetics of Yves Bonnefoy* (Chicago, The University of Chicago Press, 1984).
Nelson, Cary, 'Lyric Politics: The Poetry of Edwin Rolfe', 38 (3) *Modern Fiction Studies* (1992), pp. 733–69.
Nelson, Jason, 'Witternoon: Speculative Shell and the Cancerous Breeze', 2 *Springgun* (2010). Accessed 23 February 2021: http://www.springgunpress.com/wittenoom/
Newhouse, Muriel L. and Hilda Thompson, 'Mesothelioma of Pleura and Peritoneum Following Exposure to Asbestos in the London area', 22 (4) *British Journal of Industrial Medicine* (1965), pp. 261–9.
Ngai, Sianne, *Theory of the Gimmick* (Cambridge, MA: Harvard University Press, 2020).
Nilsson, Louise, David Damrosch and Theo D'haen, eds, *Crime Fiction as World Literature* (London: Bloomsbury, 2017).
Nixon, Rob, *Slow Violence and the Environmentalism of the Poor* (Cambridge: Harvard University Press, 2011).
North, Michael, *Reading 1922: A Return to the Scene of the Modern* (Oxford: Oxford University Press, 1999).
Nussbaum, Martha, *Anger and Forgiveness: Resentment, Generosity, Justice* (Oxford: Oxford University Press, 2016).

Nutter, Alice, *Snow in July*, BBC Radio 4, 8 January 2008.
Nye, Mavis, 'Peter Rabbit shows Mr McGregor Scrapping #Asbestos from Walls While Eating? Really?', *A Diary Of A Mesowarrior Living With #Mesothelioma blog*, Accessed 23 February 2021: https://rayandmave.wordpress.com/2018/03/19/a-diary-of-a-mesowarrior-living-with-mesothelioma-peter-rabbit-shows-mr-mcgregor-scrapping-asbestos-from-walls-while-eating-really/
Obioma, Chigozie, *An Orchestra of Minorities* (London: Little, Brown, 2019).
Obioma, Chigozie, *The Fishermen* (London: Pushkin Press, 2015).
O'Brien, Phil, *The Working Class and Twenty-First-Century British Fiction: Deindustrialisation, Demonisation, Resistance* (London: Routledge, 2019).
Osborne, Peter, 'Out of Sync: Tomba's Marx and the Problem of a Multi-layered Temporal Dialectic', 23 (4) *Historical Materialism* (2015), pp. 39–48.
Osman, Michael, *Modernism's Visible Hand: Architecture and Regulation in America* (Minneapolis, MN: University of Minnesota Press, 2018).
Outka, Elizabeth, *Viral Modernism: The Influenza Pandemic and Interwar Literature* (New York: Columbia University Press, 2019).
Oz, Amos, *To Know a Woman* [1989], trans. Nicholas de Lange (London: Vintage, 2011).
The Paleface, dir. Buster Keaton (Associated First National Pictures, 1922).
Paterson, Stewart, 'Asbestos Victims Treatment is a Scandal says James Kelman', *Glasgow Evening Times*, 19 September 2015.
Paz, Octavio, *The Collected Poems of Octavio Paz: 1957–1987*, ed. and trans. Eliot Weinberger (and others) (New York: New Directions, 1987).
Peacock, Andrea, *Libby, Montana: Asbestos and the Deadly Silence of an American Corporation* (Boulder, CO: Johnson Books, 2003).
Peacock, Matt, *Killer Dust: James Hardie Exposed* [2009] (Sydney: HarperCollins, 2011).
Pels, Peter, 'The Spirit of Matter: On Fetish, Rarity, Fact, and Fancy', in *Border Fetishisms*, ed. Patricia Spyer (New York: Routledge, 1998), pp. 91–121.
Penny, Louise, *The Long Way Home* [2014] (London: Little, Brown, 2016).
Peter Rabbit, dir. Will Gluck (Columbia Pictures, 2018).
Pett, Sarah, 'Rash Reading: Rethinking Virginia Woolf's On Being Ill', 37 (1) *Literature and Medicine* (2019), pp. 26–66.
Pfaelzer, Jean, *The Utopian Novel in America, 1886–1896: The Politics of Form* (Pittsburgh: University of Pittsburgh Press, 1985).
Pickett, Charles, *The Fibro Frontier: A Different History of Australian Architecture* [1997] (London: Lund Humphries, 1999).
Pietz, William, 'The Problem of the Fetish, I', 9 *RES: Anthropology and Aesthetics* (1985), pp. 5–17.

Pillayre, Héloïse, 'Compensation Funds, Trials and the Meaning of Claims: The Example of Asbestos-Related Illness Compensation in France', 30 (2) *Social & Legal Studies* (2021), pp. 180–202.
Pliny, *Natural History*, trans. H. Rackham, W. H. S. Jones and D. E. Eichholz. Wikisource. Accessed 24 September 2019: https://en.wikisource.org/wiki/Natural_History_(Rackham,_Jones,_%26_Eichholz)
Poet, Frances, *Fibres* (London: Nick Hern Books, 2019).
Polo, Marco, *The Travels of Marco Polo*, trans. Henry Yule, ed. Henri Cordier (London, John Murray, 1920).
Postone, Moishe, *Time, Labor, and Social Domination* (Cambridge: Cambridge University Press, 1994).
Price, Leah, *How to Do Things with Books in Victorian Britain* (Princeton, NJ: Princeton University Press, 2012).
Prose, Francine, 'Woodstock: A Town Afraid to Drink Water', *New York Times*, April 13, 1986.
Prunetti, Alberto, *Amianto: Una storia operaia* [2012] (Rome: Edizioni Alegre, 2014).
Prunetti, Alberto, 'Asbestos: The Story of a Tuscan Welder', trans. Oonagh Stransky, 41 (2) *New England Review* (2020), pp 29–38.
Quinn, Anthony, 'Category A Literature in Glasgow: How does a Literary Outsider Become the Booker Favourite? Anthony Quinn meets James Kelman," *Independent*, 7 October 1994.
Raban, Jonathan, *Waxwings* (London: Picador, 2003).
Raisin, Ross, *Waterline* (London: Penguin Books, 2011).
Reichman, Ravit, *The Affective Life of Law: Legal Modernism and the Literary Imagination* (Stanford: Stanford University Press, 2009).
Rich, Adrienne, 'When We Dead Awaken: Writing as Re-Vision', 34 (1) *College English* (1972), pp. 18–30.
Rich, Charlotte J., 'Introduction', *What Diantha Did* (Durham, NC: Duke University Press, 2005).
Richard, Jean-Jules, *Le Feu dans l'amiante* (Montréal: Réédition Québec, 1971).
Ricoeur, Paul, *The Rule of Metaphor*, trans. Robert Czerny, with Kathleen McLaughlin and John Costello [1977] (London: Routledge, 1997).
Ricoeur, Paul, *Time and Narrative*, 3 Volumes, trans. Kathleen McLaughlin and David Pellauer (Chicago: Chicago University Press, 1984–1986).
Robert, Julie, *Curative Illnesses: Medico-National Allegory in Québécois Fiction* (Montreal: McGill-Queen's University Press, 2016).
Robinson, Cedric, *Black Marxism: The Making of the Black Radical Tradition* (Chapel Hill: University of North Carolina Press, 1983).
Rodker, John, *Poems and Adolphe 1920*, ed. Andrew Crozier (Manchester: Carcanet, 1996).

Roesler, Layla, 'Allegory and Event: Two Ways of Saying the Salamander in Yves Bonnefoy', *Trans—*, 10 (2010). Accessed 24 September 2019: http://journals.openedition.org/trans/378

Rohl, Arthur N., 'Asbestos in talc', 9 *Environmental Health Perspectives* (1974), pp. 129–32.

Rolfe, Edwin, *Collected Poems*, eds Cary Nelson and Jefferson Hendricks (Chicago: University of Illinois Press, 1997).

Rooney, Brigid, *Suburban Space, the Novel and Australian Modernity* (London: Anthem Press, 2018).

Rooney, Caroline, *African Literature, Animism and Politics* (Abingdon: Routledge, 2000).

Rose, Arthur, 'Asbestos Populism in David Foster Wallace's Infinite Jest', 21 (3) *Safundi* (2020), pp. 339–54.

Rosner, David, Gerald Markowitz and Merlin Chowkwanyun, '"Nondetected": the Politics of Measurement of Asbestos in Talc, 1971–1976', 109 (7) *American Journal of Public Health* (2019), pp. 969–74.

Rubenstein, Michael, *Public Works: Infrastructure, Irish Modernism, and the Postcolonial* (Notre Dame, IN: University of Notre Dame Press, 2010).

Rukeyser, Walter Arnold, *Working for the Soviets: An American Engineer in Russia* (New York: Covici Friede Publishers, 1932).

Saadi, Suhayl, *Joseph's Box* (Ullapool: Two Ravens Press, 2009).

Sachs, Edwin O., *Fires and Public Entertainments: A Study of Some 1100 Notable Fires at Theatres, Music Halls, Circus Buildings and Temporary Structures During the Last 100 Years* (London: Charles and Edwin Layton, 1897).

Saint-Amour, Paul K., *Tense Future: Total War, Encyclopedic Form* (Oxford: Oxford University Press, 2015).

Salecl, Renata, *A Passion for Ignorance: What We Choose Not to Know and Why* (Princeton: Princeton University Press, 2020).

Samuels, Ellen, 'Six Ways of Looking at Crip Time', 37 (3) *Disability Studies Quarterly* (2017).

Scarpa, L. 'Industria dell'amianto e tubercolosi', In *XVIIe Congresso della Società italiana di Medicina interna*, ed. L. Lucatello (1908), pp. 358–9.

Schneider, Andrew and David McCumber, *An Air that Kills: How the Asbestos Poisoning of Libby, Montana, Uncovered a National Scandal* (New York: G. P. Putnam's Sons, 2004).

Schwarze, Steve, 'Juxtaposition in Environmental Health Rhetoric: Exposing Asbestos Contamination in Libby, Montana', 6 (2) *Rhetoric & Public Affairs* (2003), pp. 313–36.

Selecting Your Roof (Boston: Eternit, 1928).

Selikoff, Irving J. and Greenberg, Morris, 'A Landmark Case in Asbestosis', 265 (7) *JAMA* (1991), pp. 898–901.

Sennan Asbestos Disaster, dir. Kazuo Hara (Shisso Productions, 2016).
Session 9, dir. Brad Anderson (USA Films, 2001).
Seward, Anna, *The Poetical Works*, ed. Walter Scott (Edinburgh: James Ballantyne, 1810).
Sharpe, Christina, *In the Wake: On Blackness and Being* (Durham, NC: Duke University Press, 2016).
Sheller, Mimi, *Aluminum Dreams: The Making of Light Modernity* (Cambridge, MA: MIT Press, 2014).
Shriver, Lionel, *So Much For That* (London: HarperCollins, 2010).
Sielke, Sabine, *Fashioning the Female Subject: The Intertextual Networking of Dickinson, Moore, and Rich* (Ann Arbor, University of Michigan Press, 1997).
Silva, Roland, 'Traditional Design and Modern Architecture', in *Senarat Paranavitana Commemoration Volume*, eds Johanna Engelberta Lohuizen-De Leeuw, Karthigesu Indrapala, Leelananda Prematilleka and Senarat Paranavitana (Leiden: Brill, 1978), pp. 2514.
Sloterdijk, Peter, *Rage and Time* [2006], trans. Mario Wenning (New York: Columbia University Press, 2010).
Solbes, Eduardo and Richard W. Harper, 'Biological Responses to Asbestos Inhalation and Pathogenesis of Asbestos-related Benign and Malignant Disease," 66 *Journal of Investigative Medicine* (2018), pp. 721–7.
Sorenson, Leif, *Ethnic Modernism and the Making of US Literary Multiculturalism* (New York: Palgrave Macmillan, 2016).
Southey, Robert, *The Poetical Works of Robert Southey* (London: Longmans, Green, and Co., 1866).
Spahr, Clemens, *A Poetics of Global Solidarity: Modern American Poetry and Social Movements* (Basingstoke: Palgrave Macmillan, 2015).
A Spark may Cost a Farm (Ambler, PA: Keasbey & Mattison, 1917).
Stach, Reiner, *Kafka: The Decisive Years* [2002], trans. Shelley Frisch (Princeton, NJ: Princeton University Press, 2013).
Star, Susan Leigh, 'The Ethnography of Infrastructure', 43 (3) *American Behavioral Scientist* (1999), pp. 377–91.
Stearns, J. N., ed., *The Temperance Speaker* (New York: National Temperance Society, 1870).
Stephenson, Neal, *Snow Crash* [1992] (London: Penguin Books, 1994).
Summers, A. Leonard, *Asbestos and the Asbestos Industry: the World's Most Wonderful Mineral and Other Fireproof Materials* (London: Pitman, 1919).
Suvin, Darko, *Metamorphoses of Science Fiction: On the Poetics and History of a Literary Genre* (New Haven: Yale University Press, 1979).
Szántó, Péter-Dániel, 'Asbestos and Salamander in India', 63 *Indo-Iranian Journal* (2020), pp. 335–70.

Taylor, Analisa, *Indigeneity in the Mexican Cultural Imagination: Thresholds of Belonging* (Tucson: University of Arizona Press, 2009).

Theophrastus, *On Stones*, intro., trans. and commentary by Earle R. Caley and John F. C. Richards (Columbus, University of Ohio Press, 1957).

Todorov, Tzvetan, *The Poetics of Prose*, trans. Richard Howard (Ithaca: Cornell University Press, 1977).

Trimbur, John, *Grassroots Literacy and the Written Record: A Textual History of Asbestos Activism in South Africa* (Bristol: Multilingual Matters, 2020).

Trotter, David, *Literature in the First Media Age: Britain between the Wars* (Cambridge, MA: Harvard University Press, 2013).

Trudeau, Pierre, ed., *The Asbestos Strike* [1956], trans. James Boake (Toronto: James Lewis & Samuel, 1974).

Tweedale, Geoffrey, 'Alice: A Fight for Life – The Legacy', 67 *British Asbestos Newsletter* (2007). Accessed 23 February 2021: https://www.britishasbestosnewsletter.org/ban67.htm

Tweedale, Geoffrey, 'Hero or Villain? Sir Richard Doll and Occupational Cancer', 13 (2) *International Journal of Occupational Environmental Health* (2007), pp. 233–5.

Tweedale, Geoffrey, *Magic Mineral to Killer Dust: Turner & Newall and the Asbestos Hazard* (Oxford: Oxford University Press, 2001).

Updike, John, 'Phenomena', *The New Yorker*, 24 February 1973, p. 38.

Van Horssen, Jessica, *A Town Called Asbestos: Environmental Contamination, Health, and Resilience in a Resource Community* (Vancouver, BC: University of British Columbia Press, 2015).

Vaughn, Megan, 'Colonial Melancholia', 37 (1) *Raritan* (2017), pp. 118–28.

Veblen, Thorstein, *The Theory of the Leisure Class* [1899], intro. C. Wright Mills (Abingdon: Routledge, 2017).

Vera, Yvonne, *Butterfly Burning* [1998] (New York: Farrar, Straus and Giroux, 2000).

Vera, Yvonne, 'Crossing Boundaries', *Why Don't You Carve Other Animals?* (Toronto: Tsar, 1992).

Viney, Will, *Waste: A Philosophy of Things* (London: Bloomsbury, 2014).

Waddell, Nathan, *Modernist Nowheres: Politics and Utopia in Early Modernist Writing, 1900–1920* (Basingstoke, Palgrave Macmillan, 2012).

Wagner, J. C., C. A. Sleggs and P. Marchand, 'Diffuse Pleural Mesothelioma and Asbestos Exposure in the North Western Cape Province', 17 (4) *British Journal of Industrial Medicine* (1960): 260–71.

Wald, Alan M., *Exiles from a Future Time: The Forging of the Mid-Twentieth-Century Literary Left* (Chapel Hill, NC: University of North Carolina Press, 2002).

Waldman, Linda, *The Politics of Asbestos: Understandings of Risk, Disease and Protest* (Abingdon: Earthscan, 2011).

Wallace, David Foster, *Infinite Jest* (London: Abacus, 1996).
Warnock, Martha L. and Churg, Andrew M. 'Asbestos Bodies', 77 *Chest*, (1980), pp. 129–30.
Waugh, Evelyn, 'Love Among the Ruins: A Romance of the Near Future', *Commonweal*, 31 July 1953, *Commonweal Website*, accessed 23 February 2021: https://www.commonwealmagazine.org/love-among-ruins-0
White, Patrick, *Flaws in the Glass: A Self-Portrait* [1981] (London: Vintage, 2013).
White, Patrick, *The Tree of Man* [1955] (London: Penguin, 2010).
Williams, Jim, *Rock Reject* (Halifax: Roseway, 2012).
Williams, Raymond, *Culture and Materialism* [1980] (London: Verso, 2020).
Willis, John, '*Alice – A Fight for Life*: 25 Years On', 67 *British Asbestos Newsletter* (2007). Accessed 23 February 2021: https://www.britishasbestosnewsletter.org/ban67.htm
Wills, David, *Inanimation* (Minneapolis, University of Minnesota Press, 2016).
Winton, Tim, *Dirt Music* (London: Picador, 2003).
Wisher, Yolanda, 'My Grandmama's House Is Now The EPA', *Jacket2: Solidarity Texts*, ed. Laynie Browne, 13 April 2018. Accessed 23 February 2021: https://jacket2.org/poems/grandmamas-house
Wisher, Yolanda, 'Performance with the Afroeaters', Kelly Writers House, 5 September 2017, *Pennsound*, Accessed 23 February 2021: https://writing.upenn.edu/pennsound/x/Wisher.php
Woolf, Virginia, 'On Being Ill', 4 (1) *The New Criterion* (1926), pp. 32–45.
Woolf, Virgina, *The Years*, intro. by Susan Hill and Steven Connor (London: Vintage, 2004).
WReC, *Combined and Uneven Development: Towards a New Theory of World-Literature* (Liverpool: Liverpool University Press, 2015).
Wroe, Nicholas, 'Glasgow Kith', *The Guardian*, 2 June 2001.
Yoon, Y. R., K. M. Kwak, Y. Choi, K. Youn, J. Bahk, D. M. Kang and D. Paek, 'The Asbestos Ban in Korea from a Grassroots Perspective: Why Did It Occur?', 15 (2) *International Journal of Environmental Research and Public Health* (2018), pp. 198–209.
Zhang, Dora, *Strange Likeness: Description and the Modernist Novel* (Chicago: University of Chicago Press, 2020).
Zunshine, Lisa, *Why We Read Fiction: Theory of Mind and the Novel* (Columbus, OH: Ohio State University Press, 2006).

INDEX

1959, 52

accident, 49, 88, 121, 121, 133, 134–6, 144–5
Ackerley, Chris, 202
Acre Mill (England), 112
Aeschylus, *Oresteia*, 196
Agamben, Giorgio, 188
agential cuts, 14–15
Ahmed, Sara, xiii
Alaimo, Stacy, 14
Alder, Emily, 65, 66
Alexandre (of Paris), 97
Alice – a Fight for Life, 112–13, 116, 176
Ambler (USA), 190, 197, 198, 199, 227, 228
Anand, Nikhil, 51
Andersson, Jens A., 210
anger, 153, 176–7, 178–9
Anglicus, Bartholomaeus, 97
animacy, 83, 87–91, 97, 98, 99, 104, 152, 155, 223
   hierarchy, 89–90
Apartheid, xv, 53, 71, 72, 217, 225
Appadurai, Arjun, 83, 84–5
Appel, Hannah, 51

Arboleda, Martín, 5, 6
Arendt, Hannah, 132
Aristotle, 17
Arney, Angela, *Old Sins, Long Memories*, 209
artistic autonomy, 23–4
Asbest (Russia), 160–3
asbestos
   amosite, xiii, 53, 54, 87
   anthophyllite, 204
   ban, 223
   chrysotile, xiii, 53, 54, 87, 190
   chrysotile defence, xiii, 53, 63
   crocidolite, xiii, 53, 54, 87
   curtain, 8–13
   and development, 3, 5–6, 8, 63, 163, 205–7, 214–15, 216, 219, 226, 228
   diseases, xii–xiii, 107–8, 109–111
   dust studies, 127–8
   gas fires, 203–4, 219
   gloves, 27
   gimmicks, 21, 23
   historiography, 37–9
   housing, 205, 214–7, 219
   life, 83, 87, 202–3
   metamorphoses, 85, 93

INDEX

'nondetected', xiii, 204, 205, 218
as obstruction, 12, 152–3, 162, 167, 169, 171, 173, 227
personification of, 213
pipes, 205, 217–19
production, 52–3
promise, 48, 51, 203, 210, 217
radiators, 202–3
roofs, 205, 206–14, 219, 225–6
and snow, 190–1
story, 6, 161, 172, 176, 177, 179, 189, 205, 228
and talc, 204–5
time, 11–12, 17–19, 51, 223–4
tremolite, 204
types, 53, 54, 87, 204
woven, 44
Asbestos (Canada), 14, 74–5, 159, 168, 171
Asbestos . . . A Matter of Time, 41, 54–7
Asbestos Awareness & Support Cymru, 87
Asbestos Cement Building Products Ltd, 179
Asbestos Interest Group, 226–7
Asbestos Mountains, 85
Asbestos Relief Trust, 226–7
Asbestos Strike, 72, 168–9
asbestosis, xii, 1, 15–16, 52, 109, 111, 176, 180–1, 197
Augustine, 17–18, 53, 96
Auribault, Étienne, 177
Austen, Mary, 92

Bainbridge, James, 203
Balangero Mine (Italy), 14, 163–7
Balasi, Dudi, 226
Banton, Bernie, 176, 177, 179, 189
Bacigalupi, Paolo, *Ship Breaker*, 222
Barad, Karen, 14
Barnes, Djuna, 10
Barnes, Jeb, 227–8
Barnes, Joanne, 'Pleased to Meet You', 87
Bartrip, Peter, 37
Bass, Rick, 'With Every Great Breath', 13–14
Bazhov, Pavel, 'Šëlkovaja gorka', 85, 161–3
Bazin, Victoria, 92

Beare, Geoffrey, 179, 185
Beckett, Samuel, *Murphy*, 202
Bellamy, Edward, *Looking Backward*, 43, 45
Belvidere Mountain (USA), 157
Bennett, Alan, *The Insurance Man*, 28, 128–30, 133–7, 145
Bérard, Cassie, *Qu'il est bon de se noyer*, 74–5, 77–8, 223
Berlant, Lauren, 16, 18, 193
Bhopal (India), 192
Blackmore, R. D., 44
Blackwood, Algernon, 64–7
Blanchard, Stephen, *Gagarin and I*, 190
Blanchot, Maurice, 77
Bloch, Ernst, 41–2, 50, 205, 215, 219
Bluemel, Kristin, 28
Boltanski, Luc, 65, 66
Bond, Barbara, *Everyday Enemies*, 218–19
Bonnefoy, Yves, 'Lieu de la salamandre', 28, 87, 93, 98–100, 103
  'La Poésie français', 98–9
Bowen, Elizabeth, *Eva Trout*, 12
Bowles, Oliver, xv, 163
Boyd, Damien, *Death Sentence*, 69, 71–3
Bradbury, Ray, *Farenheit 451*, 21
Brod, Max, 127
Brody, Richard, 61
Brooks, Maria Gowen, 44
Brown, Lewis, 181
Brown, Nicholas, 23–4
Browne, Clare, 94
Browne, Thomas, 87, 94–5, 97–8
Browning, Elizabeth Barrett, 44
built environment, 28
Burchell, William, 85
Burleigh, W. H., 44
Büttner, Jan Ulrich, 97

Calvino, Italo, 'La Fabbrica nella Montagna', 157, 165–7
Cape Asbestos (Cape Plc), xiv, 38, 112, 176, 226, 228
Carel, Havi, 109–10
Carson, Rachel, *Silent Spring*, 191
Casale Monferrato, 14, 227
Cassiar (Canada), 161, 167, 169, 227

Castagna, Felicity, *No More Boats*, 217
Castleman, Barry, 37–8
causality, 25, 26, 49, 107, 114–18, 130
causation, 115, 116, 128, 152, 227
Cesaretti, Enrico, 14, 90, 193
Chamoiseau, Patrick, *Texaco*, 214–15, 216, 217
Chakravarti, Sudeep, *Red Sun*, 212
Chen, Mel Y., 88–90, 100, 103
Chernobyl (Ukraine), 191
Citizen Kane, 190
clue, 59–62
Clydeside Action on Asbestos, 138, 139
Clydeside (Scotland), 138, 139, 190, 191
Cohen, Ralph, 38
commensurability, 3, 142, 145
community, 6, 61, 83, 129, 131–2, 135, 155, 164–7, 171, 224, 227–8
Comnenus (Komnenos), Manuel, 97
compensation, 28, 76–7, 84, 113, 128, 134, 136, 143–4, 197, 204
compensatory narrative, 83, 136, 223
Concerned People Against Asbestos, 226
Cooke, William, 2, 111
Cover, Robert M., 128
Culler, Jonathan, 98
cummings, e. e., 11

D'Agostino, Bill, 'The Hill', 191
The Daily Mail, 225–6
Damrosch, David, 63
Deane, Lucy, 177
Deleuze, Gilles, 138
detection methods, 205, 217–18
detective fiction, 28
Devi, Mahasweta, 206
Devil's Dust, 174n
D'haen, Theo, 63
diagnosis, 2, 15, 83, 85, 111, 114, 119, 122, 139, 141–2, 223
differend, 2, 145
Doctorow, Cory, 50
Doll, Richard, 26, 168
Donovan, Anne, 'All that Glisters', 114, 191
Doolittle, Hilda (H.D.), 8–9
Douglas, Mary, 222
Drabble, Margaret, 114–118, 123, 124
dumps, 28, 152, 153

Durrell, Lawrence, 10–11
The Dust at Acre Mill, 112
dystopia, 6, 27, 50

Ehrenreich, Barbara, 114
Empson, William, 153, 156–7, 162, 191
encoding/decoding, 55
entanglement, 14
Eternit 14, 208, 227
Everett, Sue, *Not Welcome*, 209
Ewald, François, 48
experimental, 6–7

factories, 28, 152, 153, 179–89, 197–9
fascism, 164
Fein, John, 101
Ferns, Chris, 43–4
fetish, 84–6, 152
fibre, xii, xiii, 1, 13, 14, 19, 41, 44, 46, 53, 54, 56, 60, 72, 74, 85, 109, 116, 117, 151–2, 156, 158, 181, 183, 190, 193, 195, 197, 205, 207, 218, 226
'fibro', 215–17
fire, 4, 5, 9, 10, 19, 20, 22, 25, 37, 38, 41, 42, 44, 48, 54, 60, 64, 65, 66, 67, 91, 93, 94, 96, 100, 101, 127, 202, 203, 204, 207, 208, 210, 211, 213
Fisher, J. Alfred, 94
Fitzgerald, F. Scott, 'A 64, 67–9
Flook, Maria, 'Asbestos', 222
follow the thing, 84, 151–3
Forrester, John, 110
Frank, Arthur W., 110
Franzen, Jonathan, 120
Frayn, Michael, *My Father's Fortune*, 48, 212–14, 217
Freedgood, Elaine, 76
From Rock to Roof, 208
futurity, 47, 49, 50

Garuba, Harry, 91, 100
genre, 6–7, 37–9, 63–4, 83, 223
  mediatory function of, 27
Gervasius (of Tilbury), 97
ghost story, 74–8
Gilman, Charlotte Perkins, 45
Ginzburg, Carlo, 59
Giraud, Eva Haifa, 14

Glasgow (Scotland), 139, 141, 190, 191
Godden, Richard, 68
Goldberg, Rube, 180, 185
Gopnik, Adam, 185
Gould, Stephen J., 119–121, 123, 124
Green, Louise, 90–1
Gregson, Nicky, 156, 222–3
Guattari, Felix, 138
Gulddal, Jesper, 62
Gupta, Akhil, 51

Haigh, Gideon, 176
Hall, Stuart, 55
Hames, Scott, 142–3
Hamilton, Patrick, *Hangover Square*, 203
Hashmi, Nasser, *A Fistful of Dust*, 179, 196–8
Hatschek, Ludwig, 207
Hawkins, Anne Hunsaker, 110
Hegel, 100, 178
Holm, Isak Winkel, 129, 131–2, 145
The Holocaust, 134
homes, 202–5
horror, 6, 28, 66, 72, 76, 141, 222
Hubble, Nick, 28
Huchu, Tendai, *The Hairdresser of Harare*, 211
humility, 91–2, 93, 157, 164–5, 173, 223, 227
Hurst, Rebecca, 161–2
Hutchison, Hazel

ignorance, 4, 19–23, 187
'Improved Roofing, Asbestos Roof Coating & Cement', 207
infrastructure, 4, 5, 8, 12, 13, 27, 28, 42, 43, 46, 47, 48, 50, 51, 54, 55, 56, 57, 59, 62, 73, 77, 93, 152, 177, 204, 205, 206, 207, 218, 219
injustice, 136, 139, 145, 172, 175, 178, 179, 194, 196, 224, 228
Iovino, Serenella, 14, 90
Iroquois Theatre, 9
Irurzun, Patxi, *Ciudad Retrete*, 179, 192–4, 196
Isidore (of Seville), 97
It Pays to Advertise (Cooper Megrue and Hackett), 204

Jacques (de Vitrys), 97
Jaffe, Aaron, 19, 180
James Hardie, 176, 190, 228
Jameson, Frederic, 27, 41–2, 50–2
Jansen, Monica, 193, 194
Jarrell, Randall, 92
Jasper, James, 113
Jefferson, Alice, 112, 116, 176, 189
Jeffrey Mine (Canada), 14, 50, 74, 222
Jhabvala, Ruth Prawer, *A Backward Place*, 210
Johns, Henry Ward, 207
Johns Manville, 15, 41, 180–1, 207, 228
Johnson & Johnson, 204–5
Johnston, Michelle, 114, 167, 170, 173
Jonas, Hans, 50
Jones, Robert H., xv, 44, 163
'The Jungle', 225–6
Jurecic, Ann, 110, 119, 120
justice, 2, 28, 84, 86, 128, 131, 135, 136, 138, 139, 144, 169, 179, 195
Justice, Daniel Heath, 20

Kafer, Alison, 118
Kafka, Franz, 1–4, 85, 127–32, 133, 134, 137, 140–1, 144, 223
Kane, Pat, 139
Keasbey & Mattison, 53, 60, 190, 197, 198, 207, 208
Keaton, Buster, *The Paleface*, 8, 19–24
Keats, John, 'When I Have Fears', 187–9
Kelly, Aaron, 142
Kelman, James, 28, 128–30, 136, 137–45, 179
Kenner, Hugh, 142
Kershaw, Nellie, 1–3, 110, 130, 145, 181
Key, Laura, 68
Khanna, Ranjana, 66
The Killer Dust, 112
King, Stephen, 76
King, Stewart, 62
Kinsella, John, 'Blue Asbestos at my Bedhead', 174n
'See that Gully', 222
Kleinman, Arthur, 110
Knibbs, Henry Herbert, *Lost Farm Camp*, 85, 157–8
Ko Hung (Ge Hong), 96

Koegas (South Africa), xiv
Kunzmann, Richard, *Salamander Cotton*, 69, 70, 71–3
Kuruman, 226, 227

Langevin, André, *Poussière sur la ville*, 157, 167, 168–9
Lanza, Anthony, 167, 180
latency, 7, 13, 19, 59, 109, 172, 223
Latour, Bruno, 24–6
laundry, 195–6
Leacock, Stephen, 46
legal modernism, 128
Leshem, Noam, 226
Levertov, Denise, 102
Levi, Primo, *Il sistema periodico*, 151–2, 155, 163–5, 166–7
Levitas, Ruth, 50–1
Libby, Montana, 13–14
Lipovetsky, Mark, 161
Litvintseva, Sasha, 14, 90
Loots, François, 114
Lorde, Audre, 196, 199
Love Canal (USA), 191
Luckhurst, Roger, 66
Lucretius, 151
lung cancer, 52, 109, 111, 115
Lyotard, Jean-François, 2

McCluskey, Michael, 28
McCulloch, Jock, 37–8, 52–3, 63
McGann, A. L., *Subtopia*, 217
McLuhan, Marshall, 119, 120–1
McQueen, Steve, 194
Magashule, Elias Sekgobelo 'Ace', 225
Magnus, Albertus, 96
Maher, Ashley, 47–8
Maines, Rachel, 37–8, 93–4
Malan, Rian, *My Traitor's Heart*, 217
Mallarmé, Stéphane, *Un coup de dés*, 77
Manning, Rosemary, *The Chinese Garden*, 208–9
Mao, Douglas, 153
Marbode (of Rennes), 96
Marsh, John, 186, 187
Martin, W. R., 159
Marx, Karl, 177, 186, 205, 219
Mason, Dancy, 92

matters of fact, 25
matters of concern, 25–6
Mazzeo, Agata, 14, 15, 227
mediation, 104, 121, 142, 152, 156, 224, 227, 228
Meière, Hildreth, 4
Merewether, E. R. A., 177, 181
mesothelioma, xii, xiii, 14, 52, 74, 109–10, 112–14, 115–18, 119–24, 133, 151, 171–2, 176, 190, 193, 195, 198, 206, 214
mesowarriors, 114
metaphor, 7, 50–1
Midnight Oil, 'Blue Sky Mine', 174n
Miller, Mitch, 138–9
mines, 28, 152, 153, 155–73
miniature League of Nations, 63
Miño Pérez, Eduardo, 175–6, 179, 189
Moorcock, Michael, *Jerry Cornelius*, 208
Moore, Marianne, 28, 87, 100, 103
  'His Shield', 91–3, 98
  'Humility Concentration, and Gusto', 93
  'Marianne Moore: Poet', 92–3, 99
Moretti, Franco, 61
Mosterín, Jesús, 119, 121–2, 123, 124
Mpambani, Phikolomzi Ignatius 'Igo', 224
Munro, Alice, 'Spaceships have Landed', 158–9, 160
Murphey, Lois, *Soon*, 75–6
Murray, Nicholas, 131
Murray, Robert, 52
Musila, Grace, 210–11
Myburgh, Pieter-Louis, 225
mystery, 27–8

narrative, 9–10, 11, 12, 16–18
Naughton, John, 99
Nelson, Cary, 186, 187
Nelson, Jason, *Wittenoom: Speculative Shell and the Cancerous Breeze*, 174n
New Materialism, 14, 90
Ngai, Sianne, 21, 24, 180
Nilsson, Louise, 63
Nixon, Rob, 14, 15–16, 134
nonsimultaneity, 205–6, 209, 215, 216, 219, 224

Nussbaum, Martha, 194, 196
Nutter, Alice, *Snow in July*, 190

Ober, Warren, 159
Obioma, Chigozie,
  An Orchestra of Minorities, 209
  The Fishermen, 209–10
Osborne, Peter, 205, 219
Outka, Elizabeth, 19
Oz, Amos, *To Know a Woman*, 208

Papillon, 194
pastoral, 153, 156–7, 158, 162, 171, 172, 191, 227
Paz, Octavio, 'Salamandra', 28, 87, 93, 100–3
Pels, Peter, 84–5, 90–1
Penny, Louise, *The Long Way Home*, 69, 70, 71–3, 114
Peter Rabbit, 60–2
Pett, Sarah, 108–9
Pfaelzer, Jean, 43, 46
Phillips, Adam, 110
Pietz, William, 84–5, 90–1
Pillayre, Héloïse, 76
Pizarreño (Chile), 175
planetary mine, 5–6
pleural plaques, xii, 109, 111, 138, 176
Pliny (the Elder), 53, 96, 97, 102
Poet, Frances, *Fibres*, 190, 194–6
Polo, Marco, 87, 95, 97–8
Pomfret (South Africa), xiv
Postone, Moishe, 177
Prager Asbestwerke Hermann & Co., 1, 127
precautionary principle, 49–50
Prester (Presbyter) John, 91, 92, 93, 97, 103
Price, C. W., 177, 181
Prieska (South Africa), 72, 226, 227
proletarian literature, 5–6, 153, 192–4
Prose, Francine, 218
Prunetti, Alberto, *Amianto*, 114, 179, 192–4, 196

Quebec, 50
Quinn, Anthony, 140

Raban, Jonathan, *Waxwings*, 222
Raisin, Ross, *Waterline*, 113, 124, 191, 193, 194
REACH Ambler, 227, 228
recovery, 128–30
Reichman, Ravit, 128
Rich, Adrienne, 27, 93
Ricoeur, Paul, 7, 8, 9–10, 11, 12, 16–18, 63, 116, 121
risk, 48–50, 107
Robert, Julie, 168–9
Robinson, Cedric, 184
Robinson, William Heath, 179–85, 189, 191
Rodger, Johnny, 138–9
Rodker, John, 204
Roemer, Charles, 180–1
Roesler, Layla, 99
Rohl, Arthur N., 205
Rolfe, Edwin, 'Asbestos', 179, 180, 185–9, 193
Rolling Stones, 88
Rolls, Alistair, 62
Rooksby, W. H., 181
Rooney, Brigid, 216
Rooney, Caroline, 98
Roro Hills (India), 206
Rotterdam Convention, 206
Rukeyser, Walter, xiv–xv, 26, 160–1, 162–3

Saadi, Suhayl, *Joseph's Box*, 114, 191
Said, Edward, 100
Saint-Amour, Paul, 19
salamander, 28, 44, 85, 86, 87, 91–104, 223
  axolotl, 102–3
Samuels, Ellen, 118
São Felix Mine (Brazil), 14, 227
Schitt's Creek, 23
Selecting Your Roof, 208
Selikoff, Irving, 26, 167
Session 9, 222
Seward, Anna, 44
Sharpe, Christina, 119, 122–4
Sheller, Mimi, 8
Shriver, Lionel, *So Much For That*, 110
Sielke, Sabine, 92

Silva, Roland, 206
Sinha, Indra, *Animal's People*, 192
Sleggs, Chris, 52
Sloterdijk, Peter, 178–9, 194
slow death, 16, 17
slow violence, 14, 15–16, 17, 135, 136
The Smart Set, 67
Smith, Kenneth, 15, 180
Social Reproduction Theory, 195–6
Southey, Robert, 44
Spahr, Clemens, 188
A Spark may cost a Farm, 60
Stach, Reiner, 131
Stephenson, Neal, *Snow Crash*, 50
stereoscopic style, 129, 131–2, 136, 145
Strabo, 38, 53, 94
Summers, A. Leonard, xv, 163
Suvin, Darko, 43

talcum powder, 204
Taylor, Analisa, 101
Theophrastus, 53, 93, 95
Thetford Mines (Canada), 50, 168
Thomas (von Cantimpré), 97
Thoulon, Edouard, 49
thymos, 178–9
Todorov, Tzvetan, 61
Tomba, Max, 219
trans-corporeality, 14
Trimbur, John, 226, 227
Trotter, David, 8
Trudeau, Pierre, 72, 169
tuberculosis, 2, 134
Turner & Newall (Turner Brothers), 1–2, 38, 113, 137, 179, 181, 190, 196, 197, 212–13
Turner, Robert H., 181
Tweedale, Geoffrey, 37–8, 52–3, 63, 112, 113

Updike, John, 'Phenomena', 204
use, xii–xv, 156, 228
utopia, 6, 27

Van Horssen, Jessica, 169, 227
vanishing mediator, 19
Veblen, Thorstein, 46

Vera, Yvonne, *Butterfly Burning*, 210–11, 216
'Crossing Boundaries', 208
The Stone Virgins, 211
Viney, Will, 222

Waddell, Nathan, 43
Wagner, J. C., 26, 52, 111, 206
Waldman, Linda, 77
Wallace, David Foster, *Infinite Jest*, 50, 222
Warwick Research Collective (WReC), 6, 64
waste, 38, 42, 49, 190, 192, 217, 222–6, 228
Waugh, Evelyn, 'Love Among the Ruins, 47
White, Patrick, *Flaws in the Glass*, 216–17
The Tree of Man, 214, 216
White Mountains of Ambler (USA), 190, 191, 198
Williams, Jim, *Rock Reject*, 85
Williams, Raymond, 55
Willis, John, 112, 113
Wills, David, 88, 100, 103
Winton, Tim, *Dirt Music*, 114, 157, 171–3
Wisher, Yolanda, *Maple Street Rag*, 179, 197, 198–9
Wittenoom, 75, 157, 170–3, 227
The Wizard of Oz, 190
wonder, 2, 4, 48, 85, 91, 94, 180
Woolf, Virginia, 'On Being Ill', 108–9
The Years, xiii
Workers Accident Insurance Institute, 127, 131, 133
world literature, 6, 63–4
world-system, 6, 63–4, 69
W. R. Grace & Co., 13, 228

Xólotl, 102–3

Yates, Ken, *Dust*, 190

Zhang, Dora, 13
Zunshine, Lisa, 62
Zvarevashe, George, 210

EU representative:
Easy Access System Europe
Mustamäe tee 50, 10621 Tallinn, Estonia
Gpsr.requests@easproject.com

www.ingramcontent.com/pod-product-compliance
Lightning Source LLC
Chambersburg PA
CBHW050213240426
43671CB00013B/2323